P9-CQE-069

Futures for the Welfare State

Futures for the Welfare State

EDITED BY
Norman Furniss

INDIANA UNIVERSITY PRESS
Bloomington and Indianapolis

This book was produced from camera-ready copy provided by the editor.

Manufactured in the United States of America

Library of Congress Cataloging-in-Publication Data

Futures for the welfare state.

Bibliography: p.
1. Welfare state--Congresses. 2. Economic history--1945- --Congresses. I. Furniss, Norman, 1944-
HB846.F87 1986 330.12'6 85-45959
ISBN 0-253-32440-8

1 2 3 4 5 90 89 88 87 86

CONTENTS

PREFACE

Many of the issues in this book were discussed at a conference on "Futures for the Welfare State" organized by the West European Studies Center at Indiana University in April 1983. The chapters by Hage, Lehning, Logue, Lundqvist, Rosenthal and Schwerin are revised versions of these papers. The other chapters were written expressly for this book. The contributors want to thank Roger Benjamin, Francis Castles, Alfred Diamant, Ed Greenberg, Russ Hanson, Arnold Heidenheimer, Richard Rose, and Jerold Waltman for their valuable criticisms. This book could not have been completed without the editorial services of Keith Fitzgerald and the secretarial services of Connie Young and Mary Lake.

Futures for the Welfare State

Norman Furniss

Introduction

Anyone wishing to understand the development of social policy in advanced capitalist democracies soon confronts the terminological specter of the "welfare state." Although the term is widely used, there is little agreement on what it means. To add to the confusion, while there may not be much agreement on what the "welfare state" includes, there is a strong body of opinion that insists that it means _one thing_. This position can be traced to the theoretical arguments in the 1930s by Karl Mannheim and others that democracies must find a "middle way" between what seemed the obvious inefficiencies and appalling social costs of laissez-faire capitalism on the one hand and the political tyranny of "totalitarianism" on the other. Their answer was planning, "economic Keynesianism," or more generally state intervention. Historically, the overthrow of what Harold Laski called the "negative state" was confirmed during World War II. Today all advanced capitalist democracies are interventional states. And if all interventionist states are welfare states, then so are all capitalist democracies. And not just these: If intervention is given a concrete measure such as ten percent of G.N.P. allocated to public expenditures on health and social security programs, then almost every country in Europe, East and West, becomes a welfare state.[1]

This formulation of the welfare state as an interventionist state with the degree of intervention best measured in tax money spent is accepted by a major perspective in the study of the development of welfare state. Called by Ramesh Mishra the "Convergence Theory or Technological Determinism,"[2] its key argument is that welfare policies result from industrialism which creates new needs which in turn are met through public intervention.[3] For the first time the life cycle of work is not congruent with the life cycle of people. To sustain people when they are unemployed, sick, or too old to work, public welfare provisions are a logical answer and therefore they occur. Politics, political debate, particular historical experiences basically are insignificant as independent or even as intervening variables.[4]

Many interpretations within the "Marxist" tradition would agree with this last statement. It has been argued that all capitalist states are the same because in none has there been basic structural change. That is, power relations are not transformed; there is no production for need; there is no real redistribution of income.[5] As for the role of ideas, we are told that "in effect, the history of economic theory is the history of class struggle."[6] In sum, for many advocates of this position, "the welfare state emerged historically as the response of capital to working class struggle against the state itself... The welfare state does not represent a working class victory but rather a means of guaranteeing the maintenance of a healthy and technically skilled labor force which also plays an ideological role in the stabilization of capitalist power..."[7]

Now it is not the intention to set up a couple of strawmen, the "industrializers" and "Marxists", and then announce that the contributions to this volume effectively knock them down. As Elizabeth Trousdell, Neil Mitchell, and Stephen Valocchi describe in their bibliographic essay, the interpretations within these traditions are more divergent and subtle than a summary paragraph can accommodate. Moreover, we do not want to deny that industrialization does involve new social needs, that "capitalist" production and more particularly the international economic order do involve constraints on political action, or even as we see in the chapter by Timothy Tilton, that one can speak usefully of "functional requirements" for the development of welfare states. The proper question should be not whether a given perspective is "right" or "wrong" but whether it illuminates the issues one finds intriguing. And to begin to understand how welfare states <u>differ</u> and what <u>futures</u> are open to political action is to shift from an emphasis on the importance of economic development and its effects on social and political processes to an effort to link public policy to historically grounded patterns of state development.

This orientation focuses on problem-solving and public choice,[8] on political debate and the role of political ideas, on state action and state capacities, and on the interaction over time between relative state autonomy and social power. It underlies all the chapters in this book, and its elaboration is the particular concern of the first two. Timothy Tilton, in "Perspectives on the Welfare State," develops the reasons why it is useful to have a conception of the "welfare state" which embodies economic, political and moral issues. He then turns to explanations for why welfare states develop and again insists on the relevance of a number of factors including "the nature of the state, the character of the bureaucracy, and the mood of public opinion." At bottom, however, he argues that "it is the balance of political forces that is crucial." Douglas Ashford, in "Welfare States as Institutional Choices", not only points to the necessity of considering and comparing historical experiences. He sees their institutionalization as a "delicate and demanding political exercise."

The next two chapters deal with appropriate methodologies. A definition of "welfare policy" in terms of expenditures suggests, indeed impells, a "quantitative" approach. If, however, we define "welfare" to include the needs of social as well as economic man and "policy" to include principles and content as well as expenditures, must we then abandon research programs based on the analysis of quantitative data? For Larry Griffin and Associates ("Methodological Innovations in the Analysis of Welfare State Development") and Jerald Hage ("Techniques for Delineating Periods") the answer is no. Quantitative approaches can be fruitful if the types of data and the statistical techniques employed are broadened. The latter includes time series analysis. Griffin and Associates offer both in principle and in illustration the research potential of a pooled data matrix that combines both cross-national and time series variation. Hage argues that a focus on time periods can be combined with a consideration of changing relationship among variables. An engagement with historical experiences, far from being a bother and an impediment to rigorous social science, is broadly beneficial. The qualitative historical record provides a valuable check for the quantitative periodization of eras, while periodization may spur a reconsideration of the qualitative historical record.

Finally, to inject political variables and political debate and to take account of divergent national experiences is to raise necessarily a number of normative implications. A discussion of value premises is central to any serious debate on futures for the welfare state. The importance indeed grows as one moves from principles of welfare expansion (which could be fudged by some metaphor of "Pareto optimality") to principles of welfare contraction. As

Percy Lehning observes in "Cutting Lines We Date Not Cross: Justice and Retrenchment in the Welfare State," it is when we consider welfare retrenchment that the absence of a coherent view of what the good "welfare state" society should be is particularly troubling. Lehning proceeds to describe distributional principles that can be derived from different theories of justice. And he argues that political debate could be grounded in competing concepts of just distribution.

The contributions in Part II describe a number of "economic and social challenges" to the current operation of welfare states. These should be placed within the context of national economic management and the international economic order. The nature of this context can be appreciated by contrasting it with the international economic regime operating from the end of World War II to the early 1970s.[9] Briefly, this regime rested on expanding world trade, a diffusion of "Keynesian" economic management techniques, increasing productivity and full employment. Domestically, in Andrew Shonfield's words, there was an acceptance of "Modern Capitalism" in which a large but not nationalizing public sector aided economic coherence and fostered social welfare policies. Both aims were furthered by a public that took for granted "that each year should bring a noticeable increase in the real income per head of the population."[10]

In contrast, the international economic regime arising in the mid 1970s has been constricting. Most obviously the expectation that "each year should bring a noticeable increase in the real income per head of the population" has not been fulfilled. In the ten years since the first "oil shock" growth in the gross domestic product in OECD countries has averaged 1.8 percent, just over a third the previous rate. Moreover, yearly changes have been more extreme. In France, for example, growth in the ten years prior to 1974 ranged from 4.3 to 7.0 percent; in the ten years after 1974 the range was from 0.2 to 5.2 percent. Meanwhile in almost all countries unemployment rates soared in the late 1970s and early 1980s and then stabilized at levels that would have been considered politically intolerable a generation earlier. For a more complete statistical presentation see the Appendix, "Economic, Social and Political Indicators."

The general reaction to these trends has not been a call for more Keynesian measures, for more planning, or for more social spending. Rather, the new conventional wisdom is that salvation will come only by abandoning the policy pattern of "modern capitalism" and substituting neo-classical economic orthodoxy. Distinguishing features are presented in a useful 1977 OECD study, "Towards Full Employment and Price Stability." This report states that economic growth remains possible but only if governments recast their policies and assumptions. Governments and interest groups must recognize that beyond some spending threshold there are adverse consequences of public expenditures for economic growth, and that in many countries this threshold has been reached. Inflation, fueled by "excessive" public expenditures and by unions seeking to maintain not merely nominal but real wages, is identified as the main enemy. In general, concern focuses on low profits, or, as it usually is described, a reduced "incentive to invest." Policy implications flow naturally. Market solutions are preferred if at all feasible. Governments need to bring home the consequences of inflationary behavior. And as for full employment the OECD report concludes that "we believe the route to sustained full employment lies in recognizing that governments cannot guarantee full employment regardless of developments in prices, wages and other factors in economic life. The explanation of the paradox lies in the key role of expectations in determining economic behavior..."[11] In other words, the public must realize that to expect regular real increases in one's standard of living is to fuel inflation and to foreclose any hopes for full employment.

Underlying domestic policy changes has been a pattern of constricting economic linkages. Interdependence continues to grow, but it is given a new twist. In OECD countries the share of exports in GNP has never been higher. Even more remarkable have been advances in financial integration. According to Larsen and associates, two consequences follow. First, "economic policy multipliers" make the impact of policy changes greater if undertaken by a number of countries simultaneously. But, second, if a single country reflates or expands demand, the size of the country's <u>domestic</u> multiplier is reduced because "a significant proportion leaks abroad."[12] To stimulate economic activity in Germany, for example, would raise output in Germany <u>and</u> in her trading partners with the costs of stimulation born entirely by Germany.[13] What this imbalance between costs and benefits means is that "the performance of the overall OECD economy goes far towards determining the performance of each country individually." While national <u>rates</u> of performance continue to differ, "there is a marked tendency towards international coincidence of both business cycles and policy stance."[14] This coincidence is reinforced by the inability of exchange rate adjustments to compensate for differences in economic policy--if, say, a country were to expand at a relatively faster rate while permitting the exchange rate to fall there should be a countervailing affect on exports and imports. As Larsen and associates describe, however, this strategy is extremely difficult to implement in practice. There is a long lag time (around two years) before impacts from currency depreciation on import and export volumes are fully felt; the impact from demand stimulation is immediate. Second, "exchange rate movements induced by financial disturbances can constrain domestic policies." An effort to float a currency down easily can become a free fall given the ability of financial markets to generate movements of capital that can and do swamp the efforts of central banks. Third, national policy can be constrained by the threat of capital flight; put more delicately exchange rates "are, at times, affected by incipient capital movements induced by foreign financial disturbance or international political considerations."[15]

France provides the classic recent example. The Socialist Party came to power in 1981 with a long list of extensive and costly economic and social reforms. Social spending was increased by 20% in the first year; the minimum wage was raised; the working week was reduced; an extra week of vacation was added. More broadly, the government wanted to stimulate the economy and reduce unemployment by stimulating demand through income transfers and "Keynesian" macro-economic policies and by promoting business investment through greater credit control and nationalization. As Mitterrand stated in his "Presidential Debate" with Giscard d'Estaing, the public sector should be "the true locomotive of investment and export drive."[16] Central to this goal was the assumption that there would be a world economic recovery in 1982 yielding "positive" multiplying affects of the type described above. In the event, while France has managed to avoid a recession--GNP has never fallen--, the cost was far greater than anticipated. The blame popularly is placed on silly rhetoric or silly policies. There have been plenty at least of the former. To state that France intended a "phased break with capitalism" while at the same time encouraging private investment, or for the minister of social affairs to announce that she had far more important things to do than keeping accounts, is not likely to inspire confidence. But these are as nothing when compared to the difficulties of promoting recovery in one medium-sized capitalist country when other states including the United States were applying monetary restraint. Much of the stimulus "leaked" abroad, and pressures on the current account and exchange rate became intolerable. France has had to adopt the typical battery of restrictive policies which have stabilized the account balance and reduced inflation at the price of higher unemployment and an end to further social reform.

The question arising from this experience is whether international economic linkages now preclude major welfare state advances and may even necessitate broad retreat. The question is pressing for advanced, "social welfare" states. Because of their high levels of social spending and their historical reliance on "Keynesian" economic management, are these states particularly exposed? This is the question raised by Donald Schwerin in "Nordic Responses to 'Fiscal Crisis.'" Schwerin finds that while the Scandinavian welfare states are affected by the new international economic order, they have managed to adjust *more easily* than have many larger countries and without recourse to constricting fiscal policies. Schwerin also considers the proposition that economic adjustment must mean cuts in governmental transfers. He makes the point that this depends on the effect of government spending; whether, for example, increased expenditures lead to additional purchase of imports or whether such expenditures ultimately stimulate domestic economies.

We next turn to social and political challenges. The significance of these challenges is increased in relatively hard times. In an era of seemingly endless economic expansion states can pursue a number of policy goals simultaneously, and the it can be assumed more readily that popular reaction and the "political culture" will be at least latently supportive. But when there are fewer additional economic resources for distribution, our attention is directed more at the needs of social man. One of the most important non-transfer policies is housing. Housing policy represents well the general thrust of public policy,[17] and it can be a major force for social integration or segmentation. In "How Potent is the Welfare State?" Lennart Lundqvist describes the tension in Sweden between the desire to equalize housing opportunities for citizens and the wish to increase the opportunities for individuals to make decisions about how they want to live. The results of housing policy reflect this tension. Housing conditions have improved dramatically since World War II, and it is fair to say that there is no such thing as a Swedish "slum." At the same time the equalization of housing conditions and costs across different groups in the population is not as great as the rhetoric of the Swedish Social Democratic party might suggest.

From public policies we turn to public attitudes and behavior. Our first need is to discriminate much more carefully the incidence of popular dissatisfaction with social welfare programs among nations and among groups within nations. This task is undertaken by Bernice Pescosolido, Carol Boyer, and Wai Ying Tsui in "Crisis in the Welfare State: Public Reactions to Welfare Policies." In constructing an overall measure of public reaction the authors suggest how their findings support various models of welfare state development. They then take the essential, albeit often neglected, step of linking attitudes to political behavior. It is not the case that disillusionment with welfare state policies need result in political action. And indeed when both attitudes and propensity for action are considered, the impetus for change from the public, except perhaps in the United States, is remarkably attenuated.

In the final chapter in this part John Logue moves from professed attitudes and political action to psychological prerequisites and social action. There is a latent tension in all societies between private, individual self-interest and public, community needs.[18] Advanced, "social welfare" states were premised on individual restraint and solidarity. In "Scandinavian Welfare States Between Solidarity and Self-interest" Logue argues that these premises no longer can be assumed. He sees some types of increased service utilization and a greater propensity to evade taxes as two significant manifestations of the decline of solideristic norms. He is not complaining about the lack of stigma attached to the service use, nor does he claim that people are cheating. Rather, he argues that there has been a subtle shift in attitudes whereby, for example, the threshold for identifying oneself as too ill to report to work is lower than it was for earlier generations. With generalized benefits and the employment of universalistic criteria, not only the poor and underprivileged but also the affluent become heavy users of the welfare systems. The economic cost is far from the only concern. The greater threat is to the moral basis of a welfare society. I will raise this issue again in the final chapter.

From this discussion we must conclude that an understanding of political futures is unlikely to be advanced by simple extrapolation. We saw in Part I that welfare states have had not one past but a number of different pasts. We also advanced at least the possibility that different determinants operated in different countries. From Part II we can add to this analytic complexity a number of more concrete uncertainties. International economic constraints are more pressing. Public dissatisfaction has a significant political dimension. There is a concern that policies may not produce the anticipated redistributive or "social democratic" effects. And no longer can diffuse sentiments of "solidarity" be assumed. It is only prudent to infer from these findings that no particular welfare state, no particular welfare state type, has an automatic claim to the future. What we do see is a "repoliticization" of welfare state issues, but this time (unlike the 1920s and 1930s) those individuals and groups favoring movement toward more extensive provision or toward less reliance on "market" forces are on defensive. And they are pressed as strongly in political debate as they are in political action. A decade ago the conservative critique of the welfare state was essentially negative both in analysis--the welfare state can't work well because enough facts never will be known, because men are inherently sinful--and in prognostication--already we are on the "road to serfdom."

Today these gloomy assessments are being cast aside. Welfare states, social democracies, are to be pitied not feared. And in place of arguments about the "inevitability of ignorance" we have celebrations of capitalism and the capitalist spirit. The work of George Gilder, also discussed in the chapter by Harrell Rodgers, is representative. For Gilder, the creation of new wealth is only one, and perhaps the least significant, aspect of capitalist action. Capitalists, entrepreneurs, are "optimists, who see in every patch of sand a potential garden, in every man a potential worker, in every problem a possible profit. Their self-interest succumbs to their deeper interest and engagement in the world beyond themselves, impelled by their curiosity, imagination and faith...In the harsh struggles and remorseless battles of their lives, entrepreneurs are no saints, and far from sinless...Yet more than any other class of men they embody and fulfill the sweet and mysterious consolations of the Sermon on the Mount and the most farfetched affirmations of the democratic dream."[19] Not since R.H. Tawney have welfare state proponents written so directly on the moral component of their vision. Until they do, their defensive posture is unlikely to change.

The chapters that follow do not attempt to construct a new welfare state vision. The aims are more modest but still we hope useful for political debate. The first aim is to outline the position of the United States. Discussions of the American experience have been somewhat neglected, in part because of its assumed "exceptionism." If it was exceptional, it must be unique and therefore of little theoretical interest.[23] And since its exceptionism consists of an absence of welfare provisions citizens in most other advanced capitalist democracies take for granted, it hardly offers an inspiring "model" to be studied for possible emulation. The research thrust has been the other way--it has been the European experience that has been commended to the attention of Americans.[21] Now however, because of changes in the international political economy, the American experience cannot be ignored whether one is directly interested in it or not. The trend toward coincidence in policy stance described in the introduction to Part II threatens to become coincidence with the American policy stance. As the central player in the international political economy, American policy and its justification warrant serious consideration.

The chapters by Harrell Rodgers and Larry Griffin and Kevin Leicht intend to advance our understanding in complementary ways. In "The American Welfare State in Transition" Rodgers reviews the historical record that has led to the establishment and expansion of American Social welfare programs and offers some cogent reasons why we are likely to see their continuation albeit in an increasingly meaner fashion. In "Politicizing Welfare Expenditures in the United States" Griffin and Leicht attempt to place American policy within the general framework of "the contradictory roles performed by the democratic state embedded in capitalist society." While policy may be "exceptional" in the sense of being different, it can be understood within general theoretical categories.

The second aim, which is the concern of the final two chapters, is to raise some analytical issues that might be considered in understanding and trying to influence future political debate. In "The Welfare State: Sticks, No Carrots" Uriel Rosenthal argues that prevalent interpretations of the welfare state obscure a deeper understanding. A major problem with such interpretations is that they depart from traditional ideas about the state and its functions. That is, traditional defining features of the state (the so-called repression complex), have been largely dropped from scholarly discussions, while the more recent welfare complex receives extensive scrutiny. As the Dutch experience has shown, however, the general population, bureaucrats, and politicians do not suffer from this selective (and partially erroneous) perception about the state. They see it as a split state with the repression complex non-negotiable and the welfare complex as potentially dispensable. Rosenthal next develops a framework which includes both these repression and welfare complexes. In the course of this discussion he identifies the implications of a major tension found in any welfare state: the need or at least the tradition to use repression instruments to achieve welfare objectives. "In Welfare States between

'State' and 'Civil Society," I attempt to identify some of the continuing but at least partially controllable tensions in creating state institutions that reflect the best aspirations of civil society.

NOTES

1. Jerald Hage and Robert Hanneman, "The Growth of the Welfare State in Britain, France, Germany and Italy." In Richard Thompson (ed.) _Comparative Social Research_ III (JAI Press: 1980).

2. Ramesh Mishra, _Society and Social Policy: Theoretical Perspectives on Welfare_ (Macmillan: 1977), ch.3.

3. Basic presentations are by Phillips Cutright, "Political Structure, Economic Development and National Social Security Programs," _American Journal of Sociology_ 70 (1965) pp. 537-550, Clark Kerr et. at. _Industrialism and Industrial Man_; and Harold Wilensky, _The Welfare State and Equality_ (University of California Press: 1975).

4. For a clear exposition of this position see Robert Jackman, "Socialist Parties and Income Inequality in Western Industrial Societies," _Journal of Politics_ 42 (1980), pp. 135-149.

5. Claus Offe, "Advanced Capitalism and the Welfare State," _Politics and Society_ 1972, pp. 479-488.

6. James O'Connor, "Accumulation Crisis: The Problem and its Setting." _Contemporary Crises_ 5(1981), p. 112.

7. See the discussion in _Contemporary Crises_ 5(1981), p. 181. The not so latent "functionalist" implications are well developed by Theda Skocpol, "Political Responses to Capitalist Crises," _Politics and Society_ 10(1981), pp. 151-201.

8. This alternative perspective owes much to the work of Charles Anderson. See "System and Strategy in Comparative Analysis." In W.B. Gwyn and G.C. Edwards (eds.) _Perspectives on Public Policy Making_ (Tulane University Press: 1975); and "The Place of Principles in Policy Analysis," _American Political Science Review_ 73, 3(1979), pp. 711-723.

9. I describe the policy pattern associated with this regime more fully in "Political Futures and the New Order of Functioning." In Roger Benjamin and Stephen Elkins (eds.) _The Democratic State_ (University of Kansas Press: 1984).

10. Andrew Shonfield, _Modern Capitalism_ (Oxford University Press: 1965), p. 66.

11. "Towards Full Employment and Price Stability." (OECD: 1977), Quotation from page 185.

12. Flemming Larsen, John Llewellyn and Stephen Potter, "International Economic Linkages" (OECD: 1984), p. 49.

13. This problem, to return to an earlier theme, seems relatively unappreciated. But there is much evidence, for example, that "Germany in 1981 would have liked to expand its economy, but to do so in the face of American disinflation would have meant a sharp depreciation in the mark." Douglas Purvis, "Perspectives on Macroeconomic Performance in the 1970s" (OECD: 1983), p. 10.

14. "International Economic Linkages," pp. 50, 51.

15. "International Economic Linkages," p. 52.

16. *Le Monde* (April 16, 1981).

17. See Bruce Headey, *Housing in the Developed Economy* (St. Martin's Press: 1978).

18. For two fine elaborations with specific reference to the United States, see Daniel Bell, *The Cultural Contradictions of Capitalism* (Basic Books: 1976); and Robert Bellah and Associates, *Habits of the Heart* (University of California Press: 1984)

19. George Gilder, *The Spirit of Enterprise* (New York: Simon and Schuster, 1984), pp. 254, 256.

20. For an exception see the work of Theda Skocpol, most recently with Ann Orloff, "Why Not Equal Protection? Explaining the Politics of Public Social Spending in Britain, 1900-1911, and the United States, 1880s-1920," *American Sociological Review* 49 (1984), pp. 726-750.

21. For example, see Arnold Heidenheimer, Hugh Heclo and Carolyn Adams, *Comparative Public Policy: The Patterns of Social Choice in Europe and America* (New York: St. Martin's: 1975) This thrust is muted in the second edition of the book.

PART ONE

Toward an Understanding of Development and Change

I.

Timothy A. Tilton

Perspectives on the Welfare State

Roughly a decade has now passed since the welfare state became a popular topic for investigation by American social scientists. In 1973, James O'Connor presented a powerful neo-Marxist analysis and critique of the welfare state in *The Fiscal Crisis of the State*. Two years later, Harold Wilensky in *The Welfare State and Equality* offered a liberal diagnosis of the structure, development, and impact of the welfare state. These two trend-setting studies have arguably contributed most to structuring subsequent academic discussion. Their prominence, however, should not obscure the fact that the early and mid-1970s produced a curiously delayed, but substantial flow of American literature on the welfare state. The work of Piven and Cloward; Janowitz; Jackman; Heclo; Buchanan and Wagner; Bell; Furniss and Tilton; Heidenheimer, Heclo and Adams; and numerous others finally placed the welfare state firmly on the research agenda of American social science.[1]

Now is a useful time to assess the literature in this burgeoning area. What questions guide research? What methods yield useful results? What conclusions can be securely drawn? What directions should future inquiries take? These issues will underlie this brief survey, which I shall organize around six questions that encompass the central theoretical problems that organize research on the welfare state.

I.

WHAT IS THE WELFARE STATE

One of the central methodological imperatives of modern social science is to define the unit of analysis. What must strike any student of modern social policy, however, is the lack of a consistent definition of the welfare state. The conceptions that investigators employ, explicitly or tacitly, vary sharply in their inclusiveness. Conservative writers like Buchanan and Wagner or Friedman deplore the Keynesian fiscal policies and regulation of industry that they see as characterizing the welfare state.[2] For Wilensky, however, "The essence of the welfare state is government-protected minimum standards of income, nutrition, health, housing, and education, assured to every citizen as a political right, not as charity."[3] A host of other investigators who focus on quantitative measures of welfare state activity implicitly accept the notion that "social spending" defines the welfare state. The broadest of these studies include democratic and non-democratic regimes. To a writer like Janowitz, however, this procedure is unacceptable. For Janowitz the welfare state <u>by definition</u> entails parliamentary institutions and governmental intervention in the management of the economy. "The welfare state in my terms," he writes, "is more than a prescribed level of welfare expenditures. Moral and political issues are involved."[4]

These differences are not trivial. The narrower definitions (those focussing on "social spending") obscure the functioning of the modern welfare state in two related ways. First, they focus upon "reactive" social policy to the virtual exclusion of "preventive" social policy; for example, by studying levels of unemployment compensation rather than economic policy for full employment the quantitative study of social spending neglects the initiatives that reduce the need for ameliorative measures. Similarly, by failing to include environmental regulation as well as spending on health care in an analysis of welfare state activities, the investigator captures compensatory outlays but not preventive measures. Second, these definitions focus attention upon governmental spending, but not upon its tax structure, its regulatory activities, or its economic planning. Without a more comprehensive approach the analyst has no way of knowing whether these various activities complement or contradict one another. Progress, then, appears to require a conception of the welfare state that embraces not merely social spending, but public management and regulation of the economy as well.

The search for a generally-accepted definition of "<u>the</u>" welfare state may well prove fruitless no matter how inclusively it is cast. Wittgenstein has demonstrated the need to treat words not as depictions of "essences," but as indicators of "family resemblances," and this counsel fits admirably the concept of the welfare state. "<u>The</u>" welfare state does not exist; what exists are a range of welfare states employing a variety of policy instruments. Even if one could isolate common instruments or means, there would remain the crucial fact that different states pursue quite different objectives with these means. Whether a state aims to dampen radical potentials, shore up domestic manufacturers, ensure minimum standards of civilized life, or institute rough equality of living standards is not an incidental consideration, but a clear indication of the radically different conceptions of "welfare" or "well-being" embodied in the different manifestations of welfare states.

II.

WHY DO WELFARE STATES DEVELOP?

The overwhelming majority of studies on the origins of welfare states suffer from their reliance upon an unduly narrow conception of the welfare state. They report the growth of social spending, but neglect the development of macroeconomic policy and regulatory measures. This concentration can lead to curious findings and it can obscure anomalous results. West Germany, for example, always appears as a leader in the introduction of social insurance and in the scope of its programs, but its tardy introduction of Keynesian budgetary planning goes unmentioned and the paradoxical combination remains largely unexplored. Nevertheless, these studies of the development of social expenditures have produced a stimulating theoretical debate, one which merits further investigation.

An early and persistent theme in explanations of welfare state development treats the welfare state as a natural accompaniment of industrialization. This thesis comes in two versions, which can be labelled loosely the "social" and the "economic" variants. The social thesis betrays a structural-functionalist lineage; it emphasizes industrialization's destructive impact upon traditional families and communities and their ability to meet social needs. Whereas once the traditional family might have cared for its sick and elderly members personally, the dispersed modern nuclear family characteristic of industrialized societies is no longer able to tend to grandparents or distant relatives. In order to perform the functions necessary to the maintenance of society, modern societies have had to elaborate more complex and differentiated structures (i.e., the institutions of modern social welfare policy) in order to provide these functions. This account effectively indicates the social changes that produce a *need* for new institutions, but it fails to show the process by which the institutions and policies to meet these needs actually emerge. "Hunger does not produce bread," Bentham remarked in a preemptive strike against this sort of functionalist explanation. Although this thesis suggests one of the important situational elements that leads to the development of the welfare state, and although it helps to account for the seeming ubiquity of the welfare state in modern societies, it makes its emergence far too automatic and leaves its precise political origins unclear.

The "economic" version of the thesis stresses both the new needs created by industrialization and the new resources it makes available. Industrialization not only creates new health hazards, demands for greater education, the growth of urban centers, greater fluctuations in employment opportunities and a more elderly population, but it makes available an economic surplus that can be devoted to medical care, education, housing and urban planning, unemployment compensation, and pensions. From Cutright's early analysis to Wilensky's major study, economic growth has served as the underlying explanation of welfare state development.[5] Politics recede before the overwhelming "logic of industrialization." "Convergence" between the Eastern and Western blocs' welfare arrangements takes place; as Pryor argues, "If the basic economic circumstances (in Marxist terminology 'productive forces') are similar and if the policy dilemmas are similar, it should not be surprising that the decisions are also roughly similar. . . ."[6] In this thesis neither politics nor ideology matters.

Four major criticisms can be raised against this economic determinist thesis. First it fails to explain the substantial variation among industrialized welfare states in the extent of their provisions. Sweden's welfare state commands a far greater proportion of the nation's gross national product than does America's; this difference cannot be attributed to differences in economic development. Second, defenders of this thesis rely almost obsessively upon "social spending" as the decisive dependent variable in their studies; this concentration blinds them to qualitative differences in national programs. The differences between Sweden's active labor market policy and the United States' employment services, or the impact of universal as opposed to means-tested programs upon stigmatization and national solidarity, tend to disappear in these studies. Third, the denigration of politics and ideology contrasts sharply with the political controversy that regularly accompanies the introduction and major expansion of welfare programs. The lengthy and continuing battle over national health insurance in the United States or the British debate over comprehensive education become curious oddities inexplicable in terms of this theory. Fourth, this theory takes the content of social policy as automatic. It does not concern itself with innovation in the content of policy, but only with the amount spent upon it. The development of programs for income-related supplementary pensions or children's allowances or Head Start programs or Keynesian fiscal policy is simply assumed; the innovators who first designed them get no credit for their inventiveness. It is little wonder, then, that ideas and ideology play little role in the explanation of policy. From a constricted view of the welfare state comes a constricted view of its development.

Liberal theorists have no corner upon functionalist and determinist accounts. Writers in the Marxist tradition have succumbed to similar impulses. Piven and Cloward's early contribution, Regulating the Poor,[7] treated American social welfare policy as a functional appendage of the capitalist economy. Social welfare measures expanded in hard times in order to mollify potentially restive victims of economic hardship; then as the economy revived, spending was pared back so that workers would be forced back into the labor market (or the reserve army of the unemployed) and exert downward pressure on wages. The precise location of causation remained unclear; the poor clearly had little control over their fates, but whether the fluctuations in welfare policy resulted solely from systemic imperatives or from the conscious choices of policymakers was left unresolved. Piven and Cloward did not produce evidence about policymakers' intentions that would have removed suspicions about the essentially functionalist nature of their argument.

Works like O'Connor's The Fiscal Crisis of the State and Gough's The Political Economy of the Welfare State --and Piven and Cloward's later works --give greater scope to human agency.[8] They stress not only the imperatives of the capitalist economy, but the balance of class forces and political movements as determinants of welfare policy. O'Connor and Gough stress the contradictory demands upon the capitalist state: It must both promote the accumulation of capital and the legitimization of the social system. The capitalist state, O'Connor writes:

> must try to fulfill two basic and often mutually contradictory functions -- accumulation and legitimization. This means that the state must try to maintain or create the conditions in which profitable capital accumulation is

> possible. However, the state also must try to maintain or create the conditions for social harmony.[9]

The welfare state develops and expands in response to two functional requirements: It must invest in social capital (i.e., "expenditures required for profitable private accumulation") such as state-financed industrial parks, research and development, infrastructure, and education. It must also meet social expenses, i.e., "projects and services which are required to maintain social harmony" such as the police, armed forces, public assistance and welfare programs.[10]

This perspective raises in a more explicit fashion two central questions -- Who benefits from the welfare state? and Is the welfare state stable? -- to which this essay must return. It offers an explanation of the fact that the rich as well as the poor benefit from specific welfare programs and tax incentives.[11] It does not treat the state simply as an agency for dispersing benefits, but accents its continuing role as an imposer of sanctions. In all these respects neo-Marxist theories of the state provide a more accurate and nuanced picture of the welfare state, but they suffer from a serious flaw: they do not account for the development of social policy within the Eastern bloc. If the "growth of the welfare state is neither cause nor consequence of capitalist development, but one aspect of it"[12] then it is not clear how to account for the development of social policy within the "socialist" bloc. The boldest and most nearly correct step would be to argue that these states, too, are in the process of fostering capital accumulation and maintaining legitimacy, but this approach dissolves the capitalist/state socialist distinction into the common features of industrializing societies.

The neo-Marxist view highlights the importance of the balance of social forces and the degree of autonomy states have in implementing policy. Gough stresses that:

> In the real world the final burden of taxation is determined by the ebb and flow of class conflict, and will vary with the economic and political strength of the contending classes. Simultaneously the scale and direction of state expenditure, including that on the social services, is also largely influenced by the class balance of forces.[13]

For writers like John Stephens and Walter Korpi, who fall more within the Social Democratic tradition, the balance of social forces is crucial. Throughout his writings, Korpi insists upon the importance of working-class mobilization into trade unions and into the Social Democratic electorate as the decisive element underlying the "historic compromise" that has served as the basis for Sweden's advanced welfare state.[14] John Stephens similarly accents the fact that in Sweden, compared to the United States, Britain, and France, "a strong labor movement and a long period of socialist incumbency has [sic] led to the extension of democratic control and very significant redistribution".[15]

One can ask, however, what it is that determines the balance of class forces within a society. The list of possible determinants is lengthy and complex. The nature of industrialization, the nature of democratization, the character of the workplace and of residential patterns, the degree of organization of various classes, the ethnic and religious homogeneity or heterogeneity of classes, division over foreign policy or ideological issues, and, not least, the success of policies pursued by governments can all sway power relations.[16] It is the great virtue of Francis Castles' analysis to assert the importance of unity and division to the _relative_ balance of forces; it is not merely the strength of the left nor that of the right which is crucial, but the relation between them, particularly as that relation is affected by splits within either group. Thus Castles properly contends that "(a) party system in which the working class is undivided and the Right is weak is the condition which has permitted Social Democratic reformism . . . . to be practiced successfully in Scandinavia."[17]

Korpi, Stephens, and Castles regard the state's activities as the reflection of power relations in civil society; to understand public policy one must determine who exercises hegemony in civil society. Other writers grant the state greater autonomy. Theda Skocpol, for example, contends that the late emergence and modest scope of the welfare state in the United States can be explained largely by the distinctive nature of American government.[18] As Skowronek has shown, the American state developed slowly. The spoils system delayed the emergence of reliable administrative capacity at all levels of American government. The federal structure of American politics splintered reformist demands and patronage parties blunted class conflict. Thus the American state lacked the administrative prowess and dispersed the political forces essential to welfare-statist development.[19]

Skocpol's concentration upon state structure and autonomy is a valuable corrective to any view which reduces the state's activities to a straightforward response to social pressures.[20] Nonetheless, it is possible to exaggerate the importance of state structure; social movements democratize absolutist states; abolish rotten boroughs; gerrymander or eliminate gerrymandering; institute procedures for initiative, referenda, and recall of officials; effect civil service reform; devise new taxes; restructure local and state governments; carry out intra-party reforms; and even abolish or render negligible one house of parliament. State structure in and of itself can never be a sufficient explanation of welfare statist development, but it is a necessary element in any explanation that strives for completeness.

Neo-Marxist theories of the state allow one to see that unless states enjoy at least some autonomy from the capitalist economy, there can be no welfare state. Capitalists might dominate the state in at least three ways. First, they might fill key political and administrative positions with their minions, thus frustrating external pressures for change. Second, they may use their control of economic resources to sway elections and influence public officials. Third, they can rely on the "structural constraints" of capitalism, e.g., the potential for a strike by capital or its flight abroad, to discipline reformist politicians.[21] If any of these mechanisms or all together were fully effective, capitalists would be little inclined to grant concessions. It is because the state does enjoy at least some autonomy from the economic system --because democracy sometimes triumphs over capitalism --that the welfare state is possible.

The literature on the development of the welfare state suggests, then, that the welfare state requires a certain level of economic development and that indeed the injustices and insecurity of industrial development stimulate political "pressure" (a metaphor broad enough to encompass Bismarck's preemptive conservative policies, business-backed social insurance, Social Democratic reformism, and Communist measures) for social welfare policy. Ambitious social initiatives necessarily require a state with substantial administrative capacity. Just how specific measures become official policy remains controversial; need alone cannot explain the adoption of policy. Scholarly opinion divides over the relative importance of civil servants,[22] parties, working-class organization, and ideology,[23] both for the development and expansion of the welfare state and its specific extent, configuration, redistributive impact, and ethos. The scope of the present essay prohibits a thorough review of the evidence in this controversy, but it may be possible to shed light on the discussion by seeing how well the various determinants explain the success or failure of attempts at retrenchment in various welfare states.[24]

Any attempt to explain current retreats in terms of bureaucracy (as Wilensky's major study might suggest) must fail. There is no evidence to suggest a substantial change in the personnel of public bureaucracies, nor is there any reason to suppose a change in civil servants' impulses to aggrandizement of their spheres of authority. Public programs are not growing any younger. To a mind given to symmetry, the inability of this determinant to account for current economizing raises doubts about its cogency as an explanation of expansion. Ideology and public opinion seem more promising explanations of retrenchment. Although hard to pin down, there seems clear evidence of the resurgence of rightist ideology. Human Events is no longer regarded as a publication of the radical right; the Heritage Foundation is spoken of as a "think tank." Thatcher and Reagan lend legitimacy to the hard right; rich is chic; and a prominent Swedish Social Democrat declares his party on the defensive ideologically. Furthermore, the ferocity of the assault upon the welfare state varies with the ideological climate. In the United States, where Anthony King regards attitudes as a convincing explanation of the underdeveloped welfare state, the growth of the welfare state has been arrested, deregulation initiated, and prospects for national health insurance or other major reforms dashed by massive federal deficits. In Sweden, where "the Social Democratic image of society" has gained hegemony, the parties of the right have been unable to carry out a program of retrenchment.

There are, however, two reasons for skepticism regarding public opinion as a satisfactory explanation of retrenchment. First, Richard Coughlin's study of attitudes toward welfare policy, still the most thorough available, found little evidence to suggest the possibility of serious inroads upon the welfare state. While noting the ambiguity of popular support for the welfare state, Coughlin concluded that the existence of a wide range of social programs is firmly established not only in the institutional structure of modern society, but in the opinion structures of modern populations as well and he predicted "a greater convergence in the structure and coverage of welfare state programs in rich nations".[25] These claims may still be borne out, but they seem to underestimate both the magnitude of the offensive against the welfare state and the variation in response to this offensive. If an analyst as capable as Coughlin did not find a basis in public opinion for retrenchment, then one must not accept too readily public opinion as the key determinant.

The second problem with the explanation through public opinion is precisely whether one should regard it as an autonomous force. Jürgen Habermas has magnificently described the decline of autonomous public opinion,[26] and, less elegantly, the mass media report their power in shaping the political and social consciousness of modern populations. Even more fundamentally, one can argue that to separate "public opinion" from the workings of society and to treat it as an "independent" variable is a serious error. Public opinion is not something separate from society; it is a central part of society. Society continually re-defines itself through its interpretation of "fundamentally contested concepts" such as freedom, equality, democracy, efficiency, security, solidarity, individualism, and the elements of personal well-being. In these contests different notions gain and lose hegemony and in the process the nature of the welfare state changes. Administrators act differently when Reaganites are in the ascendancy; cheating on the payment of taxes or the receipt of benefits varies with shifts in public consciousness. Shifts in public opinion (such as the emergence of "welfare backlash") are not the _cause_ of changes in the welfare state; they are _part and parcel_ of the change.

These considerations direct attention to the forces that shape political opinion. Propaganda and mass advertising shape all modern societies and bestow powers upon their practitioners. A key question, then (and one seldom asked in previous studies of welfare development), is: Who controls the media? This question suggests research on the relationship between publicly-controlled and privately-controlled media. It encourages examining whether there is a labor press or educational establishment that can rival business-supported enterprises. It seems probable that the massive private business domination of the American media weakens the American welfare state relative to societies with more public broadcasting. It appears, too, that the formidable educational and journalistic apparatus of the Swedish trade unions undergirds the continuing strength of Sweden's welfare state.[27] More extensive research would be required, however, to confirm these relationships.

There are limits to the media's power to shape public consciousness; appearances can hold out only so long against harsh reality. In the long run it is the impact of public policy which is the key political determinant in democratic societies. For a time the media may impose the criteria by which citizens judge public policy, but eventually the citizens themselves assess the quality of their jobs, schools, health care, residential situation, leisure opportunities, and political influence. It follows that political scientists cannot neglect the quality of public policy and its impact upon the population as crucial variables in welfare-statist development or retrenchment.

Public policy for a strong and effective welfare state requires a firm political foundation, imagination, and intelligence. Without a strong basis in a left party and trade union movement, the welfare-state's successes remain tenuous. Without regular infusions of new techniques of economic and social policy, the welfare state stagnates; it becomes unable to cope with the problems its successes create. The most advanced welfare states have not figured out how to operate an economy where the traditional capitalist incentives have been diminished, vital raw materials such as oil have sharply increased in price, and human labor power has been increasingly replaced by capital. The voters realize this fact and experiment with politicians who display confidence, if not competence.

The thrust of this argument should now be clear. The literature on the welfare state has tended to focus rather narrowly on the "social spending" of the welfare state to the exclusion of its regulatory activities and macro-economic management. Industrial development serves as a necessary condition for the modern welfare state, but explains little about the particular contours of specific welfare states. The nature of the state, the character of the bureaucracy, the mood of public opinion --all these variables allow a more nuanced picture of particular developments. At bottom, however, it is the balance of political forces that is crucial --who controls more assets, who organizes more citizens, who devises and implements more effective policy.

III

WHAT ARE THE FUNCTIONAL REQUIREMENTS OF THE WELFARE STATE AND HOW IS THE WELFARE STATE EVOLVING?

In its quest to purge itself of the fallacies of functionalism, modern social science has eschewed virtually any sort of functional analysis. Despite the prevalence of the metaphors of system and machinery in political analysis, social scientists have been reluctant to investigate and to assert that certain phenomena are indeed indispensable to the operation of particular arrangements. The claim that *X* is an essential condition or precondition for *Y* is hard to substantiate empirically, but such claims are so important to politicians (engaged in, say, deterrence or economic management) that they must be faced, for practical as well as theoretical reasons.

While the analysis of origins focuses upon initiating elements and the analysis of functional requirements upon sustaining elements, the two tend to be related. Both in their beginnings and in their continued existence, welfare states require political support, an economic foundation, and administrative prowess. No welfare state can persist without support in public opinion, some party backing, and parliamentary support. Every welfare state is parasitic (in the neutral biological sense) upon a productive economy, one that generates a surplus sufficient to finance its programs. Every welfare state also requires an administrative system capable of extracting these resources from the population and redeploying them.

These conditions constitute the essential prerequisites for a modern welfare state. Their collective importance is seldom emphasized, though a variety of authors stress the importance of each individual element. Thus Piven and Cloward maintain that the American welfare state has become stable rather than prone to fluctuating directly with the business cycle because its programs now have so many beneficiaries that they engender enough political support to render them invulnerable.[28] Korpi and Stephens stress not only the political importance of numerous beneficiaries, but also the strategic value of a strong and coherent labor movement organized into unions and a Social Democratic party. The necessity of a vigorous economy was not widely observed until the recessions of the 1970s; then a host of volumes traced the "crisis of the welfare state" to a sputtering economy. Similarly social scientists long took for granted the bureaucratic capacities essential for modern social policy, but Skocpol and Skowronek have remedied this situation by emphasizing the growth of the strong state.[29]

These assertions are non-controversial; the relative importance of political, economic, and bureaucratic requisites may be disputed, but few would question the necessity of each. One enters more controversial territory when one asserts that certain psychological dispositions are essential to the welfare state, and yet, given the importance of assumptions of self-interest in modern social science, the welfare state presents a puzzle, an anomaly. Why should anyone voluntarily yield resources to anyone else, particularly a stranger? By this account, a welfare state can endure only under special circumstances. First, a spirit of altruism may infuse the population; Britain during the Second World War exemplified this pattern, it has been argued, and the subsequent erosion of its welfare state testifies to the atrophy of the wartime community. A second possibility is that the welfare state extends universal rather than means-tested benefits. Universal benefits reduce redistribution, but they give many more citizens a stake in welfare policy whereas means-tested benefits divide populations into payers and beneficiaries, imperiling the sense of solidarity from which the welfare state derives its legitimacy. These examples suggest that either universal programs or enduring altruism may be functional requisites of a vigorous welfare state.

Elsewhere in this volume John Logue suggests that the welfare state requires a delicate set of restraints and disciplines that may flourish only in the generation that establishes the welfare state. The sense of mutual solidarity, the commitment to work, the restraint in the use of public services and in the pursuit of wage claims that marked the heyday of the Scandinavian welfare states may be indispensable to the smooth functioning of welfare states, but may be eroded by their actual operation; increased wealth may not be an adequate substitute for the sense of communal obligation. This argument is hard to judge; optimistically one may take it as a warning rather than as a prediction.

A third and perhaps even more popular line of argument locates the psychological foundation of the welfare state elsewhere. The secret to its legitimacy lies, the argument runs, in a tacit or explicit compromise between labor and capital to cease disputing over the division of the economic pie and to concentrate on making it bigger and sharing the increase.[30] Unsurprisingly, some analysts conclude that a cessation of growth jeopardizes the stability of the compromise. There are two striking, but little-noticed points about this now-hoary analogy of the growing pie. First, it rests almost exclusively on rational self-interest rather than justice. It assumes that both sides simply want "more" and are untroubled by considerations of equity. Value rationality and ideology yield completely to the rationality of interests. Second, the analogy obscures the explicit terms of specific historical compromises --which prerogatives business yields, labor's acceptance of technological change, the concrete formula for "sharing" the surplus created by growth. Thus, the analogy can shed little light on the general shift of business's position from a relatively conciliatory to a more aggressive posture _before_ the economic crisis of the 1970s.

These considerations about the functional requisites of the welfare state raise questions about its likely evolution. If essential elements of its operation are changing or disappearing, then it too must change. Conversely, if the welfare state undergoes a qualitative change, it is reasonable to infer that a particular set of circumstances may have been essential to its previous configuration. Regrettably, there is even less consensus on the evolutionary tendencies of the welfare state than there is on its functional requisites. The central issues in both popular and scholarly debate are (1) whether the prerequisites of the welfare state are mutually compatible and (2) whether the normal operation of the welfare state undermines them.

The conservative "overload" theses and the radical "fiscal crisis" thesis contend that demands upon the government eventually disrupt the functioning of its economic base. Government deficits regularly appear as the mechanism of destruction. The evidence in support of these claims consists of an extrapolation of trends; if *a*, *b*, and *c* continue, disaster must follow. The trouble with such claims is that they presume enormous political rigidity. They anticipate no political inventiveness and, particularly in the conservative version, assume the inefficiency and wastefulness of public sector activity.

A more sophisticated conservative argument contends that the high taxes necessary to finance the public sector undercut the crucial incentives that drive the capitalist system: the desire to profit, to work, to save, and to innovate.[31] The government's control of resources through taxation distorts markets and destroys motivation. Workers retreat to the underground economy in order to escape taxes; speculators invest in art or coins rather than productive enterprise; talented employees reject promotion because the increased salaries do not compensate for the additional responsibilities. None of these phenomena destroys the welfare state outright, but they all gradually restrict the flow of funds to the state and impair the efficiency of the economy. Gradually the nation's economy becomes less competitive until the potential for a major crisis arises.

Evaluating this argument fairly is difficult. It rests on abundant anecdotal material and common experience, but rigorous social scientific evidence for the thesis is scarce. Furthermore, its conceptual basis is unclear: Social scientists know very little about the level of incentives required to make a capitalist economy function. Just as social democrats are hard pressed to indicate "how much equality" they want, so conservatives shy away from specifying how wide inequalities must be to stimulate economic producers sufficiently. Nor is it clear that if the capitalist economy in its present form ceases to function nothing else will take its place; it is possible to imagine alternative economies driven by alternative motivations. Nonetheless, the conservative argument strongly suggests that highly developed welfare states undermine the capitalist foundation on which they rest.

A similar conclusion is drawn by Walter Korpi, but on a different basis and with vastly greater enthusiasm. Korpi's argument is not economic, but political and psychological in nature. He contends that as people gain more power over their situations through their organizations, they come to desire still more power. Concessions, far from appeasing them, encourage higher aspirations and greater mobilization.[32] Reformist achievements breed a desire to transcend the welfare state. A successful working-class movement therefore inclines not to embourgeoisement, but socialism. Like many arguments about potentiality, Korpi's does not admit of rigorous proof; his own evidence comes from one quite progressive union within the atypically well-organized Swedish labor movement. His study points to a possible way in which the welfare state might transform itself, but Swedish metalworkers are hardly representative of all blue-collar laborers, let alone other employees, in welfare states.[33]

Considering these forceful arguments that the "crisis of the welfare state" must result in systemic change, the tenacity of the welfare state is remarkable. *Eppor si muove*. Although conditions vary significantly from country to country, stagnation and recession have not wreaked general havoc upon welfare states. Advanced ones like Sweden and Austria remain virtually intact and even the major American programs have escaped largely unscathed. Welfare states survive because they retain political support, because even in recession their economies produce sufficient resources to support them, because public administration retains (perhaps even increases) its competence, and because in the face of rightward shifts in public opinion, the solidarity which the welfare state requires persists.

The relative stability of most welfare states contrasts sharply with academic and popular expectations of greater disruption. What accounts for the disparity between theory and reality? Put simply, some analysts have erroneously equated the conditions for welfare states' growth with the conditions for their persistence and have then concluded that because the conditions for growth no longer pertain, the welfare state must collapse. The evidence suggests that welfare state expansion requires economic growth and business prosperity and a vigorous thrust from the political left. International recessions, the resurgence of the ideological right, and a more aggressive business community have effectively blocked further expansion, but the power of the right is largely a negative power. Save possibly under the peculiar political conditions of modern Britain, it cannot reshape the welfare state to its heart's desire. Business resistance, embodied in its threat to engage in an investment strike or capital flight, imperils the welfare state, but does not convey power sufficient to override the opposition of unions and the public. In Sweden the failure of a general lockout demonstrated the limits to conservative power, as did in America the Reagan administration's failure to cut Social Security and disability programs substantially.

The welfare state rests on a delicate political compromise that gives politicians votes, business profits, and labor increased wages and benefits. When all three parties to the compromise are satisfied, the public sector faces little opposition to its expansion. When one or more of the parties is aggrieved, expansion is curtailed, but it is impossible for any one - and in numerous states any two actors - to dictate a solution.

These considerations stress the material, self-interested basis for welfare states' legitimacy, but welfare states, particularly the more advanced ones where "the Social Democratic image of society" is more dominant, also have a basis in the ethical sentiments of the public. Citizens can accept the fact that economic growth may cease, at least temporarily, and willingly shoulder sacrifices, but they want assurance that the distribution of social "bads" as well as "goods" reflects their sense of justice. Because justice is an "essentially contested concept," there will be not be universal agreement upon the justice of a particular policy, but if major political groups feel that justice has been approximated, a relatively harmonious outcome follows.

IV

WHO BENEFITS?

There is no consensus regarding the impact of the welfare state on individual and collective standards of living. Some Marxist analysts see the welfare state as redounding to the benefit of property owners; liberals and Social Democrats generally contend that it has provided at least a minimum standard of the "social rights of citizenship;" libertarian conservatives assert that welfare statist intrusions hamper market mechanisms and consequently reduce living standards below what they otherwise might have been. Some of this disagreement stems from irresolvable political differences about the nature of individual well-being. Some of it results from the logical difficulties inherent in weighing current achievements against the hypothetical attainments of alternative social arrangements that "might have been". Much of it results from a failure to agree on the proper measures of living standards, a difficulty which, as I shall show, has sources in the nature of politics as well as in the nature of social scientific research.

What should social scientists measure to assess the welfare state's impact on living standards? In his study of Class, Inequality and Political Order Frank Parkin argued that the "distribution of occupational income gives us perhaps the best overall view of the reward structure, because for the great majority of the population the main or only source of income is from employment".[34] On this basis Parkin showed that Scandinavian Social Democrats have done little to reduce the inequality of market incomes. This argument, however, misses the central dynamic of welfare statist institutions - their commitment to use taxes, transfers, and public services to redistribute market incomes and thus equalize disposable incomes and living conditions after public intervention. A meaningful assessment of the welfare state's consequences, then, must direct its attention elsewhere.

Some analysts have focussed on the impact of individual programs. Thus, Bruce Headey's study of Housing Policy in the Developed Economy found more substantial redistribution to the less advantaged in Sweden than in Britain; in the United States, his evidence suggested, middle - and upper - income individuals benefited disproportionately.[35] Various studies of the British National Health Service suggest that the middle class uses its services more than working-class clients. Studies of Medicaid and Medicare in the USA show increased utilization of health care facilities by the poor. Social Security analysts note that the system's progressive benefit structure slightly outweighs its regressive tax system so as to produce a modest redistribution of benefits to the less well-off and to reduce significantly levels of poverty among the elderly.

The diversity of findings on the impact of specific programs still leaves the question of the overall effect of welfare state programs. Perhaps the most extensive study of income distribution in advanced welfare states is Malcolm Sawyer's study of Income Distribution in OECD Countries.[36] These figures pertain to the late 1960s and early 1970s and are not fully comparable because of national differences in the compilation, of statistics, but the Netherlands and Sweden seem to record the lowest degree of inequality of post-tax income, France the highest degree of inequality. The rankings for pretax inequality are not very different. The impact of social transfers makes an important difference in the incomes of the poorest sectors of the population; as Sawyer reports, "The shares of the bottom two deciles depend very largely on government policy, particularly on the level and distribution of social transfers."[37] In every case transfers significantly increase the incomes of lower deciles: for Canada, Spain, Sweden, and the United Kingdom, for example, the bottom decile has virtually no pre-transfer income, but its share of national post-transfer incomes rises to 2.5 to 4.5 per cent. The second lowest deciles get 60 to 80 percent of their incomes through transfers. The upper deciles benefit much less from transfers, but interestingly in France and the United States the top decile receives the highest share of transfer payments![38] Using Sawyer's data, Walter Korpi has calculated the redistributive effect of government budgets; his findings showed that those welfare states generally thought to be the most advanced -- Sweden, Austria, West Germany, the Netherlands, and Norway -- have the most redistributive budgets; they also have low percentages of poverty-stricken and low levels of unemployment. Clearly the more advanced welfare states reduce the economic hardship of their poorest citizens.

Wilensky, Castles, and others have attempted to capture this impact by the construction of welfare indices. These sometimes have the advantage of moving beyond merely monetary indicators, but for our present purpose they suffer from an inability to show which sections of the population benefit from governmental welfare efforts. Such measures as the percentage of gross national product spent on social services cannot indicate the distributive effects of policy; they require inferences about their consequences. These consequences may differ substantially depending upon whether the nation employ universal, categorical, or means-tested welfare programs. They may vary depending upon the degree to which different societies employ <u>preventive</u> social policy that obviates the need for certain kinds of social spending. Such measures further assume that government outlays produce increments of welfare in a relatively efficient and equitably distributed way, although the specific standard of equity goes unmentioned.

Similarly the use of data on income distribution offers only a poor approximation of an accurate portrait of relative living standards. Sawyer notes the idiosyncrasies of various statistical measures of inequality, but a more fundamental difficulty arises from the fact that monetary income increasingly becomes a less accurate indicator of individual well-being. Even if one corrects for the impact of taxes and transfers and ignores the crucial mater of individual wealth, the resulting figures on disposable income neglect the role of public services, fringe benefits, and "amenities" on individual well-being. The quality of such public services as roads, lighting, education, police and fire protection, and broadcasting, not to mention opportunities for recreation and political participation, varies substantially from country to country and even from neighborhood to neighborhood. Fringe benefits, as Titmuss' classic study of Income Distribution and Social Change demonstrated long ago, flow disproportionately to the well-to-do; company cars, stock options, subsidized recreation, free college educations and improved pension plans escape standard statistical categories although they bestow enormous and unequal benefits upon their recipients.[39] Finally, such amenities as pleasant working conditions, attractive housing and residential environments, and extensive educational and recreational opportunities substantially affect the quality of life. To capture these facets of living standards requires broader social indicators such as those used in the Scandinavian "level of living" surveys.[40] In general, these surveys show a broad and continuing equalization of living standards. After reviewing these data, Gunnar Heckscher concludes that they demonstrate that "the process of economic growth, combined with the establishment of welfare states and the leveling out of economic disparities between major social groups, has also upset traditional class structures in the Nordic countries."[41]

Is a more accurate answer to the question of who benefits then simply a matter of more detailed social surveys? While one can readily believe that the data provided by such surveys would enhance and refine knowledge, there are two reasons that weigh heavily against exaggerated expectations. First, such indicators of individual welfare leave open questions of causation, in particular the issue of whether welfare statist measures accelerate or retard economic growth. Proponents of the welfare state have long argued that macroeconomic management, "automatic stabilizers" such as unemployment insurance and means-tested outlays, and preventive social policy produce an economy more socially efficient than private markets alone can generate. Critics cite the disincentives produced by high taxation, the inept timing of counter-cyclical policy, "excessive" regulation, and the inertia of public bureaucracies as obstacles to rapid growth. To my knowledge, no comprehensive assessment of the total impact of all the relevant factors has been carried out, nor frankly, is it clear that evaluation of "disincentives" and comparable items can be anything more than estimates subject to considerable ideological manipulation. Nonetheless, without knowing how the welfare state affects economic growth, it is impossible to resolve satisfactorily the issue of its impact upon individual welfare.

The second shortcoming of level of living surveys is that they are political dynamite. Accurate statistics on disparities in wealth and income come very low on a list of conservative priorities; it was hardly accidental that the Reagan administration sharply reduced the appropriations for major statistical agencies. More progressive administrations like the Roosevelt or Kennedy-Johnson Presidencies may establish Temporary National Economic Committees or study the incidence of poverty, but the ensuing findings are not always welcome. In a classic instance the Swedish Social Democrats in the late 1960s set up a Low Income Commission, only to dismantle much of it in the early 1970s when it found poverty embarrassingly persistent despite four decades of Social Democratic rule. In short, the control of information is one of the fruits of political power, and few governments in a conservative era will choose to expose the inequalities that pervade their societies and thus risk antagonizing powerful interests. To analyze who benefits is not an abstract academic exercise, but a political act --and that fact explains why political scientists have such meager data for a more definitive sketch of income and wealth distribution in the welfare state.

In the absence of such information the safest conclusion is that the redistributive impact of public policy varies from program to program and from welfare state to welfare state. Welfare policy has significantly enhanced the condition of workers and the poor, particularly in states with strong labor movements and Social Democratic Parties and with weak, divided parties of the right. In less ambitious welfare states public policy may have done little more than simply offset the increasing inequality of market distribution, and in some "positive states" it may have actually have exacerbated inequality. Furthermore, the impact of public policy may vary historically within a specific state; prosperity and oligopoly are conducive to business acceptance of modest redistribution, but stagnation and increasing competition produce growing resistance. (In this respect, Marxists who stress a structural <u>limit</u> to welfare statist reforms within capitalist society may well be correct.) In short, there is no general answer as to who benefits from the welfare state; the answer depends on the type of welfare state and the prevailing balance of political and economic forces.

V

IS THE WELFARE STATE A "GOOD THING"?

The imprecision of this question suggests the vastness of the territory that it opens. The political theory of the welfare state has come in for extensive treatment in recent years, having been treated not only in such classic works as Rawls' *A Theory of Justice* and Hayek's *The Mirage of Social Justice*, but in a host of lesser volumes.[42] Clearly a comprehensive treatment of the ideological debate surrounding the welfare state is impossible here, but two topics merit brief consideration, first, the general resurgence of conservative opposition to the welfare state, and second, the more specific "entrepreneurial" critique.

It is not altogether clear how to account for the upsurge of libertarian conservatism, as the abundance of metaphors ("waves," "winds," "currents," "upheaval", "revolution") rather than solid analysis indicates. The failure of Keynesianism to confront "stagflation" effectively, disenchantment with some public programs and the increased taxes necessary to support them, growing international business competition, the decline of the traditional manufacturing sector, the vast resources available to right-wingers, and other factors might be cited as sources of the conservative revival. In any case it is clear that the debate over the merits of the welfare state has been reopened and that the major challenge no longer comes from the left, but the right, and specifically from a revitalized but not much refurbished classical liberal economics.

The Seventies have seen the resurrection of the conservative utopia of a "free market" economy virtually devoid of governmental intervention. In this magical world the crucial assumptions of microeconomic theory --free entry, large numbers of buyers and sellers, complete (and costless) information, no transportation costs --are taken as facts. Oligopoly is ignored. Consumers and workers are taken as rational, well-informed creatures, unless of course they join unions, in which case their choices cease to represent the actions of "market forces" and become an "interference" with markets. Labor can pursue jobs as freely and as widely as capital can pursue profitable opportunities. Government, in addition to enforcing contracts and providing national defense, may engage in modest, paternalistic efforts and correct for monopolies and neighborhood effects, but only when

Milton Friedman approves. Why people who otherwise pride themselves on their hard-headedness and practicality can subscribe to so utopian a design is an intriguing question.

The doctrine may flourish because it generally functions in much the same way that classical utopias functioned -- not as a blueprint for a new society, but as a basis for criticizing and moderately reforming existing institutions. Where it becomes a blueprint, as in Thatcher's England, the results are disastrous. In its more moderate applications it legitimates businessmen's efforts to eliminate unwanted regulations and to reassert their status as dominant social actors. In either case it too readily accepts the dichotomy between markets and politics, missing the crucial point that many welfare statist measures aim not to displace markets, but make them work better, in conditions that more closely approximate the assumptions of classical economics. Public employment services, for example, improve the functioning of labor markets by organizing information about jobs; mobility allowances reduce transportation costs for workers changing jobs; consumer legislation provides buyers with the information needed to make rational choices. The aim of the welfare state is not to abolish markets, but to make them function efficiently and in a more equitable social setting.

A second form of the new conservative critique, which I shall call the "entrepreneurial" critique, rests on a solid empirical foundation and merits careful scrutiny by proponents of the welfare state. Like their great prophet, Joseph Schumpeter, these critics often perceive the defects of the classical liberal defense of the market economy; they recommend liberal capitalism for its stimulus to innovation and "creative destruction" of outmoded production. The hero of this school is the creative entrepreneur, the inventive genius who devises new products, services, and techniques and thus revolutionizes old industries and creates new ones. For the entrepreneurial critics the symbol of the modern economy is not the new GM Saturn plant so much as smaller Silicon Valley enterprises introducing new products. They note that smaller firms contribute most new jobs and therefore stake out the future for the entrepreneurial sector --warning only that government not be allowed to suffocate these thriving new shoots in an environment of high taxes and excessive regulation. Thus, this critique, starting from a different foundation, arrives at the same prescriptions for public policy.

The entrepreneurial critique shows a tendency to blur distinctions between innovative new businesses and old-style financial manipulation or franchise operations, and it neglects the victims of economic growth, but it exposes a central dilemma for the advocates and practitioners of welfare-statism -- their Janus-headed attitude toward business. Particularly for classical Social Democrats business is both a malefactor requiring regulation and control (at least), and on the other hand it is the source of investment, new jobs, and economic growth. Long accustomed to think of business in terms of nineteenth-century cartels, large fully developed enterprises seemingly at the height of their technology, Social Democrats have been slow to make a place in both theory and practice for the Schumpeterian entrepreneur. This deficiency leaves them exposed to the entrepreneurial critique and helps explain the apparent disorientation of the modern Social Democratic parties. They do not have a formula for growth without entrepreneurship, and to support entrepreneurial activity violates theoretical norms.

Common to the classical economic and entrepreneurial critiques is their celebration of individualism. The new individual finances his education through vouchers, private scholarships, and work; maintains his health through jogging and good nutrition; hires his own security guards; counsels (and legitimizes) himself by reading _Looking Out for Number One_; and secures his retirement through his personal IRA. He prides himself on his right to spend his own income, earned not (he imagines) with the cooperative efforts of past and present generations of workers, but strictly through his own prowess. With minimal effort he persuades himself that his privileges are consistent with Rawls' standard that they redound to the benefit of the least well-off and Walzer's criterion of community standards.

This portrait fits only a small portion of contemporary society -- those well-to-do groups who can secure most of their needs through their own resources. It does not fit the marginally employed, those with unhealthy work environments, those with dangerous neighborhoods, poor schools, and incomes insufficient to save for a more comfortable retirement -- or to own their own homes. And of course, this portrait does not fit the well-to-do individual accurately. It neglects the contribution made to his skills by stimulating teachers and colleagues; it overlooks the social and cultural factors that create a market for his talents; it forgets that stripped of his material resources and left to his own devices in a developing society, prosperity might elude him. He cannot be sure that his privileges reflect his merits so much as his power and his birth. Nor can he meet Tawney's challenge that he shun acquisitiveness, cultivate fraternity with his fellows, practice solidarity, and work for a society in which everyone has an equal chance to control the conditions of his life. In short, he cannot be certain that individualism will be less satisfying than community or that he should view the state as a threat rather than as a mutual benefit association.

VI

HOW SHOULD WE CONCEIVE OF THE VALUES OF THE VALUES OF THE WELFARE STATE?

A segment of modern social science, indebted to utilitarianism and classical economics, treats the modern citizen as just such an isolated individual who strives to maximize his utility. He has material interests but no ideal interests, or if he does, they can be assimilated into the category of material interests. Having already suggested the moral emptiness of this portrait, I now want to suggest its empirical shortcomings.

Many practitioners of rational choice theory have difficulty accounting for the existence of the welfare state in general and many of its specific policies in particular. Wedded to classical economic analysis, they believe that public intervention renders markets less efficient: such intervention is therefore irrational. Yet it occurs and enjoys widespread support in an ostensibly democratic policy. How can rational actors be so consistently misguided and act so contrary to their own interests? To attribute the expansion of the welfare state to bureaucratic self-interest not only is empirically questionable, but begs the question of how these bureaucracies originated. To attribute expansion to an excess of democracy undermines the fundamental rationalistic assumptions of the theory. Nor will it do to suggest that groups, not individuals, are the source of the trouble, for this school faces the classic problem of explaining how groups cohere in the face of the widespread impulse to be a free rider. If the existence of unions and political parties is problematic, then strikes are even more perplexing, not to mention dissent based on religious or ideological commitment.

Without some sort of social content rational choice theory rapidly becomes purely formalistic. Without reference to social structure, it cannot explain why similarly endowed rational choosers divide into politically conflicting groups; in short, it cannot account for politics! When the assumption of a class society is introduced, interesting results follow as they do in the work of Adam Przeworski.

Przeworksi is able to demonstrate the working of class politics and of coalitions formed around the structure of particular programs.[43] He is most persuasive when he introduces ideological considerations as well.

The central problems with rational choice theory is its exaltation of rationalistic psychology and its consequent underplaying of ideal (or ideological) interests and of social structure. It might illuminate the free-floating, affluent, secular middle-class and its behavior. It accounts poorly for more traditional working-class voters who attach themselves to their party partly from material interests, but even more from a sense of its being "our party" and a dedication to a vaguely socialist ideology. There is no reason to think that orientations to politics should be all of a kind; on the contrary, in a class-based society with different degrees of technological development it is logical to expect different styles of politics. To capture them adequately requires a marriage of rational choice theory with Weber's emphasis on ideal interests and Marx's insistence on structural determinants. Otherwise, it is difficult to understand how that peculiarly modern phenomenon, the rationally choosing individual, devoid of family, religious, or political ties, came into existence and to appreciate that he is only one type of modern citizen along with the religious fundamentalist, the committed Social Democrat, and a host of others.

****

I have tried to show that much of the literature on the welfare state addresses six central theoretical problems. These problems, rather than any dominant theory, define this research area. Marxists, pluralists, Weberians, rational choice theorists, Social Democrats, anti-collectivists, and others contend with varying degrees of success to solve these problems. In this respect social science mirrors the politics of the welfare state --it is a shifting balance of competing forces held together by relative consensus on some issues, but separated elsewhere by seemingly irreconcilable ideological differences.

NOTES

1. Piven, Francis Fox and Richard Cloward. Regulating the Poor. Pantheon Books, 1971; Janowitz, Morris. Social Control of the Welfare State. University of Chicago Press, 1976; Jackman, Richard. Politics and Social Equality: A Comparative Analysis. John Wiley, 1975; Heclo, Hugh. Modern Social Politics in Britain and Sweden. Yale University Press, 1974; Buchanan, James and Richard Wagner. Democracy in Deficit. Academic Press, 1977; Bell, Daniel. The Politics of Post-Industrial Society. Basic Books, 1973; Furniss, Norman and Timothy Tilton. The Case for the Welfare State, Indiana University Press, 1977; Heidenheimer, Arnold, Hugh Heclo and Carolyn Adams. Comparative Public Policy. St. Martin's Press, 1975.

2. Buchanan and Wagner, op.cit; Friedman, Milton. Capitalism and Freedom, University of Chicago Press, 1962.

3. Wilensky, Harold. The Welfare State and Equality. University of California Press, Berkeley, 1975.

4. Janowitz, op. cit., p. xii.

5. Cutright, Phillips. "Political Structure, Economic Development and National Social Security Programs, "American Journal of Sociology, 71, 1965, 537-550.

6. Pryor, Frederic. Property and Industrial Organization in Communist and Capitalist Countries. Indiana University Press, 1968.

7. Piven and Cloward, 1971, op. cit.

8. O'Connor, James The Fiscal Crisis of the State. St. Martin's Press, 1973; Gough, Ian. The Political Economy of the Welfare State, Macmillan, 1979; Piven, Francis Fox and Richard Cloward. Poor People's Movements. Pantheon Books, 1977; Piven, Francis Fox and Richard Cloward. The New Class War. Pantheon Books, 1982.

9. O'Connor, op. cit., p.6.

10. Ibid., p.7.

11. Greenberg, Edward. Serving the Few, Wiley, 1974.

12. Gough, op. cit., p. 127.

13. Ibid., p. 127.

14. Korpi, Walter. The Working Class in Welfare Capitalism. Routledge & Kegan Paul, 1978; and, The Democratic Class Struggle, Federation of Swedish Industries, Stockholm, 1982. See also Rydén, Bengt and Villy Bergström. Sweden: Choices for Economic and Social Policy in the 1980s. George Allen & Unwin, 1982.

15. Stephens, John. _The Transition from Capitalism to Socialism_. Macmillan, 1979, p.174. In _Poor People's Movements_ Piven and Cloward maintain that less organized and more spontaneous obstreperousness on the part of the disadvantaged can tip the balance of social forces and effect change. They differ form Korpi and Stephens in their negative assessment of highly organized movements.

16. Elvander, Nils. _Skandinavisk arbetarrörelse_, Liber Förlag, 1980; Flora, Peter Arnold and Heidenheimer. The Development of Welfare State in Europe and America. Transaction Books, 1981.

17. Castles, Francis. _The Social Democratic Image of Society_. Routledge Kegan & Paul, 1978.

18. Skocpol, Theda. "Political Response to Capitalist Crisis: Neo-Marxist Theories of the State and the Case of the New Deal" _Politics and Society_. 10, 2, 1980, 155-201.

19. Skowronek, Stephen. _Building a New American State_. Cambridge University Press, 1982.

20. _The Case for the Welfare State_ assumed too readily that government was little more than a transmission belt for popular wishes, Furniss and Tilton, op. cit.

21. C.F., Miliband, Ralph. _The State on Capitalist Society_. Weidenfeld and Nicholson, 1969.

22. Heclo, op. cit.

23. King, Anthony. "Ideas, Institutions, and the Policies of Governments: A Comparative Analysis, Parts I and II". _British Journal of Political Science_, 3, 3 and 4, 1974, 291-314, 409-425.

24. This strategy originated in a conversation with Ed Greenberg.

25. Coughlin, Richard. _Ideology. Public Opinion and Welfare_. University of California, 1980, pp. 160, 156, 159.

26. Habermas, Jürgen. _Strukturwandel der Öffentlichkeit_, Luchterhand, 1965.

27. C.F. Linton, Martin. The _The Swedish Road to Socialism_. Fabian Society, 1984.

28. Piven and Cloward, _New Class War_, op. cit.

29. Skocpol, op. cit.; Skowroneck, op. cit.

30. See, e.g., Adler-Karlsson, Gunnar. _Functional Socialism_, Prisma, 1968.

31. Meyerson, Per-Martin. _The Welfare State in Crisis --The Case of Sweden_. Routledge and Kegan Paul, 1983.

32. Korpi, _The Working Class in Welfare Capitalism_, op. cit., p. 32ff.

33. C.F. Stephans, op. cit.

34. Parkin, Frank. Class, _Inequality and Political Order_. MacGibbon Ekee, 1971.

35. Headey, Bruce. _Housing Policy in the Developed Economy_. St. Martins Press, 1979.

36. Sawyer, Malcolm. Income Distribution in OECD Countries. OECD, 1976.
37. Ibid., p. 22.
38. Ibid., pp. 34 and 35.
39. Titmuss, Richard. Income Distribution and Social Change. Allen & Unwin, 1965.
40. Nordic Council. Level of Living and Inequality in the Nordic Countries. Nordic Council, 1984.
41. Heckscher, Gunnar. The Welfare State and Beyond. University of Minnesota Press, 1984.
42. Rawls, John. A Theory of Justice. Harvard University Press, 1971; Hayek, Friedrich. The Mirage of Social Justice. University of Chicago Press, 1976.
43. Przeworski, Adam and Michael Walerstein, "The Structure of Class Conflict in Democratic Capitalist Societies." American Political Science Review, 76(2), 1982, pp. 215-238.

II.

Douglas E. Ashford

Welfare States as Institutional Choices

Contemporary analyses of the welfare state generally view the immense explosion of social programs and social policies over the past generation as either a governmental response to irrepressible political demands[1] or as a function of economic growth.[2] These are of course the traditional distinctions of neo-classical economic analysis roughly transformed to produce demand and supply theories about the growth of welfare states. They have the distinct virtue of permitting us to make quite elaborate cross-national comparisons of governmental performance in the area of social policies and social expenditure.[3] However, these two approaches have difficulty in dealing with the internal differences among welfare states, their institutional and political contexts, the actual intentions of policymakers, and the real constraints on governmental policymaking. They treat the historical and constitutional development of western democracies as more or less identical, or at best they introduce institutional differences in highly aggregated ways.[4]

The purpose of this chapter is to suggest that the emergence and growth of welfare states was by no means a simple political process. If our concept of the welfare state is limited to the period after the major institutional commitments had been made, that is, since about 1950, we are not likely to perceive, much less to understand, critically important institutional choices that each democracy made since roughly 1890. In fact, the most intense debates over expanding social policies took place in the latter half of the nineteenth century. The traditional liberal state of nineteenth century Europe was not designed to formulate, finance and implement highly complex social policies. On the contrary, the early democratic state was intended to perform only such minimal functions as national defense, management of national debt, and maintenance of law and order. National budgets were seldom more than ten percent of national income, and few imagined them ever being more.

Seen in its full historical and political complexity, the institutionalization of welfare states was in many respects a much more delicate and demanding political exercise than the more recent conflicts and controversies over adjusting the welfare state to open-ended demands and to economic cycles. To be sure, these adaptations create political strain, but they pale before the uncertainties confronting the early developers of welfare states. Though not always articulated clearly, the leading politicians and administrators of turn of the century Europe were aware that they were making major structural adjustments in the direction, organization and values of democratic states. Possibly the greatest fault of the macro-economic and macro-sociological comparisons of welfare states is that they do not account for the diverse, and often ingenious, ways by which these policymakers began to establish new institutional capabilities nearly a century ago.

An analysis of the institutional development of welfare states is of course not intended to explain the absolute differences commonly analyzed in the more quantitative, socio-economic analyses of welfare states.[5] In their full complexity, the democratic institutional frameworks for decisionmaking, like democratic systems as a whole, are unique. On the other hand, if welfare states are differentiated only in relation to external conditions or by average performance among such systems, our research cannot include institutional differences. As a first step toward developing such an institutional theory of welfare states, I intend to describe the major institutional differences between Britain and France as they affected the construction of welfare policies from the turn of the century. There were, of course, a number of critically important institutional hurdles in developing social policies a century ago, but perhaps the two most pressing problems were to build a socially oriented and socially competent bureaucracy and to reconcile the left, meaning the nascent socialist parties and the labor movements, to the possibility of using social policies to ameliorate the most severe social problems of highly industrial societies.

If these two changes are assessed in relation to the readiness and skill of adapting earlier liberal welfare state practices to the requirements of social policymaking, the conventional interpretation of British and French progress is reversed. First, the response time of the two democracies differs significantly. Britain might be considered committed to some form of social policy reform, if not the welfare state in all its complexity, from the Poor Law Amendment Act of 1834. But even taking the more generous period of the intense social debates and inquiries of mid-Victorian Britain, roughly forty years elapsed before major social insurance programs appeared in 1911. In contrast, the early French experience was to accumulate social legislation, starting from the famous loi Roussel of 1893 providing medical assistance to school children (fifteen years before similar legislation in Britain), and continuing to workmen's compensation in 1898, the 1905 law on care for the sick, disabled and elderly and the initial pension law of 1910. Thus under much less stable political conditions than in Britain, the French laid the groundwork for their version of the welfare state over roughly the same time.[6]

Second, there are diverse measures of institutional flexibility in the formulation and implementation of early social policies. British politics erected important political and administrative roadblocks. The fledgling social programs in the Board of Education, which are in many respects the first major national agency to actively pursue social programs in Whitehall, were constantly harassed by Treasury's refusal to award top salaries to its officials.[7] The same handicap was imposed on both the Ministries of Health and the Labour after World War I. British officials seemed uncomfortable with social policies and, in fact, British government was quite willing to virtually dismantle most of the major social agencies of government after World War I,[8] a lesson that was not lost on the Labour Party officials working within the coalition government during World War II.[9] In contrast, the French state found room for socially-oriented officials from the turn of the century. In 1886, a Conseil Supèrieure de Prèvoyance was organized in the Ministry of the Interior, and in 1906 (twelve years before Britain) a Ministry of Labour was created.[10] Despite the meager performance of the French social security system, the ministry prepared the administrative foundations for an extended effort between the wars to build an integrated French welfare state, in many respects more sophisticated than the British effort because of French acknowledgement that social policies were intimately linked to achieving labor peace.[11]

Third, historical research permits us to assess the degree of institutional innovation involved in the two developments. Essentially, Britain never departed from the eighteenth century doctrine of ministerial responsibility and parliamentary supremacy. Moreover, throughout the early development of social policies, the Treasury successfully defended its dominance,in many ways much more damaging than the French administrative control of the tutelle. The interwar period is in fact the zenith of Treasury power, and many of the most damaging controls were in fact imposed in 1918 to make sure that the new social ministries did not act without Treasury endorsement.[12] In contrast, the French social security system, however inadequate, raised basic constitutional questions about democratic governance in the Third Republic. From the earliest debates, the unions demanded, and eventually achieved, autonomous organization of the social security system. Contrary to our more recent view of the suffocating power of French administration, the early funds for child allowances, pensions and workmen's compensation were organized outside government and included union and worker representation on their administrative councils.[13] In addition, the political pressure for major legislation in the first decade of the century came from the Bloc des Gauches, a combination of radical, radical socialist and socialist power, that saw social reform as directly linked to the institutionalization of French democracy against the right. The demands for a French welfare state were more confused than in Britain at the turn of the century, and the performance much inferior, but even so the emergence of the French welfare state was, and remains, indelibly linked to democracy.

Thus, there are perhaps three important indicators of the institutional capabilities of the early liberal states in response to the challenge of the welfare state: response time, organizational flexibility and political innovation. Lest the British welfare state seem too badly treated, the point should not be lost that perhaps Britain did less well in terms of these institutional measures because its material performance was better. As an institutional challenge, devising a welfare state in Britain might be seen as too easy. There was of course an immense amount of reflection and speculation about the development of new social policies,[14] but in the final analysis there was relatively little basic institutional change. Space does not permit us to explore fully the consequences of political ease of enlarging social benefits and social protection in Britain, but it may be noted that the inability of the British state to keep pace with continental developments fifty years later may be seen as the price paid for not devising a better institutional answer to the rapid growth of social policies nearly a century ago. For the moment, we can examine in more detail two critically important political transitions and how they fit into the different institutional and political development of the two countries.

ADMINISTRATIVE INITIATIVES

While it would be an exaggeration to say that the development of welfare states completely accounts for the present complexities of modern democratic states, each democracy had to devise a radically new administrative structure in order to administer the growing array of social services and social benefits. Obviously, the change was dependent on how fast social policy expanded, what kinds of departures were made on behalf of social justice and the organizational requirements of such policies. Less obviously, and integral to an understanding of how the politics of social policy takes on its distinctive forms, the kinds of organizations and the forms of bureaucratic control vary with the past administrative experience of each country. The organizational solutions of organizing the welfare state were by no means obvious to policymakers at the turn of the century. Moreover, the existing higher civil services were then, as now, well aware of their political self-interest. As might be expected, they took precautions to see that new social agencies and ministries were built in ways that would not jeopardize their administrative power.

If we consider the interaction of administrative and political structures in relation to the development of modern welfare states, the rapid growth of the British welfare state following World War II does not appear quite as rapid and embracing. Again, one needs an historical perspective on the more general problem of how the British developed a modern bureaucracy and, more specifically, how the early agencies concerned with social policy were linked to British government. Unlike France and Germany, Victorian Britain had no tradition of strong, unified civil service. The higher civil service did not take clear shape until nearly forty years after Britain was committed to developing a new form of Poor Law assistance in 1834.

Early industrial development, and consequent appearance of poverty and urban neglect, forced Britain to make social adjustments, but the initial administrative arrangements to handle the social costs of industrialization were cautious and modest. Victorian politicians were highly suspect of the new Poor Laws and, in fact, the new rules and requirements were unevenly enforced across the country.[15] The mid-Victorian preoccupation with public health and sanitation reveals the reluctance to establish strong administrative bodies, most clearly in the long struggle of Sir John Simon and the Local Government Board.[16] The early impulse was to load the financial and administrative burden of social assistance onto the localities.[17] Much the same strategy was followed in mid-Victorian Britain with the second wave of social legislation to improve public health. As national legislation on education developed, most importantly from the Education Act of 1902, the strategy of allocating the conflictual decisions to localities was once again pursued.[18] At the turn of the century the new breed of higher civil servants gave political significance to social reform and government gradually entered the more complex areas of social insurance, labor relations and employment. But over roughly the first century of growth in British social policy, the structure of the state changed little in response to social needs.

Thus, the interesting administrative question about the British welfare state is how and why it endured the inequities and inefficiencies of its own policy machinery as long as it did. There was political resistance to national intervention in social problems among all the liberal states, but finding an administrative formula for such adjustments was particularly difficult for Britain. For nearly seventy years, Parliament tolerated the inequities and insufficiencies of the Poor Laws. The temporary solution in 1871 was to assign Poor Law administration, along with a number of local government issues, to the Local Government Board,[19] but Gladstone refused to make the Board an agency of first importance, and it was never able to pay the salaries or provide the prestige that would attract the most talented civil servants. By the time that Lloyd George and Churchill were preparing the social insurance legislation of 1911, the Board had become an administrative backwater of Whitehall and actually resisted expanding social protection. There was an enormous amount of social legislation in Victorian Britain, but it was loosely integrated with national administration. It took roughly twenty years to develop the Northcote-Trevelyan proposals into an effective framework for a higher civil service, and this structure was not attuned to social policymaking.[20] As new social agencies were created, there appeared to be more effort to make sure they would not intrude on accustomed practice than to integrate them with the administrative structure of the state.

The administrative complexity of the welfare state reveals many weaknesses of British administration. Remote from the intricacies of implementation and protected by the political elite, the high civil service developed a curious relationship to the array of social services and social benefits that grew from the turn of the century. Each new social program became the basis for a new administrative departure, often under the aegis of a leading figure of the new breed of elite civil servants that emerged during the Edwardian period and thrived between the wars. The new leaders of the welfare state were such towering figures as Sir Edwin Morant for education, Sir Arthur Newsholme for health, Sir Hubert Llwelyn Smith for labor relations, and, of course, William (later Sir William) Beveridge for unemployment. They worked skillfully within the Whitehall structure, but their success was often due to their ability to circumvent cumbersome administrative practices and sometimes to their readiness to achieve their ends by subterfuge.[21] Progress was made, but with a hodge-podge of administrative devices, an enormous amount of interministerial intrigue and, most important, with numerous false starts and improvised solutions. Perhaps nothing more could be expected because these were, after all, the initial experiments in creating a democratic welfare state bureaucracy.

But the paradox within the British welfare state bureaucracy is in many ways still present in the organization of social services and in the British approach to formulating social policies. On the one hand, preoccupation with poverty, growing out of the prolonged history of the antiquated Poor Laws, helped perpetuate a giant government agency for public assistance.[22] Every country has the problem of reconciling contributory benefits with earnings, but the boundary between assistance based on earnings and on need has gradually disappeared in other countries as the diversity of social needs are recognized. Under the extreme pressures of the depression, Britain made the administration of public assistance a national responsibility, but still has not erased the early Victorian preoccupation with the "deserving" and "undeserving" poor. The shadow of the Benthamite disciple, Sir Edwin Chadwick, who was the influential secretary to the 1834 Royal Commission on the Poor Laws,[23] still hangs over the British welfare state.

The vestiges of Poor Law prejudice would be understandable were it not that British officials, including Beveridge himself, repeatedly set out to eradicate them. As in all democracies, ultimate responsibility must be laid at the door of politicians who, for good reasons, never found poverty a very attractive political issue, but one must also consider the extent to which the many reforms and reorganizations of British social security programs failed to produce an attractive and workable administrative alternative.[24] The sharply divided organization of social protection in Britain is not an intentional result of social policy, but more clearly a function of how politicians and administrators were able to assert their self-interest in relation to social policy choices. Indeed, the turbulent administrative history of what many regard as the most successful of British social services, the National Health Service, demonstrates the curious way that political-administrative linkages appear inappropriate to policymaking under the welfare state. Even the social services that work relatively well in Britain seem to be interminably at odds with administrative politics.

The French, of course, brought an entirely different administrative tradition to bear on developing their version of the welfare state. A unitary administrative structure with a large field service, French administration, though not without its shortcomings in the social policy field, was able to take the diversification of governmental activity in stride. As demonstrated in the compromises imposed on administrative plans for social security in 1947 and 1948,[25] the French bureaucracy could not ignore politics. The bureaucracy clearly wanted a more centralized and more standardized social security system, but they were effectively blocked on many important fronts by legislative directives and amendments to the initial *ordonnance* of 1945.[26] The argument is not that the political will to restrain administrative ambitions uniformly works in France any more than in most democracies, or even that legislative controls over bureaucracy are regularly successful. But the political history of the French social security system is the negotiation of acceptable compromises between political forces and administrative ideals. In this regard, the most prominent figure in creating the current social security structure, Pierre Laroque, has observed, "Social effort in France as elsewhere is largely a political affair."[27]

While much has been written about the shortcomings of the French administrative elite, their role in paving the way for the tardy, but rapid, development of the French welfare state from 1945 is important. In order to assess the administrative context, one must trace the development of bureaucratic interest in social policy at least from the Third Republic. As with the emergence of many French ministries, specialization first appeared within the Ministry of the Interior. In 1886, Henri Monod persuaded the government to establish a Conseil Supérieur d'Assistance Publique and, as Directeur de l'Assistance Publique, he became a tireless advocate of further research and inquiry into the problems of poverty.[28] His strategy was clearly to build a network of departmental and communal bureaux d'assistance publique to complement the longer standing local bureaux de bienfaisance. Monod was active in the early parliamentary debates on reforming public assistance, and clearly held the sympathy of the early socialists and radicals of the left. Amid the "wild cheers" of the Chamber of Deputies in 1903, he advocated extending the 1893 law on free medical assistance for the poor in order to construct a national policy to redirect the unreliable efforts of the local bureaux de bienfaisance toward a more equitable and state-supported system of poor relief. He brought the Chamber to its feet to applaud his claim that "public assistance is owed to those who, temporarily or permanently, are physically unable to earn the necessities of existence."[29] His approach to social reform in France is reflected in nearly all the social legislation since that time.

With the creation of a Ministry of Labor in 1906, the thrust for social reform within the French government moved to the new ministry. As in many democracies prior to and following World War I, labor turmoil in France shifted the burden of social reform to labor relations. Although the French welfare state made slow progress between the wars, it had important support from certain higher civil servants. The chain leads directly to the accomplishments of Alexandre Parodi and Pierre Laroque after the Second World War. Laroque himself is emphatic in stressing the continuity of administrative pressure for social reform, nearly all based on efforts by the Conseil d'Etat.[30] The first official in this chain is Georges Cahen-Salvador, who was an advisor to the Conseil Supérieur de Travail and the main consultant to three Ministers of Labor during the vigorous, if unproductive, social policy debates of the 1920s.[31] Cahen-Salvador was Director of Pensions in the Ministry of Labor from 1920 to 1923, where he found support from a young member of the Conseil d'Etat, Alexandre Parodi.

In 1930, Parodi relinquished his other official duties to become secretary of the Conseil National Economique, the forerunner of the post-war Conseil Supérieur de la Securité Sociale which linked the social reform activities of the Ministry of Labor to the social partners. Among Parodi's responsibilities was the examination of all projets-loi dealing with labor and social problems of the Blum government, and in this activity he enlisted another young member of the Conseil d'Etat, Pierre Laroque. In 1939, Parodi became Directeur Général of Labor, and his expertise, plus his extraordinary role in organizing the Gaullist segment of the Resistance,[32] made him a natural candidate for Minister of Labor in de

Gaulle's post-war cabinet. In cooperation with his protegè, Laroque, the 1945 ordonnance became the bedrock of the French social security system. This sequence of personal and dedicated relationships, all resting within the Conseil d'Etat, suggests that French administration was by no means uniformly inhospitable to the development of social goals.

Several institutional features of these early developments of social administration bear examination in relation to the underlying characteristics of administrative politics in the two countries. As Suleiman has pointed out for the recent past,[33] French administrative politics provides a remarkable variety of opportunities. Much the same can be observed in the constant adjustment of the prefectoral corps to changing regimes in French politics.[34] Despite the grip that French administration may hold over French politics, French higher civil servants must develop a remarkable sensitivity to changing demands and needs, while enjoying the security of their respective *grands corps*. A more positive way of viewing this phenomena is to suggest that the political sensitivity of French civil servants encourages them to take risks and to seize initiatives. The confidential and anonymous nature of life in Whitehall may have the opposite effect. To be sure, influential British civil servants are known to have favored solutions to policy problems, but they enjoy neither the organizational flexibility nor the political incentives offered to successful French policymakers. Were not these same problems still being debated in Britain, one might discount the similarity of social policymaking problems to those found in economic policy,[35] labor relations, local government[36] and industrial policy. Thus, from a policy perspective, the difficulties of innovation and flexibility in social policy seem to have a deeper political source, possibly rooted in the constitutional and institutional assumptions and foundations of British government itself.

THE AMBIGUOUS ROLE OF THE LEFT

A second major institutional hurdle was to persuade the left, both socialist parties and labor movements, that parliamentary structures could provide important social and economic relief. Contrary to some contemporary accounts of the development of welfare state, turn of the century Marxists were sharply divided over their response to early social reforms, and their political role was additionally weakened by internal disputes. In most instances, labor movements preceded the formation of strong socialist parties. Workers had begun to organize their own social protection from roughly the mid-nineteenth century. The London Workingmen's Association, for example, was by no means a revolutionary organization. Its aim was to advance the education and self-improvement of workers.[37] The Marxist wing of the British socialist movement, the Social Democratic Federation, had great difficulty coordinating its policies with the nascent Labour Party and its leader, Hyndman, left the weak coalition of 1900, the Labour Representation Committee. French workers, much weaker than the British, were more attracted to syndicalism and anarchism. Impassioned labor leaders, such as Guesde, Vaillant and Brousse, who survived the Paris Commune of 1871, were extremely suspicious of parliamentary tactics. Their successors, such as Pelloutier, Péguy and Sorel, had similarly strong views on the autonomy of the labor movement from the state.[38]

In no country were internal schisms more pronounced than in France, where the anarchism of Louis Blanqui survived as the most influential socialist doctrine well into the Third Republic. Ranged against the Blanquists were the revolutionary forces of Jules Guesde, for whom neither the Boulanger crisis nor the Dreyfus affair was adequate justification to rally to the Republic. If the French socialists were readily dismissed in French politics of the late nineteenth century, it was because ideological discord could so easily shatter their precarious unity. Nearly a decade of tedious ideological debate went into forming the tenuous rapproachment of 1898, for example, only to see the invitation of the socialist leader, Millerand, to join the Waldeck-Rousseau government plunge the socialists into chaos once again.[39] In the elections of 1902, there were two socialist parties, the _Parti socialiste francaise_ (PSF) of Guesde and Vaillant and the _Parti socialiste de France_ (PSDF) of the anarchists. Indeed, as Lefranc observes, the ultimate unification of the French socialists in 1905 in the _Parti socialiste, section francaise de l'Internationale ouvrière_ (SFIO) was only achieved under strong pressure from the international labor movement.

But the reactions of the left to growing demands for more elaborate social policy at the turn of the century should not be seen wholly in terms of the ideological splits of socialist parties. Such internal divisions were no less prominent in Britain and Germany, though more successfully overcome in order to pursue parliamentary strategies. What differentiates France from other countries is the severe problems of making a reliable alliance between the socialists and the labor movement. The CGT was

founded in 1895 under the leadership of a fiery anarchist, Emile Pouget,[40] who saw the role of unions to be the disruption of bourgeois society by means of the general strike, boycotts, and slow-downs. For the early CGT, social policy was a device to promote working class solidarity, which explains their interest in the _Bourses de Travail_ (labor exchanges) and more generally in direct worker control over social policy. In France, this long and complicated process is still not concluded, as can be readily seen in the unmanageable division of unions among the Communist CGT, the independent-minded but socialist CFDT and the conventional labor politics of the FO.

The key transitional figure in reconciling the hostility of the French labor movement with parliamentary change was Eduard Vaillant. The direct heir of Blanqui and a Communard of 1871, his career embodies the important transformation of distinctly French working class values into the early rudiments of a strategy for using social policy to advance labor's interests. Although credit for keeping the parliamentary role of the socialists alive goes to Jean Jaurès, it was Vaillant who justifiably has been called the "grandfather" of French social security.[41] No less revolutionary than the more doctrinaire Guesde, and aligned with his faction, Vaillant favored the organization of labor exchanges, the development of municipal socialism, and was a strong advocate of national insurance. He favored the formation of a Ministry of Labor, actually accomplished in 1906, and in 1896 proposed a law to organize a Conseil Supérieur du Travail with departmental branches. On Guesde's insistence, the SFIO placed harsh restrictions on parliamentary activity, but Vaillant helped construct a workable compromise with Jaurès in order to preserve the credibility and a measure of flexibility for Socialist Deputies.[42] Of course, all of these policies were part of his tactic to develop working class consciousness. As he said of national insurance, "it creates an appetite and pushes them (workers) toward a creative and rich (_fécund_) struggle, a sense of solidarity against the patron."[43] His proposals in the Chamber of Deputies were designed to achieve this end. In 1903, he was a leader in the debate over a law to transform French public assistance into a national insurance program. For example, he wanted social insurance organized at the communal level to enhance worker participation, but coordinated nationally by an Office National d'Assurance with two-thirds of its directors from the CGT.[44]

Contrary to the widely accepted image of the French socialists as estranged and remote from the development of social policy, they had clear goals and, compared to Britain, enjoyed parliamentary influence well before the British Labour Party. During the Republican resurgence of the 1880's, the Socialists were able to gain a number of seats in the Chambers of Deputies. With nearly 50 socialist Deputies, Guesde himself was elected in 1893 but retained his revolutionary posture, which was to erode his relations with Jean Jaurès. Guesde wrote, "Parliamentary action is revolutionary, whatever the policy, by fighting from the high tribune of the Chamber to recall the discontents of the workshop, the countryside and the factory and by cornering capitalists by denying or weakening their satisfaction."[45]

As the quotation suggests, the difficult problem in explaining the relation of the French left to social policy is why they cooperated as much as they did. Their proposals were quite specific, and their contributions to the political debates at the turn of the century well conceived, though naturally demanding much more than might be expected from a liberal government. Their institutional strength could not be ignored, and their dynamism attracted many able young Deputies, including Clemenceau and Briand, both of whom later left the party in search of ministerial power. In the legislative elections of 1902, the PSF held 37 seats and the PSDF 14 seats, and in the 1906 elections, as a precariously united SFIO, they continued to hold 51 seats with nearly 900,000 votes.[46] The decline of the party did not come until the fierce arguments over international socialist party during the First World War, followed by the even more disastrous split of the party over the German insurrection and the Russian revolution following the war.

Despite their ideological schisms, the skillful Jaurès and the reluctant Guesde presented numerous social proposals to parliament. Though relations with the CGT were stormy, the weakness of the labor movement enabled the socialist leaders and their parliamentary cohorts to offer alternatives to the early liberal social reforms. In this respect, their experience more closely parallels the later role of the Social Democratic Party in Germany, even though the early battle over social policy there had been preempted by Bismarck.

Much as today, the strength of the French labor movement is a function of the political and parliamentary success of socialist leaders. Growth in union membership in France tends to follow political success, as can be seen in the swelling of union ranks after the Blum government and again in the early years of the Fourth Republic.[47] The weakness of the French labor movement gave their socialist representatives more autonomy in proposing reforms, but it also underscores an important contrast with Britain. In Britain, the craft unions were strong well before the formation of the Independent Labour Party in 1893 and the Labour Representation Committee in 1900. Numerous labor leaders were elected to Parliament in the 1880s, and until the turn of the century labor leaders took the initiative in proposing social reforms. For all their reluctance to engage in party politics, the French socialist politicians were able to lead labor, while in Britain a socialist party could not emerge without a compromise with a powerful British labor movement. Paradoxically, the strong labor movement inhibited the development of more radical social policies in Britain, which explains many of the enduring political features of the British welfare state.

In the case of British social policy, as in the case of numerous other policy changes, historical timing and historical precedent are an integral part of the political analysis of the emergence of new policies. For this reason, many excellent accounts of the British welfare state, as well as several Marxist accounts of the failure of the left,[48] are politically naive. From a policy perspective, it is important to remember that the first goal of politicians, whether on the left or the right, is to win elections and to enjoy the benefits of office. The political development of the British welfare state is marked by the importance of cabinet government. Superimposing social policies on a stable and effective political structure was vastly different from the task confronting socialists in most European democracies, including France, Germany and Sweden, where social reform was inseparable from institutional development. New social policies had to reconcile organizational and institutional policy requirements with less well defined political structures and processes.

In this political sense, the problem of finding policies that might work within the framework of British democracy was a much simpler task than on the continent or in the United States.[49] Though not perceived as such, it was a more threatening task for the left. Because institutions defined the basis of political legitimacy so well, the British socialist movement, much to the dismay of its Marxist critics, could simply fit their views into an effective and reliable electoral and parliamentary structure. They did this with remarkable success. Under the skillful guidance of the secretary of the ILP, Ramsey MacDonald, the nascent socialist party had over 700,000 members by 1902, merely nine years after its foundation.[50] By cooperating with the Liberal Party, the Labour Representation Committee (LRC) had rapid success in acquiring parliamentary seats, growing from 2 MPs in 1900 to 42 by the second 1910 election. Although they did not become a formal party until 1918, their actual strength during this critical phase of the early social policy debates in Britain was less than their French counterparts.

Some decades before the Labour Party existed, British union leaders were engaged with ministers, significantly, not only to enlarge union powers but also to secure political rights with the 1867 Reform Act.[51] It is not an historical coincidence that the TUC was formed the following year. The first efforts to run parliamentary candidates for the left were organized, not too well, by a union organization, the Labour Representation League, and the affiliated membership in the TUC rose to a million workers in 1874.[52] The proud and able barons of the late Victorian craft unions were consulted by Disraeli's government and by the many Royal Commissions organized in the 1880s to resolve the future of labor politics. All this may seem far removed from the intricacies of social policy in the twentieth century, but it left an imprint on labor politics in Britain and accounts for one of the distinguishing features of the British welfare state. The left succeeded not because it directly shaped social policy, but, on the contrary, because it was relatively easy and politically advisable to divorce labor policy from social policy.

The early Labour Party leaders had little to offer in the way of new social policies, although the Webbs worked diligently to create their particular version of a socially just state. The critical political features of Fabian social reform were, first, its unrelenting elitist equality and, second, its heavy reliance on administrative manipulation and centralization. It is no disrespect to the energetic Webbs to note that many British proposals for social reform share these qualities. The Webbs made little secret of their skeptical view of mass democracy. In contemplating their tireless efforts to refashion the London County Council, Beatrice Webb considered it "a machine for dodging democracy (in a crude sense) by introducing government by a select minority instead of rule by the majority."[53] As the self-appointed "official archangels" of the welfare state,[54] the Fabians were in fact remarkably unsuccessful in bringing about major changes in British social policy. Like their Benthamite predecessors of the early nineteenth century, their high-handed ways and stringent administrative demands offended many of their potential political supporters. Many of the austere Edwardian politicians realized that their demands were excessive, including a young and ambitious minor minister, Winston Churchill. On being offered the presidency of the Local Government Board, he replied that he had no desire to be shut in a soup kitchen with Beatrice Webb.[55]

Lest we blame the Webbs too unmercifully for the political weaknesses of the British welfare state, it should be noted that the paternalistic strain within British social policy can be traced to the early Victorian period.[56] The political argument is simply that the institutional stability of British parliament, combined with the prolonged interest of Victorian politicians, such as Disraeli, in social policy,[57] made social reform a relatively easy undertaking for British socialists once they arrived in Westminister. After the turn of the century, there were few of the crippling struggles over doctrine that plagued the continental socialists. With the possible exception of MacDonald,[58] most of the Labour Party leaders of the inter-war period had few original social policies.[59] For example, proposals to relieve unemployment between the wars were well known ideas from the Edwardian period. If anything, the Keynesian views incorporated into the program of the dying Liberal Party in the 1929 election were the most daring response to the issue that dominated British social policy from 1920 until the Second World War.[60]

While this is not the place to review the violent shifts in party parliamentary strength under the British winner-take-all electoral system,[61] the enormous injustices of the electoral system were an understandable distraction for British socialists. The very mechanism of party discipline and parliamentary stability that British elections engender distracts parties from policy problems. At the very least, it encouraged the optimistic view that once in power all problems can be settled. This was clearly the case for the Labour Party between the wars. The intricacies of social policy, particularly during the persistent and crippling period of unemployment between the wars, are hardly the stuff on which political leaders can concentrate. MacDonald himself was distracted by his concern for the international socialist movement and squabbles with the ILP.[62] Bound to a testy Chancellor of the Exchequer, Philip (later Viscount) Snowden, who fervently espoused Treasury caution at every move, and to a jealous Arthur Henderson, who often made no secret of his feeling that MacDonald had cheated him from becoming Prime Minister, MacDonald, even if he had the temperament for poring over the complexities of social reform, had little encouragement or inspiration from his own colleagues.

The National Government of 1931 to 1935 left most Labour leaders in the wilderness. The disastrous election of 1931 reduced the Party to its proportions of 1910. Concern naturally focused on political recovery rather than social reform. The political situation made the Party even more dependent on the TUC, most notably Ernest Bevin, and thereby further tied Labour's social agenda to the immediate interests of the unions.63 The party was greatly embarrassed by the more radical Socialist League, where Sir Stafford Cripps, G.D.H. Cole and others tried to assemble more radical ideas.64 Although there was a significant effort to revise Labour Party thinking over the 1930s, Labour entered the wartime coalition government with few well-shaped social aims. Nor were the Labour leaders in the Coalition especially concerned with the Beveridge Plan.65 The parliamentary debates of 1943 appear to have found both the Tories and Labour unprepared. Much as had be the case between the wars, the Treasury was able to extract large reductions in proposed benefits.66 Later, the Labour Chancellor of the Exchequer, Hugh Gaitskell, fashioned the social economies of 1948 and 1949 that were again to sow the seeds of discord within the Party.

The peculiar nature of labor and socialist politics in Britain helps explain the mixture of admiration and mystification with which most continental policymakers view the British experience. Some keen observers of the British scene, such as Emile Boutmy, the founder of the Ecole Libre des Sciences Politiques, saw that the particular political and institutional configuration of British politics made the early British compromises between liberal democracy and social reform unsuitable to France.67 On the continent, the international socialist movement, especially in the inter-war period, hoped that British labor power might be harnessed to revive demoralized and divided labor movements in France and Germany, thereby distracting continental socialists from the intricacies of social policy. However the early advance of labor in Britain is analyzed, it had an important impact on the Labour Party, enabling it to take full advantage of the opportunities of British politics without hesitation, while paradoxically luring it into thinking that social policy could be easily isolated from the problems of a rapidly expanding welfare state. In fact, one could not do one without the other.

Unlike the other welfare states, Britain could make a substantial commitment to social reform as early as 1911 without violating the framework of the liberal state. Another enormous social commitment was made in 1945 without raising the intricate question of how labor would be involved in the politics of social policy. Both parliamentary and party politics placed much less pressure on the TUC and its affiliated unions to think through how the rapid expansion of social policy might affect their immediate interests.[68] The high political costs of this convenient simplification were not to become fully apparent until the disastrous labor policies of Harold Wilson and Edward Heath. The result was a curious tug-of-war that has characterized British labor and social policies since 1945 under both Labour and Conservative governments. Social policy was the great missed opportunity in British politics, for it provided a platform on which to build new foundations to reconcile labor interests in wage policy with the large issues of policymaking in the welfare state.

From the late nineteenth century onward there was a high level of inter-party agreement about the social ills of France, but the politics of French policymaking were and remain fundamentally different. Social policy could not advance without more profound institutional and political adjustments. Conservative political forces were, of course, stronger in France than in Britain, but even the right could not avoid the political problems of formulating social policy, most notably in the Fifth Republic. In short, Britain and France are politically polar cases in the transformation of liberal into welfare states. In Britain, formulating new social policy, as in the case of central-local relations,[69] was much too easy to force the system to be politically innovative. In France, new social policies were much too complex to advance without considering fundamental political relationships in the society.

As in the case of the bureaucratization of social security, the historical and institutional influences on expanding welfare varied in important ways between the two countries. Between the wars, the Labour Party badly miscalculated its appeal and in 1931 formed a coalition with the Tories that in effect sacrificed both its credibility to Labour followers and its ability to be a radical force in British politics. From the foundation of the modern Labour Party in 1918, the unions, and in particular the Triple Alliance of mining, rail and transport workers, decided on an independent course, which meant concentration of immediate union objectives of free collective bargaining rights and good working conditions. The architect of this strategy, Bevin, could barely conceal his disdain of Labour Party intellectuals and abstract political and economic planning.[70] The overall effect was that both the TUC and the Party concentrated on parliamentary strategies with relatively little thought to social reform and social reorganization. Except for the nationalization of health care that had been discussed and planned since 1918,[71] the postwar period was remarkably devoid of major new policy initiatives. Under much less favorable political circumstances, the weak French labor movement and the internally divided SFIO engaged in a lively debate over the place of social reform in socialist strategies. Many of these ideas had been debated since the Second Republic, and by the 1890s the labor unions had a relatively clear idea of how they wished to see social security organized within the French welfare state. Moreover, socialist thinking about the welfare state was never divorced from problems of achieving labor peace and labor participation.72 Perhaps the instability of French institutions made reformers think more carefully about the organization and implementation of social policies. The long struggle to achieve democratic rule made both the left and the right more sensitive to the institutional and constitutional implications of launching major new social programs.

INSTITUTIONALIZING WELFARE

As the historical and institutional sketch of the transformation of the British and French states suggests, developing modern welfare states involved major structural changes in the capabilities and norms of democratic governance. For the most part, these changes are excluded from studies that concentrate on the adequacy of performance or the responsiveness to demands. In effect, by roughly 1950, all the modern democracies had made the basic political and constitutional compromises that were to affect the policy options and policy aims over the next thirty years. Developing welfare states posed enormous political, administrative and legislative problems. Most of the precedents for these changes, as well as the contours of the welfare states as defined in postwar legislation, were based on interwar experience.

Evidence about the structuring of policy choices requires policy analysis in depth, involving party strategies, the distribution of electoral rewards and incentives, the declining strength of rural voters and the provision of rural income support (often by trade protection and cheap credit), the separation of private and social insurance (not really a major question once the high risks of social insurance were known), and the incorporation of professional interests. As new social policies appeared, most of these questions were more easily solved than either social or economic theories of the welfare state suggest. The unified opposition of economic interests or unified demands of workers, implied in Marxist theories of the welfare state, seldom appeared. In effect, there were, to use Heclo's phrase, many sequences of "collective puzzlement"[73] as the new social bureaucracies and the uncertain left tried to accommodate themselves to aid liberal political principles and institutions to the increasingly complex governmental requirements of social policies.

Accustomed as we have become to international batting averages for spending and adequacy of social protection, there is no reason to assume that all forms of comparison among welfare states should arrive at the same results. Some of the early high performers, such as Britain, underwent relatively little basic institutional change. On the whole, the party of the left, the labor movement and political leaders were agreed that new social policies should conform to the constraints of parliamentary and cabinet government. As we examine each social reform in detail, we discover an odd repetition of the same policy dilemmas: how to preserve Treasury control, how to keep clients at arm's length, how to avoid local government meddling in social policy (while simultaneously calling on local governments to implement many new Whitehall policies), how to establish a workable form of accountability and evaluation within the elevated structure of the British higher civil service, and how to assure parliamentary supervision without exposing social policies to political risks. As one surveys the dilemmas of social policymaking in Britain, there is an unmistakable pattern of institutional defensiveness. The argument is not that Britain refused to pay the costs of building a welfare state or that it was unresponsive to social needs, but simply that institutional capabilities were not substantially affected in the process.

A much less generous welfare state, France was continually involved in some sort of institutional introspection. The Moderate Republicans of the 1880s were dismayed by the loss of political vigor among the founders of the Third Republic; the Radicals and Radical Socialists of the 1890s were determined to achieve national control of social policies (education being the most controversial); and the nascent social ministries were occupied between the wars with the complex question of how labor participation and social wages could be linked to French industrial, commercial and economic policies. Despite the poor performance of the French welfare state (and this should of course be assessed in relation to social need), some fundamental institutional innovations appeared: the quasi-state agency (*établissement publique* initially created in 1901 to secularize secondary education), employer and employee participation in social policymaking, decentralized organization of social security funds, and the clear separation of social spending from national taxation and national budgets. Whether these innovations were well advised or not, they represented new departures in French policymaking that had widespread effects on building the French welfare state.

A final question might be raised over the comparative problems of working from detailed policy materials in the search for institutional innovation, flexibility and responsiveness. First, as should be clear, institutional comparisons do not explain, nor are they intended to explain, aggregate differences among welfare states. From an institutional perspective, policy analysis only provides evidence of regularities or consistencies in policymaking. Second, if direct comparison is impossible, then comparisons need broad concepts of democratic governance (accountability, representativeness, effectiveness) measured in relation to other states. In short, there is no ideal welfare state and no totally reliable path to social justice, but only approximations of these abstract concepts within given institutional contexts. Third, the conclusions are likely to be about democratic governance, its institutional parameters and limitations. There are no "best" democracies, but only highly diverse democratic structures put in place by the historical and political context of each democratic society.[74] Hence, in the final analysis comparison must be made in the light of the unique experience and unique problems of each democracy. In this respect, the welfare state is no more than another chapter in the long process of redefining democratic goals and aspirations. Were it otherwise, there would probably be no "welfare state" and possibly no democracy.

NOTES

1. Demand theories of the welfare state come in both pluralist and Marxist versions. For examples of pluralist demand theories, see Alan Walker, ed., *Public Expenditure and Social Policy: An Examination of Social Spending and Social Priorities*, London, Heinemann, 1982; and Neil Gilbert, *Capitalism and the Welfare State*, New Haven, Yale University Press, 1983. Among Marxists, demand theories seem to have gone out of fashion as the readiness of capitalist states to provide social protection increases. A more conventional Labour Party view of the open-ended nature of demands, is David Donnison, *The Politics of Poverty*, Oxford, Martin Robertson, 1982; and Frank Parkin, *Class Inequality and Political Order*, London, Macmillan, 1971.

2. Supply theories are now more numerous. Among pluralist examples, see Thomas Wilson and Dorothy J. Wilson, *The Political Economy of the Welfare State*, London, Allen & Unwin, 1982; and Richard Rose and Guy Peters, *Can Governments Go Bankrupt?*, New York, Basic Books, 1978. Socialists, in part because of their distrust of capitalist procedures, were less willing to endorse supply-side theories (the Swedes being the famous exception). Among recent changes, see James O'Connor, *The Fiscal Crisis of the State*; Ian Gough, *The Political Economy of the Welfare State*; London, Macmillan, 1979.

3. OECD, *Public Expenditure Trends* (Studies in Resource Allocation No. 5), June 1978; OECD. *Social Expenditure 1960-1980: Problems of Growth and Control*, 1985.

4. In their quantitative assessment of northern European welfare states, Peter Flora and Jens Alber, "Modernization, Democratization, and the Development of Welfare States in Western Europe," in P. Flora and A. Heidenheimer, eds., *The Development of Welfare States in Europe and America*, New Brunswick and London, Transaction Books, 1981, pp. 37-80, introduce a dummy variable, "constitutional-dualism", to attempt to control institutional change.

5. See, for example, David Cameron, "The Expansion of the Public Economy: A Comparative Analysis", *American Political Science Review*, 72: 1243-1261, December 1978 and David R. Cameron, "Social Democracy, Corporatism, Labour Quiescence, and the Representation of Economic Interest in Advanced Capitalist Society," in J. Goldthorpe, ed., *Order and Conflict in Contemporary Capitalism*, London and New York, Oxford University Press, 1984, pp. 143-178.

6. Labor relations were a major preoccupation of the moderate Republicans of the 1880s who were acutely aware that both business and agriculture

enjoyed associational privileges far in excess of those given to unions. See Pierre Sorlin, Waldeck Rousseau, Paris, Colin, 1966, pp. 97-103. In 1866, Napoleon III formed a commission of union needs and in 1869, forty-four Paris unions formed the Chambre fédérale des sociétés ouvrières de Paris.

7. The 1913 Royal Commission on the Civil Service, the last until the Fulton Report almost fifty years later, was extremely skeptical about Sir Robert Morant's claims that the budding Board of Education needed specialized, professional inspectors with decent wages. The commission included Graham Wallas, Haldane's sister, Elizabeth Haldane, the young Labour official, Phillip (later Viscount) Snowden, and the Duke of Devonshire. See Royal Commission on the Civil Service, First and Second Reports, Parliamentary Papers, ed. 6209 and cd. 6534, 1912-13.

8. There are a number of superb studies of how post-war planning disintegrated over 1981. For a summary, see Peter Fraser, "The Impact of the War of 1914-18 on the British Political System," in M.R.D. Foot, ed., War and Society: Historical Essays in Honour and Memory of F.R. Wester 1928-1971, London, Paul Elak, 1973, pp. 123-139. In addition, Kathleen Burke, ed., War and the State, London and Boston, Allen & Unwin, 1982; Paul Barton Johnson, Land Fit for Heroes: The Planning of British Reconstruction, 1916-1919, Chicago, University of Chicago Press, 1968; Kenneth and Jane Morgan, Portrait of a Progressive: The Political Career of Christopher, Viscount Addison, Oxford, Clarendon Press, 1980.

9. R.H. Tawney, an influential social advisor to Labour during World War II, forewarned the party. See his essay, "The Abolition of Economic Controls, 1918-1921," Economic History Review, 13, 1943.

10. Jean-Audre Latournerie, Le Ministère du Travail: Origines et Premiers Développements, Paris, Cujas, 1971.

11. Between the wars, the Ministry of Labour became a stronghold of the many independent socialists whom Millerand had attracted into government from the turn of the century. See Michel Guillaume, "André Fontaine, Premier Directeur du Travail," in F. de Baecque, et al., Les Directeurs de Ministère en France (XIXe-XXe Siècles), Paris, Librairie Droz, 1976, pp. 81-89. In addition, Leslie Derfler, Alexandre Millerand: The Socialist Yars, The Hague, Mouton, 1977.

12. Treasury power between the wars is associated with the long tenure as Permanent Secretary of Sir Warren Fisher from 1919 to 1939. In fear of post-war inflation, the Treasury imposed firm controls on ministerial spending in 1919. Fisher was in fact reinforced by numerous distinguished officials. See,

for example, John Wheeler-Bennett, John Anderson: Viscount Waverly, London, St. Martins, 1962, for one of the more remarkable persons whose influence stretches from Permanent Secretary of the Home Office (1922-32) to Lord President of the Council and virtual home front manager of Britain in World War II.

13. See Charles W. Pipkin, The Idea of Social Justice: A Study of Legislation and Administration and the Labour Movement in England and France Between 1900 and 1926, New York, Macmillan, 1926; and H. Dèrouin, et al., Traitè et pratique d`assistance publique, Paris, Sirey, 1914, 2 vols.

14. Space prohibits fully exploring the intense intellectual self-examination that took place in Britain from the turn of the century. Among many notable books, see Stefan Collin, Liberalism and Sociology: L.T. Hobhouse and Political Argument in England, 1880-1914, Cambridge, Cambridge University Press, 1979; Donald Read, ed., Edwardian England, New Brunswick, Rutgers University Press, 1982; Peter Clarke, Liberals and Social Democrats, Cambridge, Cambridge University Press, 1978; and Michael Freeden, The New Liberalism: An Ideology of Social Reform, Oxford, Clarendon Press, 1978.

15. See Derek Fraser, Urban Politics in Victorian England, Leicester, Leicester University Press, 1976; and E.P. Hennock, Fit and Proper Persons: Ideal and Reality in Nineteenth Century Urban Government, London, Edwin Arnold, 1973.

16. See Royston Lambert, Sir John Simon 1816-1904: English Social Administration, London, MacGibbon and Kee, 1963. In many respects, Simon made better use of the precursor to the Local Government Board, the Local Government Act Office of 1858, than did the turn-of-the-century Board Presidents. See Lambert, "Central-Local Relations in Mid-Victorian England: The Local Government Act Office, 1858-71," Victorian Studies, 6:121-150, December 1962.

17. Local responsibilities for implementing numerous British social policies in late Victorian and Edwardian Britain were substantial. Between 1870 and 1905, the cost of poor relief, born by local taxes, multiplied a hundred times. The early Unemployed Workmens Act of 1905 was basically a program of subsidized local public works. The influential Charitable Organization Society, which strongly opposed Poor Law reform, was based on local aristocracy and church groups. See Jose Harris, Unemployment and Politics: A Study in English Social Policy 1886-1914, Oxford, Clarendon Press, 1972, pp. 145-189.

18. Sir Robert Morant's success at the Board of Education depended heavily on his skirting the

inadequacies and inefficiencies of local government. See Bernard M. Allen, Sir Robert Morant: A Great Public Servant, London, Macmillan, 1934. His distaste for the unreliable local authorities was shared by most leading health and education officials of the time.

19. One of the sharpest contrasts with France, where the Ministry of the Interior played a key role in modernizing French administration, is the Local Government Board. From 1906, its Chairman was John Burns, the first labor movement official to achieve a ministerial post, a renowned labor militant, who on taking office became the most severe critic of local government, an advocate of the Poor Laws and generally an embarrassment ot the Asquith government. See Kenneth D. Brown, John Burns, London, 1977; and William Kent, John Burns: Labour's Lost Leader, London, 1950.

20. For example, it was very difficult for the early social agencies to recruit specialists and experts. See the pleas of the Second Division of the Civil Service for better pay and special recruitment, Royal Commission on the Civil Service, First Report, London, and Second Report, London, HMSO. 1912, ed. 6209 and ed. 6535.

21. Morant's reputation was made on the flood of educational reform legislation in early Edwardian Britain: the 1902 Education Act, the 1903 London Education Act, the 1904 Elementary School Code, the 1906 Education (Provision of Meals) Act and the 1907 Education (Administrative Provisions) Act. Almost unnoticed, these last two laws paved the way for nationalized health. See Sir Robert Newsholme, The Ministry of Health, London, Putnam, 1925, pp. 35-62 and 84-111.

22. The 1911 National Insurance Act did not terminate the Poor Laws. Poor relief was transferred to the overworked local authorities under the 1920 Local Government Act, and then, as this proved unworkable, the Public Assistance Committees were transformed into Unemployment Assistance Committees under the 1935 Unemployment Insurance Act. The Unemployment Assistance Board was the predecessor to the wartime National Assistance Board and the post-war Supplementary Benefits Commission. See John D. Millett, The British Unemployment Assistance Board, New York, McGraw Hill, 1940; and Tony Lynes, The Unemployment Assistance Board, London, Croom Helm, 1985.

23. See S.E. Finer, The Life and Times of Edwin Chadwick, London, Methuen, 1952.

24. Possibly the best account of recent poverty decisionmaking is Keith Banting, Poverty, Politics and Policy, London, Macmillan, 1979.

25. For a detailed account, see Henri C. Galant, *Histoire Politique de la Securitè Sociale Francaise, 1945-1952*, Paris, Colin, 1955. For a summary of strengths and weaknesses, see Pierre Laroque, *Succès et faiblesses de l'effort social francais*, Paris, Colin, 1961.

26. Officials in both parliament and government appear to have been under few illusions that substantial compromises would be needed. See *Journal Officiel, Assemblèe Consultative, Documents*, Annexe No. 554, 3è session, sèance de 24 juillet 1945, pp. 725-738, when Georges Buisson made the first parliamentary report on the *ordonnance*.

27. Laroque, *Succès et faiblesses* . . ., p. 8.

28. Henri Monod's work is available to us largely in the form of the many speeches he gave throughout France at the turn of the century while mobilizing support for his proposals, and in the parliamentary interventions he made as Directeur de l'Assistance Publique in the Ministry of the Interior for more than a decade. See, for example, his *L'Assistance obligatoire aux vieillards*, Paris, Masson, 1905 (reprint of a Senate speech) and *Bienfaisance privèe et assistance publique*, Paris, Masson, 1901.

29. *Journal Officiel, Dèbats Parlementaires*, Chambres des Deputès, 8è legislature, session ordinaire de 1903, sèance du vendredi 29 mai, p. 1843.

30. Interview, Paris, November 9, 1983.

31. See the collective memorial volume, *Georges Cahen-Salvador (1875-1963)*, Paris, Imprimerie Louis-Jean, 1980, p. 48.

32. See the tribute of Michel Debrè in the collective memorial volume, *Alexandre Parodi (1901-1979)*, Paris, Imprimerie Louis-Jean, 1980, p. 48. Until his flight to London in 1943, Parodi led a double life as a member of the Conseil d'Etat under Vichy and as a leading member of the Committee of Experts, the planning group of the Gaullist Resistance group.

33. Ezra Suleiman, *Politics, Power and Bureaucracy in France*, Princeton, Princeton University Press, 1974.

34. Douglas E. Ashford, *British Dogmatism and French Pragmatism: Center-Local Policymaking the the Welfare State*, London and Boston, Allen & Unwin, 1982.

35. Andrew Shonfeld, *Modern Capitalism*, London, Oxford University Press, 1965.

36. Ashford, *British Dogmatism and French Pragmatism*.

37. A useful introduction is the collection of labor history essays of C. J. Wrigley, ed., *A History of British Industrial Relations, 1875-1914*, Amherst, MA, University of Massachusetts Press, 1982.

38. See J. Julliard, Fernand Pelloutier et les origines du syndicalisme d'action directe, Paris, Seuil, 1971.

39. The tension between the "ministerialists" and the socialist militants occupied the party from the 1893 election onward. In fact, the socialists had reached agreement about permitting Millerand to participate in the government, but it was the unexpected appointment of Gen. de Gallifet, a leader of the bloody repression of the 1871 Commune, as Minister of War that threw their plans into disarray. See George Le Franc, Le Mouvement Socialiste sous la Troisième Republique, Paris, Payot, 1977, pp. 105-110.

40. The CGT was linked more closely to the anarchist strain of French socialism. See Christian de Goustine, Pouget: Les Matins noirs du syndicalisme, Paris, Editions de la Tete de Feuilles, 1972.

41. Maurice Domanget, Vaillant: Un grand socialiste 1840-1915, Paris, Table Ronde, 1956, p. 161.

42. Lefrance, Le Mouvement Socialiste..., p. 123.

43. Domanaget, Vaillant..., p. 167.

44. Journal Oficiel, Débats parlementaires, session ordinaire de 1903, 8è legislature, séance de vendredi 29 mai 1903, pp. 1777-1781, for the debate on Vaillant's amendment. See also his book, Assurance sociale, Paris, Imprimèrie Centrale de la Bourse, 1901.

45. Lefrance, Le Mouvement Socialiste..., p. 56.

46. Lefrance, Le Mouvement Socialiste..., p. 146.

47. Lefrance, Le Mouvement Socialiste..., p. 133 fn. Politics continues to serve as a mobilizing agent for the French labor movement. See G. Adam and J.D. Reynaud, Conflits du travial et changement social, Paris, Presses Universitaires de France, 1978.

48. The standard works, such as Maurice Bruce, The Coming of the Welfare State, London, Batsford, 1961, and Derek Fraser, The Evolution of the Welfare State, London, Macmillan, 1973, are of course country studies. The omission in Marxist critiques of the role of the left, such as Ralph Miliband, The State in Capitalist Society, London, Quartet Books, 1969, is less easily rationalized because the politics of labor and socialists party politics are integral to understanding the weaknesses and strengths of the left in Parliament. His critique is revealing testimony of how estranged British socialist politics has become from its European counterparts.

49. As Martha Derthick notes, in Policymaking for Social Security, (Washington, Brookings Institution, 1979, p. 110), the American labor movement had little interest in the radical reforms of the 1930s until

their electoral importance became evident after the war.

50. David Marquand, *Ramsay MacDonald*, London, Jonathan Cape, 1977, p. 75.

51. On the union leaders' involvement with the debate over the 1867 Reform Act, see B.C. Roberts, *The Trades Union Congress, 1868-1921*, Cambridge, Harvard University Press, 1956, pp. 28-41. Roberts provides an excellent account of how various Royal Commissions on labor relations worked unsuccessfully with the Liberal government and received promises of more favorable treatment from Disraeli.

52. Roberts, *The Trades Union Congress...*, p. 80 and p. 93.

53. Quoted in W. H. Greenleaf, *The British Political Tradition: The Ideological Heritage*, London, Methuen, 1983, p. 398.

54. The phrase was coined by H.G. Wells, who, like many other younger intellectuals of the Edwardian period, found himself uncomfortable with the Webb's elitism. Both Cole and Tawney had difficulties accepting the Webb's political strategy.

55. The reason why he would be so confined was that the Local Government Board has responsibility for administering the Poor Laws, and Beatrice Webb was, as we shall see in more detail below, intensely committed to major reform through her membership on the Royal Commission on the Poor Laws and the Relief of Distress.

56. See David Roberts, *Paternalism in Early Victorian England*, London, Croom Helm, and New Brunswick, Rutgers University Press, 1979.

57. See Paul Smith, *Disraelian Conservatism and Social Reform*, London, Routledge and Kegan Paul, and Toronto, University of Toronto Press, 1967.

58. David Marquand's subtle revisionist work, *Ramsay MacDonald...*, makes clear how preoccupied he was with the socialist international in the post-war years, even to the extent of neglecting domestic policy problems. Though certainly not seen as a distraction by socialists, international problems were equally important in occupying Leon Jouhaux, the inter-war leader of the CGT. See Bernard Georges and Denise Tintant, *Leon Jouhaux: Cinquante ans de syndicalisme*, Paris, Presses Universitaires de France, 1962, tome 1.

59. Labour Party politics were again pre-empted by the severe strikes and labor unrest which placed the Party in an ambiguous position. For a summary of the Party's strategy, see Richard W. Lyman, "The British Labour Party: The Conflict between Socialist Ideals and Practical Politics between the Wars," *Journal of British History*, 5:140-172, November 1965. The notable exception was Sir John Wheatley on housing.

60. Contained in the famous "Yellow Book" or the Liberal party platform, Britain's Industrial Future, London, Liberal Party, 1928. Assembled by an aging Lloyd-George, it synthesized important discussions that had been going on over much of the 1920s among a group of extremely able men, including Keynes. See Greenleaf, The British Political Tradition..., pp. 170-179.

61. Then as now, 30 percent of the vote was a magic threshold, but the spatially concentrated vote of the left meant larger numbers of lost votes. For example, with nearly 31 percent of the vote in 1931, the party only acquired 46 seats (plus six unendorsed candidates), while in 1923, 31 percent produced 191 seats. See F.W.S. Craig, British Electoral Facts 1885-1975, London, Macmillan, 1976, p. 13 and p. 17.

62. MacDonald never succeeded in healing the split within the ILP organization over shifting to a more revolutionary posture. See Marquand, MacDonald..., pp. 450-557. The disastrous defeat of 1931 silenced the more militant socialist wing of the Party until the rise of Aneurin Bevan.

63. Much has been written about the effects of declining union activity with the Party. With the exception of the 1929 election, trade unions sponsored half or more of Labour Party candidates from 1900 to 1935. After the war, the proportion drops precipitously to roughly a third. See Craig. British Electoral Facts..., p. 86. Of course, the significance of this change for social policy rests on how active union leaders were in this regard once they gained influence from the top of the party organization.

64. There are several accounts: James Jupp, The Radical Left in Britain 1931-1941, London, Cass, 1982; Elizabeth Durbin, New Jerusalems; The Labour Party and the Economics of Democratic Socialism, London, Routledge and Kegan Paul, 1985; and the relevant chapters of Philip Williams, Hugh Gaitskell, London, Jonathan Cape, 1979.

65. Jose Harris, William Beveridge: A Biography, Oxford, Claredon Press, 1977, pp. 419-488. Also Kenneth O. Morgan, Labour in Power 1945-1951 Oxford, Clarendon Press, 1984; and Paul Addison, The Road to 1945: British Politics and the Second World War, London, Jonathan Cape, 1975, pp. 211-228.

66. The Treasury sought and obtained the near halving of child benefits 1944; pensions were smaller than Beveridge anticipated, and there was no revision of unemployment insurance. The skeptical views of the Treasury are outlined in a hastily prepared economic analysis of the Beveridge Plan by a Subcommittee of the Committee on Reconstruction, (Phillips Committee), Report, PRO CAB 87/3, January 1943; and in the Chancellor's report, Financial

Aspects of the Social Security Plan, PRO C 87/3, January 11, 1943, which formed the basis of his speech to Parliament the next month.

67. Emile Boutmy, The English People: A Study of their Political Psychology, London, Putnam, 1904.

68. One need not accept the marxist conclusions of Ralph Miliband, Parliamentary Socialism: A Study of the Politics of Labour, London, 1961, in order to see the political effects on the labor movement.

69. For an analysis of how strong, central institution permitted great simplifications of central-local relationship in Britain, see Douglas E. Ashford, Politics and Policy in Britain: The Limits of Consensus, Philadelphia, Temple University Press, 1981.

70. Allan Bullock, Life and Times of Ernest Bevin: Trade Union Leader, 1881-1940, London, Heinemann, 1960, pp. 255-257 and 509-524.

71. Plans for nationalization of health were well advanced in the 1920s and favored by both the first and second Chief Medical Officers of the Ministry of Health, Sir Charles Newsholm and Sir John Newman. See Newsholm's postwar report, Local Government Board, 47th Annual Report, Parliamentary papers, 1917-1918, cd. 9169. Richard W. Lyman, "The British Labour Party: The Conflict Between Socialist Ideal and Practical Politics between the Wars," British Journal of History, 5:14-172, 1965, notes that the Labour platform did not mention nationalization until 1934, and then devoted only three pages to it.

72. Sorlin, Waldeck Rousseau; David J. Saposs, The Labor Movement in Post-War France, New York, Columbia University Press, 1931.

73. Hugh Heclo, Modern Social Politics in Britain and Sweden, New Haven, Yale University Press, 1974, p. 305.

74. Compare with the concept of institutions as organization choices in James G. March and Johan P. Olson, American Political Science Review, 73:734-745, September, 1984.

III.

Jerald Hage

Techniques for Delineating Periods

An Example with the Growth of the British Welfare State

Historians have been sensitive to the problem of periods or eras for a long time. The basis for separating a nation's history into one or more periods, however, is an analytical problem that historians have not necessarily solved. The usual approach is to take major events such as wars or revolutions -- the Napoleonic Wars or the Second World War -- or else changes in the constitution -- the 4th Republic or Weimar -- as the basis. But are these genuine and significant breaks with the past? Dramatic though they may be, they do not necessarily signify a real alteration of society. We have here a basic methodological issue that is worth some attention: By what criteria can we say that a particular periodization is meaningful? One objective of this paper is to suggest some methodological criteria for delineating temporal periods.

In considering the theoretical problem of how to select cycles and periods in the analysis of societies, it is useful to combine this issue with another one that has recently emerged in the social sciences, namely that of parameter shift. The best example of the latter is the problem of stagflation in most post-industrial societies. Whereas unemployment and inflation were previously strongly negatively related,[1] now it appears that these economic variables have a much weaker relationship, i.e. the coefficient has decreased in strength. To be more precise, the amount of stable unemployment needed in the period up to the 1960's before inflation would decline was about 5.5 percent in Britain. Now Britain has unemployment averaging about 12 to 13 percent and still has inflation of five or six percent. This change in the trade-off is called a parameter shift. Economists are still trying to explain the reasons for it.

Williamson, an historical economist, as another example, has developed a model of economic growth that explains a number of economic parameters including differential wage rates, migration and the like. His model for predicting economic growth in the United States works extremely well for the time span from the 1870's until the First World War and then breaks down. To be able to say that the period of 1870-1910 forms a coherent whole in the growth of the American economy is a critical intellectual insight. We are immediately led to ask a whole series of new questions once we shift our focus from the idea that the model "breaks down" to the idea that the relationships between the variables are relatively constant. My theoretical glass is thus half-full! The problem of parameter shift has also been noticed by a few sociologists who have referred to this phenomenon as social change.[2] Duncan states in the last paragraph of his book _Introduction to Structural Equation Models_[3]

> We can conceive of two populations (or the same population at two points in time) in which the same structure holds -- that is, the model is the same and the numerical values of the coefficients are the same. We can also imagine that the model is the same, but one or more coefficients are different. It is this latter kind of variation (over time, or between different social universes), in particular, that ought to be especially amenable to study with tools like those introduced in this book. If we can find situations or time periods where only a few coefficients differ, we may have some hope of coming to understand the impact of these differences -- our models can help directly with that -- and perhaps of making useful conjectures as to their origins.

Essentially the same meaning is attached: alternations in the size of the coefficients indicate that one cause or explanatory variable becomes more important than another in different temporal periods. Laslett has suggested that this should be the focus of historical research and is the task of the theorist, that is, the task is to explain changes in the _strength of_ relationships.[4]

As sociologists have increased the number of longitudinal studies they have begun to discover period effects. For example, Ragin, Coverman, and Hayward show that the meaning or purpose of strikes changes from the period of 1902-1918 to the period 1919-1938 in Britain.[5] The importance of certain variables in explaining successful outcomes also changes. The explanation for this historical change is that the unions moved from being a challenger to a member of the political system. Similarly, Schram and Turbett in reexamining the impact of riots on welfare benefits, find differences in two periods.[6] Finally, and more recently, Hicks shows a Nixon period effect in the analysis of American government expenditures.[7] In most cases, though, the choice of periods appears to be either an accidental discovery or somewhat arbitrary. We would like to be able to specify the temporal limits to our theoretical models, and even more, we would like to be able to explain why the parameter appears to be shifting. If we can do so, we might then be able to generalize our theoretical models to include more than one temporal period. Finally, in the future we could conceive of our developing indications of when our forecasts are more likely to be incorrect.

Parameter shifts and the breakdown in the ability of modern econometric models to accurately forecast has caused despair in some who see social science being discredited. Instead, as the current work in sociology suggests, there are new intellectual opportunities here that can deepen our understanding of history and expand the sophistication of our theoretical models. Indeed, the idea that the essence of social change is a shift in parameters is an attractive one.[8] Describing historical periods or eras by fundamental shifts in the relationships between variables would appear to be a major innovation in thinking about history. To specify social science models by conditions of space such as culture, and conditions of time such as a specific era, would considerably enrich our theoretical understanding. And this is an important point. As Duncan has noted, the logic of differences between populations and between temporal periods is essentially the same.[9]

The conceptualization of meaningful chunks of time will become increasingly interesting to sociologists and political scientists as they become more concerned about comparative macro sociology. I believe that as sociologists focus on this analytical level, they find historical imagery extremely attractive as Laslett argues.[10] What are some of the components of historical imagery? First, there is an emphasis on time. Change can accumulate slowly, sometimes over many decades. But change can occur quickly and rapidly at specific moments. Thus, the element of time can be analyzed as a conjuncture of forces at specific moments, implying some multiplicative process on non-linear combination of variables. Next, the forces are usually specific to the cultural space and historical moment. Again, we see in this imagery the implicit idea of parameter shift. Periods of time are described by relatively unvarying relationships, but then, suddenly, the importance of specific factors -- social forces, the state, crops, etc. -- alters with quite dramatic effects. These considerations are particularly relevant in considering the development of welfare states. Their evolution has been over a long period of time, and their determinants have been said to include all the major socio-economic, structural, and political factors.

This discussion suggests that we need to develop new methodological techniques so that we can attempt to capture the richness of historical eras in our statistical analysis. How does one quantify this imagery? It would appear to be impossible to encapsulate this qualitatively rich imagery in a standard regression program. But, this is our objective. For how does one remain convinced that the historian has indeed made the correct judgment without some way of portraying the complex interactions of variables that wax or wane? Being able to measure and test this provides additional evidence for the historians' arguments.

In summary, in both history and in the social sciences there is a set of methodological problems that are cognate. In history, we want to delineate specific time periods by focusing on complex interactions that are different from other eras. In the social sciences, we want to know what the temporal bounds to our models are; that is, when parameters shift. So, historians and social scientists face the same problem; and an analysis which is suited to identifying significant periods allows us to find a solution to both problems. Temporal analysis forces us to ask when relationships break down and why. And, it allows us to view historical periods as a set of interrelated variables with unique coefficients, a good analytical way of conceptualizing them. This would be one way of understanding Berkhofer's view of history as the analysis of time; chunks of time are viewed as periods when the parameters are reasonably stable.[11] These periods may last a century or only a few years; regardless, we have a systematic way of delineating the beginning and the endpoint.

To imply that the solution to our methodological problem is an easy one would be incorrect. We have to establish a number of guidelines on how to decide about when a parameter shift has indeed occurred. The first part of this paper explores the basic methodology and provides some rules as to how it can be used. The second part looks at a particular case, the analysis of the growth of welfare expenditures in Britain. In the analysis we must be concerned with trying to validate the empirical analysis with qualitative materials. While the example is a specific one, the technique employed is quite generalizable to other cases.

THE METHODOLOGY OF PERIODIZATION

The need for a methodology of periodization is demonstrated by the variety of temporal analysis approaches that have been tried. One of the most common is to select some period of time such as a decade and then recompute the coefficients.[12] The difficulty with this approach is that the choice of periods is arbitrary. Furthermore, it will tend to exaggerate the amount of change since each decade will be different. Another approach is that of Box-Jenkins. Their procedures do not link periods with parameter shifts but instead only document discontinuous change in some variable or correct for random fluctuations due to seasons, white noise or whatever.

An example of the difficulties presented by failing to consider qualitative factors from the historical record can be seen in an article by Ragin, Coverman and Hayward in which they chose 1919 as a moment when labor unions had more power.[13] Historically this does not make as much sense as either 1911, when the Conservatives began to consult with the T.U.C. on all social matters -- indicative of their being part of the system -- or 1924, when the first Labour Government was formed. One suspects 1919 was chosen more because of the need to have an equal number of time points for the sake of analysis. Similarly, Schram and Turbett do not make clear how and why their time point is chosen.[14] Nor do Rubinson and Ralph provide a convincing argument for their choice of periods in an analysis of school expansion and economic development.[15]

Rather than arbitrarily selecting a particular bench mark, we should develop a series of procedures by which periodization can be made more meaningful. The crux is to identify when the relationships between a number of key variables change. This can be detected by a careful examination of the residuals in the best and most complex model. (We might parenthetically note that "best" means the most variance explained coupled with a reasonable Durbin-Watson value, while "complex" means the number of explanatory variables, especially of different theoretical orientations.) Whenever there is a long, sustained shift in the residuals then we know we have a parameter shift. A hint of this procedure is suggested in the recent article by Hicks who observes a large swing in the residuals associated with the Nixon administration.[16] These periods can then be selected empirically. The model can then be refitted within each period.

A simple example is provided in Figure One. This is the plot of the residuals for a one-variable model that relates industrialization to welfare expenditures in Britain (a common explanation for the growth of the welfare state.) Since industrialization is often cited as the major explanatory factor for the degree of development of welfare state, the example is significant. As can be easily seen, there are three sub-periods which are hidden in the data analysis. Figure One also demonstrates how much new information one receives from a careful examination of the residual pattern.

Another approach is to look for large oscillations that may have disturbed the regression analysis. If they are found, they can be used to periodize the "longue durée", to use the favorite term of the French historians, into meaningful periods. Oscillations can be distinguished from swings by the short number of time points and the size of the change in the residuals. Since the residuals are standardized, we can move directly to the concept of the speed and magnitude of change, important ideas in historical imagery. An example is provided in Figure Two which represents the impact of education demand on education expenditures in Germany. The huge oscillation that occurs in the middle of the Weimar Republic disrupts the analysis.

If our theoretical model is a good one, then the residuals should weave back and forth across time -- and frequently so -- with small departures from the predicted line. But our models are seldom that good. Instead there are quite distinctive periods for which they fit better or worse, as evidenced in the residuals.

The advantage of examining the residual patterns is that they tell us <u>when</u>, in terms of specific dates, social science models are no longer working. They force us to recognize internal periods within our analysis, a most useful insight. What is being proposed might be considered as a variation on the analysis of co-variance, except that the problem is to divide the sample into distinctive periods rather than distinctive sub-populations. The logic is the same as Duncan has observed.[17] Once this has been accomplished then we can begin to understand how we can move to a consideration of historical imagery and, although this may appear to be less certain, the ways in which variables wax and wane and even interact non-linearly across time. Thus, the procedures proposed here are more analytical and not as descriptive as the more well-known time series techniques such as the Box-Jenkins methods. The delineation of significant eras is always relative to the specific structural equation model; it may not be relevant to other social and historical problems. In this analysis, welfare expenditures are perceived as an indicator of state responsiveness and state activism.[18] The central question is -- are there periods when the state is more or less responsive to particular independent variables such as welfare need, political power, and economic development?

In the analysis of state responsiveness, a variety of economic and political variables has been used to explain the rise of the welfare state. We can construct complex models with these suggested variables and then distinctive periods within particular models can be analyzed with reference to basic structural changes in the society or unique historical events. For example, when political variables are employed, do we find that distinctive periods are related to the emergence of a left political party, its growth in power, or is it related to a distinctive event such as the left capturing control of the state? The same logic applies to economic variables. As the number of variables increases, so does the complexity of the analysis. With multiple explanatory models, we should find a convergence in the delineation of periods. The periods are then defined relative to the interaction of a number of forces. Finally, insofar as the variables themselves are complex indices, and refer to basic aspects of society, the periodization becomes more convincing.

Figure One, which displays the residuals for the impact of industrialization on state responsiveness as measured by welfare expenditures shows three distinctive periods. Between 1871 and 1904, the British state is not very responsive to the growth in the economy. Between 1905 and 1927, the state is increasingly responsive; there is a parameter shift. Finally, the era 1928 to 1965 forms another distinctive period with perhaps the last few years forming a new parameter shift.

I choose industrialization as the first example because it is the standard explanatory variable in the literature.[19] Even though the zero-order correlation is moderate (r=.42), we see that it obscures distinctive time periods. This raises questions such as: What causes the changes in state responsiveness to further industrialization in different time periods? Why doesn't the Great Depression hit state responsiveness more? In other words, with periodization we can best judge whether major economic events have an impact. When they don't is equally interesting.[20] Once the periods are detected by distinctive residual patterns, then separate equations can be derived for each period. This then provides the specific parameter size. The parameter shift is made explicit. We now have a new intellectual problem, namely: Why are there three periods in Britain and what causes them?[21]

Let us take another example which focuses on two variables: the effects of the power of the industrial working class and the agricultural service class on state responsiveness.[22] One theoretical reason for examining these two variables is to ascertain if the periods correspond to changes in the nature of the political system. Theoretically we can delineate the following distinctive periods. The first is the emergence of elections and the creation of political parties. Authorities might disagree, but in England this is roughly the period of the 1860s to 1900. The second period is the emergence of a working class party and its growing power. The third major change begins when that working class party either participates in a coalition or, more decisively, gains control of the state.

In Figure Three we observe an interesting but quite different pattern in the residuals. State responsiveness tracks fairly well until 1904 when it begins to shift. This change is associated with the emergence of the Labour Party. There are steady and then sharp increases in state responsiveness until 1933. This is when the Labour Coalition fell apart and the depression was at its worst. There is a steady decline relative to the growing power of the industrial working class until about 1952. Clearly the legislation of the Attlee government starts a new period of steady and rapid growth <u>relative</u> to the power of the industrial working class and the power of the agricultural and service sectors.

The very high correlation $r^2m=.95$ hides a great deal of additional information. (Much of this reflects auto-correlated error.) New questions are raised, and we begin to see how various political events can or cannot affect responsiveness. What is critical is that analysts must remember that we are describing the <u>relative</u> relationship between two or more variables. The power of the industrial working class waxes and wanes during these periods. But state responsiveness is also influenced by various other events or variables.

Obviously, no one would want to build such a model with a single variable or even two. I only use these examples to indicate how suggestive the residual analysis is and how important it is to search for configurations or patterns. In a sense, examining the residuals is a form of deviant case analysis. It also alerts the researcher to outliers. The time series of public expenditures can be vulnerable to outliers. The most recent measures are frequently the largest. Given the statistical model of regression, the fitted equations give most weight to the largest scores which, if the most recent, can considerably distort the analysis. We might note in passing that we have taken a number of precautions including computing expenditures as a percentage of GNP which reduces the outlier problem considerably.

As one includes additional variables, the residual patterns should become less distinct. As one captures more of the causal forces, then ideally the size of the error term diminishes, i.e., the residuals are closer to the predicted model. If this happens, our model is approaching a more complete explanation. But this may not happen because of the sheer complexity of the phenomenon. There are all manner of random shocks that can impinge on the residuals. Oscillations and outliers provide a way of detecting the presence of such shocks.

In this study, we have quantified concepts such as social need, industrialization, economic class power, and vote shifts, as well as other variables in an attempt to capture the complexity of state responsiveness. In Figure Four, we see the impact of all four of these variables. We can see that the periods are less extreme deviations -- a good sign -- indicating that we are measuring some, if not all, of the major forces that influence the willingness of the British state to spend money on welfare services broadly defined. But there is also more oscillation, reflecting the waxing and waning of social forces and the conjuntural imagery of the historian. We can still see distinct periods and we will explore their meaning in the next section. When there is an extended period oscillation, it is usually best to treat these as a distinctive era, perhaps an era of instability or state indecisiveness.

Figure Four also illustrate another issue, the difficulty of deciding where to begin a time period. When there is some judgment involved, one can try several different periodizations and examine which describes the behavior of the trajectory most adequately. In this instance, I first chose four distinct periods: 1871 - 1900, 1901 - 1918, 1919 - 1953, 1954 - 1965. After careful reconsideration of the residuals, I decided it might be more accurate to classify the periods as follows: 1871 - 1907, 1908 - 1953, 1954 - 1965. The reason for our indecision is the sudden and rapid increase in negative residuals between 1900 and 1907. The problem is whether this positive swing is a distinctive era or the beginning of the swing. Both are reported in the following analysis.

In choosing between alternative periodizations one must be mindful of both theoretical and statistical reasons, both qualitative and quantitative evidence. Short time spans, say less than twenty years, do not provide stable estimates. For this reason the second periodization would be preferable on statistical grounds. In weighing the quantitative evidence, one would examine the size of the betas, trying to avoid those above one, indicating non-linearities. Also, the size of the Durbin-Watson statistic should be used as a measure of the presence of second and higher order auto-correlated errors. The consistency of the qualitative evidence is equally critical. Here one asks whether the periodizations make historical sense. Since the Labour Party comes into existence in 1906, the second periodization is preferable for historical reasons. These criteria and the reasoning above are illustrated in the second part of this paper.[23]

There is another observation that is worth making. Note that in the contemporary period, the residuals are becoming larger. This is a sign that the model is about to crash. So, the residuals even in short spans can be quite informative. We need to do further research to determine whether the rapid swing in the residuals is a leading indicator of the ineffectiveness of the model for forecasting. If so, residual analysis could become a very powerful tool in the up-dating of models or at least in the acknowledgment of their limitations.

Refitting our regression models within the distinctive periods detected in the patterns of residuals has a number of advantages. First, it reduces the number of years involved in the analysis making the linear assumptions of regression analysis more plausible. Second, it usually reduces the problem of second and higher order auto-correlated error. Third, it allows us to test the relative importance of traditional periodizations found in the analysis of state responsiveness. Fourth, it allows us to test the adequacy of our analysis over our entire 88 year period. In several instances we found that our analysis was inadequate and had to be replaced by the period analysis because of outliers or major oscillations. Fifth, the dialectic between the period analysis and the analysis of the longue durée leads to an appreciation of how much the partial correlations are affected by a few large scores or outliers. Sixth, and most critically, we are led to a new set of problems -- the differences between the variables that create the origin of a new period, and the variables that reflect the slope of a period or trend.

There are several limitations, however. To have some confidence in the period analysis, one needs at least twenty time points in a five variable model. Sometimes the periods are of shorter duration. The configuration of what constitutes a period is sometimes open to debate depending on how oscillations from a trend line are viewed. For this reason our analysis below of two alternative periodizations is instructive. In this way the reader can judge for him or herself the appropriateness of our analysis.

There are several concluding observations that can be made. First, the longue durée, in Britain at least, is covering quite distinctive periods or eras. Admittedly, this is an unusual data set since it contains yearly observations for almost a century. Many time series sets are only twenty-five years or less. In these, the problem of periods are probably not important, although Schram and Turbett argue for periodization in a shorter space through the use of a pooled time series technique.24 The residuals should be examined for outliers, swings, and the tendency of the regression model to move towards large errors in prediction. In general, when doing period analysis one would want to have the models with the most variables that contributed to an explanation of the dependent variable. These would come closest to modeling the complexity of history.

Second, the swings in the residuals lend themselves to a direct and interesting theoretical interpretation. This will become more evident in the part below when the betas are interpreted in light of historical and qualitative evidence. Residual analyses allow us to capture the waxing and waning imagery that I suggested was so attractive to sociologists interested in comparative macro sociology. We have previously noted that the state was becoming more or less responsive to particular social forces when the residual is other than a parallel line or is oscillating in a short band. The one difficulty is that misinterpretations may occur due to the interactions of various unmeasured variables which in turn indirectly influence the pattern of correlations or betas.

Third, last but not least, we are presented with opportunities to test previous historical insights about periodization. Thus we find some support for the importance of the Lloyd George government being a distinctive element and less support for some other periodizations. This then leads to the next issue -- how one analyzes the periods once they are detected in the residuals.

ANALYSIS

British welfare expenditures present us with an excellent historical case with which to test the methodology of periodization. Much has been written about the growth of the British welfare state and there is, therefore, a wealth of qualitative materials available.[25] More critically, some of the literature argues that there was a significant break when Liberal Government came to power in 1906.[26] This argument needs to be tested. Most historians look at legislation or expenditures and then decide that a particular period began. This is a parallel procedure to the descriptive techniques found in time series analysis. What is missing is an analysis of changes in the independent variables that cause expenditures to increase or decrease. The designation of historical periods becomes more compelling if in fact there is a significant change in the coefficients of variables -- that is, co-variance -- used to explain state responsiveness measured by welfare expenditures and/or legislation. Beyond this, however, the focus on social legislation is itself suspect. In other words, what is important is an understanding of causal relationships. Regression analysis makes this connection explicit.

A TWO VARIABLE POLITICAL MODEL

Even though one normally prefers the most complex model possible, it is also true that sometimes one would like to relate parameter shifts to basic changes in part of the society. Under these circumstances, one may prefer to focus on only some delineated set of variables that are relevant to the basic changes. For example, we may want to see whether fundamental changes in the political system result in the state altering its responsiveness to political and social forces. To illustrate this problem, we will examine again the periodization of two political variables, the economic power of the industrial working class and the agricultural and service classes (FI and FAS, respectively).[27]

When state responsiveness vis-a-vis economic class power is broken into periods, we find that roughly four periods emerge. The periods are established on the basis of the residual patterns. (See Table One.) The first distinctive period is 1871-1906. In this period there is a very rapid growth in the number of Lib-labs as they were called, that is, "labour members" of the Liberal Party. In the same period, state responsiveness is a positive function of both working class power and power of the agricultural-service sector. The second period roughly represents the first period of growth in the strength of the

Labour Party until the crisis of the party in 1932 - 1933. The period from 1933 on represents the steady growth in the power of the industrial working class until the Labour Party finally takes control of the state for an extended period of time. From a theoretical perspective it would be preferable to have 1907-1955 as one distinctive period. An examination of the residuals (Figure Three) indicates some oscillations, suggesting that our breaks are not necessarily the best empirical cutting points. Here we see how theoretical insight and qualitative evidence can be used to check our judgments.

Once the periods are selected, then the model is run for each period just as would be done in co-variance. Our task is to examine the relative size of the betas or partial correlations and ascertain if there are parameter shifts. The betas for each of the four periods are reported in Table One. In the first era the betas for both economic classes are positive and strongly so. This is interesting for a number of reasons. The emergence of widespread suffrage, and the development of "modern" political parties in Britain largely occurs in the 1870s and 1880s. Although the T.U.C. was founded in 1869, it did not begin to elect MPs until much later. In short, it is useful to think of the period of 1870-1906 as the growth and emergence of middle class politics. This provides, perhaps, the best understanding of the meaning of the Liberal Party during this era. The Liberal Party represented both working and middle class interests, but surely focused more on the latter until 1906.

In what sense can we say that increased welfare expenditures or, more specifically, welfare legislation was desired by the industrial working class? The first significant point to be made is that British politics was not class based until the turn of the century. Labour candidates and the T.U.C. began to put forth a "socialist" program only at the turn of the century. Indeed, the reforms of 1906-14 were specifically designed to appeal to working class interests. The Liberals responded with the social legislation as a way of blunting the appeal of this platform much as Bismarck did in the 1880s.[28]

The National Committee of Organized Labor on Old Age Pensions specifically campaigned for social legislation. While it was never a major election issue, the back-benchers did agitate for social legislation in Parliament. Beyond this, both local governments and the Friendly Societies found themselves increasingly overburdened with demands for expansion of benefits. Thus, industrial working class interests became reflected in overloads on the traditional solutions to the problem of welfare need.

But once the Liberals came to power, a major turning point occurred and we find that from then on the power of the shopkeepers and the service sector had a negative impact on the growth in expenditures. As noted above, there was widespread agreement about the need for reform, which helps explain the legislation of the first few years. But as the legislation continued it created opposition to it. This is, of course, another way of describing turning points. Enough is accomplished so that in the future there are calls for a dismantling; a counter-reaction occurs. The formation of the Labour party in 1906 represents a structural transformation of the political system. The growth of the Conservatives who represented the middle classes, landowners and shopkeepers, and other service sector owners and employees provided the alternative class based party. The decline of the Liberal Party was the decline of the one attempt at a coalition that cut across the concerns of several economic interests.

The probable impact of the depression and the war indicates that in the third period, the state was unresponsive to both social classes but especially to the power of the agricultural and service sectors. It might also be noted that in this period and in the previous one the constant is positive, suggesting that the state was becoming more responsive over time but due to factors not included in our model. Another observation to make is that in several of these periods, the betas are above one. This indicates strong interaction effects and suggests the problem of non-linearity, the imagery of the conjuncture of forces. Some of this is a consequence of the multi-collinearity which exists in the data. The growth of industrial working class power was steady throughout the 1930s and through the 1940s. Despite this, its impact on government expenditures declined while that of the agricultural and service sectors grew. This may seem strange but it is important to remember that the level of the variable -- working class power -- is not necessarily the same as the co-variation between it and state responsiveness. Put in other terms, relative to their numbers, the industrial working class had more impact on welfare expenditures in the period marked by the emergence of the Labour Party than during the institutionalization of their power in the post-second World War period.

In the fourth period, the one when there is a dramatic swing in the amount of state responsiveness, we see that the negative association with economic class power grew larger and became positive for the other economic class. How can these two things be true simultaneously? Regression analysis explores whether variation in one variable leads to variation in another. Here we see that as the state became much more responsive, it was <u>not</u> doing so relative to changes in the power of the economic classes, or, if so, it did it in a manner contrary to what one would suppose. My interpretation is that once the major legislation is in place, expenditures grow by a different logic -- a bureaucratic one and the principle of incrementalism -- and not in response to changes in the relative power positions of the two economic classes as we have defined them. The age of program is frequently related to the size of the program.29

Our co-variation across time does suggest an interesting political pattern. As the power of the industrial working class grew, the state became less responsive to it in the sense of variation. However, the growth of power resulted in the origin of two significant growth periods, that of 1907-32 and that of 1953-65 even though changes in state responsiveness are increasingly less a function of changes in class power. To put it in other terms, <u>the growth in power leads to significant historical moments, which manifest themselves in increased expenditures even though variations in power are not always strongly responded to</u>.

Several observations can be made about this methodological procedure. It is not arbitrary and has reasonably clear guide-lines. Different people might make different judgments about beginnings and endings of periods but since the equations are run separately, there is an internal check on the choices. One problem is the number of cases. In some periods the number of years is small. For example, in the analysis of state responsiveness to our two political variables, the power of the two economic classes, the last period is only twelve years. But it is also the period that has the strongest swing and most definite and sharpest increase in state responsiveness. The small number of years means the possibility of unstable parameters but the residual pattern should alert one to the fact that it is a transition period and it has its own special meaning.

Even a two variable model (in this instance economic class variables, when related to some theory of the nature of the political system and how it evolves over time), provides some important insights. I doubt that most analysts would have come to the conclusion about the changing impact of political forces across time as a consequence of changes in the nature of the political system and its changing rules of the game without this methodological technique. Also, our analysis puts the thesis of incrementalism into a new light. Only after the left has taken control of the state and passes the legislation does bureaucratic logic determine growth. The flip side of this interpretation is that our political model of two variables, at least relative to the problems of welfare expenditures, is very much time bound by 1952. After this, it does not predict well. This example illustrates how critical it is to relate the periods and the specific betas back to qualitative materials about the historical flow of time in Britain. Most of the analysis is based on the changes in the political system because of the nature of the variables used to explain state responsiveness.

A FOUR VARIABLE POLITICAL AND ECONOMIC MODEL

What happens when one adds more variables? One must recognize that inevitably the pattern of residuals changes. One might assume that these are the special problems of quantification, but these are generic in any analysis. Historians who do not explore certain hypotheses are in danger of imputing more influence to other variables than truly exist even if they are assessing matters qualitatively. This is one reason why history can be constantly reinterpreted. The methodological issues of the variable analysis become clearer when we shift to a model with two economic variables -- need and industrialization -- and the two political variables, the ones previously employed. The periodization changes as well, with 1920-1952 beginning one period rather than a break occurring in 1932. Adding more variables reduces all but one interaction effect, which indicates that our assumptions about linearity are much more plausible. The R^2 are improved in general, and the problem of auto-correlated error is eliminated in all but one period. These results imply important ideas about the nature of the historical eras that have been delineated. They also indicate how much we must be aware of our statistical assumptions when using time series analysis.

A comparison of the betas for the class power variables in Tables One and Two provides additional quantitative evidence about these eras as useful chunks of time. The betas are smaller in Table Two, indicating that they had been inflated. The betas for the two political variables in Table One indicate how powerful the indirect influence of economic variables can be. Adding industrialization to our analysis reduces, in particulars, the importance of the power variables in most periods except the last one. In the first period, most of the variation is explained by industrialization but negatively so. What this suggests is that when the rate of growth in industrialization slowed, the state spent more on welfare and vice-versa. Welfare expenditures in the era prior to the first Lloyd George government were largely counter-cyclical. Here we see how parameter shifts can give us quite a different interpretation. Need had some positive impact but surprisingly little.

However with the election of 1906 and the rise of the Labour Party, the small power of the industrial working class was translated into a very big change in state responsiveness. The impact of the economic power of agricultural and service sectors was also positive. Industrialization and need are essentially weak explanatory forces by comparison. The very large beta for FI indicates that there is a very strong interaction, especially with FAS. The small number of cases would also suggest instability as well. Statistical instabilities evoke very interesting historical images; we now have an explanation for the parameter shift.

The third period also differs greatly. During this period of unemployment, state responsiveness was a function of need and industrialization. The power of the agricultural and service class was a strong negative influence. During this era, the Labour Party was attempting to gain control of the state but did not succeed. The negative impact of changes in the power of the agricultural and service sectors is especially interesting. It suggests that the power of the center and right stopped growth rather than the alternative view that the power of the left increased state responsiveness. At first the center supported the idea of health and welfare insurance as we have suggested above, but as it grew, they became opposed to these expenditures.

Finally in the fourth period the welfare bureaucracy proceeded of its own accord and responded negatively to changes in any of these four social sources. Again, it is worth repeating how the sharp swing in the residuals provides additional information that helps us to understand the specific period at hand. All the negative coefficients and the pattern of the residuals indicates that our explanatory model ends in 1952. We do not have a good explanation for state responsiveness after this timepoint.

Earlier we observed that the betas can be inflated when other variables are not included because of various indirect relationships. Obviously industrialization and expansion in the power of the industrial working class have some connection. But they represent quite different interpretations in the existing literature. Their combination in a single model provides a more complex interpretation. My general experience has been that as one adds variables from different modes of explanation, there frequently is a significant change in the coefficients. But, adding more variables from the same intellectual tradition does not have this impact.

Another way of studying periods is to compare the betas within eras with those over the longue durée. There are a number of theoretical reasons for doing so. Such an analysis allows one to understand which variables are important for changes in the slope, per se. The above discussion dealt primarily with the variables that explain variation of each slope within each of the eras. Also a comparison across all periods with the longue durée makes apparent how much of the partial correlation in the later analysis is a consequence of a few outliers.

As can be seen, the strength of the industrial working class was concentrated in one short period just after the birth of the Labour Party. This variable largely accounts for the change in slope as well as the growth in state responsiveness. Once the legislation was in place, and especially during the Depression and after the World War II years, it was not a factor. In contrast, the negative impact of the power of the agricultural and service sectors was true of the entire period after the First World War. Need simply averaged out.

Industrialization's lack of relationship obscures several distinct periods that reflect the quite different ways in which the state responds to need. Prior to the legislation of 1906 welfare expenditures were countercyclical. From 1908 until the Attlee government, the government spent more when industrialization grew faster. Part of the reason for this was because expenditures became increasingly based on a tax and, therefore, more dependent upon economic expansion. I am emphasizing industrialization because it has been used as the major explanatory variable by a number of economists and sociologists.[30] Its impact has been overestimated because of the tendency either to ignore power or to measure it in very simple ways.

A FIVE VARIABLE MODEL

In a larger study we considered a variety of other variables including modernization and industrial conflict.[31] In general, the various factors were not important in explaining the growth of welfare expenditures. One other variable did become critical and that is the size of the vote shift between parties (a cubic function was used). The results of periodization with this variable are reported in Table Three. Theoretically, the vote difference variable looks at the responsiveness of the state as a function not of the absolute vote but of vote shifts. A negative sign indicates a shift to the left and a positive sign means a shift to the right. This model considerably improves the amount of variance explained. As explained previously, this is also the model that we decided to use to explore two separate periodizations as a check on our judgment and as a way of illustrating how important qualitative and quantitative evidence is in making the choice between two sets of time periods. We are concerned with improving the stability of the betas, reducing the extent of auto-correlated error, and increasing the amount of variance explained. But, we are also concerned with tapping fundamental changes in society and having them substantiate the choice of timepoints. A comparison between two sets of time periods allows the reader to understand better both the strengths and limitations of the methodology of periodization.

The major change in coefficients between the two periodizations occurs in the betas for industrial working class power (FI) and vote difference (VTF). These shifts are a consequence of adding in the years 1900-1907. This is the era in which labor's power is growing rapidly but the state is not responding to these changes in the political system. The year 1906 was a landslide election for the Liberals, so paradoxically, given our classification of the Liberals as a rightist party, this shows up as a massive shift to the right in votes and a strong positive correlation for this variable. These shifts in betas are, of course, a function of outliers. <u>What is an outlier is a question of how the periodization is made.</u> At the same time outliers are real data. This second periodization, we believe, is the more accurate one. It captures better the very dramatic changes taking place in the political system and the society.

The second period in the second run combines most of the second and third periods of the first periodization. There are not many changes in the size of the betas except for the reduction of the negative coefficient for the power of the agricultural and service sectors (FAS). Industrial working class power is the dominant force. Since this is the period of steady growth in their power as we have measured it, this makes much more sense historically. This second periodization then reflects the basic stages in the transformation of the British political system.

Which periodization is correct? From a statistical perspective, the second periodization is to be preferred. It eliminates the one short period. The first period despite its greater length has a much higher Durbin-Watson value indicating less auto-correlated error. Although the middle period has a low D-W value, it is one in which there are oscillations. In addition, a reading of the qualitative evidence supports the second periodization. It corresponds, as we noted above, to changes in the political system. The second period began with the emergence of the Labour Party and the social legislation from 1906 - 1911. The shifts in the parameters for industrialization and the power of the two economic classes all make sense in light of the historical record. Thus the qualitative evidence supports and strengthens the choice just as the quantitative analysis poses new questions of the historical record. Note that the key is to combine qualitative materials with this regression analysis as a way of understanding the flow of time.

One might ask about the appropriateness of regression analysis given the observed non-linearities, the waxing and waning of historical forces. For short periods of time, regression analysis is a useful approximation. The comparison of the betas of the separate eras with the partials over the entire century makes clear how much can be hidden in an analysis over a long time period. Analyzing the residuals and breaking the data into periods is a critical correction. I believe it is a most useful technique for historical sociologists.

Several final observations need to be made. We have demonstrated that there are parameter shifts. Very few of the variables ever retain the same sign in each period. We can observe the presence of non-linearities when the betas are above one. In this instance much of this problem has been eliminated. The last period should be excluded as one that is too short and probably a transition but an era in which the explanatory model no longer seems to work, a fact which is itself informative.

CONCLUSIONS

The methodological procedures for periodization appear reasonably generalizable to most situations. By ransacking the residuals in a long time series one may find swings. If these swings are of twenty timepoints or more or if a number of oscillations also make a distinctive period, then they reflect a probable parameter shift. When the models are refitted within each period identified by the swings or oscillations, then we can measure the extent of this shift. In the case of Britain, there are several distinctive periods. In each, different causal forces proved to be critical. The swings in the residuals themselves provide additional information that can enrich the analysis.

Decomposing the analysis into separate periods also often solves a number of statistical problems associated with statistical analysis of time series data. Over shorter periods, the linear assumptions are more easily met. Usually the Durbin-Watson values are higher indicating less serious inflation due to auto-correlated error. The analyst becomes sensitive to the problem of outliers and avoids having the findings dominated by them. For those who are interested in statistical models, the reasoning is very similar to co-variance. The major difference is that we are dividing the sample into meaningful temporal units rather than sub-samples. Also we are doing this on the basis of the patterning of the residuals.

It goes without saying that any analyst should study their scatter plots before they do much interpretation of the data. However, few do. In cross-sectional data this is perhaps less fatal. In time series analysis and especially over a long sweep the analysis is subject to severe criticism. We have discovered quite distinctive periods, considerable parameter shifts, much auto-correlated error, and a lot of non-linearity. To ignore scatter plots and residual patterns is to make basic and fundamental errors.

The question is how does one interpret the changes in the relative importance of particular variables. These should be related back to fundamental shifts in the institutions of society which are relevant to the period at hand. In this instance we have tried to develop a theoretical model about changes in the political system and found that -- within limits -- it did seem to help is to understand the periodization.

Great events can be reexamined in the light of the analysis. Within bounds, the Lloyd George government is a turning point. But it is clear from the last analysis that the real shift started prior to it and indeed produced it. More striking -- by its absence -- is any impact of wars and depressions on state responsiveness as we have measured it.

Although there is some judgment involved in the choice of periods and some statistical constraints as well, the analyst can experiment with alternative choices. Usually one choice will emerge as superior when considered in the light of the historical record and in view of various theoretical insights. Regardless, the procedure can be replicated and, therefore, it is open to empirical verification. The choice of several alternative periodizations allows for a testing of the robustness of the analysis which is itself desirable. Thus the procedure is neither arbitrary nor a descent into raw empiricism.

We would appear to have a technique that allows us to combine qualitative and quantitative evidence, numbers and documents. The periodization of time series analysis provides a new and rich tool for understanding better how the march of time can be analyzed. Perhaps more than any other empirical technique of which I am aware, ransacking residuals makes one aware of the historical imagery of the waxing and waning of social forces and the contextual flow of the historical process.

TABLE ONE

Economic Class Power
and State Responsiveness

Longue Duree[a]	FI	FAS	const.	R^2	D-W
1871-1965	.24	-.24	+	.29	1.42
Periods[b]					
1871-1906	.91	1.15	-	.54	1.16
1907-1932	.41	-.59	+	.89	.54
1933-1952	-.29	-1.20	+	.84	.78
1953-1965	-.58	.35	-	.75	1.11

a computed by G.L.S., partial correlations
b computed by O.L.S., betas

TABLE TWO

Economic Class Power, Welfare Need,
Industrialization and State Responsiveness

Longue Duree[a]	FI	FAS	NWH	IP	const.	R^2	D-W
1871-1965	.22	-.22	.11	.04	+	.29	1.42
Periods[b]							
1871-1907	-.07	.14	.10	-.73	+	.64	2.16
1908-1919	1.74	.96	-.18	.18	-	.96	2.26
1920-1952	.00	-.68	.16	.26	+	.80	.65
1953-1965	-.83	-.30	-.34	-.42	+	.91	2.02

a computed by G.L.S., partial correlations
b computed by O.L.S., betas

TABLE THREE
Economic Class Power, Welfare Need,
Industrialization, Vote Shift
and State Responsiveness

Longue Duree[a]	FI	FAS	NWH	IP	VTF	const.	R^2	D-W
1871-1965	.20	-.30	-.07	-.03	-.45	+	.42	1.69
Periods[b]								
1871-1900	.12	.23	.17	-.65	.01	+	.83	1.48
1901-1918	1.25	.11	-.12	-.22	-.26	+	.96	1.41
1919-1953	.18	-.07	.07	.05	-.38	+	.91	.94
1954-1965	-.89	-.38	-.25	-.54	.09	+	.95	2.23
or								
1871-1907	-.51	.18	.0	-.68	.52	+	.67	2.18
1980-1953	1.15	.11	.13	-.19	-.18	+	.95	.69
1954-1965	-.89	-.38	-.25	-.54	.09	+	.95	2.23

a computed by G.L.S., partial correlations
b computed by O.L.S., betas

FIGURE ONE

Residual Plot for Industrialization

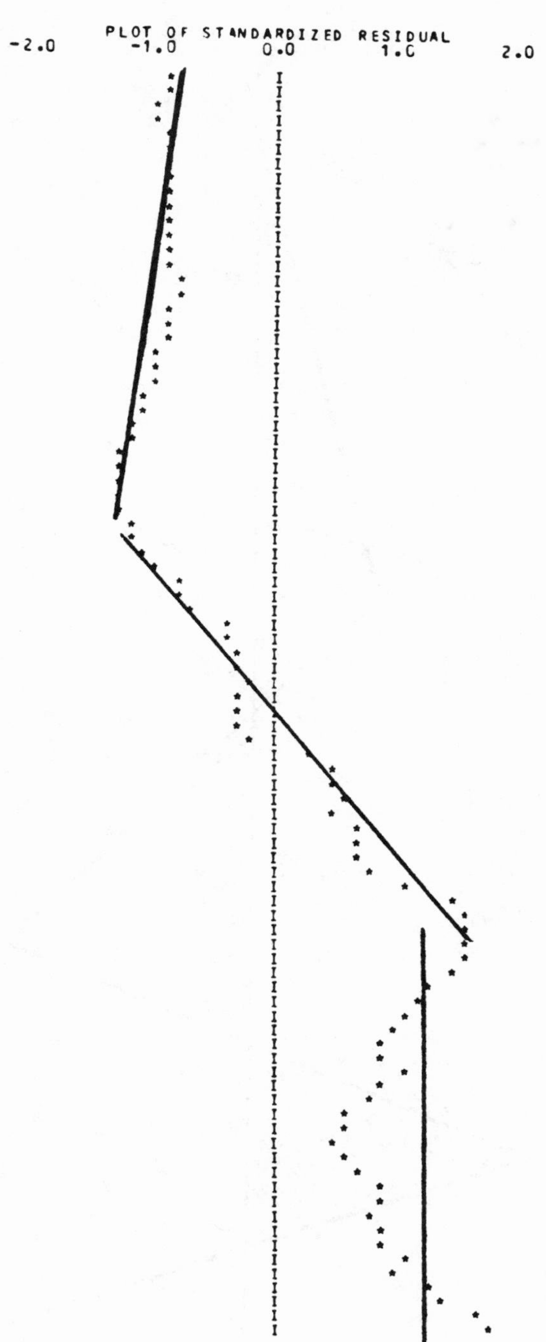

FIGURE TWO

Residual Plot for Economic Class Power

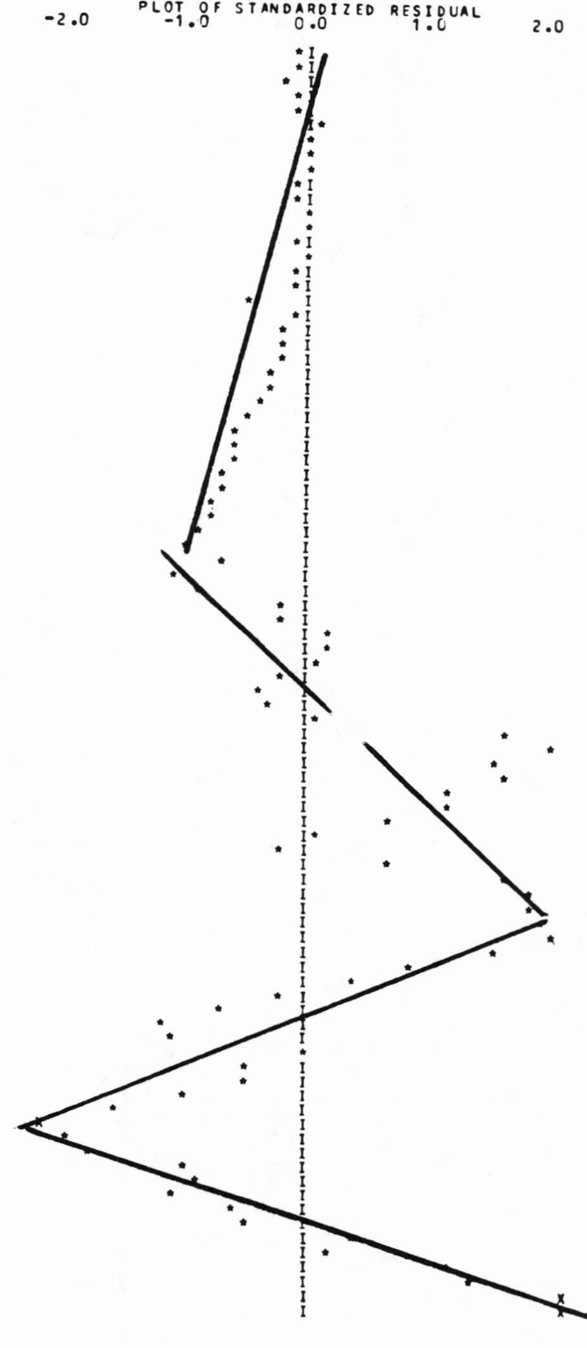

FIGURE THREE

Residual Plot for Economic Class Power, Need, Industrialization and Vote Shift

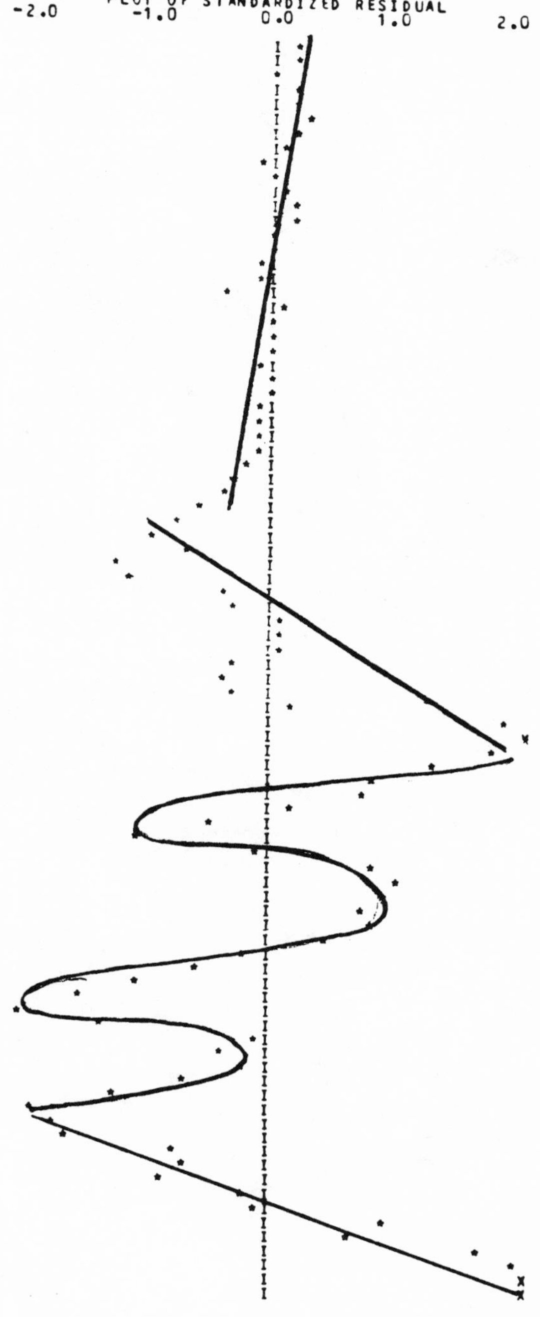

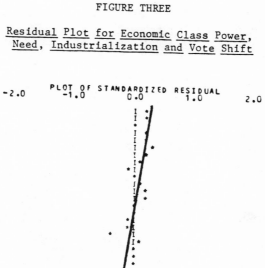

FIGURE 4

Residual Plot for Economic Class Power, Need, Industrialization and Vote Shift

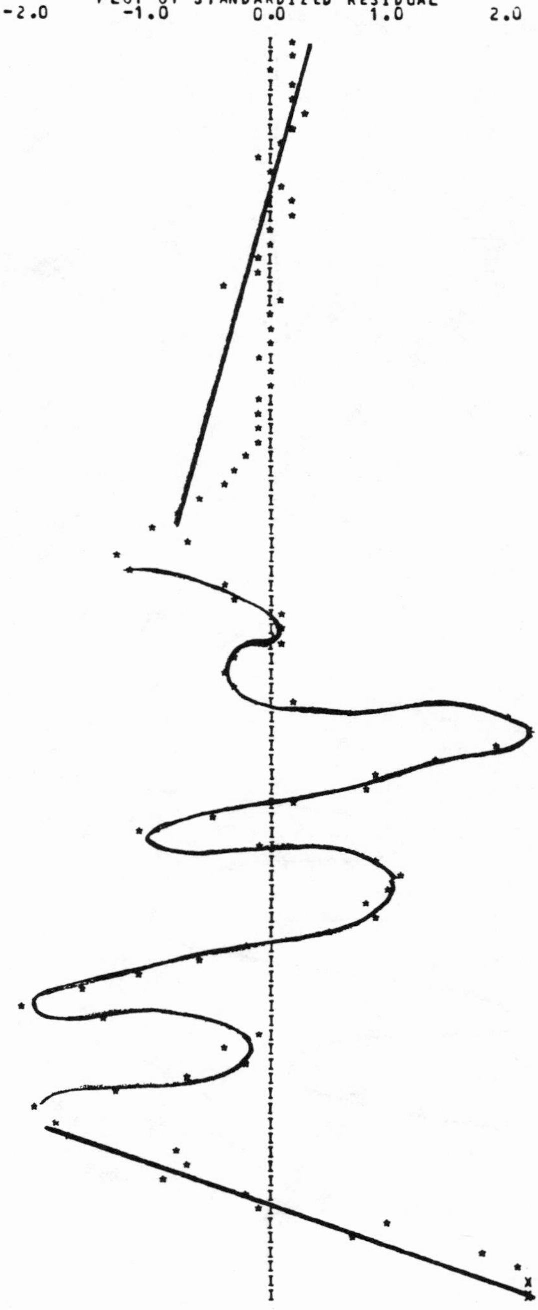

NOTES

1. Phillips, A. W. "The Relation Between Unemployment and the Rate of Change of Money Wage Rates in the United Kingdom: 1861-1957." Econometrica New Series 25, pp. 283-299, 1982.

2. Duncan, Otis Dudley. introduction to Structural Equations. New York: Academic Press, 1975; Hernes, G. "Structural Change in Social Processes," American Journal of Sociology, 82: p. 513, 1975.

3. Duncan, op.cit., p. 167.

4. Laslett, Barbara. "The Place of Theory in quantitative Historical Research," American Sociological Review, 45: pp. 214-228, 1980.

5. Ragin, Charles, Shelley Coverman, and Mark Hayward. "Major Labor Disputes in Britain, 1902-1973: The Relationship Between Resource Expenditure and Outcome," American sociological Review, 47: pp. 238-252, 1982.

6. Schram, Sanford and J. Patrick Turbett. "Civil Disorders and the Welfare Explosion: A Two-Step Process," American Sociological Review, 48: pp. 408-414, 1983.

7. Hicks, Alex. "Elections, Keynes, Bureaucracy and Class," American Sociological Review, 49: pp. 165-181, 1984.

8. Hernes, op. cit.

9. Duncan, op. cit.

10. Laslett, op. cit.

11. Brinkerhoff, Robert Jr. A Behavioral Approach to Historical Analysis. New York: The Free Press, 1969.

12. Flanigan, William and Edwin Fogelman, "Patterns of Democratic Government: An Historical Comparative Analysis," in John V. Gillespie and Betty A. Nesvold, eds., Macro-Quantitative Analysis, Beverly Hills: Sage, pp. 441-473, 1971.

13. Ragin, Coverman, and Hayward, op. cit.

14. Schram and Turbett, op. cit.

15. Rubinson, Richard and John Ralph. "Technical Change and the Expansion of Schooling in the United States, 1890-1970." Sociology of Education, 57: pp. 134-151.

16. Hicks, op. cit.

17. Duncan, op. cit.

18. This is part of a larger study which has been recently completed. See Hage, Jerald, Edward T. Gargan and Robert Hanneman. State Responsiveness: The Rise of Social Expenditures in Britain, France, Germany, and Italy from 1871-1968. Unpublished manuscript, University of Maryland.

19. See, e.g., Aron, Raymond. Main Currents in Sociological Thought II. Garden City, N.J.: Doubleday, 1967; Wilensky, Harold. The Welfare State and

Equality: Structural and Ideological Roots of Public Expenditures. Berkeley: University of California Press, 1975.

20. One word of caution: when a single variable is run, then the force of other variables can impact indirectly via the error term. Thus, this periodization represents the direct influence of industrialization and the indirect influence of all other variables operating via the error term and industrialization. This suggests, of course, too simple a theory about state responsiveness but it does nicely illustrate parameter shifts and how much periods can tell us about societal change.

21. Those familiar with time-series procedures might wonder why we have not used some G.L.S. procedure to reduce the auto-correlation, which is substantial. When estimating parameters for the full time series we do use a G.L.S. regression model because there is substantial auto-correlation. When we are concerned about periodization we cannot because these procedures involve computing a rho which factors out a portion of the common variance altering the residual pattern. O.L.S. remains sensitive to the interplay of all the forces -- which is what is desired for the detection of periods -- and therefore is employed.

22. For a description of how the variables are measured see Hage, et. al., op. cit.

23. One way of conceptualizing the alternative periodizations is as a sensitivity test on the robustness of the chosen periodization. This is extremely important because it means that we have a check on our judgment. Thus, the procedure becomes much less arbitrary.

24. Schram and Turbett, op. cit.

25. See, e. g., Fraser, Derek. The Evolution of the British Welfare State. London: Macmillan Press, 1973.

26. Hay, J.R. The Origins of the Liberal Welfare Reforms, 1906-1914. London: Macmillan Press, 1975.

27. See fn. 22.

28. Hay, op. cit., p. 36.

29. Aron, 1967, op. cit.; Wilensky, 1975, op. cit.

30. E.g., Musgrave, P.W. Sociology, History, and Education. London: Methuen, 1970; Pryor, Fredrick, et al., Public Expenditure in Communist and Capitalist Nations. London: Allen & Unwin, 1968; Aron, op. cit.; Wilensky, op. cit.

31. Hage, et al., op. cit.

IV.

Larry Griffin
Pamela Barnhouse Walters
Philip O'Connell
Edward Moor

Methodological Innovations in the Analysis of Welfare-State Development

Pooling Cross Sections and Time Series

INTRODUCTION

Researchers have approached the study of welfare-state development from a variety of conceptual and methodological perspectives. Many analyses, often employing a Weberian comparative approach, attempt an historically grounded interpretation of welfare policy in one or a few nation states.[1] While certainly representing causal examinations and occasionally relying on descriptive quantitative data, these studies are of course not rooted in quantitative "model fitting". The second very general approach, with which we are most concerned, extensively uses quantitative analytic techniques to address issues of theoretical importance.

Two strategies appear most often in the quantitative literature. The first is some form of cross-national design, either for a single time point or period, or a panel design, where the researcher has cross-national information for two or more time periods.[2] The objective of such designs, of course, is to provide the analyst with information on country-to-country differences in variables assumed to be causally linked so as to answer the following sort of question: to what degree are differences across countries in a causal variable (say, left party strength) related to differences across countries in an outcome variable (say, transfer spending)? The second strategy within the rubric of "quantitative" welfare studies employs historical variation within one or a few states to answer the following question: to what degree does change over time in the causal variable induce change in the outcome variable? The prime concern here is to explain country-specific historical processes.[3] For those handfuls of time-series studies which use more than one nation, the researcher attempts to explain how dynamics <u>within</u> countries differ <u>across</u> countries in a manner not unlike that used by qualitative analysts.[4]

The power and richness of a properly contextualized qualitative analysis is obvious. Our purpose in this chapter, however, is both to review the relative strengths and weaknesses of the two quantitative approaches and to proffer a design that exploits the utility of each, so we will say nothing further about the qualitative methodologies.[5] Since all subsequent discussion hinges to a degree on the organization of a cross-nationally and temporally variable data matrix, it would clarify our discussion to describe how it looks. Assume for the moment we have observations on a number of variables for N nations for each of T temporally ordered time points (say years). For purposes of illustration, let us assume that all cells of this matrix are non-empty. That is, that data have been obtained on the exact same set of variables for each nation, and that, within nations, this set of variables has been compiled for each time period. We then "stack" the year-by-variable matrices for each nation, rather than the nation-by-variable matrices for each year, but the data could just as readily be organized in the alternate manner. The stacked year-by-variable matrix would look as follows:

nation 1 (1) $y_{11}\ x_{111}\ x_{121} \cdots x_{1K1}$,

(n=1) (2) $y_{12}\ x_{112}\ x_{122} \cdots x_{1K2}$,

.
.
.

(3) $y_{1T}\ x_{11T}\ x_{12T} \cdots x_{1KT}$,

nation 2 (4) $y_{21}\ x_{211}\ x_{221} \cdots x_{2K1}$,

(n=2) (5) $y_{22}\ x_{212}\ x_{222} \cdots x_{2K2}$,

.
.
.

(6) $y_{2T}\ x_{21T}\ x_{22T} \cdots x_{2KT}$,

.
.
.

nation N (n=N)

(7) y_{N1} x_{N11} x_{N21} ... x_{NK1} ,

(8) y_{N2} x_{N12} x_{N22} ... x_{NK2} ,

.
.
.

(9) y_{NT} x_{N1T} x_{N2T} ... x_{NKT} ,

where N indexes nations, T indexes time, and K is the number of variables.

Now, the most commonly used quantitative designs, either simple or panel cross sections (here nations) or single nation time series, ignore possible sources of variation in the data matrix. In most cases, the researcher is not faced with a decision about which way to slice the year-by-variable-by-nation matrix, but has instead filled in only one portion of the possibly available data (e.g., the study is designed as a single nation study, or as a cross-national examination at a single point in time). In cross-national designs nations are the unit of analysis, and the sample size equals the number of nations. In terms of how we have laid out our data matrix, this is equivalent to selecting out the row for time t for each nation and ignoring the other NT-N rows. Such an approach necessarily ignores temporal variation in the causal process of interest, which has been one of the most persistent criticisms leveled against their use.[6]

A simple cross-sectional model with two independent variables might look as follows (n=1 to N, T is fixed at some time point):

$$(10) \quad Y_{nT} = a + b_{1T} X_{n1T} + b_{2T} X_{n2T} + e_{nT}.$$

Estimation of such models with ordinary least squares (OLS) regression is relatively straightforward, providing that the routine OLS assumptions are met: the units are independent, the errors are uncorrelated among themselves and with the regressors, and the process is constant across all countries (all n's) in the sample (e.g., small and large states, capitalist and socialist states, etc.). _To infer historical causation from cross-sectional regressions_, however, requires an additional "strong" assumption about the process being modelled, that it is in an "equilibrium" state.[7] That is, the process must be _assumed_ to be a function exclusively of the (generally unknown and unspecified) historical conditions which established the process initially[8] and which keep reproducing it in exactly the same manner through time. Moreover, this must be assumed because it cannot be demonstrated with cross-sectional analysis or even panel designs (in which change in the dependent variable is modelled by including a lagged value of the dependent variable as one of the regressors).

The alternate way to slice the data matrix is to examine longitudinal variation within a single nation, and ignore possible variation among nations. Time-series analyses are logically equivalent to cross-section designs, except that the unit of analysis is years instead of nations, and the sample size is equal to the number of years for which data are available. Referring back to our layout of the year-by-variable-by-nation matrix, using a time-series design is equivalent to selecting out only one of the nation sub-matrices. The same exact model that could be fitted to cross-sectional data could also be fitted to time-series data, except that in the former case the relationships are estimated across nations at a single point in time, and in the latter case the relationships are estimated across time within a single nation. The subscripts in the two models would differ accordingly. A simple two-variable time-series model might look as follows (t=1 to T; N is fixed):

$$(11) \quad Y_{NT} = a_N + b_{N1} X_{N1t} + b_{N2} X_{N2t} + e_{Nt}.$$

In principle, regression models can be fitted to time-series data by the same methods used to fit linear models to cross-sectional data (i.e., OLS, again, if all of its assumptions can be satisfied)[9]. The analog in time-series analysis of the assumption of equivalent processes across units for cross-sectional analysis is the assumption that the process is constant throughout the entire time period of interest. If one has reason to suspect that this is not the case, the years can be divided into two or more separate time periods, with separate estimates of the model coefficients for each. The major advantage that time-series models offer over cross-sectional designs, of course, is that time is introduced explicitly into the analysis. This is of obvious paramount importance if the theoretical process under consideration is intrinsically an historical one.

Despite the power of a time-series analysis in addressing historical questions, it typically exhibits severe shortcomings, some seemingly embedded in the very nature of the analytic procedures used and in the data themselves, and others that stem from the particular application of time series in a substantive context. Among the former, the most serious limitation is that time series tend to model and then estimate short-run adjustments (or changes) in an outcome variable as an independent variable changes. (The time lag generally is not modelled to be greater than a few years.)[10] Among the latter is how generalizable are the results of a time-series analysis of only one or several nations to a theoretically derived population of interest. _If the results of a time-series analysis are used to infer "general" causative processes specified to exist across all nations in that population_, the analyst must simply make the assumption that the estimated causal structure is essentially constant cross-nationally. That, too, is an exceedingly "strong" belief, and, barring examination of other states, is held in the absence of knowledge.

Although one may fit the exact same theoretical model to time-series and cross-sectional data, the estimated coefficients often do not agree.[11] The possible discrepancy between cross-sectional and time-series coefficients is not necessarily a problem, but may indicate that one has sampled different realizations of what one had assumed was the same underlying causal process. In particular, Firebaugh suggests that such discrepancies tend to occur because: (a) cross-sectional data _may_ "measure long term cumulative effects, whereas time-series model short-run adjustments; (b) ...cross-sectional and time-series data differ in lag structures; (c) ...variables omitted from the analysis have different effects across units than over time; (d) cross-sectional data are out of equilibrium."[12] The major point to be made here is that an inconsistency of results between time-series and cross-sectional models is not unexpected, and is not necessarily the result of sampling error, measurement error, or aggregation bias.[13] Such discrepancies nonetheless highlight the importance of taking advantage of the possibility of analyzing both sources of variation whenever possible in macro-level research, and of trying to determine the reasons for the inconsistency.

The research designs that have been discussed thus far have exploited only one of the two possible sources of variation that are available, in principle, for the study of macro-level processes. Researchers with data on multiple states for multiple years have sometimes tried to take advantage of this richer data set by pooling the data across periods ("pooled cross sections")[14] or across states ("pooled time series").[15] Each unit in this "pooled cross-national, time-series" data matrix is treated as a separate observation, the total of which equals the number of nations multiplied by the number of years for which the data were compiled, or N*T.

In addition to the standard OLS requirements, the major assumption that underlies most applications of pooled cross-sectional, time-series models is that the relationships of interest are invariant across time and space. Conceptually, this is equivalent to the assumption that the estimates of each of the T separate cross-sectional equations and the N distinct time-series equations are equivalent (e.g., $b_{k1} = b_{k2} = \ldots = b_{kT}$ for all k). These assumptions are easily tested by computing the relevant T cross-sectional and N time-series coefficients and by seeing if the differences among estimates (with the set of N or T coefficients) are statistically significant. If the values are statistically equivalent, then the estimates may be pooled into one combined model.[16] This crucial assumption of constancy of the theoretical process may be unreasonably restrictive (it is in our data, see below). But along with greater statistical efficiency,[17] the resulting (assumed or demonstrated) spatial and temporal invariance of the pooled parameter estimates also explains their attractiveness to researchers. <u>To the extent that these strong assumptions are true</u>, the analysts can make quite sweeping general inferences about putative theoretical processes which are not unduly conditioned by country-to-country or year-to-year peculiarities. If these assumptions are only modestly violated, moreover, the researcher can minimally describe the essential workings of a relatively general process, while admitting that its estimates are not precise for all (or even any) nations or time periods.

Assuming, though, that the differences in the coefficients across countries (or time) are statistically significant, the availability of temporally- and spatially-variable data can be used to "explain" those nation-specific (or time-specific, for the T cross sections) estimates in a higher-order cross-national (or time-series) analysis. That is, differences <u>across</u>, say, countries in estimated <u>within-country</u> processes can be explicitly modelled as a function of other cross-nationally variable, temporally-invariant properties. We present an illustrative higher-order analysis in section E below.

To summarize our discussion thus far: the two quantitative approaches to the study of welfare-state development (a) have different strengths and weaknesses; (b) will not necessarily generate the same estimates of the causal process assumed to exist; and (c) should be combined in some fashion so as to maximize the potential explanatory power of each, as pooled cross-sectional, time-series models can do, when creatively used, for example, in a higher-order analysis. Below we illustrate these points with an analysis of welfare spending in twelve nations for the years 1961-1976. The nations, basically a non-representative sample of our population of interest, advanced capitalist democracies, are as follows: Australia (A), Canada (C), Denmark (D), Finland (F), Germany (G), Ireland (Ir), Japan (J), Netherlands (Ne), Norway (No), United Kingdom (UK), and the United States (US). Given our population of theoretical concern, our choice of specific nations to be analyzed was dictated by the availability of extant time-series data. Our choice of years, too, was largely necessitated by data availability. This latter limitation is not crippling, however, given the alterations in the world political economy which began in the late 1960s to early 1970s. Our analysis is largely expository by intent, but it is nonetheless theoretically grounded and we want to emphasize that whatever substantive inferences can be drawn should not be generalized to any other nation state or time period. Data sources and variable operationalizations are contained in the Appendix.

ANALYSIS

We begin with a specification of the determinants of welfare spending derived generally from neo-Marxist interpretations of state policy (see Griffin and Leicht in this volume) and from past research on the topic.[18] The following six variables, representing a variety of politico-economic influences and fiscal constraints on transfer outlays (TRANS), are included in all of our regression equations: military spending (MIL), percent of the labor force unemployed (UNEMP), gross domestic product per capita (GDPPC), volume of strike activity (VOL -- person days lost due to strikes per 10,000 workers), the inflation rate (INF), and left party representation in the cabinet (LEFT -- Canada, Japan, and the US are argued to have no left representation in the executive so their scores for this variable are zero throughout the entire time period). TRANS and MIL are standardized, following convention, by GDP.[19] We omit from this analysis two variables of documented importance cross-nationally: percent of the population "elderly" and the age of the social security system, because Wilensky argues that both properly should be considered as dependent on economic development (our GDPPC measure), military spending, and the redistributive and opportunity ideologies of governing elites (tapped by our LEFT variable).[20] Cutright also posits that social insurance program experience is a consequence of economic development.[21] Given these theoretical assumptions, our results are unbiased estimates of the reduced form of the posited causal structure; that is, our regression equations do not incorporate those mechanisms which may mediate, or "explain," how GDPPC, LEFT, and the other exogenous variables affect transfers (through increasing the proportion of elderly, for example). Our estimates, therefore, are correct but unexplicated; thus, a full-blown analysis of transfers would require the addition of these two omitted variables. We assume throughout this chapter that the effects of these six regressors are linear and additive. Finally, we assume all of the regressors affect transfers contemporaneously, that is, we do not lag any of our variables. Modest experimentation relaxing this assumption did appreciably change our general results.

A. PARTITIONING VARIANCE

In addition to theoretical concerns, we use an assessment of the observed variation in the variables across the 12 nations, and through the 16 years, to guide our choice of variables to be included in the equation. Table 1 presents the proportion of variation in each variable which exists _across_ countries (column 1) or through time (column 2).

The statistics in column 1 were obtained by regressing, in the pooled data matrix, each variable against a set of N-1 country dummy variables (i.e., 1 for country n=1, 0 otherwise). The R^2 in that equation represents, in effect, the cross-nationally invariant (or "country free") variance attributable uniquely to year-to-year changes in the values of each variable summed over N cross sections. The proportions in column 2 similarly reflect the time-invariant (or "time-free") variance attributable uniquely to country-to-country differences in the values of each variable summed over T time periods, and were obtained by regressing each variable against T-1 time dummy variables (e.g., 1 for t=1, 0 otherwise).

The information contained in Table 1 is important for our subsequent analyses for several reasons. First, the table shows vividly where the bulk of the _pooled_ (i.e., across nations and through time) _variance_ is or is not housed. Most of the pooled variance in most variables is situated between countries, rather than through time. This is particularly the case for MIL and UNIONIZATION, a variable not included in our TRANS equations. Variations in INF and GDPPC, on the other hand, are predominantly a function of year-to-year changes rather than cross-national differences. The statistics presented in column 3 are the proportions of the pooled variance accounted for by the _additive_ combination of year-to-year and country-to-country differences in the variables' values. They are always less than 1.0, and in some cases, especially

LEFT and VOL, substantially so. Coefficients less than unity may initially seem puzzling, but are explicable. The between-time between-country variance is assessed assuming that each and every country in the analysis is subject to an identical time trend (or the lack thereof), i.e., that the movement through time of any given variable is constant for all countries. Likewise, for each and every time period, cross-national differences in the variables' values are assumed to be identical. For some variables (MIL, GDPPC, UNIONIZATION) these assumptions appear to map reality. For other variables, however, again especially LEFT and VOL, they do not. Statistically, coefficients less than unity reflect statistical interaction between time and countries. This means, substantively, that growth paths of the variables through time differ from one country to the next.[22]

The second element of importance contained in Table 1, and the one motivating our discussion of this table, is its potential use in equation specification. Theoretically, UNIONIZATION should play an important role in welfare policy, especially in social democratic countries.[23] Yet column 2 suggests that given this time period, there simply is generally too little within-country, through-time variation to analyze meaningfully. In other words, there has been very little movement through time in UNIONIZATION for these 12 countries considered as a set.[24] (To verify this assertion we added UNIONIZATION to our country-specific time-series equations and obtained, for most countries, statistically significant negative regression coefficients, completely implausible findings.) There is massive between-country variation in UNIONIZATION (column 1), and later in this chapter we attempt to show how to capitalize on this to explain within-country differences in causal processes. One message contained in Table 1, then, is that the researcher should pose only those questions which realistically can be answered with the actual data contained in the matrix. The pooled design is a powerful tool aiding that process.

A final point of importance can be demonstrated with TRANS. Of the total variation in TRANS, 23.7 percent is situated within countries, attributed to changes through time. This implies that even were we to explain 100 percent of the temporal variance in TRANS for all 12 of the countries included in our sample, we would nevertheless have explained "only" 23.7 percent of its total or pooled variation. What is completely untouched by within-country time-series examinations of TRANS is, of course, differences in the levels of TRANS which exist across countries. Even perfect explanations of within-country welfare outcomes explain the total TRANS variation only to the extent that the pooled variance is captured by, or attributable to, changes in TRANS levels through time. We are not in any sense disparaging comparative time-series analysis; we are saying, however, that researchers should be aware of precisely what it is they are explaining with their within-country (or their cross-national) models. Again, pooled models, used appropriately, force the researcher to confront this.

B. CROSS-NATIONAL ANALYSES

To return now to our hypothesized causal model, we are pooling cross sections and time series, so the general structure of our equation is:

$$(12)\ TRANS_{nt} = a + b_1\ MIL_{nt} + b_2\ UNEMP_{nt} + b_3\ GDPPC_{nt} + b_4\ VOL_{nt} + b_5\ INF_{nt} + b_6\ LEFT_{nt} + e_{nt}.$$

Equation (12) thus posits that for every n (n=1, 2,...12) and t (t=1,2,...16) the posited structure is assumed to represent accurately the operative causal process. (Here none of the coefficients are subscripted by n or t, reflecting the assumption that all are constant and equal for all n and all t.) We begin now to test the realism of these "strong" assumptions. In Table 2 we present OLS regression estimates of T cross-sectional models; that is, we estimate the same regression equation across the 12 countries for 16 years, from 1961 to 1976. In abstract equation form, we are analyzing:

$$(13)\ t=1961:\ Y_{n1} = a_1 + b_1\ X_{n1} + e_{n1},$$

$$(14)\ t=1962:\ Y_{n2} = a_2 + b_2\ X_{n2} + e_{n2},$$

.
.
.

(15) t=1976: $Y_{n16} = a_{16} + b_{16} X_{16} + e_{n16}$.

These T equations may be summarized by a single equation:25

(16) $Y_{nt} = a_t + b_t X_{nt} + e_{nt}$.

The coefficients should not be taken seriously. We have only 12 observations per year and the variables are too collinear for comfort (which led us to exclude UNIONIZATION even from this analysis; it is heavily correlated with LEFT). Both conditions combine to render both low adjusted R^2's and, for the vast bulk of the estimates, statistically insignificant coefficients. (Because of this we do not present either R^2's or t-statistics).

The main reason why the estimated structures should not be taken very seriously, however, is that they are extraordinarily unstable across years. The magnitudes vary considerably by year and some coefficients change signs more often than not. UNEMP, for example, changes signs 10 times in 16 years, and GDPPC 8 times. Table 2 thus shows all too painfully that there is no "general" or accurate cross-national model which holds even for these 16 years. Still more dramatically, there are very few periods of contiguous years which display sign stability. In Table 3, row 1, we present a simple unweighted average of the year-specific coefficients. That is probably the best estimate of the "general" causal cross-national parameters because idiosyncratic yearly fluctuations are averaged out. But here even the signs of the mean estimates are not replicated in any single year (at best only four of the coefficients from any t regressions are the same as the average estimates).

The lack of a "general" model does not trouble us; we did not expect to find one and we did not. What is quite disturbing, though, is the extreme instability of the T set of coefficients. If a researcher had chosen, say, 1966 (as did Wilensky26) to measure these concepts, s/he would have concluded that MIL, LEFT, VOL, and INF stimulate TRANS, while UNEMP and GDPPC retard it. If, on the other hand, 1969, only three years later, were chosen, two of the "stimulants" would be adjudicated "retardants," and one of the 1966 "retardants" would be accorded the status of "stimulant". Because much analysis of welfare outcomes is cross-national, and because the utilized year, or small group of years, is chosen generally with an eye toward data availability rather than anything theoretically inspiring about that particular year, we should be extremely cautious about reporting or making inferences concerning general time-invariant processes from static cross-national regressions. 1970, for example, is not an acceptable proxy for the entire post-war period, or for the period of years specifically in our analysis, or, for that matter, for 1969 or 1971.[27] This general point has been made by others in different substantive contexts.[28] Finally, to the extent that panel designs are based on an arbitrarily chosen time period, or are dictated by data availability, they too offer little hope for uncovering processes generalizable to the entire period covered by the panels.

Careful scrutiny of period average and yearly patterns of collinearity can mitigate to an extent this extreme instability. Equation re-specification and re-estimation, in an almost iterative way, can actually lead to models of great stability. The analyst should emphasize most strongly the average coefficients across all years because these more accurately reflect the causal process over the entire period than does any single year's estimate. For example, we experimented with two distinct five-variable models and a four- three- andtwo-variable model. The average of the sixteen coefficients for the most stable equation is presented in row 2 of Table 3. If these estimates are to be believed, over the sixteen-year period, levels of TRANS were higher in those countries where LEFT parties were relatively stronger in the cabinet and lower in "rich" nations and in countries with high rates of INF. Remember that this analysis pertains only to the component in TRANS, LEFT, INF, and GDPPC which lies between nations. Any static cross-national regression slopes are silent about possible sources of variation which are functions of time within countries.

Regardless of the theoretical accuracy or stability of the estimates generated by averaging equations, two important problems remain. First is the issue of specification: to the extent that the excessive cross-national collinearity has forced us to exclude pertinent variables from the equation, the estimates in row 2 are biased. While specification bias is always a real possibility in any quantitative study, the likelihood of the presence of the bias is high in data of this sort. Secondly, even if the coefficients are unbiased, they should be understood as precisely what they are -- average cross-national estimates, which are static (though yearly data were employed to estimate the period-specific coefficients) -- and not for what they are not, inferential evidence about historical processes. They have absolutely no necessary implication for within-country, time-series processes, or even for the average of the N time-series coefficients, as we shall see below.

The belief underlying averaging coefficients is that idiosyncratic yearly coefficients, themselves rooted in idiosyncratic yearly values of the regressors, will be smoothed out by the averaging process. An alternative procedure is simply to average the values of the variables themselves across all years and obtain just one cross-national regression coefficient; that is, to simply regress the 1961-1976 mean of TRANS on the independent variables' 1961-1976 means. Our specification of this option is represented by the estimates presented in row 3 of Table 3. The "means" analysis is exclusively cross-national in scope. Indeed, the actual information summarized in row 3 is not even contained in our pooled data matrix. We have one value of the mean of each variable (though, of course, it is derived from time-series information) and 12 observations.

It is instructive to compare the equations represented in rows 2 and 3 of Table 3. The "means" equation (row 3) coefficients are larger than the average of the T coefficients (row 2). Kuh argues that this is to be expected because the cross-sectional "means" regressions "will reflect long-run adjustments," which are cumulative.29 More important, perhaps, than magnitude differences, are sign consistencies; the coefficients in the two rows are of the same sign. This, as well as their interpretation as "long-run" coefficients, should be of some comfort to analysts of the welfare state who often have at their disposal only period means, rather than actual yearly values. Any ordinal-type rough inferences which may be drawn from row 2 can also be drawn from the means analysis, as they will be essentially identical. Regression of means, however, shares with the averaging-of-coefficients approach problems of collinearity (in our data, VOL and UNEMP are correlated at .85 and should not be put in the same equation), and the subsequent specification troubles.

C. TIME-SERIES ANALYSES

We return now to the pooled cross-national, time-series data matrix to ascertain how general are the estimates of the N within-country time-series TRANS models. We will estimate 12 equations of the general form:

(17) n=1: $Y_{1t} = c_1 + d_1 X_{1t} + U_{1t}$,

(18) n=2: $Y_{2t} = c_2 + d_2 X_{2t} + U_{2t}$,

.
.
.

(19) n=12: $Y_{12t} = c_{12} + d_{12} X_{12t} + U_{12t}$.

These N equations can also be summarized by a single equation:

(20) $Y_{nt} = c_n + d_n X_{nt} + U_{nt}$.

Note that the regression coefficients, the d_n's, are properties of the specific countries analyzed in the equations summarized by (20). That is, they are time invariant, because they are assumed to be constant for every year within each of the N countries, but are potentially cross-nationally variable. We use these country differences in regression estimates in a later analysis in this chapter (Section E).

To see how consistent or diverse are the coefficients linking TRANS to within-country variation in the same six variables used in the T cross-sectional regressions, we simply estimate equation (20) above 12 times, once for each country in the sample. The signs of the OLS coefficients are presented in Table 4.[30] The signs of the country-specific time-series estimates generally exhibit much greater stability than did the T cross sections. MIL, UNEMP, and GDPPC are quite stable across the 12 nations, with very few sign changes. The signs of the coefficients of VOL, LEFT, and INF, however, are volatile, and variation in signs of the INF coefficients appears systematic; only in relatively social democratic countries are these coefficients negative. We are unsure what, if anything, to make of this pattern, but we attempt to partially explain variations in sign and size of the GDPPC and LEFT coefficients in Section E.

The averages of each of the six coefficients across all nations are presented in row 4 of Table 3. How applicable are these average coefficients for any given country? Several answers to this question are possible. The signs of the averaged coefficients are replicated exactly for three nations: Australia, the Netherlands, and Japan (excluding the LEFT coefficient comparison in the latter case because Japan has had no left representation in the executive and therefore no variance on the measure); another three countries (Germany, Norway, and Canada) are discrepant on only one sign. The mean estimated structure, moreover, is quite similar to that of

Australia in terms of the actual magnitude of the coefficients (data not presented). In this case, then, the "general" (or averaged) model seems to fit the observed country-specific patterns reasonably well. Substantively, the averaged estimates imply that TRANS is reduced by MIL (a fiscal trade-off), VOL (probably an artifact of averaging random noise currently passing for genuine effects because the only two significant VOL effects, for the UK and the US, are positive -- see Table 5 below), LEFT (again possibly an overall artifact -- see Table 5); and are increased by UNEMP (a proxy for societal "need" and the growth of the surplus population, both of which exert pressure for expanded transfers), INF (possibly the pegging of transfers to inflation rates;[31] and GDPPC (the economic resource base of the society). With the exception of the two possible statistical artifacts, the estimates are theoretically plausible in addition to exhibiting reasonable stability across countries.

Yet no single estimated country-specific time series from either the N equations using the "common" regressors (Table 3) or a trimmed down version of equation (12), modelling explicitly country-specific TRANS dynamics (see Table 5), is identical to the average of the coefficients presented in Table 3, rows 4 and 5. These coefficients, obtained by estimating versions of equation (12) modified for each country by retaining only those influences significant in Table 4 and then re-estimating with the appropriate (i.e., OLS vs. GLS) estimation technique, evoke markedly different processes underlying transfer outlays by country. In some countries (Ireland, the UK, and the US), the determination is multi-causal. For other nations, Denmark, Germany, Norway, and Japan, for example, the crucial causal processes are estimated to be remarkably simple, relying only on societal wealth or "needs". Here, too, the coefficients, with the possible exception of the negative LEFT effect in the Netherlands, are quite plausible.

Since the set of estimates is not radically divergent, the analyst is faced with a quandary. On the one hand, the country-specific slopes present a more accurate representation of the causal mechanisms driving TRANS in any single nation, but they do so by destroying the unmistakable generality which does exist in the estimated causal structures. In this sense, parsimony is sacrificed for what may be hair-splitting accuracy. Given that both appear to be reasonable approximations of the theoretical process of interest, the choice as to which to use would seem to depend on the intent of the study. Those searching for trans-national generalizations will find them in Table 3, rows 4 and 5, at least as those generalizations pertain to the twelve nations and time period under investigation. Those seeking divergent paths of welfare-state development -- for even such a seemingly "homogeneous" group of nations -- will find them in Table 4, and especially so in Table 5. No unambiguous solution to this dilemma is apparent. This of course contrasts strongly with the T cross-national regression results, where it is clear that temporally-invariant laws do not exist, even over such a "short" time in history.

That consideration brings us to the final question raised by Tables 4 and 5. How similar are the average cross-sectional and average time-series results? Comparison of the average cross-national slopes and the average time-series slopes (in rows 1 and 4 of Table 3) indicates that the two sets of results presented in Tables 2 and 4 have very little in common. Only three of the averaged coefficients have the same sign (UNEMP, VOL, and INF); MIL, GDPPC, and LEFT have different signs. Even coefficients from the cross-national specification which yielded the most stable coefficients of the T cross sections (row 2, Table 3) differ pronouncedly from those obtained with an identical specification in N time-series models (see Table 3, row 5). The averaged time-series slopes (over 12 countries) agree with the average of the 16 cross-sectional slopes on the sign of only one variable, INF. The positive GDPPC and negative LEFT coefficients in the time series persist in the trimmed time-series model, and are opposite in sign from those estimated in either row 2 or from the cross-national "means" equations (row 3). This is not to say that the averaged T cross-national coefficients are wrong. It is, however, compelling documentation that cross-national averages of variable values or slopes cannot be used to infer historical processes of welfare-state development generally or for any particular nation, _even when both the cross-national analyses and the time-series analyses pertain exactly to the same countries and time periods._[32] Simply put, the analyses are directed toward explaining different components of the pooled variation.

D. POOLING CROSS SECTIONS AND TIME SERIES

We have demonstrated that neither cross-sectional analyses nor time-series analyses, considered singly, are capable of examining the entire variance in TRANS, which varies both historically and spatially. Thus a design which includes the omitted dimension of both of the above approaches can potentially be used to capture and analyze the full extent of the variation in the outcome under consideration. This, of course, is accomplished by pooling cross sections and time series. Moreover, more efficient and precisely weighted estimates of the influence of the independent variables across T cross sections and N time series than those thus far discussed can be obtained by using simultaneously, in one estimating equation, all of the information contained in the full array of the N*T (in our case, 12 by 16) data matrix. The equation is then estimated over 192 cases as if the observations were just a continuous string of data, unbound either by time or space. Equation (12), above, represents the mathematical expression of this (as presented) trans-national, trans-temporal structure. We know already that the assumption of this equation -- constant regression coefficients for every nt observation -- is not, in our case, plausible. But estimation of equation (12), and elaborations of it, are useful for a number of reasons.

First, because a much larger number of observations is used in the pooled regression analysis than in either the T cross sections or the N time series, the resulting OLS estimates will have smaller sampling variability, thereby increasing the statistical significance of the coefficients. Second, the greater number of observations allows the inclusion of a much larger number of regressors than is possible with only N cross sections or T time periods. Third, country or year differences (or both simultaneously), adjusted for the presence of the continuous variables of theoretical interest, can be readily assessed by the simple addition of N-1 country dummy variables and T-1 year dummy variables in the equation. Finally, estimates of the pooled matrix yield weighted averages of the regression slopes (the b's) across nations, across time periods, or across both simultaneously. The last set of coefficients is not obtainable from any manipulation of either the T cross-sectional coefficients (because country-to-country variation is used in those analyses), or of N time-series coefficients (because yearly variation is used in those analyses).

To illustrate the potential inherent in the pooled matrix we estimate four models linking TRANS to the independent variables. Model 1 (M1) is simply equation (12). It is most restrictive in that all coefficients (including the intercept) are assumed constant and equal for all N*T observations. Country and time effects are assumed zero, meaning that the adjusted means of TRANS are restricted to be the same for all nations and years. Model 2 (M2) adds N-1 country dummies to equation (12). Inclusion of the "nation effects" purges the pooled matrix of cross-national variation in all variables, effectively allowing us to analyze "pure" time-series variation in TRANS, MIL, GDPPC, etc. The coefficients estimated by M2 will approximate the average of the N time-series coefficients because there, too, the regressions pertained only to the time-series variation. M2 allows only for intercept differences across the 12 nations (i.e., the "a" in equation (12)); the regression slopes remain constrained to be the same for all countries. Model 3 (M3) adds T-1 time dummies to equation (12). Estimation of this equation thus purges the pooled data matrix of its time-series variation. The regression estimates obtained with M3, therefore, will approximate the results of the average of the T cross-national coefficients, which also represent "time-free" coefficients. And, as in M1 and M2, only the intercepts are allowed to vary from year to year, reflecting annual changes in TRANS adjusted for the effect of the original six variables. The regression slopes are again constrained to be constant for all 16 years. Finally, Model 4 (M4) includes both time and country dummies additively (i.e., we do not allow country and time interactions, though for some purposes, for example, the U.S. during the Vietnam War years, this might prove substantively interesting. See our discussion of column 3 of Table 1 for the interpretation of this equation). Again, only the intercepts are allowed to vary across time and nation; the slopes remain constrained to be constant across all time periods and nations.

Both the OLS and GLS estimates of the four models are presented in Table 6. The coefficients are sensitive to estimation techniques, MIL, and in Model 4, GDPPC, especially so. Since our intent here is expository, we will limit our comparison of the pooled OLS coefficients to the average cross-national and time-series slopes presented in Table 3, which were also estimated with OLS.[33] Comparisons of both M2 and M3 with M1 suggest that M1 should be abandoned as too restrictive. The additional variance in TRANS explained by M2 is statistically significant, meaning that significant differences in the TRANS means across nations exist after controlling for the effects of the six regressors. The M3 - M1 comparison indicates marginally significant time differences in the adjusted TRANS means. The explained variance for M2 is considerably higher than that obtained with M3, echoing the results in Table 1 that show greater cross-national variation in TRANS than time-series variation.

The estimates of M2, which pertain only to the time-series variation in the pooled matrix (because cross-national variation has been expunged by the introduction, in M2, of the country effects), suggest that, over time, MIL, and perhaps VOL, significantly decrease, and UNEMP and GDPPC significantly increase,

TRANS. Taken as broad conclusions, these are in almost complete accord with the averages of the N time-series coefficients reported in row 4 of Table 3. This, of course, is expected, as both procedures actually model the same time-series component of the pooled data matrix. (The pooled estimates, however, are more efficient than the coefficients averaged over N time series for the reasons discussed above.) The sign of only the INF coefficient differs across the two approaches to the estimation of the time series, and it is not significantly different from zero in Table 6.

OLS estimates of M3 pertain only to the cross-national variance in the pooled matrix, and, as expected, are quite similar to the average of the T cross-sectional estimates presented in row 1 of Table 3. Only INF's coefficient is not same-signed. M3 implies that MIL, LEFT, and INF stimulate TRANS, while VOL and GDPPC depress it. M2 and M3 tell different stories about the causal factors driving TRANS, just as did the averages of the T cross-national and N time-series regressions, because they are analyzing different components of the observed variation in the pooled data matrix, with M2 pertaining <u>only</u> to the time-series variation and M3 <u>only</u> to cross-national variation.

Finally, OLS estimates of M4, containing both country and year dummies, tell still another story. M4 analyzes the variation in TRANS and in the six regressors under the assumption that country and year do not interact (see Table 1). The coefficients in M4 report the estimated linkages between TRANS and the regressors under the conditions that all variables in all countries behave identically through time and that cross-national differences in these variables are constant for every year. Only UNEMP and INF register significant influences, with TRANS increasing with increases in UNEMP and decreasing with increases in INF. Substantively, M4 most closely resembles M2, which assesses the efficacy of the regressors in the twelve time series. The major discrepancy between M4 and M2 concerns the GDPPC coefficient; it is significant and positive in M2 (as it was in the averaged N time-series equations) but not significant in M4.

It may make little sense, in terms of increasing the explained variance, to add, as we did, the time dummies to M2 to obtain M4 because the addition of fifteen variables indexing time adds nothing to the explanatory power of M2. Moreover, M4 embodies stronger restrictions than do either M2 or M3 (though weaker ones than M1) in that the assumptions of constant cross-national differences for every year, and identical time paths for every country, may be (and, given our earlier analyses, probably are) incorrect. On the other hand, M4 allows for more sweeping generalizations -- literally across time and space, while still allowing for temporal and spatial differences in the adjusted TRANS means (unlike M1) -- and is assumed to generate disturbances with more desirable statistical properties (see footnote 33) than either M2 or M3.

What can we infer about welfare-state development from Table 6? The safest conclusions, we believe, to draw from these genuinely pooled analyses are not substantive, but methodological. First, although all four models make the identical "strong" (and, in the cases of M1, M2 and M3, certainly unrealistic) assumption that causal processes are constant across whatever unit is allowed to vary, the coefficients estimated by the four equations differ sharply. Only VOL maintained the same sign across each of the equations. MIL exhibited little consistency. Second, the analyst should comprehend precisely what component of the pooled variation is being analyzed by which model, and should use that knowledge in choosing the model most suitable to answer the substantive question being posed. If, for example, an analyst wished to estimate only cross-national effects with the pooled matrix, M3 would seem to be the logical choice. Third, in these data at least, we again see dramatically that no "general" trans-national trans-temporal determination of transfer outlays exists. This is completely consistent with our earlier analysis, but perhaps is more forcefully brought home since these very discrepant results are obtained with four pooled models which _seem_ to be analyzing the same set of data in a way the T cross sections or N time series obviously did not, and which differ among themselves only with respect to what is, for our purposes here, the theoretically trivial specification of purely additive time and country effects. Let the consumer of quantitative welfare state literature beware.[34]

E. EXPLAINING DIFFERENCES IN COUNTRY-SPECIFIC EFFECTS CROSS-NATIONALLY

We now wish to move to a higher order of analysis to demonstrate the research potential of a pooled data matrix combining both cross-national and time-series variation. Table 1 demonstrated that the variation, over these nations for this time period, in some variables was housed almost exclusively either through time (INF, to a degree) or across countries (UNIONIZATION, for example). Such patterns pose problems of equation specification: if UNIONIZATION, for example, has almost no time-series variation, we should not expect it to affect TRANS within nations over time, and we should not even attempt to assess its impact. Moreover, inclusion of UNIONIZATION in the T cross-national regressions is not feasible either since it is highly correlated with variables already included in the model (i.e., LEFT) and an intelligible interpretation of its influence is not possible without severely misspecifying the welfare equations. Yet we know that UNIONIZATION is important theoretically, that it is somehow implicated in welfare state development. What is to be done?

No fully adequate response to this question is possible given the conditions just described. Those, after all, are the observed empirical patterns for these nations over these years. It is possible, however, to turn these defects in the data at one level of the analysis (the one with which we have been thus far concerned) into virtues -- desirable properties of the data -- in a higher order explanation of welfare-state development. Recall the country-specific time-series estimates signed in Table 4. Assume for the purpose of this exposition that the differences implied there are "real"; that is, not just insignificant deviations from each other or from some averaged or pooled estimates. These slopes, of course, represent the sensitivity of transfer outlays to particular politico-economic events or conditions <u>within countries across time</u>. As such, they represent a property of the country in precisely the same way as does the 1961-1976 mean level of transfers for each nation. Both statistics, in fact, can be used to pose issues pertaining to country-to-country differences: why does the mean of TRANS over the entire time period differ from one nation to the next? And why do the <u>within-country time-series</u> regression slopes of, say, GDPPC on TRANS differ across countries, again for the same 1961-1976 period? If we were to conclude our analysis after examining only the time-series variation (by estimating either N within-country time-series equations or M2 of the pooled equation) we would be unable to offer more than crude explanations of the country differences in transfers over a substantially larger number (N=12) of cases than is normally entertained by qualitative welfare analysts. Yet viewed from the perspective outlined above, the GDPPC coefficient differences across countries become conceptually familiar, as one of variation in one property of a country inducing variation in another property of a country.

More formally, we argue that the within-country, time-invariant (by assumption) but cross-nationally variable regression slopes can be modelled as a function of any other time-invariant, cross-nationally variable property as follows:

(21) $\hat{b}_n = g + hX_n + v_n'$

where b represents the estimated coefficients from the N time-series regressions and x_n is any time-invariant property of country n. Note there is no t subscript in equation (21) because we are dealing with attributes which differ solely across n countries; time is no longer in equation (21), though obviously it was a factor in obtaining the bs and the Xs. (The latter is considered time-invariant, but such an assessment necessarily requires examining the value of X over time.)

To illustrate our procedure, we posit that two specific within-country time-series regression coefficients, those assessing the efficacy of LEFT and GDPPC on TRANS, are determined by several variables indexing the organizational strength (either in trades-unions or in political parties) and collective action of the working class. We do not have space to develop this much further, but on the surface the argument seems plausible: in strongly unionized capitalist democracies, for example, the effects of LEFT and of GDPPC on TRANS should be higher than in those countries that lack a strong working-class organizational base. Likewise, we also posit that the left's ability to extract transfers from the state will be greater in those nations where the working class has been willing and able to muster the collective resources necessary to strike to shut down production. We are therefore arguing that while UNIONIZATION may have little direct importance in stimulating TRANS _within_ countries, given its exceedingly small variation through time for this period, _country differences_ in UNIONIZATION may partially shape the _differential cross-national contexts_ within which, _over the entire period_, other actors or forces increased TRANS. And, similarly, the differences _across nations_ in LEFT representation or dominance in cabinets, _during the entire period_, may, again partially, shape the nation-specific processes pegging TRANS to economic development (GDPPC). This is not a conventional argument about statistical interaction; the 1961-1976 means of LEFT domination, UNIONIZATION, and strike VOL are, by definition, constant for any t within the period, and the computation of within-country, over-time UNIONIZATION*LEFT variables, for example, is statistically impossible and substantively nonsensical. Now we see that the defects in UNIONIZATION, its essential invariance through time and its substantial variation across countries over the entire period, are precisely the properties we desire in an analysis of this sort. It _demands_ temporally-invariant, cross-nationally variable attributes.

In Table 7, we present five regression estimates of the empirical and substantive form of the abstract equation (21). In all cases, the dependent variables are within-country time-series regression coefficients, which differ across countries, and the independent variables are all within-country means, which also differ across countries.[35] The number of observations, as in any cross-national analysis, is N (or 12, in our case). The regression coefficients generally support our hypotheses. In nations with higher average levels of labor militancy (VOL) over the 16-year period, the left, <u>within</u> those countries, appears better equipped to increase TRANS. Likewise, in heavily organized countries, and in countries with a strong left presence, again as averaged over the years 1961-1976, the stimulative impact of GDPPC on TRANS within nations is greater, arguably reflecting the contextual power of the left or of trades-unions to transfer some of the fruits of industrialization to those forgotten by, or actually impoverished by, private capital accumulation.

Of all the analyses discussed in this chapter, those summarized in Table 7 are the most experimental and, however plausible, tenuous. Table 7 contains only bivariate regressions; the collinearity problems of highly aggregated cross-national data remain; the statistical properties of slopes-as-variables are not fully known and estimation procedures are not completely developed. But whatever caveats these imply, and they are certainly not trivial, this analysis represents, we think, the potential utility of higher-order quantitative theoretical work not possible with any other sort of data. However tentative, this represents the power of simultaneously examining variability across time and space.

CONCLUSIONS

Theoretical propositions about welfare state development are generally posed without concern for how those propositions are to be empirically tested. A theorist might hypothesize, for example, that industrialization increases "welfare effort".[36] This is an important proposition both for reasons of theory and compassion; it fully deserves substantial empirical examination. But note: the proposition, as posed above, is "data free"; it does not specify whether industrialization and an expanded welfare apparatus covary historically within a single society or whether country-to-country differences in levels of industrialization lead to cross-national differences in transfer payments. The theorist has the luxury of being independent of the vexing issue of what sort of data <u>ought</u>, normatively, to be used to test the accuracy of this hypothesis. The data analyst does not.

We attempted, in the analysis presented in this chapter, to see whether (among other things) the industrialization thesis is empirically valid. Our conclusion is that it is and, simultaneously, it is not. Cross-national analyses for twelve nations, for the period 1961-1976, either averaging coefficients or variable values, either pooling data or not, decisively reject the hypothesis. Time-series analysis, over the same 1961-1976 period, over the same twelve countries, and using an identically specified causal model, just as decisively accepts the hypothesis.

The message of this chapter is multi-faceted and starkly clear. Theorists should more precisely pose their propositions; in particular they should, if possible, couch them in terms of the real-world units, time or nations, researchers must use in empirical analysis. Until that (possibly ideal) condition is reached, data analysts should understand the consequences of analyzing one or another unit. We have attempted to show that the choice of unit can have profound consequences indeed. Given the possibility that inferences based on different units can lead to completely contradictory empirical findings, researchers need to analyze data that can vary both across countries and across time. Finally, we have also attempted to show that simultaneous examination of country-to-country differences and within-country processes can lead to higher order theoretical explanation, and possibly, to a merging of cross-national-analytic and historical-analytic perspectives.

APPENDIX

Operationalization and Sources of Variables Used in the Analysis.

(1) TRANS: Transfer expenditures expressed as a proportion of GDP, both in current national currency units. Transfer expenditures include government outlays to households of social security benefits, social assistance grants, unfunded social security payments, and other current transfers to private non-profit institutions serving households. In general, OECD statistics of transfers in the new series of national accounts (SNA) were used, although old SNA series were used for Denmark, Japan, Ireland and Norway. In the case of Ireland it was necessary to estimate the values in the old SNA for the years 1974-76 by regressing the old against the new SNA series over the years 1970-73, when both series overlapped. Transfer expenditures are from Organization for Economic Cooperation and Development. _National Accounts Statistics; Detailed Statistics_, Volume 2. Paris: OECD, 1984. GDP is from OECD, 1984.

(2) INF: Inflation; the rate of change of the Consumer Prices Index (CPI) expressed as a percentage. CPI is from International Monetary Fund, _International Financial Statistics._ Washington: IMF, June 1984.

(3) GDPPC: Gross domestic product per capita. GDP is from OECD, 1984. Population is from IMF, 1984.

(4) VOL: Number of strikedays lost per 10,000 non-agricultural workers. Strikedays are from (a) International Labour Office, _Yearbook of Labour Statistics_. Geneva: ILO, 1954, 1958, and 1983; and (b) Bureau of Labor Statistics, _Handbook of Labor Statistics_. Washington: GPO, 1983. Non-Agricultural Labor-Force is from OECD, _Labour Force Statistics 1962-82._ Paris: OECD, 1984.

(5) UNIONIZATION: Total number of union members expressed as a percentage of the non-agricultural labor force. Union membership for Australia, Canada, Denmark, Germany, Norway, Sweden, the U.K., and the U.S. were taken from Bain, George S., and Robert Price, _Profiles of Union Growth: A Comparative Statistical Portrait of Eight Countries_. Oxford: Basil Blackwell, 1980. Other national sources are as follows: **Finland:** Central Statistical Office of Finland: _Statistical Yearbook of Finland._ Helsinki: Central Statistical Office of Finland, various years. **Ireland:** Central Statistics Office, _Statistical_

Abstract of Ireland. Dublin: Government Stationery Office, various years. **Japan:** Statistics Bureau, Japan Statistical Yearbook. Tokyo: Statistics Bureau, various years. **Netherlands:** Netherlands Central Bureau of Statistics, Statistical Yearbook of the Netherlands. The Hague: Staatsuitgeverij/CBS-publications, various years.

(6) UNEMP: Number of unemployed expressed as a percentage of the active labor force. Unemployment is from (a) United Nations, Annual Statistical Yearbook. New York: UN Statistical Office, various years; and (b) Commonwealth Bureau of Census and Statistics, Official Yearbook of the Commonwealth of Australia. Canberra: Commonwealth Bureau of Census and Statistics, various years. Sources for the active labor force are the same as for (5).

(7a) LEFT: The number of votes received by left-wing or left-of-center parties with cabinet representation, expressed as a percentage of the total number of votes received by all parties with cabinet representation. Voting data are from Mackie, Thomas and Richard Rose, The International Almanac of Electoral History. New York: Facts on File Inc., 1982. Cabinet Composition is from Europa Publications, The Europa Yearbook. London: Europa Publications Ltd., various years. Party Ideology is from (a) McHale, Vincent, Political Parties of Europe, Volumes 1 and 2. Westport, Conn.: Greenwood Press, 1983; and (b) Day, Alan, and Henry Degenhardt, Political Parties of the World. Detroit: Gale Research Company, 1980.

(7b) LEFT MAJORITY: The percentage of years in which left-wing parties with cabinet representation held a majority of the popular vote received by all parties with cabinet representation (i.e. LEFT greater than 50 percent).

(7c) LEFT DOMINATION: The percentage of years in which the cabinet was entirely left-wing (i.e. LEFT = 100 percent).

(8) MILS: Military expenditure expressed as a percentage of GDP. Military Spending is from Stockholm International Peace Research Institute, SIPRI Handbook. London: Taylor and Francis, various years. GDP is the same as for (1).

Table 1. Proportions of Variance Situated Between Country, Between Time, and Between Time, Between Country (N=192)

	Between-Country	Between-Time	Between-Country and Between-Time
TRANS	.639	.237	.876
MIL	.909	.036	.945
UNEMP	.707	.170	.877
VOL	.375	.078	.453
LEFT	.480	.078	.558
INF	.119	.622	.741
GDPPC	.297	.668	.965
UNIONIZATION	.900	.015	.915

Table 2. Annual Estimates of Cross-National Models of Transfers/GDP (N=12)

	Independent Variables					
Year	MIL	LEFT	VOL	INF	UNEMP	GDPPC
1961	-.255	-.035	.0035	-1.782	-1.205	.0019
1962	.541	-.003	-.0190	.116	.258	-.0012
1963	.541	.009	.0001	- .446	- .764	-.0013
1964	.724	.005	.0050	.253	-1.260	.0003
1965	.502	-.005	.0045	- .832	-2.104	-.0006
1966	.837	.002	.0079	.159	-3.073	-.0005
1967	.002	-.031	-.0581	.318	8.031	.0042
1968	.741	-.032	-.0310	-1.390	5.222	-.0091
1969	-.141	.019	-.0024	.844	- .810	.0007
1970	.528	.012	-.0029	- .042	- .044	-.0008
1971	.398	.023	.0288	.448	- .151	-.0001
1972	.664	-.008	-.0048	2.201	.080	.0017
1973	-.869	.039	.0027	3.909	.054	-.0046
1974	-.693	.039	-.0076	- .499	1.402	-.0009
1975	-.218	.058	-.0060	- .409	1.203	-.0010
1976	-.360	.064	-.0012	- .306	.526	-.0007
# of bs + =	10	10	7	8	8	5
# of bs - =	6	6	9	8	8	11

Table 3. Coefficients Averaged Over 16 Yearly Cross-National Regressions and 12 Within-Country Time-Series Regressions, and Coefficients from the Cross-National Means Equation

	Independent Variables					
	MIL	LEFT	VOL	INF	UNEMP	GDPPC
(1) Means of coefficients from 16 cross-national regressions (N=12)	.184	.010	-.005	.159	.460	-.0002
(2) Means of coefficients from 16 cross-national regressions (N=12)	--a	.023	--a	.214	--a	-.0006
(3) Cross-national regressions of means of variables (N=12)	--a	.074b (2.79)	--a	-.1.79 (2.36)	--a	-.0028 (2.32)
(4) Means of coefficients from 12 time-series regressions (N=16)	--a	-.006	--a	-.016	--a	.0015

[a]Variable omitted form the equation.

[b]T-statistics in parentheses.

Table 4. Signs of the Regression Coefficients of Equivalent Time-Series Models for Twelve Countries, 1961-1976 (OLS)

	Independent Variables					
Country	MIL	LEFT	VOL	INF	UNEMP	GDPPC
A	–	–	–	+	+	+
C	–	a	–	+	+	–
D	–	–	–	+	–	+
F	–	+	+	–	+	+
G	–	–	–	–	+	+
Ir	+	+	+	+	+	+
J	+	a	–	+	+	+
Ne	–	–	–	+	+	+
No	–	–	–	+	–	+
S	–	a	+	–	+	+
UK	–	+	+	–	+	+
US	+	a	+	+	+	+

[a] Variable omitted from the equation due to zero variance.

Table 5. Regression Coefficients of "Trimmed" Time-Series Models for Twelve Countries, 1961-1976.[a]

	Independent Variables						
Country	MIL	LEFT	VOL	INF	UNEMP	GDPPC	rho[d]
A	-.210	--[b]	--	.131	.629	--	-.01
C	-.920	c	--	.129	.665	--	-.31
D	--	--	--	--	--	.0014	(.03)
F	--	.004	--	--	.347	.0004	(.20)
G	--	--	--	--	1.36	--	(.00)
Ir	1.08	.030	--	.101	.595	--	-.04
J	--	c	--	--	2.68	--	(.24)
Ne	-4.24	-.037	--	--	--	.0004	-.10
No	--	--	--	--	--	.0012	(-.09)
S	--	c	--	--	2.02	.0010	-.34
UK	-.628	.005	.001	--	--	.0006	.17
US	--	c	.001	.057	.473	.0009	(.20)

[a] All coefficients significant ($p \leq .10$, one-tailed test). Uniformly high $\overline{R^2}$ omitted from table due to their non-comparability across countries.

[b] Variable estimated to be non-significant in Table 4 and omitted from the equation.

[c] Variable omitted from Table 4 due to zero variance.

[d] ( ) = GLS estimation; OLS otherwise.

Table 6. Estimates of Pooled Cross-Sectional, Time-Series Models of Transfer/GDP (N*T = .192)

	Independent Variables							
	MIL	LEFT	VOL	INF	UNEMP	GDPPC	R-2	rho
M1. Fully Constrained								
OLS	-.093 (.600)[a]	.021 (3.11)	-.003 (3.44)	.102 (1.37)	.145 (.806)	.0006 (3.30)	.232	.847
GLS	.623 (2.93)	.007 (2.16)	-.000 (.914)	.067 (1.88)	.443 (3.48)	.0009 (1.88)	b	.038
M2. (M1 + N-1 Country Dummies)								
OLS	-.489 (-2.07)	-.002 (.595)	-.001 (1.53)	-.018 (.432)	.674 (5.11)	.0009 (6.99)	.865	.724
GLS	.046 (.262)	.001 (.941)	.000 (.114)	.018 (1.17)	.507 (6.89)	.0007 (5.22)	b	.156
M3. (M1 + T-1 Time Dummies)								
OLS	.335 (2.12)	.021 (3.37)	-.002 (2.78)	-.284 (2.87)	-.074 (.397)	-.0010 (3.15)	.343	.842
GLS	1.04 (5.03)	.005 (1.68)	-.001 (1.30)	-.011 (.278)	.122 (.892)	-.0006 (2.25)	b	.021
M4. (M1 + (N-1 Country Dummies + T-1 Time Dummies))								
OLS	-.290 (1.17)	-.004 (.971)	-.0001 (1.58)	-.089 (-1.83)	.635 (3.52)	.0001 (.228)	.871	.738
GLS	.007 (.039)	.000 (.170)	-.000 (.028)	.008 (.440)	.252 (2.81)	-.0011 (3.27)	b	.157

[a] t-statistic.

[b] R-2 not reported; not comparable across equations.

Table 7. Cross-National Bivariate Regressions of Selected Within-Country Time-Series Coefficients on Working Class Strength and Collective Action

Panel A: Dependent Variable = Coefficient of GDPPC[a]

eq. no.	Independent Variable[b]	Regression Coefficient (t-statistic)	Correlation
1	Mean Unionization	.149 E-04 (1.37)	.396
2	Mean Left Representation	.915 E-05 (2.27)	.582
3	Mean Left Majority	.937 E-05 (2.47)	.616
4	Mean Left Domination	.898 E-05 (2.38)	.602

Panel B: Dependent Variable = Coefficient of LEFT[c]

eq. no.	Independent Variable[b]	Regression Coefficient (t-statistic)	Correlation
5	Mean Strike Volume	.726 E-04 (3.01)	.776

[a] The coefficient for each country is taken from its "full" time-series model, the signs of which are shown in Table 4. Estimates are based on the full sample (N=12).

[b] Values of the independent variables are country-specific means of the annual values over the 1961-1976 period.

[c] The coefficient for each country is taken from its "full" time-series model (see Table 4). Estimates are based only on cases that exhibit variation in LEFT (N=8).

NOTES

1. Heclo, Hugh, Modern Social Politics in Britain and Sweden: From Relief to Income Maintenance. Yale University Press, 1974; Korpi, Walter, "Social policy and distributional conflict in the capitalist democracies: a preliminary comparative framework." West European Politics 3:296-313, 1980; Orloff, Ann and Theda Skocpol, "Why not equal protection? Explaining the politics of public social spending in Britain, 1900-1911, and the United States, 1880s-1920." American Sociological Review 49:726-50, 1984; Quadagno, Jill S. "Welfare capitalism and; the social security act of 1935." American Sociological Review 49:632-47, 1984.

2. Wilensky, Harold, The Welfare State and Equality. Berkeley: University of California Press, 1975; Cutright, Phillips "Political structure, economic development, and national social security programs." American Journal of Sociology 70:537-50, 1965; Jackman, Robert, Politics and Social Equality: A Comparative Analysis. New York: Wiley, 1975; Jackman, R., "Socialist parties and income inequality in western industrial societies." Journal of Politics 42:135-49, 1980: Cameron, David, "The expansion of the public economy: a comparative analysis." American Political Science Review 72:1243-61, 1978; Katz, Claudio, Vincent Mahler, and Michael Franz "The impact of taxes on growth and distribution in developed capitalist countries: a cross-national study." American Political Science Review 77:871-86, 1983.

3. Isaac, Larry and William Kelly. "Racial insurgency, the state, and welfare expansion: local and national level evidence from the postwar United States." American Journal of Sociology 86:1348-86. 1981; Devine, Joel A. "State and state expenditures: determinants of social investment and social consumption spending in the postwar United States." American Sociological Review 50:150-65, 1985; and Griffin and Leicht, this volume.

4. Domke, William, Richard Eichenberger, and Catherine Kelleher. "The illusion of choice: defense and welfare in advanced industrial democracies, 1948-1978." American Political Science Review 77:19-35, 1983.

5. Stinchcombe, Arthur. Theoretical Methods in Social History. New York: Academic Press, 1978.

6. See, e.g., Firebaugh, Glenn. "Cross-national versus historical regression models: conditions of equivalence in comparative research." Comparative Social Research 3:333-44, 1980; Schoenberg, Ronald consequences of dynamic misspecification." Social Science Research 6:133-144, 1977; Bach, Robert L. "Methods of analysis in the study of the world-

economy (Comment on Rubinson, American Sociological Review, August, 1976)." American Sociological Review 42:811-14, 1977.

7. Brunner, Ronald and Klaus Liepelt. "Data analysis, process analysis, and system change." Midwest Journal of Political Science 16:538-69, 1972; Firebaugh, op.cit.

8. Schoenberg, op. cit.

9. The most troublesome of the routine OLS assumptions for purposes of fitting time-series models is the assumption of independence of errors. Often the data that are of interest show some regular trend over time, and frequently the errors in models that are based on trended data are correlated over time (autocorrelation). If the OLS estimation procedure reveals that autocorrelation is present, the parameters may be estimated by the application of a generalized least squares (GLS) procedure that adjusts the data for the estimated correlation among the errors.

10. It is possible to circumvent this assumption if the researcher has a sufficiently long series (e.g., Walters, Pamela Barnhouse and Richard Rubinson "Educational expansion and economic output in the United States, 1890-1969: a production function analysis." American Sociological Review 48:480-93, 1983), or if the researcher is willing to make strong statistical and theoretical assumptions about the dynamic process being modelled (e.g., Griffin, Larry, Michael Wallace, and Beth Rubin "Capitalist resistance to the organization of labor before the New Deal: Why? How? Success?" Unpublished, 1985).

11. op.cit.; Kuh, Edwina. "The validity of cross-sectionally estimated behavior equations in time series applications." Econometrica 27:197-214, 1959.

12. Firebaugh, op.cit., 334.

13. Ibid.

14. See Pampel, Fred C. and Jane Weiss, "Economic development, pension policies, and the labor force participation of aged males: a cross-national, longitudinal approach." American Journal of Sociology, 89: 350-72, 1983; Pampel, Fred C. and John Williamson, "Age Structure, politics, and cross-national patterns of public pension expenditures." American Sociological Review, forthcoming; Friedland, Roger and Jimy Sanders, "The public economy and economic growth in Western market economies." American Sociological Review, 50: 421-437, 1985.

15. See Hibbs, Douglas A., Jr. "Industrial conflict in advanced industrial societies." American Political Science Review 70:1033-53, 1976.

16. For example, see Pampel, Fred C. and John Williamson, op. cit.

17. By statistical efficiency, we mean that the regression estimates will be more precise, though in

principle unchanged in absolute magnitude, in the sense that their sampling variability will be less as the number of observations increase. The number of observations in a pooled matrix is N*T, whereas in the cross-section and in the time-series, there exist only N and T observations respectively. In our own analysis, to be discussed below, for example, we have 12 countries, each measured for 16 years. When we pool these data, we have NT observations, or 192, rather than either 12 or 16 cases.

18. Especially, Wilensky, op.cit.

19. By standardizing by GDP we are also controlling for at least one source of heteroscedasticity, which biases the estimate of the sampling variances of the OLS regression coefficients and renders statistical tests of significance biased. Estimated errors obtained from the OLS regression are heteroscedastic if their variance increases or decreases with the values of a regressor.

20. Wilensky, op.cit.

21. Cutright, op.cit.

22. Hibbs demonstrates this with respect to strike volume. See his "On the political economy of long-run trends in strike activity." British Journal of Political Science, 8: 153-75, 1978.

23. Stephens, James D. The Transition from Capitalism to Socialism. London: Macmillan, 1979.

24. Only Finland exhibited substantial time-series variation in UNIONIZATION for the years 1961-76, which accounts for most of the miniscule historical movement we do see (and this series is subject to changing classificatory schemes). Had a researcher been unaware of this s/he might simply have added UNIONIZATION into within-country time series predicting TRANS equations and been stuck in the uncomfortable position of attempting post-hoc to explain unintelligible coefficients actually representing nothing more than the statistical artifact of severely truncated variance in UNIONIZATION. Another indication of this is the country-specific coefficients of variation for UNIONIZATION. The coefficient of variation averaged over the 12 nations is only .059. Compare this to another indicator of working-class mobilization and action, strike volume, which has a coefficient of variation, averaged over the 12 countries, of 1.203. LEFT's mean coefficient of variation is .727.

25. Firebaugh, op.cit.

26. Op. cit.

27. This year-to-year instability in the estimated coefficients also illustrates quite dramatically that the "strong" assumption of equivalence through time embedded in pooled cross-sectional design is, at least in our data, quite unrealistic.

28. Kuh, op.cit.; Smith, Ronald. "Military ex-

penditure and investment in OECD countries, 1954-1973." Journal of Comparative Economics 4:19-32, 1980.

29. Kuh, op.cit., 207-208.

30. Five of the countries exhibit significant autocorrelation, which biases the standard error of the OLS coefficients and, hence, tests of statistical significance. OLS estimates, however, remain unbiased. We chose to present the OLS coefficients because the procedure used to remove the autocorrelation (GLS transformation of the variables) would destroy the comparability in country-specific estimates. In any case, the GLS estimates do not differ markedly from those obtained with OLS and are no more comparable to the averaged cross-national estimates than are the OLS estimates. We correct, where necessary, for autocorrelation in Table 5.

31. Tufte, Edward. Political Control of the Economy. Princeton: University Press, 1978.

32. Conceptually the cross-national and time-series models are perhaps subject to differential specification bias and lag structures (Firebaugh, op.cit.). It is conceivable, therefore, that once these complexities were explicitly modelled, the time-series and cross-national estimates might be reconciled. In principle, though, most cross-national analysts do not lag their independent variables and do not include in their models many exogenous variables which we have ignored entirely. In estimating our T cross-national equations we have therefore simply followed the precedents established by others.

33. The OLS models appear to be autocorrelated, but that is partly a function of the country-to-country differences in the structure of the errors. The average of the OLS country-specific estimates of the degree of autocorrelation is only .075, suggesting no significant autocorrelation. Thus it is not clear if GLS, assuming a constant rho across countries, is necessary or even desirable. By including both N-1 country effects and T-1 year effects, M4 is often assumed by some econometricians to purge the errors of their extraneous country and time components, leaving only a random component uncorrelated across time and space. Appropriate modelling and estimation of the disturbances in the pooled equation is a highly technical matter often involving specialized software. The interested reader is referred to Hannan, Michael T. and Alice A. Young, "Estimation in panel models: results on pooling cross-sections and time series." Chapter 2 in David R. Heise (ed.), Sociological Methodology. San Francisco: Jossey-Bass, 1977, and the references contained therein.

34. More fundamental modifications (of equation

12), which relax the assumption of constant slopes across all n countries or t time points, are easily accomplished by computing interaction terms between a regressor (say, VOL) and a particular country or year (say the U.K. -- see Table 5). Moreover, those N or T coefficients which are not significantly different from some "pooled" estimate (GDPPC in the N time series is a likely candidate) can be "fixed" to be constant for all units, but all other coefficients allowed to vary over all N or T (again, VOL for the U.K.). Some coefficients can be constrained to be zero for some or all countries, etc. A properly specified version of equation (12), which allowed for serious attention to the disturbances, and was estimated with the pooled data matrix, could reproduce the results presented in, for example, Table 5. The pooled equations do not have to be as restrictive as is often believed.

35. The independent variables in such an analysis need not be limited to period means. They could, for example, be specified to be some measure of inequality (variances, quintiles, ratios), sums (e.g., the number of racial riots during some period), or even regression coefficients. For such a higher order analysis, the only properties necessary for statistical estimation are time-invariance and cross-national variability. Likewise, the regression estimates used in equation (21) need not be point estimates; they could just as easily be the minimum or maximum values of the regression slope's interval range, as that is established by the standard error of the coefficient itself. Finally, this particular exposition of a higher order analysis exploiting both within-country through-time variability (to obtain the slopes and means) and cross-national differences therein could easily be extended to obtain temporally-variable, cross-nationally invariant properties as yearly attributes. Thus, for example, the T cross-national regression coefficients presented in Table 2 represent a time-series which could be regressed against other temporally variable, but cross-nationally invariant, attributes, such as the price of oil or the geo-political attitude of the Soviet Union toward the NATO nations.

36. Wilensky, op. cit.

V.

Percy B. Lehning

Cutting Lines We Dare Not Cross

Justice and Retrenchment in the Welfare State

There is an ongoing debate on the organization, structure and goals of social security.[1] Since the onset of the current economic slow-down, this debate has become even more intense. The costs of social security have become an increasingly heavy burden for the taxpayer and the economy. This is a major reason why several proposals have been circulated which advocate a significant reduction in the size of existing programs. A more fundamental debate is underway on possible changes in the financial structure of social security, changes which might bring about a system that is more in line with budgetary possibilities and economic realities. The primary cause of the fiscal problem is, of course, the failure of the economy to maintain steady growth, stable prices and full employment. Discussions about the fiscal problem have been transformed into a more general debate on the overall purposes of the welfare state. With the cessation of economic growth, one of the essential shortcomings of the welfare state has painfully emerged: its extremely diffuse ideological and theoretical base. "The welfare state has yet to develop a single coherent and compelling theory to guide its political practice," wrote Furniss and Tilton in 1977.[2] This situation has not changed. At a time when there is still no coherent theory to guide the welfare state's political practice, and when economic growth has stopped, it may be useful to reconsider Wilensky's argument that economic growth is the ultimate reason for the development of the welfare state.[3]

The rapid expansion of social policies during the post-war period was facilitated by a degree of persisting economic growth that was as unexpected to the welfare state's founders as it was to its critics. We will restrict our empirical discussion to recent developments in the Netherlands. One indication of welfare state growth can be seen in public expenditures. From 1965 until 1978 the share of public expenditures as a proportion of national income rose by more than 20%. The share of public expenditures in the net national income increased from 40% to 50% in 1977 and finally, to 65% in 1980.

The economic crisis, together with the prospect of an uncontrollable and unmanageable process of increases in public expenditures, have led to a more fundamental reappraisal of the welfare state. The indictment against it that has gained most currency involves one or more of the following three counts: *excessive costs*; *ineffectiveness*; and *overregulation*.[4]

The economic crisis and the subsequent indictment against the welfare state have led the Dutch government to launch a well-organized operation aimed at large-scale cutbacks in public spending. A task force of civil servants was formed in 1980 to develop scenarios for a 20% cutback in government expenditures. A goal of a 10% cutback was set for expenditures for social security, public health and income of public sector employees. The task of the civil servants involved a fundamental overhaul of government policy. The civil servants, however, were not provided with any political advice on the principles in terms of which of those policy changes should be discussed. The only mandate was that costs should be reduced. In 1981 and 1982, two sets of *Memoranda on the Reconsideration of Public Expenditures* were sent to Parliament.[5] The present government program has been substantially influenced by these memoranda. In general, the tenor of these documents can be described as one of advocating a reduction of the influence of government. Deregulation and privatization are the most frequently used terms in these memoranda. More specifically, the leading theme of these reports is the need to push back the *social welfare state* in the direction of a *social security state*.[6]

The central question posed in this article is whether retrenchment proposals (as for instance those formulated in the *Memoranda* and especially those regarding social security) can be evaluated from the perspective of contemporary theories of justice. Different conceptions of justice give distinct answers to problems of distribution, to questions on the extent of property rights, and to questions on the proper limits of government intervention in these rights. It is my thesis that such theories can give guidelines for a *just* cutback policy.

THE TWO TIER SYSTEM

The basic proposal of the Memoranda on social security involves a complete overhaul of the social security system. The renovation suggested consists of the replacement of the present Unemployment Insurance Act, the Sickness Benefits Act and the Disablement Insurance Act by a single two-tier system.

The starting point for this system is a differentiation of benefits according to relative need. The need of individuals is calculated according to their personal circumstances: do they have to look after a family without an earned-income; and, are there other wage-earners in the family? The division between the two tiers is as follows. The first tier consists of a so-called "individualized" flat-rate benefit for each person, which amounts to an equal percentage of the minimum wage level. The second tier consists of a "supplementary" benefit. The first tier protects individuals against the loss of income that lies below the level of the minimum daily wage; an allowance will be added if more than one person is dependent on that benefit. In this way, relative need is taken into account. The second tier supplies, in addition to the first tier benefits, a supplementary benefit that protects against the loss of income above the minimum level and is related in a specific way to actual lost earned income. The rule for the benefit level in this second tier is that the higher the original earned income, the lower, relatively speaking, the supplementary benefit will be. This is the so-called "sliding-scale" system.

The total amount of costs that will be saved on expenditures for social security will depend on the level of allowances that will be given in the first tier according to need and, at the same time, on the ratio that will be chosen for taking account of the lost earned income in the second tier. Regardless of the exact percentage that will eventually be chosen for the flat-rate benefit and the kind of sliding-scale that will implemented for the second tier, high savings in expenditures will result. When a comparison is made to the existing system of benefit regulations, it becomes clear that significant income differences will occur if the proposed changes are adopted. Savings will occur first because all benefits above the minimum standard of living will be pushed down in the direction of the social minimum, and second because all benefits at the social minimum standard of living will stay at the same level as the existing benefits, but individual need will be taken into account more than is presently the case.

In general, the result will be a system in which the existing insurance idea of a benefit is replaced by the idea of a sliding-scale. At the same time, the concept of solidarity with the least-advantaged is given more attention.

The growth of social security expenditures in the Netherlands is mainly due to an increase in the number of persons who claim benefits under the Unemployment Insurance Act and the Disablement Insurance Act. A major result of the new system will be that the disabled group will, as a group, receive less income. But within this group there will be a more equal distribution of income. The "most-advantaged" disabled will be pushed down in the direction of the "least-advantaged" disabled. At the same time, the disparity in income between those who receive benefits and those who are earning income will grow.[7]

HOW TO CUT BACK IN A JUST WAY: HARD QUESTIONS IN HARD TIMES

These proposals can be interpreted as attempts to solve a concrete distribution problem: How to develop new distribution rules for allocating social benefits if the social security fund is cut by 10%. There are theories of justice that generate principles for solving distribution problems. Although the civil servants, in their proposals, apply a specific interpretation of the need principle (cutbacks should not lead to benefits below the minimum standard of living), they do not refer to any theory of justice or even to an explicit evaluative principle as a guideline in the reconsideration project. This is surprising since policy proposals made, for instance, with regard to a desired income policy, do, in fact, make explicit references to contemporary theories of justice.

In other words, the civil servants did not derive their cutback proposals from an overall theory about the good society. They offered no arguments to support either their decision to apply the need principle or the content of their specific proposals. There are, however, several reasons why the suggested cutback options should be evaluated by means of theories of justice. The example of the ratio between active and inactive people in the present Dutch welfare state, a ratio that has become the core of many contemporary policy problems, can show the usefulness of such an evaluation.

The ratio of the working population to the dependent population is a crucial determinant of the level of benefits a given rate of tax will support.[8]

The total group of inactive people for whom benefits and old-aged pensions have to be provided has grown quickly and is still growing. Closely related to this ratio problem is the question of how to maintain the income position of the inactive people. In the Netherlands that position, has been rather favorable. In 1979, the average income of those who were receiving welfare benefits was only 30-36% lower than that of employed people. The benefits that are paid under the Unemployment Insurance Act, the Sickness Act, and the Disablement Insurance Act, in other words, have been close to the original net earned incomes.

It is not surprising that this ratio has come under attack by those who are in favor of a fundamental change in the Dutch social security system. With rising unemployment and disability figures, the amount and duration of benefits granted to these groups has moved to the center of public controversy. Opinions about benefits levels and eligibility conditions have grown further apart over the years. Critics claim that the present system provides a double disincentive for a person to perform productive work: There is less need to work to avoid the misery of poverty; and, there is less incentive to earn income, much of which will be taken by the government to support welfare programs. In general, critics argue that benefits should be substantially below the wage last received in order to retain an incentive for people to take up productive work. (One should add, however, that the empirical base for these opinions about the disincentives and their effects, is rather weak.)

The ratio between active and inactive people is usually discussed from the viewpoint of the efficiency of the labor market and the costs of the welfare state. This chapter approaches this issue from another direction I will stress the necessity, when searching for the outline of a new optimal social security system, of not only taking into account the criterion of efficiency, but also aspects of _justice_.

More specifically, on the basis of a theory of justice, it should be possible to reach a conclusion on the justice or injustice of the following distributions:

- -- income within the group of employed persons,
- -- income within the group of inactive persons,
- -- income _between_ these two groups

We are interested in determining whether or not theories of justice are also applicable to problems of the distribution of benefits in the social security system. If they are not, _which principle of_ justice should be used when comparing the incomes of active and inactive people? Next, there is the question of whether different kinds of inactive people (sick, disabled, unemployed, aged) should be treated in the same way. These questions are seldom posed explicitly. However, answers to such questions are critical if one wants to reach, for instance, a considered judgment about the mechanisms that regulate the ratio between social security benefits and earned income, or, on a more general level, have an opinion as to the normative tasks of the social welfare state.

Social security has increasingly become recognized as a basic human right. Indeed, social security was recognized as such in the Universal Declaration of Human Rights of 1949. Since then, this right has been enshrined in one way or another in the constitutions of a number of states.[9] For instance, since February 1983, the right to a secure means of subsistence and entitlement to social security are explicitly stated in the constitution of the Netherlands. As a result of the extension of the coverage of social security and the recognition of access to social security as a human right, the various social security systems in Western Europe have developed into a major government responsibility. However, although social security has become a structural component of the welfare state, its construction has been determined by factors such as economic growth, pressure of rival interest groups, and the behavior of civil servants. Policy makers tended to take advantage of the steady economic growth and full employment of the period up to 1973 to develop the social security system based on these diverse demands. This resulted, certainly in the Netherlands, in a system in which nearly all risks are covered. However, an analysis of the growing cost of social security might have given rise, as early as the sixties and seventies, to serious doubts about the justification for an increase in some of the component costs, such as, to name but a few: certain methods of guaranteeing minimum social benefits; certain indexing systems; and the extent to which the impact of demographic factors had been taken into account.

A reconstruction of the social security system in the future is unthinkable without a fundamental reappraisal of the social security system with reference to an overall vision of what we want and expect of a "social welfare state". A theory of justice which formulates distribution principles could be helpful in developing such a vision and in formulating priorities when revision is inevitable.[10] In reappraisals, insufficient distinction has been made between fundamental shortcomings of the economic system on the one hand, and the inherent defects of the social security system on the other. After all, the social security system is not in itself responsible for the economic crisis, even though it may have contributed to some of its adverse effects.11

Politicians are searching for a stable ratio between the public and the market sector. But without guiding principles as provided by theories of justice, such searches will not yield much of value. No proposal for a reconstruction of the social security system will survive the parliamentary and extra-parliamentary discussion and actions if it does not fulfill at least two conditions of legitimacy. First, the conception underlying the proposal reforms (that cuts are necessary) should be accepted by a majority of the population. And second, the particular cutbacks in social security should be compatible with the considered judgments of that same majority on what a just distribution of policy benefits and burdens would be. The task facing policymakers is to develop social-economic policy that takes into consideration the position of active as well as inactive people, that aims at reconstructing the social social security system, and that, at the same time, will pass the test of legitimacy.

In the following pages I will examine the main aspects of three contemporary theories of justice. The thesis advanced is that such theories can help in developing principles for _just_ cutbacks. Cutbacks without such principles, or without any principles whatsoever, raise the prospect of unacceptable and thus ineffective policy measures; measures which do not take into account notions of efficiency and justice.

THEORIES OF JUSTICE: MAIN ASPECTS

In theories of justice the relation between active and inactive people in an economy is dealt with in different ways. In this paper, I will discuss the major aspects of three different theories of justice: the _theory of the minimum standard of living_ developed by Hayek and Friedman; the _theory of equal individual welfare_ by Tinbergen; and the _theory of compensating inequalities_ by Rawls.

According to the theory of Hayek and Friedman, who can be interpreted as representing _classical liberalism_, active people live under the regime of the desert principle (rewards are related to contribution), while the inactive people (aged, sick, disabled and unemployed) live under the system of the social minimum. According to the theory of Tinbergen, who represents _democratic socialism_, the active people live under the rule of compensating wage differences, while the principle of need is applied to certain specific groups of people, for instance, the disabled. According to Rawls, the philosopher of the welfare state, the minimum level of income of the least-advantaged should be maximized, whether or not they are active or inactive.

The theory of Hayek and Friedman consists of two parts. The first part deals with the primary distribution of income between persons. This distribution becomes increasingly asymmetrical as the income-earning capacities, the contributions to the process of labor, and the propensities to risk-taking are divided more unequally. There is no reason, according to Hayek and Friedman, for the government to influence the primary income distribution so long as the exercise of economic power on the market is excluded and market failure only exists in the short run. Income differences based on bequest are allowed. The absence of a distribution policy is a necessary condition for the maintenance of individual freedom and the market order. .Friedman is clearly in favor of the principle of desert determined by valued market contributions. In contrast, Hayek argues that the primary distribution of income, which is an unintended effect of actions of market parties, is arbitrary from a moral perspective, and accordingly, a judgment in terms of justice is inappropriate. His plea for nonintervention is directly linked to his principle of freedom. Hayek argues that each partial intervention in a given income distribution will lead eventually to a situation in which public policy encompasses all income categories. In his view, such an inclusive income policy is unjust. It interferes with free and unhindered contracting; it distorts the allocation of goods; it is always arbitrary because people can never unanimously agree on an optimal distribution of income; and it never fits actual situations because there is always a shortage of policy information.

The second part of the theories of Hayek and Friedman deals with a uniform minimum standard of living for the inactive people. They agree that a minimum standard of living is an efficient way to cope with poverty and to prevent the decline of a free economy because it makes unnecessary compulsory insurance against the risks of sickness, old age, disability and unemployment, as well as government interference by means of redistributive subsidies and regulations. Both writers are opposed to policies in which social security is used as a vehicle for redistribution of income, and both agree that in a free market society only a voluntary system of private insurance is appropriate.

Within this general plan here are options. Hayek argues that the minimum standard of living must be related to the average level of wealth in a country. A lower rate of economic growth demands, in this interpretation, a downward correction of the minimum standard. In contrast, Friedman launches his well-known idea of a negative income tax. Applied to the Dutch situation, this would imply that the conspicuous costs of social security implementation and the so-called "hidden costs of policy," would be eliminated.[12]

The Social-democratic argument is based on fundamentally different principles, Tinbergen argues that a just economy is realized when the total welfare of all separate individuals is equal. In 1946, he argued that a distribution is fair when it is based on the "exchange principle", which implies that in a just economy individuals will not be willing to exchange their social position for anyone else's. This principle assumes that an exchange of positions is feasible, that individuals possess the capacity of empathy, that the process of exchange has a determined solution and that, finally, it is completely evident which elements play a role in the trade-off of exchanging individuals.

In his early work Tinbergen considers this exchange principle to be the basis of distribution policy. However, in later publications he argues that the exchange principle is not feasible and therefore is utopian. That seems indeed to be the case! Individuals are too diverse, not only on the level of their innate capacities, but also on the level of learned capacities, such as their capacity for enjoyment, for the exchange principle to work. Income policy is always too global to make effective use of the exchange principle. With these sorts of reservations in mind, Tinbergen has searched for a narrower idea of equal individual welfare. He deals now with the equal welfare of different professional groups (plumbers, carpenters, political scientists, etc.) The individuals in each professional group, he maintains, are equivalent. Their utility functions have an identical shape. The variables in these functions have the same relative weight. In all of the sections of the labor market the active people desire to earn an income which compensates them financially for the time they had to spend learning or training for the job, for the responsibilities of the job itself, and for the stress the job produces (which is caused by the difference between the actual level of training and the level which is demanded by the employer). Income differences which are the product of tradition, differential economic power and differences in intelligence, are unfair. Tinbergen argues that this concept of just income differences is compatible with the view that the labor market should function efficiently. For instance, the remunerations for unpleasant work, dirty work with a low status in the occupational hierarchy, should be higher. In contrast to Hayek and Friedman, Tinbergen supports a statutory income policy. It is this kind of statutory policy which, by means of a function classification, is able to differentiate according to the inconveniences of the jobs.

Tinbergen has, on purpose, not fully developed a theory of justice. Utility is but a part of the happiness of individuals. Earned incomes (of employers etc.) are only part of all incomes. The just distribution forms only a portion of the reasonable or optimal distribution, which is also connected with the other goals of economic policy. Recently, Tinbergen has developed his theory more thoroughly in close collaboration with the Dutch economist, Jens Pen. Tinbergen first turns his attention to the distribution of wealth. Justice demands that such income (rent and profit) should be reduced if they over-compensate the 'psychic' income of owners of wealth. Rents and profits should be tolerated, however, if they are compensation for earlier postponement of consumption. Second, Tinbergen now regards the income of the inactive persons as a compensation for inconveniences. However, he is concerned only with the incomes of those who are, or have become, permanently inactive: the disabled; the long-term unemployed; and the aged.

The treatment of temporarily inactive persons is not specified in Tinbergen's theory. Due to their inconveniences, the disabled have a right to an income which is higher than the modal income in the economy. The aged have a right to an income which is, at the most, equal to this modal income. One would have expected that Tinbergen would make his arguments also applicable to these groups. Empirical research in the Netherlands has shown clearly that inconveniences in these groups exist. The disabled lack, for instance, daily contact with former colleagues. They hate the burden of control exercised by the bureaucracy on which they are dependent for their benefits. The longer that they are inactive, the more they lose status and self-respect. Tinbergen notes, however, that his theory of justice is <u>not</u> applicable in these cases. The granting of exceptional allowances of a compensatory nature for disabled persons is incompatible with another important aim: maintenance of the incentives for active people and a bearable premium burden for them.[13]

John Rawls, advances a third perspective in which one can speak of a just economy when there is an equal distribution of primary social goods unless an unequal distribution of any or all of these goods can be shown to be to the benefit of the least-advantaged. In this economy, the following principles of justice should be implemented. First, each person has an equal right to a fully adequate scheme of equal basic liberties which is compatible with a similar scheme of liberty for all. Second, social and economic inequalities are to be arranged so that they are both attached to offices and positions which are open to all under conditions of fair equality of opportunity, and are to the greatest benefit of the least-advantaged, consistent with the just savings principle.

In this chapter, I am especially interested in the distribution of income and wealth. Who is to be identified as the representative least-advantaged person? What is the definition of the least fortunate group in Rawls' theory? According to Rawls, one strategy is to choose a particular social position, say that of the unskilled worker, and then to count as the least-advantaged all those who have the average or less than average income and wealth for that particular social position (according to Pen and Tinbergen's scheme, this group consists of those who are in the fourth lowest income decline). A second alternative involves a definition solely in terms of relative income and wealth, with no reference to social position. Thus, all persons with less than half of the medium income and wealth may be taken as the least-advantaged segment. (In the Netherlands, for example, this segment lies around the fifth income decile.) The effect of Rawls' difference principle (the principle of compensating inequalities) can now be shown. An equal division of income between representative persons is to be called just where the lowest 30% receive 30% of the income. An unequal distribution of income is just only if it can be demonstrated that this distribution will guarantee, in the long run, an improvement of the absolute income position of the least-advantaged. The position of the worst-off is, in Rawls' theory, the Archimedean point of reference. The difference principle has some peculiarities. It is indifferent to changes in the income distribution of the upper seven deciles. It does not preclude beforehand a movement away from an initially equal distribution; And it prohibits a deterioration of the income position of the least-advantaged in the short-term but it allows for a stabilization of that position if this is necessary for an improvement in the long-term.

Rawls adds that the first two points are required because some inequalities are necessary to promote a situation where individuals will desire to take specific social positions, work as efficiently as possible, and, best promote the general interest. In relation to the third point, Rawls remarks that the distribution of income is related to the growth of productivity. This implies that the government should maximize the income of the least-advantaged making sure that the amount of the public expenditures is adequate to realize the system of liberties and opportunities (the first principle of justice); and that the amount of savings remains sufficient to allow for a just economy for future generations. In short, it is clear that Rawls is not opposed to a distribution policy that takes into account those measures that are necessary for a growth policy, a policy, in other words, where a trade-off is made between equality and efficiency.

A necessary consequence of the difference principle is 'big' government. The task is fulfilled within a market economy and a political democracy. The government's tasks are accomplished by four different branches (allocative, stabilizing, transfer, and distributive). The transfer branch guarantees a social minimum either by family allowances and special payments for sickness and unemployment, or, more systematically, by such devices as a graded-income supplement (i.e., a negative income tax). The task of the distribution branch is to preserve an approximate justice in distributive shares by means of taxation and the necessary adjustments in the rights of property. It imposes a number of inheritance and gift taxes, and sets restrictions on the rights of bequest. The purpose of these levies and regulations is to gradually and continually correct the distribution of wealth and to prevent concentrations of power which are detrimental to the values of political liberty and equality of opportunity. For Rawls, the scheme of taxation to raise the necessary revenues could consist of a proportional expenditure tax, but he is also willing to accept a proportional income tax.[14]

JUSTICE IN A TWO-TIER SYSTEM

A consideration of these three theories of justice together with the proposals for a reconstruction of the Dutch social security system leads to the following conclusions. To the extent that the proposals advocate a contraction of the public sector in favor of the market sector, one can conclude that there is some compatibility of the reform efforts with the theories of justice elaborated by Hayek and Friedman. The visible costs of social security (not the hidden policy costs) will be brought down. However, the two-tier system should be rejected in the light of the theories of Hayek and Friedman, because the government continues with its policy of redistribution (sliding-scale) and regulation. According to their theories, the just solution would be to re-privatize social security. Insurance freedom would be restored and there would be ample room for private insurance activities.

The Memoranda of 1981 and 1982 place a long list of items on the privatization agenda. In the light of Hayek and Friedman's theories, social security should certainly be included on this agenda. More specifically, the two-tier system is incompatible with Hayek and Friedman's theories because it severs the relation between paid premium and level of benefit (especially in the case of the higher benefits). On the other hand, the two-tier system seems to be more compatible when it takes the (Anglo-Saxon) idea of a national minimum seriously and when it provides an incentive for people to use private insurance against social risks (above the modal income positions).

The reform proposals which would differentiate according to need seem quite compatible with Tinbergen's theory. The inclusion of social security, which would remain in the revamped system, is also an element in the optimal economic regime in Tinbergen's work. The level of the benefits should not provide any incentive for people to become or remain inactive. For that reason, benefits should not be higher than 80% of the last earned income, Tinbergen remarked in 1959, a statement he recently repeated.[15] In that sense, it seems he could readily agree to a leveling down of the benefits allowed under the present Unemployment Insurance Act. Continuing this line of argument, the two-tier system might be seen as another means to lower the costs of unemployment benefits paid by the government. I have stated earlier that the principle of need plays a central role in the proposals for the two-tier system. As we have seen, it is also important in Tinbergen's theory. But, Tinbergen demands that this need principle be elaborated so that it takes into account the particular inconveniences of specific groups of inactive persons. The two-tier system does not provide such an elaboration.

A judgment based on Rawls' theory must depend, almost totally, on the macro-economic consequences of the cutback policies. In general, Rawls would consider it admissible that the cutback policy result in larger income differences within the group of employees above the group of least-advantaged, and/or that the policy be accompanied by a deterioration of the relative position of the worst off, if it could be shown that the absolute income position of the least-advantaged does not deteriorate; and that the inequality is necessary to improve the long-term prospects of the least-favored (i.e., that economic growth will take place and/or that unemployment will decrease).

Unfortunately, the Memoranda on the Reconsideration of Public Expenditures have nothing to say about macro-economic prospects. Therefore, it is impossible to come to a considered judgment of the reform proposals from the perspective of Rawls' theory. Contrary to Glazer's statement that the Rawlsian theory of justice provides a legitimation of supply-side economics, my opinion is that such a judgment on economic policy is impossible without quantitative and qualitative measurement of the macro-economic consequences of that policy.[15] Thus, for us to judge reform proposals by means of Rawls' theory, it would be essential to have knowledge about the long-term consequences of the two-tier system. It is clear, however, that Rawls would agree with the protection of the least-favored as provided in the two-tier system. Also, the deterioration of the position of a part of the group of disabled persons (the 'best-off') in the direction of the least-advantaged could not be rejected out-of-hand by Rawlsian theory. Finally, the possibility of an increase in income differences between active and inactive people would be compatible with Rawls' theory so long as these increased inequalities led, in the long-term, to a higher absolute income position for the least-advantaged.

LEGITIMATE CUTBACKS

After this confrontation of three theories of justice with the proposals of the Memoranda, one should be able to make a considered judgment on the justice of the proposed retrenchment policy. All three theories agree on the following points:

- that it is just that a minimum standard of living should be guaranteed,
- that it is necessary to take into account the trade-off between principles of justice and efficiency, and, that the minimum standard of living cannot be determined without taking into account the actual scarcity situation
- that income differences should not be based on differences in power.

In addition to these specific points of agreement, there is another, more general similarity. All three theories require a lot of information before clear-cut judgments on specific policy proposals can be made. In the theory of Hayek and Friedman, the primary income distribution should reflect the marginal productivity of individuals. In Tinbergen's theory, the differences in earned-income should be related to the differences in inconveniences among active persons. If the inactive people are included in the theory, one should also have information on their inconveniences. To make a judgment based on Rawls' theory, one needs information about the effects of the economic policy on the long-term position of the least-advantaged.

The three theories of justice would, however, not always come to the same conclusions when confronted with a specific retrenchment policy. In the two-tier system, for instance, the position of the least-advantaged is not always guaranteed in each theory. In Hayek's theory, for instance, a drop in buying power of those who receive benefits would be just in a situation of economic downturn.

In this chapter, I have focused on the position of the inactive people and the way social security treats them. In general, it seems to be the case that theories of justice pay most attention to distribution problems regarding those who are earning an income. When inactive people are taken into account, these theories focus most carefully on those who own wealth. However, the fundamental changes that are taking place in the economies of western industrialized countries, as shown in the transition from employment in agriculture and industry to services, the growing numbers of people working in public services, and, perhaps most importantly, the growing numbers of people who are unemployed and have no prospect of getting back to work, are hardly dealt with in theories of justice.

It has not been my intention to examine all possible methods of cutbacks in the area of social security. Here, the perspective has been on the cutback proposals set forth in the *Memoranda on Reconsideration of the Public Expenditures*. Alternative proposals would also have to be confronted with principles of justice. Proponents of the proposed policy change in the Netherlands have claimed that the time has run out for a discussion on the legitimate aspects of alternative cutback proposals. In my opinion, a public and careful political discussion is, and always will be necessary *prior* to the moment of making binding political decisions.

Careful discussion and development of rational arguments are important when expansion of welfare programs in times of economic growth is at issue. Such discourse is even more critical when fundamental changes in the tasks of the welfare state are at stake. A confrontation of fundamental policy proposals with theories of justice (theories that give an interpretation of a just distribution of the policy burdens), will contribute to the development of a consensus; a consensus which is crucial for successful retrenchment without risking deterioration into a situation of welfare backlash.

THEORETICAL SHORTCOMINGS AND THE FUTURE

Several interrelated shortcomings of normative political theory have emerged in the process of confronting theories of justice with the reconsideration of the social security system. As stated before, the expansion of the social welfare state has not been guided by an encompassing theory. The same can be said of the period of contraction. The current development can best be described as a movement _backward_ from a social welfare state in the direction of a social security state (a type of state reminiscent of the ideas Beveridge originally developed, where the centerpiece consists of the guarantee of a social minimum standard of living). This movement is led by civil servants who, in their _Memoranda_, employ instrumental ad hoc arguments. It is supported by politicians of practically all political parties who, on the one hand, have failed to bring their ideologies up-to-date, and who, on the other hand, demand that citizens pay more attention to what they can do for themselves and ask less from the state.

However, the necessary fundamental debate on where we should go from here (a critical discussion to develop a coherent vision on the future of the welfare state) is lacking, while the need for such debate is more pressing than ever. It is, for example, claimed that, once the economic crisis has passed, the original ideas about the welfare state can again be applied. This claim seems to me to be fundamentally flawed. The present crisis in the welfare state is certainly not due only to an economic or financial crisis. Even if there had been no crisis at all, a re-thinking of the goals and functions of the welfare state would have been necessary. Did the welfare state accomplish what was originally intended? If not, what lies at the source of its failure? Is, indeed, the state the appropriate instrument for steering society in the desired direction?

In regard to these questions, political theorists have failed to develop a coherent vision. The pursuit of justice and the attempt to constrain market effects are not mirages. In a world of scarce resources, it is unthinkable that the questions of who gets what based on what distributive principles will become irrelevant to the political agenda. Theories of justice seem to have been limping behind the actual situation of shrinkages.

In general, the aim of the welfare state can be formulated as that of trying to achieve a general equality of living conditions. Income distributions of different kinds (primary, secondary and tertiary) have very often been focused on in attempts to reach this goal. There are sufficiently developed normative theories that can be used to come to a judgment on the justice of particular primary income distributions. However, when we turn to the secondary income distribution (the primary distribution together with social security benefits), normative theories are, as we have seen, less developed. The common element in all three theories of justice dealt with here consists of a guaranteed property right for everyone: a right to an income on the minimum level of social well-being regardless of the worth attributed to human capital in certain periods of time. But the question of how to deal with inactive persons above this minimum level is not considered adequately.

There is even less theoretical development regarding the tertiary income distribution (the secondary distribution plus the benefits of public services). In this area, the most important instrument of reaching the goal of the welfare state involves the provision of public services like health care, education, housing, and public transportation.[17] As we will see in the chapter by Lennard Lundquist in this volume, the use of these public goods is certainly not in accordance with the original intentions: those who have the greatest need for them are not using them the most. The distributional effect is, in other words, different from that originally intended.[18] What kind of normative evaluation should be given as regards this situation? Should these goods no longer be provided as public goods? Should these kinds of goods be privatized?[19] Viable alternatives have not been formulated on what the strategy of justice in this field requires.

Related to this is the problem that the three theories of justice are not specific enough in regard to questions of how different groups should be treated (i.e., the least-advantaged disabled, the long-term unemployed, and the aged, etc.). Further, we have seen that these theories require a lot of information before a considered judgment on a proposal can be given, and before a clear differentiation among them can be made. At this point, only general conclusions seem possible. Finally, there is the question of whether these theories of justice can make a meaningful contribution to opinions on distributive justice in "real life"? Is there any congruence at all? Empirical studies that deal explicitly with what is considered fair in "real life" have been undertaken only recently.[20] Research into the degree of congruence between elaborate normative principles derived from theories of justice, and normative ideas on distribution in daily life could contribute to the development of a consensual reconstruction of the welfare state.[21]

NOTES

1. In this article we understand social security basically to consist of regulations concerning Disablement and Unemployment Benefit Acts. These regulations form only a part of the overall social security system.

2. Norman Furniss and Timothy Tilton, The Case for the Welfare State: From Social Security to Social Equality, Bloomington: Indiana University Press 1977, p. 24.

3. Harold Wilensky, The Welfare State and Equality, Berkeley: University of California Press, 1975.

4. See: Hugh Heclo, "Toward a New Welfare State?" in Peter Flora and Arnold Heidenheimer, eds., The Development of Welfare States in Europe and America; New Brunswick, N.J.: Transaction Books 1981, p. 383-406.

5. Memoranda on the Reconsideration of Public Expenditures, Second Chamber, session 1980-1981, document 16,625, numbers 1,2,3,4, The Hague, Government Printing Office (in Dutch).

6. For this distinction see Furniss and Tilton, op. cit..

7. The present Dutch government (which is since November 1982 a coalition of the right-of-center Christian Democratic Party and the Liberal Party) has taken the proposals formulated by the civil servants in the Memoranda on social security as their official government policy. From 1982 onward measures are taken which are intended before the parliamentary elections of Spring 1986 to produce new social security system. The proposals the government is implementing differ only slightly from those formulated in the Memoranda.

8. For an American discussion on this ratio, see in particular, for the number of aged, the articles by Peter G. Peterson on the "Crash of Social Security" and its "Salvation" in the December 2 and December 16, 1982 issues of the New York Review of Books. See also the subsequent discussion in the March 17, 1983 issue.

9. For instance, see Carl Wellman, Welfare Rights, Totowa, N.J.: Rowman and Littlefield, 1982.

10. Percy B. Lehning, "Property Rights, Justice, and the Welfare State" in Acta Politica, vol. 15, 1980, p. 319-356.

11. G.M.J. Veldkamp, "Social Security and the Economic Crisis", in Social Security and the Economic Crisis, Proceedings of the European Institute for Social Security, E.I.S.S. Yearbook 1980-1981, Part II, Deventer, 1982, p. 133-146.

PART TWO

Economic and Social Challenges

VI.

Don S. Schwerin

Nordic Responses to 'Fiscal Crises'

Limits and Strategies

INTRODUCTION

There is concern for the futures of the welfare state. This book otherwise would not be written. The idea of the successful welfare state seems inextricably tied to the Scandinavian social democracies, several peripheral, thinly populated and historically poor states in Northern Europe. Until recently, at least, these rather special political economies seem to have combined equalization of personal incomes and life chances with enviable economic growth rates, in spite of -- or because of -- the public sectors implied by equality norms. It is the apparent faltering of these welfare states that for many foreign observers has put the idea of social democracy and social welfare in peril. If welfare states have no future in Scandinavia, then where do they?

One does not have to search far for predictions of doom. The Economist says that the Norwegian economy "is in a mess." The Danish economy is "crumbling" and the Swedish "consensus is breaking down." This is not just foreign sniping. Scandinavian conservatives feed and embellish these assessments for domestic political consumption. This conservative offensive is thriving again in Sweden after the Social Democrats' return to office in September, 1982, but is more subtle now in Denmark, under its bourgeois government since September, 1982, and in Norway since the election of the Conservative government in September, 1981.

It is conventional to conclude that the smaller European countries are so dependent on foreign trade that domestic business conditions are produced abroad. Domestic policy has little to do with recessions and booms. Domestic policy-makers can only tinker on the margins to ameliorate or exacerbate the prevailing economic cycle imported from abroad. By this reasoning, neither the current straits of the Nordic economies nor the futures of the Scandinavian welfare model are in the hands of Nordic authorities.

I develop this reasoning below and sketch a preliminary evaluation of external and internal constraints on Nordic economic performance. Two companion questions require discussion in any treatment of the futures of the welfare state: can economic adjustment be consistent with welfare state priorities, or are we facing a necessary dismantlement of welfare states; and, are there characteristics of (Scandinavian) welfare states which can facilitate adjustment, or does adjustment require institutional change? I come back to these questions after examining the political economics of adjustment and reviewing the reaction of the Nordic governments over the last several years.

I begin with a brief review of Nordic economics in the world economy. Britain's free trade policy during its period of economic expansion in the late nineteenth century pulled the Nordic economies, via commodity exports, into the European market. The returning flow of technology and capital contributed to a base for sustained economic growth and increase of personal incomes. Nordic production and export of semi-manufactured goods and finished products joined export sales of timber, pine tar, fish and iron ore to bring the economies into international commerce. Industrial demand for foreign investment goods and materials, along with demand for imported consumer products, completed the circle of opening the small Nordic economies to external markets.

This expansion of import suppliers and export buyers underpinned Nordic economic growth but at the same time increased the exposure of these small economies to the economic winds blowing across the North Sea and the plains of Europe. Success in penetrating foreign markets and earning foreign currencies carries increased vulnerability to what happens in those markets. Just as bullish foreign economies provide an easy stimulus to slumbering domestic production, so too do economic doldrums in foreign capitals feed back into the home economy as factories producing for foreign customers shut down. The dependence of small nations on large neighbors is familiar enough: when X sneezes, Y catches cold. The United States and Canada, Britain and Ireland, Germany and Austria, are examples. Regional markets with their implications of dominance by large countries, of course, are still with us. What is new is that even the big neighbors are dependent on each other, the small neighbors have more diversified markets, and the rhetoric of political domination has been overtaken by railings against the tyrannies of disembodied international financial markets and acephalic exchange rate regimes, and the inequities of GATT. The lesson read from all this is that individual nations, and certainly small nations, may have little control over their domestic economies. For "domestic economy," read "unemployment" and "inflation". When governments cannot manage their domesticeconomies to produce jobs for their citizens and stand for the value of workers' savings, social policy is reduced to safety net services, often offering a net with steadily larger mesh.

Any small open economy must adjust its domestic incomes to prevailing wages and prices in the external economy. In theory, a small open economy faces the same conditions as does the individual producer in a perfectly competitive economy. It cannot sell its products if its prices lie above the uniform market price; yet it can make its price competitive only by squeezing its own margin (wages and profits) in the short term (and by increased productivity in the medium term). And if it cannot sell its goods, it cannot buy goods. Imports are bought by the proceeds of export sales. In special circumstances, a country's currency itself is in demand, for purposes of international exchange for example, and so becomes an export commodity. The alternative to competitiveness for a small economy is an Albania-like existence. Small closed economies are backward and poor. The larger an economy's domestic market, however, the greater the scope for growth in the home market, capital accumulation, economies of scale, price competition among producers, and technological innovation, mostly for reasons which have nothing to do with the assumptions of perfectly competitive markets. The result is much greater sensitivity to international conjunctural movements. The margins for deviating from foreign wage and price trends, especially on the high side, are much tighter for small open economies than for large closed economies. Since exchange rates translate foreign prices into domestic money and vice versa, domestic producers and wage earners watch assets and incomes move back and forth across the frontier as the domestic currency moves up and down vis a vis foreign currencies.

BALANCE OF PAYMENTS: CURRENT ACCOUNTS AND CAPITAL ACCOUNTS

External constraints on domestic economic policy revolve around the balance of payments. The balance of payments is made up of a current account and a capital account. The current account records the import and export of goods and services while the capital account includes flows of capital finance in the form of long-term investments and loans, short-term bank credits, and short-term import-export credits. The "balance" of payments is seldom an actual balance. The stock of foreign exchange reserves expands and contracts as capital account transactions overshoot or undershoot the balance on current account transactions. The idea of a balance comes from the necessity to cover current account deficits with compensating imports of capital. Likewise, current account surpluses are often accompanied by capital export in the form of trade credits.

The current account, more specifically, is made up of: the import and export of goods, the import and export of services, and the payment and receipt of interest, dividends, and transfers. Goods trade is also called visible trade, while trade in services and flows of investment incomeare referredto as "invisibles". Note here that the trade account is only part of a nation's current account. A country may run a deficit on its trade transactions but recover ground in its sale of services. Since shipping revenues are counted as sales of services, the sea-faring Nordic countries have historically offset trade deficits by running a surplus on the service account. However, since the Nordic countries have historically also been capital importers, they have paid interest and dividends to foreign banks and investors. Finland's surplus on its trade and services account, for example, has in recent years been nullified by sizeable deficits in its balance of foreign investment. Payment of interest to foreign lenders is not necessarily a sign of reckless extravagance. The label "extravagance" may be an inappropriate description if the issue is whether to borrow to finance a hydroelectric project. Norway, for example, is paying enormous interest on debt incurred in the early- and mid-1970s to finance development of its North Sea oil, though fortunately not so much as the revenues from the sales of the oil produced by the investment.

Whether owing to the failure to sell enough goods and services or to servicing earlier debt, deficits on the current account must be paid by running down the country's stock of foreign exchange, accumulating additional foreign exchange by borrowing abroad, or by acquiring foreign exchange through unrelated capital inflows. A good example of the last is the substantial import of private capital to the United States to take advantage of the high real interest rates and active real estate markets. This capital inflow has kept the U.S. dollar at a high value which, in turn, has reduced imported inflation but also has contributed to an enormous trade deficit. This current account deficit is then financed by the foreign capital attracted to this country by the Reagan-Volcker tight money policy and the tentative economic recovery. This is an example of unrelated capital flows. Other governments, the Danish for example, push domestic interest rates higher than they would otherwise choose explicitly in order to encourageprivate businesses to go abroad for their capital and bring home foreign exchange to cover a current account deficit. The Danish case is complicated by the fact that domestic rates are also supported by large-scale public sector borrowing on the domestic financial markets. Still other governments (e.g., the West German) use attractive real interest rates and the lure of currency appreciation as bait to appeal more directly to foreign financial investors.

There are limits to how much and how long a current account deficit can be offset by capital imports. The limits are not absolute as are the limits of financing a deficit from finite reserves. The limits are trade-offs. Current borrowing means increased debt service later. Unless the economy has moved to a surplus in the interim, the debt servicing itself must be financed and rolled into the country's outstanding debt. The demands on trade performance in goods and services steadily increased as the debt burden grows. Servicing a current deficit that is regularly compounding means that a country must ask more and more competitive performance of its export industries. A healthy trade surplus shrinks the roll-over of the deficit on investment income.

Building a healthy trade surplus just to pay off foreign debt, however, can mean export competitiveness at the expense of wages, profits, consumption andinvestments -- in short, domestic incomes and demand. A competitive export sector under these conditions may also suffer declines in the number of firms, employees, and investment, as well as in total revenues. Squeezing the profitability of the export sector, even if the aim is to improve the country's competitiveness in foreign markets, eventually drives resources either into protected home markets or out of the country, as in the case of capital flight and export of labor.

While debt service constrains domestic policy, the availability of foreign credit in recent years has not been a real constraint. International capital markets have been flush with liquidity in the wake of the 1980 oil price rise and consequent slow-down of investment activity in OECD countries. Banks were anxious to place inactive funds, even in what turned out to be nonperforming loans to countries like

Brazil, Argentina, and Mexico. The Nordic countries had no difficulty finding external financing. The cost of foreign borrowing, on the other hand, can increase. Denmark suffered the embarrassment of having its credit rating downgraded in 1982 and having to pay an increased risk premium.

Attracting capital imports means a tight money policy and high domestic interest rates. The immediate trade-off is a cooling of the domestic economy. Unemployment increases and plant utilization declines. This may help restore balance on the current account, depending on the income elasticity of imports and the stickiness of domestic wages and profits. Management of domestic credit becomes trickier if the inflow of capital overshoots, adding to the stock of foreign exchange and also money supply figures. Monetary authorities are pushed to tighten further the regulation of domestic credit to avoid importing inflation or unwanted monetary stimulus. Switzerland and West Germany from time to time take determined action to "sanitize" their capital inflows.

If we add exchange rate changes, the picture becomes more complex. Capital imports via foreign investment in domestic securities increase the demand for the domestic currency and can exercise an upward pressure on the exchange rate. Exchange rates are popularly thought to move up and down with surpluses and deficits on the trade account. Countries running trade surpluses experience an increased foreign demand for their currency to pay import bills, and a consequent upward pressure on their currency, and vice versa. Exchange rate variations remain sensitive to trade balances and changes in trade balances, of course, but financial flows on the capital account can reverse the direction exchange rates should move on the basis of trade balances alone. The U.S. provides a spectacular example. American monetary policy since 1979 turned a long-standing pattern of U.S. capital export into substantial capital import. An increase in the value of the dollar followed, beginning in the last quarter of 1980. The current account began to plunge in the middle of 1982. Since the end of 1983, a massive U.S. current account deficit has coincided with an exceptionally strong U.S. dollar. The costs of currency appreciation pushed by capital imports are real. A Data Resources report suggests for the United States that if the U.S. dollar had stayed at its 1980 value, "we would have had more than 1 million additional people employed and our trade deficit would be $25 billion lower."[1] Clearly, a policy of financing a fiscal deficit through capital imports is constrained by the production and employment consequences of currency appreciation.

These consequences depend, in turn, on the openness of the economy and on political sensitivities.

SOME POLITICS OF ADJUSTMENT

The balance of payments summarizes a country's current and capital transactions with the outside world. It is the conduit for external constraints on domestic policy. It funnels price and volume changes on world markets into the domestic economy and recycles the effects of earlier deficits. The consequences of deficits on the current account are real and cannot be ignored, at least by countries whose foreign transactions make up a substantial proportion of the economy. Bringing domestic economies into line with foreign wages and prices is called "adjustment." Exposed economies must, within some latitude, adjust wages, prices, interest rates, and exchange rates to bring national income levels into line with the national product, expressed in common currency. A persistent current account deficit indicates that a country is consuming goods, services, and capital beyond its means.

Current account deficits mean that domestic incomes must be reduced in favor of foreign incomes, and domestic household incomes are more dispensable than capitalist incomes. The technical problem is to reallocate resources to the export- and import-competing sectors in order to increase the production of the exposed sectors relative to the sheltered sectors and to do this without increasing the relative prices of factors in export production. This reallocation between sectors can happen autonomously in response to changes in the relative profitability and relative prices of export and home sectors. Workers and capital are drawn to the export- and import-competing markets when higher profits and higher wages are to be made. The tricky part of adjustment policy is to effect this reallocation in spite of market incentives. Just as the government runs counter-cyclical fiscal policy, so must it run counter-cyclical industrial and labor market policy. And the implications are political as well as economic, which means that the constraints on policy and instruments are political as well as economic.

Adjustment policy tends to focus on improving the trade balance. International trade in commodities seems more price competitive than trade in services.[2] Prices and volumes in goods exports seem to move in familiar ways, and policy-makers think they know how to make exported goods more price competitive. The demand for services seems more fickle. Reputation and judgments of quality rank along side price in the buyer's mind. Even where policy-makers know what accounts for export demand for services, they are not always sure of how to meet the requirements. Further, most trade in services is not covered by GATT and is subject to a variety of protectionist measures. Services are still traded predominately in national markets.

What governments think they can do about trade deficits on the supply side is to bring the rate of export price increases below that of their competitors. There are four components to export prices: (1) profits, (2) wages, (3) productivity, and (4) exchange rate. Capital costs are not included here since monetary policy is usually tied up by the demands of the capital account. Domestic supplier costs can be broken down into the same components as export prices and respond to government policy in roughly the same way, while usually only revaluation among domestic policy instruments can influence the prices of imported materials. Wages rates combine with productivity (plus non-wage labor costs) to make up per unit labor costs. Profit margins added to per unit labor costs give the unit price in national currency. The exchange rate then translates this price in national currency into prices in foreign currencies. These are the prices potential foreign customers must pay.

On the import side, governments aim at reducing the import of consumer goods either by making these goods more expensive relative to home-produced products, making import-competing industries more price competitive, or simply reducing households' total consumption and hoping that imports suffer a disproportionate share of the cutbacks. Protectionism reduces actual quantity of goods allowed for import as well as increasing import prices.

Alternate adjustment policies have both demand and supply-side effects. Incomes policy involves attempts to negotiate moderate wages in exchange for profit reinvestment and price controls on the supply side, and relies on reductions in real wages to temper demand for consumer imports. Fiscal constraint and tight money policy slow the growth of aggregate incomes and cool expectations of wage and price increases in order to lower employment pressure, dampen wage demands, and slow up price increases on the supply side, and count on the demand side taking care of itself. Both incomes policy and fiscal-monetary policy operate on prices and demand through incomes. Whether explicit or implicit, incomes regulation feeds through to prices for export goods and import-competing goods. Devaluation, on the other hand, operates on incomes through prices. Devaluation increases the prices of imported goods to domestic consumers, thus reducing real incomes, and reducing the foreign -- but not domestic -- prices of export goods. This, in turn, should increase the volume of export sales and so increase the domestic currency incomes of export producers. True to supply-side thinking, export producers will then reinvest their profits and increase productivity.

The political content of adjustment policy is obvious. Whether government does nothing, pushes an increasing debt service burden onto successive governments and generations, or applies some mixture of incomes policy, fiscal and monetary policy, and devaluation, it is making both distributive choices about who wins and who loses and choices affecting how much there is to distribute. Government measures to influence the allocation of resources imply choices with regard to distribution of incomes. Choices among policies imply price and volume trade-offs in the demand for labor, for example. Incomes policy reduces real prices of labor while maintaining a high volume demand. The cuts in real wages are spread over a large pool of employed workers. Incomes policy takes the view that the economic hard times are cyclical and that what is needed is a bridging maneuver which maintains employment and domestic demand. Budget cuts backed up by tight money take the opposite view, that what is needed is structural reform: "a cold turkey" shift of factor incomes from labor to capital and a reversion of national expenditure from household and government consumption to private investment. Proponents of the latter view welcome occasional recessions in order to shake out excess labor and reestablish labor market discipline. They argue that the growth rates coming out of a health-restoring recession compensate for the human misery and loss of aggregate incomes induced by government policy. "Bridging" proponents calculate that sustained growth even at lower rates beats the aggregate growth of boom-bust economies, especially when descriptions of recoveries are in the future tense.

The burdens of adjustment policy are not borne equally, nor are they necessarily intended to be spread evenly. The success of devaluation, for example, rides on slowing the recovery of real wages and incomes for workers and households while approving the restoration of profits to export- and import-competing industries. Wage controls masquerading as incomes policy hold wages back with no quid pro quo guarantee that industry's improved margins will be used to regain markets or, alternately, that increased profits will be reinvested in some way proportionate to the workers' sacrifices. Incomes regulation through fiscal constraint and tight money lays the greatest burden on marginal workers and rewards holders of capital.

Just as inflation favors borrowers, deflation favors lenders. Reallocation policies necessarily redistribute incomes.

The political constraints on adjustment policy come from interests seeking to protect their incomes. Interest cleavages run horizontally between labor and capital and vertically between exposed export- and import-competing sectors, on the one hand, and the sheltered domestic sectors, on the other. Other interest cleavages run between lenders and borrowers and between fixed-income and variable-income groups. The political coalitions change with the adjustment strategy and policies employed. What is not to be missed is that adjustment to external constraints, whether through technical currency devaluations, statutory wage-price controls, or cuts of social spending, affects individual incomes and assets. Adjustment policy is political in the basic sense of deciding who gets what.

SPILLOVERS: OIL, DEFLATION, AND TRADE

Denmark, Finland, Norway, and Sweden exported goods and services equal to 36, 32, 46, and 32 percent, respectively, of their GDP in 1982. They imported goods and services at about the same proportion. The imports of the average OECD country (on a weighted basis) were about 20 percent of its GDP. (The figure for the US was 11 percent.) When economies like those of Germany and the United States are growing, the Nordic countries grow also, creating more sales, more jobs, more consumption, and more investments. Growth in any one economy spills over to its trading partners. Assuming conventional multipliers and elasticity of import volume growth with respect to GNP of around 1-1/2 to 2, "a $1 stimulus to a typical economy may, when the effect is at its peak, raise output in that country by $1 1/2 and activity abroad by another $1 to 1 1/2. Thus, total OECD output expands by $2 1/2 to 3, but the initiating country sees only $1 1/2 of that."[4] When several countries are each priming their economic pumps, without taking into account the home effect of what their neighbors are doing, there is a tendency to overshoot. The total stimulating effect can be much greater than any one country counted on.

What goes up, can come down. When a country decides to cut big government or fight inflation or turn around a current account deficit by cooling domestic demand, the felicitous multipliers and elasticity coefficients run backward. Foreign economies as an aggregate will steal the lion's share of the intended policy effects, whether they want to deflate or not. Unhappy with the initial results, the first country may step a little harder on the economic brakes. And, again, when several countries deflate at the same time but without coordinating their cutbacks, the combined effect can throw their economies into recession.

The OECD has called 1980-1982 a period of "synchronized deflation". It started with an increase in the price of oil from $12.98 in 1978 to $19.00 in 1979 and $31.51 in 1980. Real GDP growth in the OECD dropped from a 4.8 percent from 1976 or 1978, to 3.1 percent in 1979, then to 1.2 and 1.6 percent in 1980 and 1981, and finally to a trough of -0.2 percent in 1982. A similar slowdown and then actual shrinking of the economy happened in 1974 and 1975 after the first OPEC price shock. OECD growth went from 6.1 percent in 1973 to -0.2 percent in 1975.

The oil price increases hit the European economies roughly the same as if they had devalued -- but only on the import side. The OPEC price hikes increased import prices for petroleum and petroleum-based goods. Moreover, the import price increases were on essential products for which there were limited local substitutes. The only way to reduce the oil import bill in the short term was to reduce total demand and this meant, in effect, shutting factories down. Few policies are as effective in reducing oil imports as recession. Making matters worse, the "normal" devaluation's positive side was missing. Exports did not become relatively cheaper. With most countries deflating, no one country could gain much competitive ground on its neighbors. OPEC's oil price hike looked more and more like a one-sided tax assessment; one-sided because OPEC revenues were only partly returned to the OECD economies through reverse purchases of consumption and investment goods. Most governments chose to tighten belts and reduce living standards at home to pay the foreign oil tax. They aimed to reduce both oil and non-oil imports and to slow the increase in domestic costs to gain a competitive edge in export markets and generate a trade surplus. This "synchronized deflation" snowballed. The OECD estimates that the four major European economies gave up growth equal to 5 1/2 percent of GDP between 1980 and 1982. Most countries managed only to hold their competitive foreign position as each tried to out-deflate the other. Deflation in the industrialized countries slowed, stopped, and then reversed the growth of world trade. The volume of world trade increased at about 6 percent per year in 1978 and 1979. From 1980 to 1983, growth rates dropped to 1.5, 0, -2.0, and 0 percent, respectively. Industrialized countries slowed their import of consumer and investment goods from other industrialized countries, cut their import of oil from OPEC and other oil-exporting countries, and reduced their imports of other commodities from everybody, hurting especially non-oil third world countries. Industrialized countries as a whole (OECD plus Comecon) cut the dollar value of their imports. The dollar value of imports of "sixteen debtor countries" -- mostly newly industrialized countries (NICs) -- dropped even more sharply, from $202 billion in 1981 to $174 billion the following year, partly as a result of the appreciation of the dollar.

NORDIC EXPORTS IN A TOUGHER WORLD

External conditions for the Nordic countries worsened after 1979. How each country fared depended on the product mix it exported and to whom it exported. Domestically, it depended on each country's adjustment of incomes. One measure of a country's success in adjusting to external circumstances is how well it does in its foreign markets. Relative export performance, or change in market share, is one indicator. This is the difference between the growth of a country's markets (i.e., growth of its customers' imports from all suppliers, by volume) relative to the growth of the country's exports to that market. It is performance in the manufactured goods markets,(i.e., excluding food, raw materials and energy),which is the most responsive to domestic adjustment policy.

The manufactured markets for the Nordic countries expanded over 10 percent in 1979 and then dropped to between 2.5 and 3.5 percent annual growth in 1980 through 1983. Growth was slower in 1980 and 1981 than for the average OECD economy but held up better in 1982, which was the particularly slow year for other OECD countries. Among the Nordic countries, Finland was faced with the slowest market growth, attributable to the slow growth of its largest single market, the Soviet Union, which takes about a quarter of Finland's exports. Sweden's markets followed more nearly the OECD pattern while Denmark trailed after slightly. Norway's markets were more volatile, growing the fastest of the Nordic countries in 1978 and 1979 and in 1982 and 1983, but the slowest in the years in between.

Relative export performance compares actual exports with market growth. OECD countries lost market shares in the bullish 1979 market and the following two years. Only at the bottom of the trough in 1982 did the OECD hold its own, before recovering lost markets in 1983. Overall, the Big 7 OECD economies did considerably worse than the OECD mean. The Nordic countries, on the other hand, did better. Among the Nordic countries, Denmark consistently maintained or won market shares. After a bad year in 1979, Finland did even better. Norway was the laggard, losing market shares each year from 1979 until 1983. Sweden started out on the same downward path as Norway but recovered dramatically in the wake of the 1982 16 percent devaluation.

The puzzle is that the Nordic countries managed to improve their market shares while rejecting tight fiscal policy, the conventional remedy for restoring external balance. The Nordic countries, and the small OECD countries generally, were far less inclined than the Big 7 to contract fiscal policy during the recession. The OECD divides changes in "general government financial balances" into discretionary and automatic changes.[5] Automatic changes, or built-in stabilizers, reflect budget changes following from variations in economic growth. Discretionary budgetary changes "reflect both deliberate policy interventions and fiscal drag." Changes in financial balances, whether discretionary or automatic, move the balance toward either surplus (contraction) or deficit (expansion). Leaving aside the United States, the remaining six Big 7 economies chose to use fiscal policy to contract government stimulus of the economy in 18 of the 24 years represented between 1981 and 1984 (six countries times four budget years each). The automatic stabilizers in these countries moved toward expansion in 21 of the 24 opportunities. Discretionary policy in 16 of those 21 recession years went to the other direction, toward contraction of fiscal stimulus.

This is the conservative fiscal policy one would expect more from small economies imposing domestic discipline in order to survive in international markets. Smaller countries, however, did not follow this prescription. Built-in stabilizers over a period of three years (1982,1983) for a sample of ten smaller OECD countries moved toward expansion in 27 of the 30 budgets, roughly the same proportion as in the larger countries. Discretionary policy interventions, on the other hand, were also expansionary in 16 of the 27 recession years, 59 percent versus 24 percent for the large countries. Large countries chose to contract fiscal policy even when automatic stabilizes signalled recession. Discretionary policy in these countries was counter-cyclic in only 7 of the 24 budget years (29 percent), compared to 18 of 30 budget years (60 percent) for the small countries. Discretionary policy in Denmark, Norway, and Sweden was distinctive even among the smaller countries. Discretionary policy was expansionary in 7 of the 9 budget years (78 percent), including one budget in which the built-in stabilizers moved towards restriction. (The United States is also distinctive: discretionary policy was expansionary in three of the four Reagan budget years, making Reagan's fiscal policy exceptional among the Big 7 and more expansionary than even Mitterrand's choices in France.)

Wages, prices, and exchange rates are the major variables explaining relative export performance. While fiscal policy may have been expansionary, labor costs per produced unit in the Nordic countries increased at roughly the same rate as in the OECD as a whole. Using government expenditure to support domestic demand did not push up unit labor costs relative to competitors. Unit labor costs in local currency in Nordic countries on average increased 33 percent, compared to 35 percent on average in the OECD. The Nordic countries did not manage unit labor costs by pushing workers into unemployment lines. Unemployment slid up in each of the Nordic countries, but, again, to a lesser extent than in comparable economies. The Nordic countries' labor cost performance, however, was not matched by competitive pricing, at least not before exchange rate changes taken into account. Nordic export prices of manufactures in local currency (i.e., Finnish marks, Norwegian crowns) increased 16 percent faster from 1979 to 1983 than in the OECD as a whole. Nordic export prices rose 45 percent, compared to 39 percent for the OECD. Denmark and Sweden were on the high side, at about 52 percent increases each, while Finland was close to Norway, and was below the OECD mean at 42 percent and 32 percent, respectively.

Comparing the increase of export prices with the increase of unit labor costs gives an indication of whether national policies put the adjustment burden on labor or capital. Subtracting percent increase in prices from percent increase in labor costs gives positive differences when profits are squeezed and negative differences when wages are squeezed. On average, the OECD increased labor costs 35 percent between 1979 and 1983 but raised prices 39 percent, a difference of 4 percentage points on the negative side. That is, exporters on average raised prices, and potentially profits, at a faster rate than unit labor costs increased. Contrary to expectations about social democratic welfare states, Nordic countries on average squeezed labor even harder, to a negative difference of 12 percentage points. Some of the increase in prices over and above the increase in unit labor costs can be marked up to energy price increases. Assigning the average OECD difference of 4 percentage points to cover accelerating energy costs still leaves the Nordic squeeze on labor at a net of 8 percentage points. Of the three countries with the greatest negative differences (squeeze on labor) in the fifteen countries, two were in Scandinavia: price increases in excess of unit labor costs in Belgium, Denmark, and Sweden were -27, -23, and -27 percentage points respectively. The greatest positive differences (squeeze on profits), on the other hand, were +19 and +11 percentage points, in Britain and Canada, respectively.

Devaluations complete the Nordic picture of expansionary fiscal policy and favoritism of profits. Relative unit labor costs convert unit labor costs in local currencies to US dollars. In local currencies, average OECD unit labor costs increased 35 percent from 1979 to 1983. Converted to US dollars, unit labor costs actually decreased 3 percent from 108 in 1979 to 105 in 1983 (where the 1970 level equals 100%). On average, Nordic unit labor costs dropped even more, 7 percent, from 108 to 101. The average, however, conceals polar differences between the Nordic countries. Relative unit labor costs in Denmark and Sweden, on the one hand, dropped 20 and 27 percent respectively, while relative unit labor costs in Finland and Norway, on the other hand, increased 9 and 4 percent, respectively, from 1979 to 1983.[6]

THE WORKINGS OF DEVALUATION

Devaluation, as adjustment policy, splits Denmark and Sweden from Finland and Norway. Devaluation, of course, makes the difference in the conversion of unit labor costs and export prices from local currency to common currency ("relative" costs and prices). It is no surprise that relative unit labor costs dropped sharply in Denmark and Sweden while increasing modestly in Finland and Norway, or that relative export prices increased in Finland but declined in Denmark and Sweden. What is not obvious, but which is related to devaluation strategy, is why Swedish-Danish export prices in local currencies increased 52-53 percent while Norwegian and Finnish prices rose only 32 and 42 percent, respectively, or why export prices rose so much faster than unit labor costs in Denmark and Sweden, while in Finland and Norway prices and costs increased at a fairly constant rate.

Sweden's devaluations were abrupt and very obvious. Sweden's bourgeois government devalued 10 percent on September 14, 1981, and a year later on October 8, 1982 the newly elected Social Democratic government devalued a further 16 percent, amid loud protests from Finland and Norway. Sweden's "effective" exchange rate (i.e., the trade-weighted average value of the crown against other currencies) dropped 20 percent from 1979 to 1983. Since the Swedish crown had appreciated about 6 percent from 1979 to the announcement of the first devaluation, the drop from September 1, 1981 to November 1, 1982 was closer to a full quarter of its value.

Denmark devalued 22 percent in the same period. But the value of the Danish crown slid slowly through the entire period, attracting only a fraction of the attention that accompanied the Swedish devaluations. The difference is that the Danes had to consult with its other West European partners in the European Monetary System (EMS) before the value of the crown could move outside a narrow range. For example, Denmark attempted to use the occasion of Belgium's 10 percent devaluation in March, 1982 to get approval for a cut of its own. Denmark's EMS partners rejected this demand, allowing only a token 3 percent devaluation. Sweden, on the other hand, could unilaterally realign its crown vis a vis a basket of currencies. It was precisely the unilateral character of the 1982 devaluation that upset Sweden's neighbors.

The Norwegian crown had appreciated nearly 20 percent from 1970 to 1977, having followed the German mark upward during the years that Norway had been a member of the European currency snake. Norway devalued within the snake in 1978 and then left the European exchange rate regime when it changed into EMS, with the value of the Norwegian crown still about 10 percent above its 1970 level. After 1979 the Norwegian and Swedish crowns tracked each other on an upward course for better than a year prior to Sweden's first devaluation. Norway's crown, buoyed by oil exports, continued to inch upward after Sweden's 1981 devaluation until the summer of 1982. Norwegian authorities then guided the crown downward until, with a final devaluation of 3 percent on September 6, 1982, the crown was about 10 percent below its July level. Then came the Swedish devaluation and the Norwegian crown bounced back up. The Norwegian crown oscillated up and down before returning to an upward path finishing in 1983 a couple of percentage points above its 1979 level, while the Swedish crown finished in 1983 20 percent below its 1979 level.

Norway devalued before Sweden's 1982 move and had its competitive gain wiped out. Finland had to devalue after the Swedish surprise in order to preserve its competitive position. The Finnish mark had depreciated about 15 percent in the three years prior to 1979 but then regained nearly 10 percent from 1979 until October 1982. When Sweden devalued, Finland quickly decided it had to follow. About 12 percent of Finland's trade is with Sweden directly, and about 35 percent of Finland's exports are forest products which compete against Sweden. Finland's effective exchange rate dropped 11 percent from September to November 1982. Against the Swedish crown, however, the Finnish mark had still appreciated.

These details should not obscure the main point: Denmark and Sweden substantially devalued after 1979. Denmark did so in a discreet manner; Sweden devalued in a particularly aggressive fashion. Sweden's Prime Minister, Olof Palme, detailed three adjustment strategies when he presented his government's program in November 1982. The first strategy involves expansion of domestic demand, the sort of policy his previous government had adopted in the mid-1970s to "bridge over" the first OPEC recession. However, according to Palme in 1982, in anything other than a short-term recession in world trade, this strategy feeds inflation, undermines export competitiveness, and soon flounders on current account deficits. The constraints on a small open economy eventually force a reversal of policy.

A second strategy, according to Palme, is contraction of domestic demand. Palme, a bit unfairly, claimed that the preceding bourgeois governments in Sweden sought to recover export competitiveness by cooling domestic demand and reducing inflation. Palme claimed that the only results were unemployment, under-utilization of industrial capacity, and a sinking standard of living. A reduction of domestic demand was not compensated by any increase in export demand. Palme's third strategy of course, was devaluation: "The increased export competitiveness as a consequence of devaluation will make it possible in the next year to make a definitive break with the downward trends in production, employment, and investment." The industrial recovery, which would permit the expansion of private and public service and protection of social welfare programs, is rooted in the "strengthening" of the export and import-competing sector. "Strengthening" in this context means restoration of profitability. A devaluation strategy poses several technical and political problems. The immediate effect is that import prices go up in local currency and export prices go down in foreign currencies. It is important that the devaluing country's terms of trade (ratio of export prices to import prices) go down, which at other times is unwelcome news. The principle is then that import volumes will go down in response to the increased prices and export volumes will go up in response to lower prices to foreign customers. Whether the volume changes are sufficient to offset the revenue per unit changes and make devaluation an eventual trade balance success, depends on the relative elasticities of demand regarding imports and exports. Even if devaluation successfully stimulates export demand, higher export volumes (at lower prices) can draw in higher priced imported materials, producing an offsetting foreign exchange flow. More certain, however, is that imports on order are immediately more expensive and that exports on order are immediately worth less in foreign exchange. Even assuming that volumes will adjust sufficiently, it takes time, during which there can be a substantial outflow of foreign exchange. Equally certain is that the local currency value of foreign debt must be marked up in the wake of a devaluation, and more domestic currency set aside to service it.

A government that chooses to bring domestic incomes into line with the value of national production by devaluing its currency must be prepared to reject demands for compensating income hikes. The increase in prices for imported goods feeds directly through to the cost of living, as expressed in the consumer price index. Workers find that their take-home pay buys less than before. Pensioners and others on fixed-incomes suffer a deterioration in real income. And businesses in the sheltered sector -- those which produce primarily for the home market and which face no significant import competition -- find that their costs have gone up and their sales have perhaps declined. If these domestic incomes are adjusted upwards, through an indexing scheme, for example, then the expected improvement of export competitiveness will be nullified. For devaluation to work, real incomes must fall.

The built-in discrimination between exposed and sheltered sectors means that enforcement of real income reduction is targeted on selected groups. The winners in a devaluation are producers in the exposed (export- and import-competing) sectors. Devaluation moves resources from the sheltered to the exposed sectors by making productive activity in the exposed sector more profitable. Import-competing businesses find that their competition has, in effect, raised prices. Exporters find that their prices to foreign customers lie below the prices of many of their competitors. And workers in these industries know that their employers can afford wage increases.

Devaluation works best when exporters raise their prices just enough avoid giving their profits away unnecessarily to their foreign customers (which would make them the chief beneficiaries of the devaluation), but not so much that they lose the volume increases necessary to maximize total revenues. Import-competing businesses likewise should seek that price where they take away the lion's share of the importers' customers without jeopardizing profits.

Import prices in Denmark and Sweden moved as intended. A comparison of changes in import prices and the consumer price index gives an indication of whether domestic prices increased on the coattails of the imported goods. Danish import prices during the years of greatest devaluation increased from 33 to 44 percent faster than the CPI, the index price of a basket of goods usually weighted heavily with goods from the sheltered sector. A slower relative increase of import prices would have indicated that domestic competitors were taking advantage of the import price increases to raise their own prices. Indeed, there may have been some catch-up by domestic businesses after the crown had stabilized in 1983 when import prices increased only half as much as the CPI. Likewise, import prices in Sweden in 1982 and 1983 rose much more sharply than the CPI, although the difference in 1983 was down from the previous year. Import prices, in Finland and Norway relative to the CPI, moved as expected for countries with appreciating currencies. Domestic prices, as reflected in the CPI, increased substantially more rapidly than import prices.

Export price changes (in local currencies) relative to changes in the CPI suggest that Danish and Swedish exporters cannot be accused of giving away their profits to foreign customers. Export prices in Denmark in 1981 and 1982 increased about 25 percent faster than the CPI, and in Sweden in 1982 and 1983 export prices increased 20 to 50 percent faster than the CPI. After the Danish crown levelled out in 1983, export price increases dropped to three-quarters of the CPI increase. The price constraint Danish exporters felt in 1983 was pressing all along on Finnish exporters. Export prices increased at a slightly lower rate than the CPI from 1980 on. Norwegian export prices, of course, are biased by the movements in the price of oil, first the price explosions in 1979 and then the slightly falling price. In 1982 and 1983, Norwegian export prices increased at only about half the rate of the CPI.

The record is clear. Devaluation opened the way for Danish and Swedish exporters to increase prices, and to increase prices at a faster rate than wages or other input costs. The squeeze on labor and the advantage to profits that I noted above are intended consequences of a devaluation strategy. Devaluation creates incentives for factors of production to move to the exposed sector but does not assure an equal distribution of the income gains between those factors, principally labor and capital. Profits come first. There is no guarantee that profits will trickle down to labor, especially when high unemployment biases the income distribution against labor.

Devaluation generally did not succeed in reducing import volumes. In only one of the five devaluation years (1980, 1981, 1982 for Denmark and 1982 and 1983 for Sweden) did the relative increase in import prices have a noticeable effect on import volumes, and that was 1980 in Denmark with the first shock of higher import prices. Sweden managed to reduce import volumes 6 percent in 1981, but that cannot be credited to devaluation. Finland also was able to cut import volumes by 6 percent in 1981, without the assistance of devaluation. Export volumes, on the other hand, responded positively to devaluation, even given the price taking of Danish and Swedish exporters. In each of the five devaluation years, exports increased faster than would otherwise have been expected. Again, however, Finland managed impressive export performance in 1979 and 1980 without devaluation.

The trade balance combines the effects of changing prices and volumes on the import and export sides. The summary judgment on Denmark's devaluation is mixed. Denmark did cut its trade balance deficit from 19 billion crowns in 1979 to 10 billion two years later, but the deficit climbed to 13 billion in 1982. The success story for Denmark's trade balance was in 1983, with a cut in the deficit to 4 billion crowns. This, however, had more to do with Palme's second strategy, contraction of domestic demand, than with a strategy of sliding devaluation.

Sweden's technical success is unequivocal. After a typical worsening of the trade balance in the first year, Sweden's trade balance has moved strongly into the black in 1983. The trade balance went from a deficit of 6 billion crowns in 1982 to a surplus of about 9 billion crowns in 1983. Political costs accompanied Sweden's technical success. Palme campaigned in 1982 on a platform of four election promises to restore the value of pensions, unemployment compensation, sick pay, and state subsidies to municipal child-care programs. His government delivered on the letter of the promises. Yet the spirit of the campaign promises was violated by the 16 percent devaluation, which increased the prices of imported goods by 16 percent, and a 1.3 percentage point increase in the value-added tax. Palme's government was laid open to charges of betrayal. Labor was mollified by a tax deduction on union dues, a jobs and public works program, and, most importantly (for union bosses), action on a wage-earners investment fund financed by profits. That was good enough for starters. Labor's demands in wage negotiations in general have been consistent with the devaluation strategy. But with the latest election behind it, labor's patience with accumulating profits can be expected to wear thin.

CONCLUSIONS

I return to the three questions I posed in the introduction. I have used much of this paper to describe the foreign positions and strategies of the Nordic countries after 1979 without directly evaluating the relative importance of internal and external factors. Any debate on whether external factors are important is fruitful. One might as well ask whether General Motors should try to sell cars or just see to it that staff cafeterias are stocked. Likewise, assertions that small open economies face peculiar problems are unrewarding. The distinctiveness of small open economies surely must be exaggerated when the Financial Times can use France as "an eloquent example of the limits to government action in a country which keeps its borders open to flows of capital and technology,"7 or when Paul Volcker can use language in Congressional hearings which could be confused with the concerns of a Danish central banker. This is not to say that openness is not important. On the contrary, nearly all industrial economies are so internationally integrated that the label of "open economy" is no longer distinctive.

If the question is whether domestic policy can make a difference, the answer is clearly yes. Devaluation obviously can make a difference. Contractionary domestic policy can work too, as can incomes policy. Under some circumstances, a policy of domestic expansion can work. Precisely how it will work depends on complementary measures and the country's starting political and economic situation. We can be even more certain that choice of strategy will make a difference in who wins and who loses.

This also answers the question of whether, given that domestic policy can be effective, countries are constrained to adopt the same domestic policy. Clearly not. Finland did not devalue as did Denmark and Sweden, nor does it have Norway's oil. Yet, Finland earned a positive balance on trade of goods and services (granted, offset by net interest payments on loans and repatriation of profits). Even if there were a final reckoning day for nations -- and there is not -- when their "bottom lines" had to balance, there would remain differences in who in the country would have to come up with the cash. Nations must adjust, more or less, but when and how they adjust, how efficiently they adjust, and who bears the distributive burdens of adjustment, are matters of political choice.

The second question is whether economic adjustment to the contingencies of the 1980s requires dismantlement of the welfare state. If governments so choose, they can dismantle the welfare state under the pretext of adjustment requirements. But this is not the question. If the question is whether governments can continue to pay transfer payments at the present or higher rates to larger proportions of the population, my answer is another "it depends". It depends, for instance, on whether expansion of government spending jeopardizes economic growth. It depends also on whether fiscal expansion worsens the trade balance by stimulating imports while saddling export industries with inflated labor and materials costs.

It is usually assumed in this sort of debate that transfer payments eat away at economic growth. This may be true if pensioners and unemployed workers mailorder expensive wines from France. More usually, however, transfer payments go into consumption, mostly of domestic goods, and a little into savings. That means that transfer payments end up as domestic wages, rents, and profits, and some money gets used to finance investment.

Note the significance of this simple observation. The challenge of the 1980s to welfare states lies in the international integration of markets. Fully integrated markets, especially with inflexible exchange rates, severely limit the extent to which individual countries can effectively stimulate their economies in recessions and contract in booms. It would be as if Michigan were to try to go it alone and stimulate its economy back to growth. How much of each dollar of additional state spending would be used to pay for lettuce from California, grapefruit from Texas, hotel rooms in Florida, brokerage fees in New York, and cars from Japan? On the other hand, if transfer payments or, better, government spending generally, does remain substantially in the domestic economy, it means that there is some scope for expansionary fiscal policy to stimulate domestic growth. Finland is not Michigan. Finland and the other Nordic countries may be able to use familiar counter-cyclic policy to generate domestic incomes. Even Michigan can affect where its spending dollar ends up. Road-building and local public works projects typically draw on local labor and materials and leave more in the state economy than many alternative uses. Government consumption also has a low import intensity compared to using tax relief to stimulate the consumption of high-income households or entice corporate expansion. The Nordic countries as well as the other smaller OECD countries clearly did not think that counter-cyclic policy was doomed to fail. As I pointed out above, the smaller OECD governments after 1979 pursued counter-cyclic policy in spite of the supposed futility of stabilizing a small open economy. It was the larger countries with supposedly greater capacity to operate a domestic economic policy which elected not to fight but to flow with the conjunctural streams.

Government spending which neither pays for itself in economic growth nor is covered by domestic borrowing or increased taxes, threatens to show up in the capital account as foreign borrowing and in the current account as debt service. Public sector deficits directly invoke a foreign economic constraint when they require foreign borrowing. The extent of foreign borrowing necessary is the deficit on the current account, which is equivalent to the shortfall of domestic savings. Gross domestic savings is what is left of income after consumption which can then be used for investment or lending to someone else. Sectors whose revenues are sufficient to cover their consumption and their own investment become suppliers of savings, or net lenders. Sectors which either have investment needs in excess of their own savings or are simply consuming in excess of their revenues become net borrowers. The government when it runs a deficit is a net borrower. If net borrowing exceeds net lending in an economy, the difference is made up by importing capital. Failure of fiscal policy to generate domestic recovery is now compounded by high domestic rates to attract foreign capital, nullifying an expansive monetary policy as a spur to recovery.

This is why the question of whether governments can implement counter-cyclic policy is critical. If governments can steer expansion of demand into domestic growth, continued welfare spending need not draw down the stock of lendable funds and so contribute to a balance of payments deficit. If they cannot, government deficits can directly affect the foreign balance.

Indirectly, government fiscal policy, including its welfare spending, affects the foreign balance through its effects on domestic incomes and prices. Stimulation of domestic demand which inflates domestic wages and prices disproportionately increases imports while pricing exports out of foreign markets. Deterioration of the trade balance then becomes the foreign economic constraint on increased welfare spending. Protectionism is attractive to some because it allows a government to pump up the domestic economy, increasing employment without drawing in imports. However, protectionism offers no solution for deterioration of export competitiveness. Devaluation, on the other hand, addresses the import side of the trade balance by making imported goods more expensive. This reduction of real national income is offset by increased economic activity attributable to the economy's lower relative prices, which, in turn, produces an increase in incomes in local currency.

Governments can respond to both the direct and the indirect foreign constraints on fiscal policy by targeting government spending on activities which have a low import intensity and holding a package of devaluation and wage-price controls in reserve. Exchange rate changes are the small countries' first line of defense against the integration of markets which threatens to deprive small countries of fiscal policy autonomy. Paradoxically, it is the openness of trade to other markets that makes devaluation and revaluation effective. Further, it is the stabilization of exchange rates which is thought to facilitate international trade.

Governments need to slow down welfare spending if: such spending leaks abroad and worsens the trade balance; devaluation is out of the question; protectionism is ruled out; and all possibilities of international coordination of recovery are exhausted. Military spending, for that matter, should be cut back under such circumstances. What about deficits? Deficits recycle savings. Deficits are worrisome: if the savings being recycled are foreign savings; or if the recycled savings are net lending that otherwise would have gone to investment in real capital that would lower unit costs in the production of goods for which there would be buyers. As pointed out before, government spending is not money put down a rat hole, except maybe when it goes to pay off foreign debts on consumption. Government spending takes money from a combination of private savings and household consumption, non-financial private corporations, and financial corporations and shifts it to wages, services, supplies, interest payments, debt retirement, loans to home buyers, development projects, and industrial reconstruction. Any evaluation of net gain or net loss must compare what actually happens with the money the government taxes, borrows, and spends with what the taxed and lenders would have done with it. Hasty responses that what the government does is necessarily suboptimal compared with private choices will not do. Studies must be done on a case-by-case basis, and even then they are so contaminated by violations of necessary conditions in mixed economies as to be technically unfeasible, leaving aside biases attributable to initial property and income distributions.

I suggest that reduction of welfare spending should not be a reflex action, regardless of its appeal to many. The alternative to welfare spending in slack economies is deflation. Deflation may slow the flow of imports, depending on whose incomes are hit, but it is hardly a solution to reducing the unit costs of export goods. Deflation means low turnover, low capacity utilization, low profits, and high unit costs. Other than reducing import demand, the sole rationale of deflation is wage bashing. Deflation invites revival of class antagonisms by relying on lengthening unemployment lines to sap the resolve of organized labor.

There are three things amiss with this discussion. One is the equation of the welfare state with generous spending on transfer payments. A common theme in this book is that the meaning of the welfare state may be something other than government spending. Granted, openness of markets may require some trimming of spending ambitions in times of international recession. But if, on the other hand, the welfare state is fundamentally about solidarity and equality, then the welfare state in economic hard times needs buttressing, not dismantlement.

A second casual assumption that may be amiss is that the external economy in the 1980s will continue to be depressed and that the domestic policy problem is to somehow stimulate the home economy when growth in the rest of the industrialized world remains stagnant. The last decade should have taught us not to extrapolate current trends without qualification. This is my qualification. Wars, domestic unrest, changes of governments, coincidence of elections, natural catastrophes, fading memories of inflation, and so forth can turn synchronized deflation to synchronized reflation.

This discussion can be faulted for dealing with symptoms and not the problem. I have taken adjustment of the home economy as the problem while the problem more properly is the appalling failure of governments to coordinate national policies. Deflation and reflation need not be simply synchronized in the OECD's use of the words, meaning disorderly and sometimes excessive, but synchronized in the sense of being mutually anticipated and coordinated. The appropriate home economy is not Belgium or Sweden but the larger OECD market. Political coordination has not kept pace with integration of markets. Unemployment is the visible consequence. The US is large enough to reflate autonomously but not large enough to avoid a huge trade deficit or to single-handedly reflate the European economies. France showed what can happen to a moderate sized country which breaks ranks and reflates -- both asynchronous and uncoordinated -- while Germany demonstrates the effects of synchronous but uncoordinated reflation. Neither model bears emulation.

The third question I anticipated in the introduction is whether the characteristic institutions of the Nordic welfare states facilitate or hinder adjustment. Put differently, do corporate institutions and corporate bargaining facilitate the adjustment of incomes between labor and capital, between exposed and sheltered sectors, and between present and future consumers? The question is one of comparative institutional performance and is central to evaluation of what we have come to think of as

Nordic social democracy. As important as the question is, the adjustment strategies of the Nordic countries of the last several years give little opportunity to for a definitive answer. By and large, the Nordic countries have not tested their corporate institutions in the most recent cycle. The most salient political fact of the last several years has been the restoration of parliamentarism, even when this has meant strong cabinet dominance as in Sweden. The retreat from corporate bargaining has been most apparent in the atrophy of tripartite labor-management-government wage and price determination. Quite naturally, the political rhetoric accompanying the shift from negotiated incomes agreements to "market" determination of wages and prices has been most colorful in Denmark and Norway, where bourgeois governments have succeeded social democratic administrations. Even in Sweden, though, the Palme Social Democratic government has disappointed or simply side-stepped the LO, the mostly blue-collar labor federation, on a number of occasions, despite the complaints of bourgeois newspapers and politicians that the government is beholden to it. Corporate incomes bargaining is out of favor in Nordic countries for the present. Closer analysis may show that it is not corporatism that is in suspension, but simply that tripartite balanced bargaining which enlists the political support and organizational brawn of labor to restrain wage costs in return for promises of jobs and investment. More common is exploitation of weak labor markets to under-cut labor's bargaining position. The aim seems to be a fundamental revision of wage-profit shares and wage structures. Corporatism in the sense of producer-government bargaining to regulate administered markets may be relatively unaffected.

NOTES

1. The Financial Times (February 1; 1984), p. 14.

2. The most familiar attempt to improve the services account is to limit the foreign exchange citizens can buy for foreign travel. French citizens in 1982 were enraged when they thought they were condemned to vacationing on the Riviera after the government applied restrictions on the foreign exchange citizens could buy for foreign travel. New Zealanders are told by their central bank that if they use credit cards abroad they face the possibility that the central bank will not approve the eventual claim on New Zealand dollars.

3. For reasons of comparability and standardization I draw heavily in OECD data in the following pages. In several instances I use also statistics prepared by the OECD staff. The principal source is OECD Economic Outlook, various numbers.

4. OECD Economic Outlook (No. 33), p. 17.

5. OECD Economic Outlook (No. 34: 1984), pp. 134, 148.

6. One currency which did not change against the US dollar, of course, was the US dollar. Unit labor costs in the US increased 31 percent, in common currency (US dollars) as well as in local currency (US dollars), compared to the average 3 percent drop in the OECD as a whole.

7. The Financial Times (March 1, 1984), p. 11.

VII.

Lennart J. Lundqvist

How Potent Is the Welfare State? Housing Policy Effects in Sweden

Commonly used as it is, the concept of "welfare state" at times seems to embrace almost any organized society on the globe. However, there are some common elements which constitute its essence. A social welfare state is based on certain values: equality, liberty, solidarity, and social security, to name the most central ones. The welfare state uses the collective powers of the state to redress the distributional inequity caused by unregulated markets. And the social welfare state tries to broaden citizen participation wherever decisions affecting them are made.[1]

Analytically, the welfare state is defined as providing a considerable degree of equality to its citizens in basic conditions of living as well as in actual participation in decision-making.[2] But if one concentrates on equality in basic living conditions, what policies and actions of the state do affect the distribution of welfare among citizens? Traditionally, social security and income maintenance programs have been emphasized. However, other interventions of the state affect the basic living conditions of individuals and groups, regardless of whether redistributive effects are sought or not.[3]

This certainly holds for the housing sector. Food, clothing, and shelter form a classic triad of basic living conditions. And if welfare policies are seen as results -- more or less stable -- of conflicts over what pattern of distribution should prevail, the area of housing certainly involves such conflicts of interest. Who should build and provide housing for whom, and on what terms?[4]

HOUSING POLICY AND THE DISTRIBUTION OF WELFARE: A FRAMEWORK FOR ANALYSIS

Conflicts over the distributive issues just mentioned are central to housing policy. In order to analyze the distributive effects of such policies, one must first develop more carefully the notion of which distributional conflicts are central to housing. Next, it is necessary to establish what the objects of state intervention are, as well as at which stages in the distribution of purchasing power and pricing of dwellings such interventions are made. Third, one must identify the measures taken to redistribute purchasing power or to manipulate dwelling prices. It is also necessary to account for measures having redistributive effects on housing. Fourth, there must be a discussion of the scope and intensity of welfare state intervention to allow us to hypothesize about the redistributive effects in housing.

Because new production is only a small portion of the already existing stock, housing policies must concern both new production and the use of the existing stock. Conflicts over housing thus concern both <u>production</u> and <u>consumption</u>. Three further dimensions of conflict can be identified. One has to do with the quantity and quality of residential benefits to be enjoyed by households and individuals, i.e. with housing standards. Another comprises the question of how, where, when, and by whom decisions should be taken and responsibilities assumed for housing decisions, i.e. the distribution of housing powers. The third relates to housing costs; "how should the sacrifices corresponding to the distribution of standards and powers be distributed over time and among different groups of citizens?"[5] Combining these dimensions, we arrive at a six-fold classification of the distributional conflicts giving rise to -- and affected by -- housing policies (see Figure 1).

If measures are taken to solve these distributional conflicts in housing, what should their targets be? Concentrating for a moment on standards and costs, two targets immediately present themselves, i.e, households and dwellings.[6] Measures can be taken to regulate the distribution of housing standards according to specific household criteria. Housing policy can change the households' purchasing power through, for example, housing allowances or tax regulations. Policy measures may also concern the distribution of standards, for example, by setting criteria on what an "appropriate" dwelling quality will be. This, in turn, may affect housing prices, especially if getting subsidies is made dependent on fulfilling the quality criteria for new housing production.

Of course, there are many other welfare state policies outside the housing sector which have effects on both the purchasing power of the households and the price of the dwellings. Social security transfers affect purchasing power. Price controls and interest rate regulations affect dwelling prices. Furthermore, welfare state policies of different kinds do affect the housing market, causing prices to fluctuate in ways which may or may not be intended by policy-makers. This points to the dilemma of policy evaluation: how does one determine the exact influence and effects of housing policy on the distribution of housing standards and costs? The most important thing to note here, however, is that interventions can be directed towards both household purchasing power and dwelling prices.

Figure 2 indicates that welfare state interventions in housing can be made at different stages, using many different measures. The explicit objective of housing allowances is to affect purchasing power with regard to housing. Allowances can be linked to household income and household size, as well as to specified housing standards. They may be fairly general with -- in principle -- all households above a certain size eligible for support. They may also be more specific, with individual means-testing of households who apply for the allowances.[7]

Factors of dwelling production -- land, materials, capital, and (to some extent, at least) labor -- can be subjected to price regulations. Direct production subsidies can be used; state "loans" may be written off immediately upon completion of the dwelling. Dwelling standard regulations do have upward or downward effects on dwelling production costs.

The capital costs of production affect housing consumption costs. By regulating the terms of the loans, the state influences the price of dwelling. The same is true for interest subsidies. Rent regulations -- "rent controls," "cost rents," "fair markets rents," etc. -- are often used to keep the price of dwellings down. Rent-setting practices, such as cost-pooling and rent-averaging, affect dwelling prices, and the distribution of costs among the households. Sales price regulations in the form of, for example, maximum prices for certain types of dwellings, lead to price levels other than those which would prevail in an unregulated market. Housing management costs may not be reflected in the price of the dwelling; the state can provide direct support to, maintenance and repair activities of ailing public housing companies.

The measures discussed so far can be linked clearly to effects on household purchasing power or on dwelling prices. However, when one looks at tax regulations, the effects are not determined. Regulations making it possible to deduct mortgage interests from taxable income increase a household's purchasing power by increasing the disposable income available for, say, housing consumption. Furthermore, this effect is more pronounced the higher the income of the household. This, in turn, affects the distribution of housing standards. It makes better quality dwellings -- which are usually more expensive -- look relatively "cheaper" to the high income households in terms of "net" price for housing consumption. Sales prices on the housing market adjust to these tax effects. The end result is a certain distribution of housing standards, which may correspond to what households with different purchasing powers can afford. Even if real estate taxes are linked to the assessed value of the dwelling, they affect households differently, depending on different marginal tax rates and different degrees of mortgaging. Capital gains taxes may, at least in principle, keep dwelling prices down. However, they can often be evaded by side-payments and other non-contractual agreements between seller and buyer. Furthermore, if sellers can evade the tax by investing their capital gain into another dwelling, their purchasing power is strengthened, and the dwelling prices may even increase over time. This would, of course, benefit those households who have more purchasing power as regards the distribution of housing standards.

It is the argument of this paper that inconsistencies in the use of housing policy measures and the effects of tax policies on housing prices and household purchasing power detract from the potential of welfare states to achieve a distribution of housing standards and housing costs consistent with that state's basic objective of equality. To assess the validity of this argument, we need a basis for judgment. It is necessary to know both the dominant principle of distribution in a country's housing policy, and the degree to which this principle permeates housing policy and the housing sector of the country.

Two opposite principles of distribution can be identified. Merit alludes to the households' ability to pay. With this principle that distribution of housing standards and costs is best which corresponds to the distribution of household purchasing power. Proponents of this principle generally accept the view that purchasing power is determined by the forces of a competitive market. Individuals do acquire unequal amount of wealth. They should also be allowed to follow their preferences as individual customers on the housing market, using their ability to pay to acquire whatever standard of housing they want. Need implies a different sort of criterion. It suggests housing standard requirements which define certain housing as lacking or "unfit". With a principle of need an "appropriate" housing standard can, and should be, identified by the welfare state. In other words, distribution according to need -- however this is defined -- implies welfare state interventions in the housing market to satisfy the preferences of its citizens -- expressed by citizens through politics -- concerning who should enjoy what standard, regardless of their ability to pay.[8]

Evidently, the scope and intensity of state intervention in housing may differ; the distributive principles just mentioned hint at the well-known distinction between _marginal_ (or residual) and _institutional_ welfare policies. Whatever the intensity and scope, however, the aim of the welfare state is to counteract the distributive effects of unfettered markets. In housing, the expected result would be decommodification of housing as a good. When judging the welfare state potential in this respect, both the actual scope and intensity of measures taken to decommodify housing, and the actual "degree to which goods are distributed according to need rather than ability to pay," must be examined.[9]

The definition just quoted is too broad, but also too narrow, to be useful in this context. It was developed for welfare state measures in general, not specifically for housing. It addresses only the household aspect (i.e., the socio-economic status of individuals), according to which distribution should proceed. As pointed out earlier, housing policies must also be directed towards dwellings. Furthermore, the use of "commodification" and "decommodification" as concepts in analyses of housing policies is problematic. First, there is a tendency to use an "empirical" definition: Owner-occupied housing is identified as commodified, and public rental -- non-profit -- housing as decommodified.[10] A related tendency is to make profit the dividing line; whenever someone makes a profit somewhere out of housing, we have a case of commodification or "privatization" in the housing sector.[11]

A definition of these distributive principles should not include what we expect to find by using these concepts in our analysis. Furthermore, the definition should include all the relevant aspects of housing that can be manipulated through a comprehensive welfare state housing policy. I attempt to make a comprehensive classification in Figure 3. In this figure I take the multi-faceted problems of distribution in housing into account. The three basic conflict dimensions (standards, powers and costs), are subdivided into different aspects. For each of the subdimensions of conflict, different distributive principles can be posited.

In other words, we are in a position to establish "ideal types" of commodification and decommodification. These are envisaged as opposite ends of a continuum of possible combinations of distributive principles. A situation where commodification prevails is distinguished by the following characteristics. Access to dwellings is based on merit (i.e., ability to pay). Space and equipment standards are biased; those who can pay get a better standard. The same is true for housing powers; ownership provides a far more comprehensive freedom of disposal and security of tenure than does tenancy. Costs tend to be distributed in a way which favors dwellings with restricted access and high standards. They also tend to be distributed in a way which favors households with a higher ability to pay. At the other end, we find a situation of decommodification. Need determines access. Standards, powers, and costs are distributed neutrally among dwellings, and incomes.

Now, an institutional welfare state policy towards housing can be defined as one in which measures are consistently arranged and used to achieve a distribution tending towards the decommodification end of the continuum. Need would be the leading distributive principle, together with income and tenure neutrality in the distribution of standards, costs and powers in housing. Measures to redistribute purchasing power for housing would cover a large part of the population, not just the "truly needy". Prices of most dwellings would be manipulated, not just a small quota designated for those in "real need".

However, even allegedly institutional housing policies may have their potential of redistribution thwarted. With a large number of values to be distributed among both dwellings and households, inconsistencies are bound to appear in a country's housing policy. For example, measures to distribute standards among dwellings in the housing stock and new production may be inconsistent with objectives and measures to redistribute housing costs among households. The effects of tax regulations may also confound intended housing policy effects.

Sweden provides a case in point. Ever since the introduction of the new "social" housing policy after World War II, the intention has been to provide well-equipped, modern, spacious dwellings to _all_ households at reasonable costs. Space is defined _as a_ minimum standard which may seem modest to some observers; there should not be more than two persons per room (with the kitchen and living room excluded). If this space standard is not achieved, there is "over-crowding". The costs of housing should be such that a family with "normal" income should be able to enjoy the minimum space standard without the support of housing allowances. It is also an explicit objective that housing costs should be tenure neutral; dwellings of the same "use value" should cost the same, regardless of tenure. To achieve these objectives, state interventions in housing finance cover all housing production, regardless of tenure. At the same time, measures are differentiated to achieve true tenure neutrality in the distribution of costs. Housing allowances are given to all households within specified income brackets, regardless of what tenure they are living in. At issue, then, is whether this "institutional" housing policy has resulted in a distribution of standards and costs resembling the decommodification end of our distributive continuum.

SWEDEN"S HOUSING POLICY: THE MAIN MEASURES OF REDISTRIBUTION

Under the present system of housing finance, all dwellings can have part of their production costs covered by subsidized state loans. These subsidies cover part of the payable interest, including that on the first mortgage. The portion covered is largest in the first year, and then gradually diminishes. The rate of decrease is more rapid for owner-occupied dwellings than for rental ones, the objective being to neutralize the tax effects of mortgage interest deduction for homeowners. State loans are also differentiated among tenures and owner categories in terms of the percentage of production costs covered by such subsidized loans. The first mortgage is 70 percent, and state loans cover between 22 and 30 percent, depending on tenure and owner category. Private rental housing is least favored while public rental housing is most favored with 100% percent of its production costs covered by subsidized loans.[12]

Indeed, public rental housing has been used as a vehicle for providing and distributing dwellings in accordance with policy objectives. Run on a non-profit basis, the Municipal Housing Companies provide housing for people regardless of their level of income. The system of rent-setting is geared towards lowering rents. First, the costs of a company's total stock are pooled and the necessary rent incomes determined. Next, the rents are averaged so that dwellings of the same standard have the same rent, regardless of age. This system of rent-setting is supposed to achieve two things. First, the non-profit character of the companies keeps the general rent level down. Second, the rent-averaging makes it possible to hold down the rents for newly produced, and thus more expensive dwellings. Furthermore, the principle of "similar utility value" is also applied to private rental dwellings. Dwellings in that stock thus cannot cost more to rent than dwellings of the same standard in the non-profit public stock.[13] In recent years, public housing companies have demanded heavy rent increases to be able to keep housing standards at an acceptable level. This has caused Bourgeois and Social Democratic Governments to give extra support to public housing. From 1979 to 1981, subsidized state loans to maintenance and repair totalled 1.4 billion Swedish Kronor. For 1983, the state subsidized public housing loans on the financial market up to a total of 0.9 billion Swedish Kronor.[14]

The increase in public housing's share of the Swedish housing stock has indeed been remarkable. In 1945, the total stock comprised 2.1 million dwellings. Only 4 percent constituted public rental housing. During the next 35 years, the public rental stock increased to more than 750,000 dwellings, constituting approximately 20 percent of the total stock of 3.8 million dwellings,. During the same period, the number of private rental dwellings remained about the same, or around 700,000-750,000. Indeed, public housing took the brunt of the Million Dwelling Program from 1965 to 1974. It represented 37 percent of the one million dwellings completed, and its annual share of new multi-family housing production remained above two-thirds.

As just described, public rental housing is allocated according to need rather than ability to pay. No capital input is required, and the whole cost of production is subsidized. The increase in such housing could be interpreted as a trend towards decommodification. At the same time, however, there has been a concomitant and growing increase in the number of new owner-occupied homes. This trend was especially marked in the 1970's. By 1980, this form of housing -- which requires capital inputs for access, and has high total costs -- represented 1.6 million dwellings, or 43 percent of the total stock.[15]

In 35 years, the Swedish housing stock thus increased from 2.1 to 3.8 million dwellings. Huge state subsidies were provided. Direct state coverage of mortgage interest quadrupled between 1975 and 1981, going from 1.8 to 7.2 billion Swedish Kronor. It is remarkable that in the same period, housing production decreased. The explanation seems to be that production of rental dwellings fell off much more rapidly than production for home ownership.

Since total production costs for the latter are larger, and since production costs in housing have risen very rapidly, it is only natural that the increase in state expenditures has been so marked.

The state also supports housing consumption through housing allowances, which are provided to retired people as well as to families with children. Between 1975 and 1981, such household support doubled from 3.1 to 6.0 billion Swedish Kronor.[16] When comparing these figures with those for direct interest subsidies, it becomes clear that some rapid change has taken place in the last years. While housing allowances accounted for almost two thirds of the main direct governmental subsidies to housing in 1975, their share constituted only 45 percent of state expenditures for the main direct forms of subsidies in 1981.

We have indicated that government also supports housing indirectly. The major form of such indirect support is the homeowners' right to deduct mortgage interest payments from their taxable income. Technically, this was never deliberately intended as a redistributive measure in housing. In practice, however the tax effects of deductions are formidable agents in redistributing housing standards and costs. Before taking these effects into account, however, we should look at the present distribution of housing standards -- in terms of space -- within the existing stock of Swedish housing, and among different types and categories of households.

THE DISTRIBUTION OF SPACE IN DIFFERENT TYPES OF HOUSING IN SWEDEN

Is there any visible trend towards more spacious housing in Sweden, following the introduction of the modern "social" housing policy after 1946-47? If so, is it distributed equally or unequally among dwellings with different principles of access? In other words, have policy intentions become housing reality? As pointed out earlier, the total housing stock amounted to around 3.8 million dwellings in the early 1980's. In the preceding three decades, 2.3 million new dwellings were produced. It is thus appropriate to say that the housing production of the last 30 years represents the dominant part of the housing available to the population.

Up to 1971/72, housing production was dominated by small dwellings. More than two thirds consisted of dwellings with three (or fewer) rooms and a kitchen; 40 percent of the dwellings produced had only two rooms (or fewer) and a kitchen. Beginning in 1971, there was a quite visible break in the earlier pattern. Dwellings with four or more rooms and a kitchen increased their share very rapidly. By

1977/78, they accounted for 70 percent of all new production. After 1979, smaller apartments have again increased their share, but they still have not reached more than 40 percent. It is notable that these rapid shifts in new housing production toward more spacious dwellings occurred at the same time that total production decreased. Between 1972 and 1981, the annual number of new dwellings was cut in half, or from 104,000 to 51,500.[17] This certainly has had an impact on the composition of the housing stock with respect to space standards. Dwellings with four rooms or more have increased their share of the housing stock from 29 percent in 1970 to almost 40 percent in 1981.[18] This important shift in new housing production in the 1970's coincides with another. The earlier dominance of dwellings in multi-family housing was broken. Beginning in 1972, the share of one- and two-family homes in new production rose rapidly, from 30 percent in 1971 to 70 percent in 1976 and to almost 75 percent in 1978. Their share remains a significant 60 percent in 1981.[19]

Under certain circumstances, such a shift could have important consequences for the distribution of housing standards: (1) if the increase in dwellings with many rooms is concentrated to the one- and two-family housing sector; and (2) if that sector is guided by the principles of commodification rather than decommodification. As it turns out, the composition of new housing production in the one- and two-family homes sector has been dominated by dwellings with four rooms (or more) and a kitchen. Indeed, such dwellings have represented 85 percent or more of new production in this sector since the mid-1960's. The overall production boom of the 1970's in this sector was accompanied by an increase in space standards. Dwellings with five, six or more rooms increased their share to more than 50 percent after 1972/73.[20] The multi-family housing sector reveals a quite different pattern. After falling from more than two thirds of new production in the early 1950's, new production of dwellings with two or fewer rooms and a kitchen remained, on the average, more than 50 percent throughout the period. Dwellings with four or more rooms and a kitchen have never represented more than 15 to 20 percent of new dwellings in multi-family housing.[21]

The figures for new production in the last three decades are indeed telling. Of the 2.3 million dwellings produced, 37 percent had four or more rooms and a kitchen. However, only about 12 percent of the new dwellings in multi-family housing were of that size. While more than 700,000 of these more spacious dwellings were built in the one- and two-family housing sector, only around 170,000 were produced in the multi-family housing sector. Total figures for the respective sectors were 850,000 and 1,450,000 dwellings.[22] The implication is clear; families with greater need for housing space would find it much more difficult to obtain adequate space in the multi-family housing sector, and much easier if they settled for a home rather than a flat. At issue, then, is which distributive principle is dominant in each sector of housing.

There is a very clear pattern in this respect. In the one- and two-family homes sector, owner occupancy and cooperatives have held around 95 percent of new production throughout the last 30 years. These tenures require capital inputs for access, while rental tenure does not. In multi-family housing, cooperatives have constituted 25 percent of new production throughout the period. Public rental housing's share increased from 50 to 70 percent during the Million Dwelling Program years. Lately, its share has fallen off, while that of cooperatives has increased. For private renting, the share has decreased throughout the period.[23]

These trends in multi-family housing are quite interesting from the viewpoint of distributive principles. As was shown above, public rental housing seems to present a close approximation to a distribution according to need. No capital is needed for access. No profit is made from rent incomes. In cooperatives, capital is needed for access, but rents are set so that they only cover costs. Cooperative dwellings can be bought and sold at market prices and can thus be hard to come by for lower income households. As for private renting, rents are set according to the "utility value principle", with non-profit public housing as the price-leading sector. However, private landlords can -- and do -- make a profit from renting. Furthermore, housing allocation in the private rental sector goes through the Municipal Housing Exchanges to a much lesser degree than is the case for public rental housing. Thus, the principles of allocation are probably not as neutral in relation to tenant income as they are in the public rental sector.[24]

In summary, there was substantial growth in space standards in Swedish housing in the 30 years up to 1981. This growth was particularly pronounced during the 1970's. Furthermore, it was to a large extent concentrated to the one- and two-family homes sector. In 1980, 62 percent of the dwellings in this sector had four or more rooms. At the same time, 59 percent of the dwellings in multi-family housing sector had only two rooms (or three) and a kitchen.[25] The growth has been <u>tenure</u> biased. Space standards have grown most rapidly in dwellings where access is governed by <u>ability to pay</u> rather than <u>need.</u> But has the growth also been income biased? Does the distribution of standards among households follow a more neutral pattern, and if so, is this the result of the "social" housing policy?

THE DISTRIBUTION OF HOUSING SPACE STANDARDS AMONG DIFFERENT TYPES OF HOUSEHOLDS IN SWEDEN

The number of households in Sweden increased by almost half a million in the 1970's reaching 3.5 million in 1980. This increase is mostly due to the splitting up of larger households. One- and two-person households increased from less than 1.7 to 2.25 million between 1970 and 1980, i.e. to 64 percent of all households. Families with four or more persons decreased from 26 to 21 percent of all households. The share of very large households (five persons or more), was cut from 9 to 6 percent of all households.[26]

Figure 4 shows that overcrowding -- defined as the share of households having more than two members per room, kitchen and living room excluded -- decreased from almost half a million to less than 150,000 households during the 1970's. At the same time, high standard of housing space -- defined as the share households enjoying more than one room per member, kitchen and living room excluded -- more than doubled. In 1980, more than 900,000 Swedish households were enjoying this high standard of housing space. Indeed, the pattern revealed by analyses of the regular census is one of rapidly increasing housing standards. During the last two decades, overcrowding has decreased from 35 to less than five percent among Swedish households. In the same period, the share of households enjoying high housing space standards increased from less than 10 to more than 25 percent.[27]

Analyses of the "Level of Living" surveys done by the Stockholm Institute for Social Research also seem to confirm that standards of housing space have indeed increased in Sweden during the last decades. The data base is unique. It includes panel data, the core of the survey covering the same people for three years (1968, 1974, 1981). It thus provides a great opportunity to follow the dynamics of the distribution of housing standards in the population. In 1968, 15 percent enjoyed high space standards, while 18 percent were overcrowded. By 1981, 30 percent enjoyed high standards of space, while only three percent were overcrowded.[28]

But is this increase in housing standards tenure neutral? In order to enjoy high standards, households quite clearly have to move into dwellings where money determines access. Seventy-eight percent of singles in owner occupancy enjoyed high standards of housing space in 1978, as compared to 11 percent in tenancy and 20 percent in cooperatives. Forty six percent of the families with one child living in owner occupancy enjoyed high space standards, as compared to only 3 percent in cooperatives and tenancy. Indeed, larger families are more prevalent in owner occupancy. Households with four or more members constitute 40 percent of all homeowners, but only 10 percent of all households in cooperatives and tenancy.[29]

This tenure-biased distribution of dwellings with high standards makes it necessary to have money for access. Thus, the distribution of households with different incomes, but similar needs for housing space, among different types of sizes of dwellings becomes of great interest. Can we find out if distribution is income-biased too? The "Level of Living" data classifies households according to "social group", the basic principle of categorization being the occupation of the head of household. Frykman's analysis, which is relied upon here, uses eight classes. The Roman numerals in Figures 5 and 6 should be read as follows; I corresponds roughly to upper class, II to middle, and III to lower class in terms of socio-economic characteristics. (See Figures 5 and 6.)[30]

The data reveal a very differentiated development of space standards among different socio-economic classes from 1968 to 1981. It is clear that blue collar workers are more often overcrowded, and enjoy high standards less often than do upper and middle class white collar employees. This is true not only for working, but also for retired households. Lower class retired households more often live with normal, and less often with high housing standards, than the average for all households. There are also some interesting differences over time among working households. Blue collar workers have escaped overcrowding; in fact, this category is the only one increasing its share in normal standards. They have not, however, moved into high standard housing in the same way upper and middle class white collar employees have been able to do. Is this connected, in any way, to the housing careers of different socio-economic groups in terms of their living in dwellings with different principles of access? The answer seems to be in the affirmative. Blue collar workers decreased their share of all households. Their distribution among different types of tenures changed very moderately. However, they constituted the only category increasing its share of households in tenancy, (i.e., need accessible but often low space standard housing). During the same period, the share of homeowners increased among upper and middle class households (white collar employees I and II, and employers II --see Table 1).31

These differences between the lower and other classes are borne out even more clearly in Table 1. White collar employees (II) were the ones who purchased money accessible owner occupancy housing from 1968 to 1981. Every second new homeowner came from this category. In fact, 8 out of 10 new homeowners came from the middle or upper class households (white collar employees I and II, and employers). In contrast, only 1 out of 25 new homeowners came from the blue collar working class. Furthermore, the increase in home-ownwership among working class households was concentrated in households with children, while the increases among middle and upper class households also included other types of households. It is also notable that this limited increase in working class home-ownwership was far less pronounced than for other categories. Blue collar working class families with or without children were close to the average rate of home-ownwership in 1968, but were lagging behind in 1981. The other actively occupied classes in most cases had home-ownwership rates above the average in 1981.32

This concentration of upper and middle class households in owner occupancy has certain implications for the household income profiles in need and money accessible housing. Table 2 shows that high income earners dominate among homeowners, and those with lower incomes among tenants. From our point of view, this becomes all the more interesting when one compares the distribution of housing standards among households with similar needs for housing space but different amounts of money to spend on housing. Figure 7 shows the share of different income brackets for families with one and two children, and living in different forms of tenure. Quite obviously, there are differences. High income families are predominately found in owner occupancy. Low income families of the same size are mostly living in rental tenure.

In summary, there has been a remarkable improvement in housing space standards for Swedish households in the last two decades. Overcrowding of households has declined from about 33 to only 3 percent. The share of households enjoying high space standards has increased to nearly one third of all households. By 1976, Sweden had the highest number of dwellings per 1,000 inhabitants in Europe (431 per 1,000). During the 1960's and 1970's, the size of dwellings increased fastest in Sweden. From 1961 to 1977, average useful floor space in new dwellings increased from 69 to 113 square meters. Comparative figures for West Germany, which came closest to Sweden, were 73 to 96 square meters. As a 1980

European Community report points out, it should be remembered that the rapid increase in dwelling size taking place after 1970 coincided with the very swift increase in the share of single family homes in new construction. In fact, no other nation in Western Europe experienced such a shift as the one taking place in Sweden.[33]

The growth of housing space is, however, unevenly distributed among Swedish households. Working class people are still more often overcrowded, and less often enjoy high space standards. Two things seem of crucial importance in this context: the distribution of space standards among dwellings with different forms of access; and the income distribution among different socio-economic groups. Spacious dwellings dominate in owner occupancy, where money determines access, but form only a limited part of the rental stock, where the dominant principle for access is need. Since access to high standard housing is made very much dependent on the economic resources of the households in need of spacious dwellings, it is only natural that the distribution of such dwellings seems to follow the pattern of ability to pay rather than that of need. From the viewpoint of housing policy, these patterns could perhaps be justifiable, if housing costs really followed housing standards. At issue, then, is whether housing policy support is tenure neutral and income neutral. Do dwellings with the same space standard cost the same, regardless of housing tenure or household income? As we shall see, this is not necessarily the case in Sweden.

THE DISTRIBUTION OF HOUSING COSTS AMONG SWEDISH HOUSHOLDS

The housing policy in force since 1974 spells out two objectives for housing costs. First, families with "normal" incomes should be able to enjoy the space standard appropriate for their particular household size. Second, housing support from the state should be "tenure neutral", or rather, "neutral to type of housing". Households needing five rooms and a kitchen should absorb the same costs for that standard regardless of whether they live in a one-family home or in a flat in a multi-family building, and regardless of whether they are owner-occupiers or tenants.[34]

The second objective is of utmost importance here. Is the present policy actually neutral to types of housing or forms of tenure? Or are some forms of housing favored, thereby favoring the households who manage to get into such housing? Since we are primarily concerned with space standards here, let us compare the distribution of housing costs among families with children (households with an objectively measurable need for housing space). The data available for such a comparison can be drawn from the Housing Standards and Housing Cost surveys made in 1978. Comparability is not complete: renters' expenditures on electricity are not included, neither are their individual expenditures on maintenance and repairs to their flats. As for homeowners, the value of their own work on the house is not estimated.

The 1978 survey indicated that more than two out of three families with children live in owner-occupied housing. The socio-economic pattern described earlier is again visible; homeowners had much higher gross incomes than renters. However, homeowners also had much higher gross expenditures for housing; they were almost twice as high as those for average renters with children. This is reflected in the much higher gross housing expenditures/gross income ration for homeowners. On the other hand, homeowners have a very large difference between gross and net housing expenditures, the latter being less than two thirds of the former. As a result, the ratio of net housing expenditures to gross income was about 12 percent for the average 1978 homeowner with children. For the renter, the net housing expenditures/gross income ratio was percent. On this score, then, homeowners and renters came out approximately even at the end of the 1970's. However, it should not be overlooked that the actual net expenditures were larger for homeowners.[35]

It cannot be said for certain, however, that any group is favored as long as the size of dwellings is not controlled for. It may well be that the differences between money and need accessible housing depend very much on this variable. However, further analysis of the 1978 data seem to confirm the original pattern. Homeowners have higher gross incomes than renters for all dwelling sizes. Their gross expenditures, and the differences between gross and net expenditures, are larger than for renters. In some cases, the end result is striking. For families with children, living in four rooms and a kitchen, the net expenditures/gross income ratio is almost the same, regardless of whether their housing is need or money accessible; 11 percent for renters and 12 percent for homeowners. Evidently, homeowners enjoy a lowering of gross expenditures not experienced by renters in comparable dwellings.[36]

The analysis can be taken one step further by looking at the space standard actually enjoyed by renting and homeowning families with children. According to the survey data, the number of room units (kitchen included) per 100 persons for families with children was 115 in tenancy, and 145 in owner occupancy. If we combine all the items in this discussion, we find that for families with two children, the average net cost per room unit for renters was 2,100 Kroner, as compared to 2,250 Kroner for homeowners. The corresponding gross figures were 2,500 and 3,700 Kroner, respectively. We must conclude that tenure is crucial in determining how standards and costs are distributed among Swedish households. First, we have seen that one-family housing is the type which offers the best standard in terms of space. Indeed, larger families have very little to choose from in terms of spacious dwellings in other forms of tenure than owner-occupied one-family homes. Second, we have seen that this type of housing is almost exclusively distributed according to ability to pay, the dominant tenure being owner-occupancy. Third, we have seen that such housing is expensive in terms of gross expenditures. Not only must the family find money to buy the house -- something which at least in the existing stock may require considerable amounts of savings or money acquired by other means -- but it must also have a high and sustainable income to meet the monthly gross expenditures. Fourth, we have found that home-ownership has spread most rapidly among the upper and middle classes. They are the ones who have settled in the many new and spacious homes produced during the latter part of the 1970's. Fifth, we have shown that home-ownership enjoys a much larger difference between gross and net housing expenditures than does tenancy. Housing costs are reduced much more for economically resourceful households, since they dominate among homeowners. Thus, such households not only enjoy a higher standard but also a relatively more favorable net/gross expenditures ratio.

Nor do the benefits end here. Ownership means legal title to real estate. A house can be sold on the housing market, at whatever price the owner can get. No such option is open to the tenant. So while the homeowner can enjoy a capital gain from his house, the tenant cannot. This factor must be taken into account when housing cost distribution is analyzed. In times of rapidly rising prices for family homes, the owners can look forward to considerable capital gains. If these are taxed only slightly or not at all, the homeowner's housing costs may turn out to be quite different from gross expenditures. Even with an effective capital gain of less than 40 percent, the owner of an average-sized house broke even in terms of final housing costs in 1978. Actually, the final housing costs of home-ownership were transformed into a benefit from 40 percent and upwards in the effective capital gain, assuming such market value increases as those common in the 1970's.[37] Furthermore, if one applies this analysis to the families with children we have looked at earlier, some interesting trends appear. For homeowners living in homes of 86 - 100 square meters (or roughly 3 rooms and a kitchen), the break-even point came when effective capital gain was 38 percent of the market value increase. For owners of larger homes (161 - 180 square meters, or 6+ rooms and a kitchen), the break-even point came even earlier at an effective capital gain of 28 percent.[38] Since we have already shown that the owners of such large homes also have a higher ability to pay from the beginning, the conclusion must be made that the final distribution of housing costs is very unequal. Those with the best ability to pay enjoy the highest standard, and, in relative terms, they have the smallest costs.

Admittedly, such a conclusion cannot be based only on observations from two years. However, data provided by official sources show similar patterns and trends over the entire period from 1958 to 1980. Regardless of whether one looks at running prices, or uses 1978 prices as a basis, the differences in final housing costs for renters and homeowners have increased up to the early 1980's. The trend was especially marked after 1970.[39]

The picture seems clear. Housing standards and housing costs are not distributed according to the principle of need. On the contrary, they seem to have become increasingly distributed according to ability to pay. High space standards -- admittedly investing high gross housing expenditures -- have, to an increasing extent, been enjoyed by the upper and middle class households. At the same time, this high standard has been increasingly concentrated to that part of the housing stock where money is the key to access (i.e., owner occupancy). With owner occupancy one can expect a considerably larger reduction of gross housing expenditures, making homeowners come out almost even with renters in net terms. In addition, homeowners can look forward to capital gains which further decrease their final housing costs.

THE IMPACTS OF HOUSING POLICY ON THE DISTRIBUTION OF STANDARDS AND COSTS IN SWEDISH HOUSING

Given this picture, we can look more closely into the impacts of Swedish housing policy. Why is one of the most "advanced" welfare states not powerful enough to impel a trend towards decommodification in housing? Why is it that policy intentions do not become housing realities? The tentative answer formulated earlier in this paper is that inconsistencies in housing policy and its implementation, compounded by the double-edged effects on dwelling prices and household purchasing power stemming from tax policies, undermine the aim of achieving an equitable distribution of housing standards and housing costs.

The most glaring inconsistency in Swedish housing policy concerns the distribution of housing space standards. Despite the objective of providing spacious dwellings for all at reasonable costs, larger dwellings have not been distributed neutrally among tenures. Public rental housing has been favored when it comes to housing finance. Subsidies have covered all production costs, and have disappeared at a slower rate than for owner occupancy. Rents have been determined on a non-profit basis. It thus seems fair to say that this form of housing comes closest to the distributional formula of decommodification. The opposite holds for owner occupancy. Money is necessary for access. Gross housing costs are high. Homes can be bought and sold at market prices, and the ability to pay determines what standard a homeowner can get. Thus, owner occupancy seems to come closest to the distributive formula of commodification.

The key is that larger dwellings have been produced almost totally within the <u>owner-occupied</u> sector. The average share of 4- and 5-room dwellings and larger has been close to 90 percent throughout the period after 1960. In public rental housing, the average share for such apartments has been as low as 12 percent. The distribution of space standards among dwellings has thus been severely tenure-biased. This bias has been such that it is reasonably correct to talk about a trend towards commodification of housing space in Sweden. High space standard has been concentrated in dwellings where the principle of access is ability to pay.

This inconsistency has been especially marked after the 1974 housing policy decision. Then, the Million Program with its enormous production of public rental housing came to an end. At the same time, however, the objective of appropriate standards for all at affordable costs was retained. What really changed in 1974 was the way in which appropriate standard was to be determined. During the Million Program years, the increase in space standards was determined by collective choice; every household should enjoy the space standard recognized as minimum by the Parliament. By 1974, this had been reached by a majority of the households. Instead of deciding on a new, and higher minimum standard, the Parliament retained the existing one. Consequently, space standard increases would be left to individual choice. At the same time, however, the system of finance was set up in such a way that <u>all</u> housing would be subsidized, thus including housing with higher standards than the official minimum.[40]

Still, this would not explain the increasing concentration of production to the one-family homes sector, especially since the system of housing finance set up in 1974 explicitly strived towards tenure neutrality in cost distribution. However, the objective of neutrality was based on somewhat shaky assumptions. It presumed a small difference between market levels and subsidized levels of interest. Furthermore, the break-even point between owner-occupancy and tenancy would come at a marginal tax rate which was set remarkably low already when the system of finance was introduced. Rising interest rates, and higher marginal tax rates, could tip the balance in favor of owner-occupancy.

This is what happened during the 1970's and early 1980's. With inflation, interest rates increased, thereby increasing the sum deductible from taxable income. Incomes also increased with inflation. More and more households experienced higher marginal tax rates, since state income taxes are progressive. Furthermore, inflation led to soaring production prices for new homes. This also contributed to larger interest payments, and thus to larger sums deductible from taxable income. No wonder, then, that the indirect governmental support to housing through the tax effect of mortgage interest deductions became the fastest increasing support to housing in Sweden in the later part of the 1970's. From 1975 to 1981, this support more than quadrupled, going from 2.7 to 11.5 billion Kroner.

Even if one looks only at the development of interest subsidies in the system of housing finance, one may question whether tenure neutrality is achieved. From 1977 to 1981, total subsidies to owner-occupancy more than tripled, while subsidies to tenancy and cooperatives less than doubled. If one looks at the average subsidy per dwelling, the following pattern is revealed. For owner occupancy, the increase was 90 percent in the four-year period. As for tenancy, the increase in average dwelling subsidy was less than 40 percent.[41] This occurred despite a more rapid growth in production costs for rental housing during the period. It would seem as if housing policy did not achieve tenure neutrality with regard to the costs of new dwellings. To some extent, this is due to inconsistency between policy objectives and the techniques used to achieve them; housing policy just has not been aggressive enough in tackling the problems of housing finance caused by inflation and increasing interest rates.

Housing policy inconsistencies aside, the most formidable agents in redistributing housing standards and costs have been the tax regulations. These have made distribution both tenure and income-biased. Tenure bias derives from the fact that only owner occupancy offers households the possibility of deducting part of the housing costs (the mortgage interest payments) from taxable income. Income bias derives from the fact that deductions -- up to the 1983-85 tax reform -- were "worth more" to those with higher incomes because the tax effect of deductions increases with higher marginal tax rates.

Table 3 illustrates these effects. If a household with an income somewhat above average could choose among dwellings of equal standard, it would be foolish to opt for rental tenure. Admittedly, gross housing expenditures are higher. But of far more importance to the household, is the fact that the net (and thus final) housing costs are lower, even in the first few years, when no effective capital gain can be made. Thus, the tax effect explains the large differences between gross and net housing expenditures found typical of home-ownership. Cost distribution becomes tenure-biased.

The household income bias of housing cost distribution in the late 1970's illustrated in Table 4. The familiar pattern from above is again visible: the higher the income, the more prevalent was home-ownership. Furthermore, the higher the income, the more common were deductible deficits from home-ownership. These deficits increased with income. In turn, this led to larger tax effects the higher the income of the household. Since we have shown earlier that the higher income earners also have the highest housing standards, we must again conclude that they have been favored when it comes to the distribution of housing costs. Tax regulations tend to put owner occupancy in a more advantageous position than other tenures. Before the 1983-85 tax reform they also tended to favor households with higher incomes. Their purchasing power was relatively more increased by the effects of mortgage interest deductions than that of households with lower incomes. Housing costs thus become distributed in an income biased manner.

This analysis seems to show that housing policy inconsistencies, compounded by the effects of tax regulations, did lead to a situation in Swedish housing in the early 1980's much closer to commodification than decommodification. There has been a remarkable increase in housing standards, but the distribution is clearly tenure and income-biased. The same is true for the distribution of housing costs. We are forced to conclude that these features have detracted so much from the potential of housing policy that the equitable distribution sought has not been achieved.

HOUSING AND THE FUTURE OF THE WELFARE STATE: WHAT PRICE DECOMMODIFICATION?

The issue arising from the developments just described is two-fold. Is any welfare state able to reverse the trend towards commodification and bring the distribution of housing standards and costs more in line with the principles of equality and solidarity? Or is the development in housing leading to a reemergence of a class society, hostile to these values? Is the welfare state -- through housing -- literally building its own mausoleum? In some thought-provoking essays, Jim Kemeny has argued that what has here been called the commodification of housing should be seen as one of the central elements -- if not *the* central one -- in the process of privatization now visible in many welfare states. The privatization results in a lessening of support for collectivist solutions to social welfare issues.[42] One implication which could be drawn from this analysis is that efforts by welfare state proponents to alter the pattern of distribution now emerging stand very little chance of success; political support for the welfare state is declining as home ownership and commodification proceeds in housing as well as other parts of society. Great Britain seems to be a case in point. Following their victory in the 1979 elections, the Conservative Government launched one of its few popular "privitization" policies. Public housing tenants were granted the right to buy their dwellings for owner occupancy, at the same time as subsidies to housing were cut more than any other program of social welfare. In 1982 alone, more than 200,000 council house dwellings were sold to tenants.[43]

What about Sweden? Unfortunately, the evidence provides no definite answer. Admittedly, there seems to be a negative correlation between a high share of owner-occupied dwellings in new production and voter support for the Social Democrats (i.e., the principal architects of the Swedish welfare state). The correlation is, however, quite weak and the pattern differs between regions.

The tendency seems to be that the more ardent proponents of privatization and commodification (the Moderate Conservatives), gain most where owner occupation constitutes the largest share of new housing. This is especially true for metropolitan areas. However, the Social Democrats have experienced their largest gains in communes with high owner occupancy shares outside the metropolitan areas. At the same time, their largest losses have come in metropolitan owner occupancy suburbs. In fact, the Conservative's 15 best communes are almost all metropolitan suburbs, dominated by owner occupancy. In contrast, no fewer than 10 out of these 15 communes appear among the Social Democrats' 15 "worst" communes between 1970 and 1982.[44]

The analysis can be pushed a bit further. In the metropolitan area of Stockholm, the Social Democrats incurred their largest losses in the northern suburbs, dominated by owner occupancy. Their best districts were in the southern suburbs, dominated by rental multi-family housing. The researchers conclude that in this process of political polarization, ". . . the intensive production of owner-occupied homes during the 1970's plays an important role . . . New large areas have been developed, with a bourgeois hegemony, and where the privatized economy, founded on high incomes and large tax deductions on the family's home, combined with strong pressure from the social environment, has produced a Conservative upswing."[45]

To some extent, this upswing may have been a result of the Conservative stand on tax reform. For whatever the Swedish welfare state proponents are doing, they are not awaiting the attacks passively. The tax reform being implemented between 1983 and 1985 contains two main features. Marginal taxes will be lowered to 50 percent for the majority of income earners by 1985, and the tax effect of mortgage interest deductions will be maximized to 50 percent for *all* home-owners, regardless of income. The reform was a result of an agreement in April 1982 between the then governing Center and Liberal parties, and the Social Democrats. The third governing party, the Conservatives, did not adhere to the agreement. They wanted a quicker reduction of marginal tax rates, and a continuation of the earlier rules for tax deductions.[46] In the subsequent September 1982 elections, the Conservatives made large gains, while the Center and Liberals incurred losses. In fact, the Liberals were almost annihilated as a force in Sweden's political life.

The political costs of trying to come to grips with one of the main factors in commodification (tax deduction rules), have thus already become visible. But will the actual effects of the reform be as dramatic as the opponents contend? The discussion around the 1982 agreement was almost chaotic. While an official Cabinet document asserted that no more than 40,000 income earners and homeowners would be affected, some economists argued that as many as 800,000 would be losers. If these were all homeowners, half of the homeowning population would be on the losing side! Naturally, all homeowners with incomes above the "breaking point", (where marginal tax rates are higher than 50 percent), and with deductible mortgage interests, will find the tax effect of their deductions diminishing. But this may well be compensated for by the decrease in the overall tax burden. Some high income homeowners with moderate tax deductions may come out almost even in terms of disposable income, as the reform takes full effect in 1985 (even if they do not increase their income at all between 1983 and 1985). Should they increase their income by the rate foreseen in the tax reform, they will even make a small real gain in disposable income.[48] One should not forget, however, that high income earners with no tax deductions are the real winners; they stand to gain much more than their peers with heavy mortgages. Thus one effect of the reform will be to make it comparatively advantageous to rent rather than to own your home if you are a high income earner. This is, of course, true only if no capital gain could be made from owning one's house. One effect of the protracted discussions on changing deduction rules in the early 1980's has been to bring the small home market almost to a standstill. Home prices do not seem to have increased much in nominal terms from 1980 onwards, thus going down in real terms. One predicted effect of the tax reform is a comparatively large drop in prices for larger homes. A nation-wide survey of house prices in June 1982 seemed to confirm this pattern.[49]

The final effects of the tax reform on the distribution of housing standards and costs have yet to be seen. However, the political upheaval surrounding its enactment points to the centrality of housing in welfare state politics. It further points to the tension within the democratic welfare state between the drive for equitable distribution and the quest for liberty. The first implies thoroughgoing regulation and comprehensive redistribution schemes. The second points, at least partly, in the direction of allowing citizens to follow their own preferences.

In terms of housing policy, this may lead to a tension between distribution of standards and costs on the one hand, and distribution of housing powers on the other. To achieve neutrality and equality in costs and standards, the welfare state may have to intervene quite substantially in the market, twisting and bending peoples' preferences. Some households may be helped, others may find their possibilities decreased when it comes to their deciding how and where to live, and how much to spend on housing. Since the welfare state, by definition, strives to give its citizens more scope to decide for themselves, the equitable distribution of standards and costs can indeed come into conflict with the objectives of participation and influence.

In the end, then, it is the welfare state's ability to maintain a balance between equity and individual liberty which determines how potent it will be in the realm of housing. If anything, the Swedish -- and even more so, the British -- example indicates that allowing a biased distribution of standards and costs to proceed too far may lead to enormous political costs when attempts are made to return to a more equitable pattern.

ABLE 1 Number of Home-Owners in Different Socio-Economic ousehold Categories, and Different Categories' Share of the ncrease in Home-ownership in Sweden, 1968-1981 (Source: Frykman, ., "Vem bor i ägd bostad?", Att bo (March 1983). p. 25

Socio-Economic Category of Household	No. of Owner-Occupierse in Household 1968	1981	Percentual Change in No. of Owner-Occupiers in 1968-1981	Household Category's Share of In-crease occupiers
lue Collar orkers (III)	324	342	+ 6	4
hite Collar mployees (II)	161	389	+142	47
hite Collar mployees anagerial rofessional (I)	93	207	+123	23
mployers (II)	100	146	+ 46	9
etired (II)	47	85	+ 81	8
etired (III)	101	144	+ 43	9

ABLE 2. Percentage Share of Gross and Disposable Income in Different ncome Brackets for Households in Different Forms of Tenure in Sweden, 1978 Source: National Housing Board SUI 1982:10: calculations by the author).

Form of tenure	Household income in a 000 sw. cr.								
	Gross					Disposable			
	-60	60-80	80-100	100-120	120-	-40	40-60	60-80	80-
wner ccupancy	43	53	56	58	75	35	49	54	80
ooperatives	8	11	12	13	8	12	12	13	6
enancy	49	36	32	29	17	53	39	33	14
otal	100	100	100	100	100	100	100	100	100

TABLE 3. Calculation of Housing Costs for Dwellings of Equal Standa Different Tenures, for Households with Incomes Solightly above the Ave in Sweden 1982 (author's calculations).

	Owneroccupied home 115 square meters produced 1981		Rented flat (pu 115 square me produced 19
1 Total production costs	460,000		506,000
2 State subsidized loans	437,000		506,000
3 Own capital (all borrowed)	23,000		--
4 Capital costs	60,000		
5 Interest subsidy (to owner)	32,000		
6 Interest paid (and deductible by owner)	27,000		--
7 Municipal tax on house	1,800		
8 Imputed rent income from ownership	8,000		
9 Extra deduction for owner	1,500		--
10 Deductible deficit [(6) + (9) - (8)]	21,700		
11 Rent	--		25,500
12 Running costs	10,000		3,000
13 Tax effect of deduction (marginal tax rate 0,7)	15,200		--
14 Housing costs			
14a - gross expenditures [(6) + (7) + (12)]	39,000	[(11) + (12)]	28,50
14b - net expenditures [(14a) - (13)]	23,800	[(11) + (12)]	28,50
15 Market value increase [0.03 x (1)]	13,800		
16 Effective capital gain (0 in the first years)	--		--
17 Final housing costs [(14b) - (16)]	23,800		28,50

TABLE 4. Distribution of Taxable Income and Deductible Deficits from Homeownership, and Tax Effects for Homeowners in Different Income Brackets in Sweden, 1979 (Source: Swedish Official Statistics, SM N 1982:7 Riksrevisionsverkets taxeringstatistiska undersökning taxeringsåret 1980, pp. 196 ff).

	Income Bracket, 1 000 Sw Cr			
	-50	51-80	81-100	101-200
1 Number of income earners	3 434 824	1 985 580	469 885	348 653
2 Number of homeowners	516 943	578 085	215 363	215 270
3 Percentage of homeowners (2 in % of 1)	15,0	29,1	45,8	61,7
4 Number of homeowners with taxable income from ownership	309 971	104 299	19 999	14 524
5 Percentage homeowners with taxable income from ownership (4 in % of 2)	59,9	18,0	9,3	6,7
6 Average taxable income from homeowners (Sw Cr)	1 365	1 464	1 694	1 783
7 Average tax effect (Sw Cr)	+ 468	+ 907	+ 1 321	+ 1 426
8 Number of homeowners with deductible deficit from homeownership	170 337	466 942	194 388	200 473
9 Percentage homeowners with deductible deficits from homeownership (9 in % of 2)	33.3	80,7	90,2	93,1
10 Average deductible deficit from homeownership(Sw Cr)	3 364	7 661	9 294	13 650
11 Average tax effect (Sw Cr)	- 1 152	- 4 920	- 5 736	- 10 824

TABLE 5. Changes in the Share of Eligible Voters for Swedish Political Parties 1970-1982, in Areas with High or Low Shares of Owner Occupancy in New Housing Production (Source: Elmgren et al, 1983, p. 16)

Political parties	Metropolitan areas: Share of owner occupancy in new housing production		Non-metropolitan areas: Share of owner occupancy in new housing production	
	High	Low	High	Low
Moderate Conservatives	+18,1	+14,8	+9,2	+8,9
Center Party	- 6,6	- 2,8	-4,4	-3,4
Liberals	-10,7	-13,0	-6,6	-6,9
Social Democrats	- 1,5	+ 0,1	+2,6	+2,0
Leftist Communists	+ 1,2	+ 1,7	+0,4	+0,5
Others	+ 1,7	+ 1,7	+1,6	+1,5
Number of communes	25	33	98	123
Number of eligible voters (1000)	352	1823	1276	2679

	Consumption	Production
Standards	The quality and distri-- bution of the existing housing stock	The size, quality and distribution of new housing production
Powers	The distribution of rights and duties in housing stock management	The distribution of rights and duties in housing construction
Costs	The distribution of expenses and other sacrifices necessary for housing consumption	The distribution of expenses and other sacrifices necessary for housing production

Figure 1. The principal distributional conflicts to be addressed by a welfare state's housing policy (Adapted from Gustavsson. See note seven.)

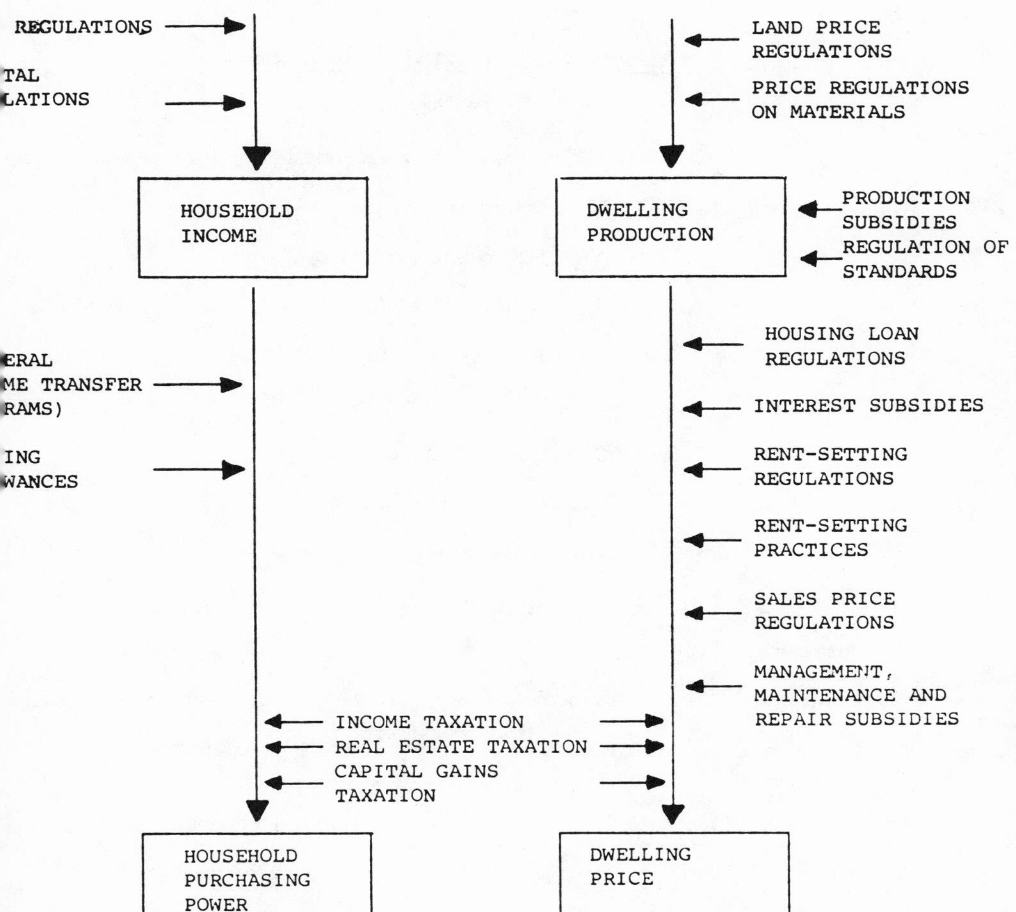

gure 2. State Interventions into Different Stages of the stribution of Household Purchasing Power and Dwelling Price rmation (Adapted from Korpi 1980, p. 302).

OBJECTS TO BE DISTRIBUTED IN HOUSING

A HOUSING STANDARDS

A1 Access to dwellings

A2 Space standard

A3 Equipment standard

B HOUSING POWERS

B1 Freedom of disposal

B2 Security of Tenure

C HOUSING COSTS

C1 Dwellings

C2 Households

PRINCIPLES OF DISTRIBUTION

	COMMODIFICATION		DECOMMODIFICATION
A1	Merit = ability to pay	A1	Need
A2	Tenure and income biassed	A2	Tenure and income neutral
A3	Tenure and income biassed	A3	Tenure neutral
B1	Tenure biassed	B1	Tenure neutral
B2	Tenure biassed	B2	Tenure neutral
C1	Tenure Biassed	C1	Tenure neutral
C2	Income and Wealth biassed	C2	Income and tenure neutral

Figure 3. A Classification of Objects to be Distributed, and Principles of Distribution, in Housing Policies of Welfare States

1970

	1rkmm	2rk	3rk	4rk	5rk	6rk	7+rk	sum
1 pers	378	242	94	34	12	4	3	771
2 pers	107	349	260	118	44	14	8	902
3 pers	20	161	211	120	52	16	8	590
4 pers	5	73	170	137	73	25	13	497
5 pers	1	15	57	60	38	16	11	198
6 pers		3	16	20	13	6	5	63
7+pers		1	5	10	7	3	3	28
sum	512	843	813	499	239	83	51	3050

1980

	1rkmm	2rk	3rk	4rk	5rk	6rk	7+rk	sum
1 pers	351	464	194	73	30	11	7	1148
2 pers	45	291	373	207	101	35	20	1090
3 pers	6	47	171	149	89	36	17	525
4 pers	2	14	101	170	127	64	26	515
5 pers	1	3	21	49	46	28	17	169
6 pers		1	4	10	9	6	6	37
7+pers			1	3	3	2	2	13
sum	405	820	865	660	407	183	94	3498

Figure 4. Number of Households According to Dwelling Size and Household Size, in Sweden, 1970 and 1980 (Source: Eriksson & Lindquist, 1982. p. 51. Marked squares in lower left indicate overcrowding, marked squares in upper right high space standard). in 1,000's.

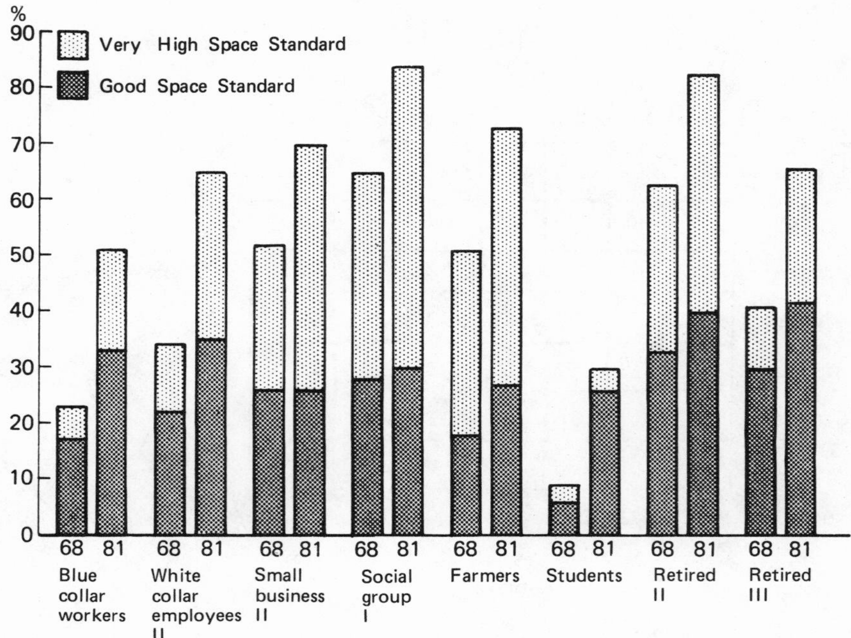

Figure 5. The Distribution of Good and Very High Space Standard among Different Swedish Social Groups in 1968 and 1981. (Source: Frykman 1984, p. 221).

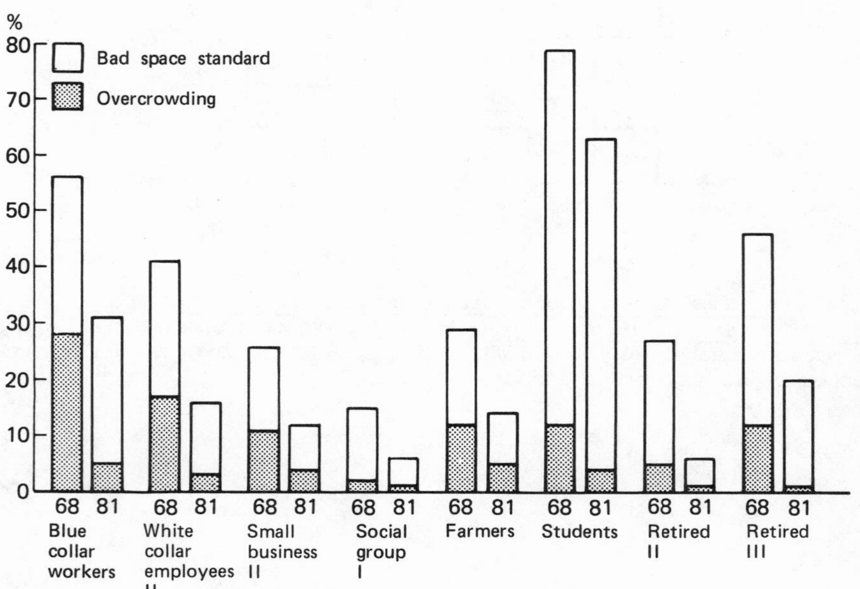

Figure 6. The Distribution of Bad Space Standard and Overcrowding among Different Swedish Social Groups in 1968 and 1981. (Source: Frykman 1984, p. 222).

NOTES

1. Norman Furniss and Timothy Tilton, The Case for the Welfare State: From Social Security to Social Equality, (Bloomington: Indiana University Press, 1977), pp xi, 5, 20.

2. Walter Korpi, "Social Policy and Distributional Conflict in the Capitalist Democracies: A Preliminary Comparative Framework," West European Studies, 3 (1980), p. 299.

3. Ibid., p. 301.

4. Cf. Peter Marcuse, "Determinants of State Housing Policies: West Germany and the United States," in Fainstain, N I & S S (eds.), Urban Policy under Capitalism (Beverly Hills: Sage Urban Affairs Annual Review, Vol. 22, 1982), pp. 85 ff.

5. These ideas have been developed by Sverker Gustavsson in e g, "Vad är det vi vill veta?", PLAN 33 (1979), pp. 467 ff; and "Housing, Building, and Planning," in Leif Lewin and Evert Vedung, (eds.), Politics as Rational Action. Essay in Public Choice and Policy Analysis (Dordrecht: D Reidel, 1980), p. 170 ff.; and "Three Basic Questions in Political Inquiry," Scandinavian Political Studies 4 (1981), p. 210. It is important to note that housing is also part of the overall distributional conflict over how society's total resources should be distributed among different purposes and sectors. Cf. Marcuse, p. 84 f.

6. This dualism is of longstanding importance. It is reflected in, e.g., the German housing policy and its distinction between Subjekt - and Objektförderung. See GEWOS, Wohnungsbesitzarten in der Bundesrepublik Deutschland - Beurteilungen von Erfahrungen und Konzepten (GEWOS GmbH: Hamburg, 1981).

7. Cf. the discussion of different forms of state intervention found in Stuart Lansley, Housing and Public Policy, (London: Croom Helm, 1979), pp. 34 ff.

8. Gill Burke, Housing and Social Justice (London: Longman, 1981), pp. 148 ff. For a further discussion, see Sverker Gustavsson, "Demands and Needs for Housing," paper for the British-Swedish Seminar on Housing Policy, Gävle, Sweden, September 13-16, 1982, esp pp. 2 ff.

9. Gösta Esping-Andersen, "Politics Against Markets: De-Commodification in Social Policy," paper for the Arne Ryde Symposium, Department of Economics, Lund University, August 24, 1981, p. 2, (quote), pp. 8 ff.

10. Michael Harloe, "The Recommodification of Housing," in Michael Harloe and Elizabeth Lebas, (eds.), City, Class, and Capital (London: Edward

Arnold, 1981), pp. 17 ff. Harloe says he is "concerned with the changing boundaries between housing provision via the market criteria of access and housing provision via need- oriented criteria," p. 25. However, he tends to jump to owner-occupied and "social" council housing without discussing the theoretical implications of his concept.

11. Jim Kemeny, The Myth of Homeownership, (London: Routledge & Kegan Paul, 1981), pp. 65 ff.

12. Swedish Cabinet Proposal 1980/81:63, p. 9f.

13. For a more detailed treatment of these measures, see my "Housing Tenures in Sweden," in Fritz Ijmkers & Hans Kroes, Buitenlandse Vormen van Woningbeheer (Delft: RIW-instituut voor volkshuisvestingsondertook, 1982) and "Strategies for the Swedish Public Housing Sector," Urban Law and Policy, 6 (1984) pp. 220 ff.

14. Cabinet Budget Proposal 1982/83:100, Part 16, p. 28; Cabinet Proposal 1982/83:50, Part 5, pp. 12 ff.

15. Riksbyggen, Fakta i bostadsfragan 1981 (Stockholm: Riksbyggen 1981), pp. 8, 11; SABO, SABO-boken 78/79 (Stockholm: SABO 1978).

16. Swedish Cabinet Proposal 1980/81:63, p. 3; Swedish Cabinet Budget Proposal 1982/83:100, Part 16, p. 17.

17. Swedish Official Statistics, SM Bo 1982:6.2, Bostadsbyggandet 1981, (Stockholm: National Central Bureau of Statistics, 1982), p. 16.

18. Jan Eriksson & Margareta Lindquist, "För vem planerar vi bostäderna?," Byggindustrin 33/1982, p. 51.

19. Bostadsbyggandet 1981, p. 16.

20. Swedish Official Statistics Bostadsbyggandet 1968 (Stockholm: National Central Bureau of Statistics, 1969), p. 28 f; SM Bo 1980:6.2, Bostadsbyggandet 1979 (Stockholm: ibid, 1980), p. 24; SM Bo 1982:6.2, Bostadsbyggandet 1981 (Stockholm: ibid, 1982, p. 24.

21. Ibid.

22. Ibid.

23. Bostadsbyggandet 1981, p. 17.

24. For an in-depth analysis of the differences in allocation of public and private rental housing in Sweden, see Marianne Wiktorin, Kommunal bostadsförmedling - Serviceorgan eller bostadspolitiskt medel? (Stockholm: Byggforskningsradet T9:1983), esp. ch.5.

25. Eriksson & Lindquist, p. 51.

26. Ibid.

27. Ibid, p. 52.

28. Tofte Frykman, "Boendeförhallanden 1967-1981", in Eriksson, R. and R. Aberg (eds.), Välfärd i fe

rändring. Levndsvillkor i Sverige 1968-1981 (Stockholm: Prisma 1984), p. 215.

29. National Housing Board, Hushallstyper, inkomster och boendekostnader (Stockholm: NHB Statistik/Utredningar/Information 1982:10), pp. 5, 10.

30. Frykman, pp. 220 ff.

31. Ibid., p. 229 f. 32. Ibid., p. 321 f.

33. Economic Commission for Europe, Major Trends in Housing Policy in ECE Countries, (New York, United Nations, ECE/HBP/29, 1980), p. 10. Cf. David Donnison and Clare Ungerson, Housing Policy (Harmondsworth: Penguin 1982), p. 53 ff. On the other hand, it may be argued that the average size of Swedish dwellings is not remarkably high in international comparison. The high space standard is also due to the comparatively small average size of Swedish households; see Erik Hemström, Utrymmesstandarden i internationell jämförelse. Nagra kommentarer utifran internationell statistik (Gävle: The National Swedish Institute for Building Researce, Working Paper, June 1983).

34. Swedish Cabinet Proposal 1974:150, Riktlinjer för bostadspolitiken m, p. 349 ff.

35. Swedish Official Statistics, SM Bo 1980:6, Bostads- och hyresundersökningen, Del 2: Hushållsdata för flerbostadshus, and SM Bo 1980:10, Del 3: Lagenthets- och Hushållsdata for småhus, Stockholm: National Central Bureau of Statistics, 1980) passim.

36. Ibid, passim.

37. Rune Wigren, Bostadspolitik och smahusvag, (Gävle: National Swedish Institute for Building Research, Working Paper, February 1983), p. 28.

38. Swedish Official Statistics, Bostads- och byggnadsstatistisk arsbok 1979 (Stockholm: National Central Bureau of Statistics, 1980),p. 154, and ibid, 1980 (Stockholm: National Central Bureau of Statistics 1981), p. 164. Cf. Tables 10 and 11.

39. Wigren, p. 29 ff.

40. See Gustavsson, "Housing, Building and Planning," pp. 175 ff.

41. Derived from data in Swedish Cabinet Budget Proposals each fiscal year, and budget applications from the National Housing Board each fiscal year.

42. Jim Kemeny, "Home-Ownership and Privatisation," International Journal of Urban and Regional Research, 4 (1980), pp. 372-388; and "Privatisering eller kollektivisering i boendet? Teoretiska fragor om välfärdsfördelning och urban struktur," Sociologisk forskning 20 (1983). This arguement is made from a different direction by John Logue in his contribution to this volume.

43. For an account, see my From Tenancy to Home Ownership. A Comparative Study of Tenure

Conversions and Their Effects (London: Croom Helm, 1986), which compares the British experiences of council house sales with those of Condominium conversions in the U.S. and conversion to ownership flats in West Germany.

44. Bo Elmgren, Hans-Eric Holmqvist and Stig Lundgren, Socialdemokratin och 70-talets val (Stockholm: Socialdemokraterna, Utredningsrapport 1/83, 1983), pp. 12, 15 ff, 29.

45. Ibid, p. 22.

46. Axel Hadenius, Spelet om skatten (Stockholm: Norstedts 1981), pp 264 ff.

47. Dagens Nyheter, October 30, 1981: "Kompromiss om villaägare: 40,000 väntas förlora"; Svenska Dagbladet, April 6, 1982: "Bankekonomer i rapport: Minst 820,000 förlorar pa skattereformen."

48. National Tax Board, Skattereformen - 1983 ars inkomster - 1984 ars taxering (Stockholm: Riksskatteverket, brochure 1982).

49. Svenska Dagbladet, January 27, 1982: "Färre villor, sänkta priser." "A nationwide brokerage firm reported an average drop in house prices by 6.7 percent for 1981. However, another survey from June 1982 reported a recovering market, with the exception of larger homes. Svenska Dagbladet, June 23, 1982: "Aterhämtning pa villamarknaden. Prisnivan ökar - Fler köper hus."

VIII.

Bernice Pescosolido

Carol Boyer

Wai Ying Tsui

Crisis in the Welfare State

Public Reactions to Welfare Policies

The welfare state is in "crisis". Something is amiss, Mishra tells us, since "the long and extraordinary combination of full employment, economic growth and rising social expenditures seems to have come unstuck."[1] Yet, explanations of the crisis, solutions to the problem and, in fact, the very nature of dilemmas in the public provision of welfare remain the subject of heated debate. That the "crisis" means different things to different people reveals something about the inherent problems in welfare state politics. From the perspective of government policy-makers, welfare professionals and academics, there has come a large, critical and prescriptive literature that we will describe in terms of competing theoretical or ideological perspectives. What is less discussed is where and to what degree the public aligns with any of these views.[2] Debates about the future of welfare policies often rely on assumptions about public dissatisfaction with current government efforts. But how does the public evaluate government action in social programs? And exactly where does the locus of disapproval, if any, lie?

Our aim is to explore the extent and implications of the public's disapproval of the welfare state.[3] To evaluate the "crisis" in the public mind, it is necessary first to separate out the ideologies of crisis and see which, if any, fits with the public's notion. We then go one step further. It is not enough to see how individuals line-up with the differing positions; we need in addition to know their propensity for engaging in political action. If the current crisis represents a watershed in the history of the welfare state and not just an impasse, whose demands will the government be likely to face? With what types of political action will these people be willing to confront the government?[4] These questions do not imply that a public choice model operates in social policy-making. The ideologies of crisis provide frameworks for how political systems work, how they change, and what type of action the public needs to take to have their opinions incorporated in policy decisions. Our discussion of who is discontented with government action, coupled with what political action they are willing to take, allows us to assess the "legitimacy crisis", its implications for the future of the welfare state, and the utility of competing theories for understanding both.

We will study these issues through a comparative analysis of the public's appraisal of welfare state. We identify those groups in each country evaluating government action negatively and link their disapproval with political behaviors. Ideological theories on current policy development 1) provide different perspectives on public reactions, 2) imply diverse models of political action, and 3) suggest the type and direction of changes that might occur. In the first section, we outline three theoretical perspectives based on different explanations of the development and functioning of the welfare state, each of which expects different groups to evaluate the government's performance negatively. Next, we examine these contentions using data from eight western democracies: United States, Great Britain, West Germany, The Netherlands, Austria, Italy, Switzerland and Finland.[5] Finally, we link these findings and the theoretical perspectives to political action (both institutional and non-institutional) and conclude with a discussion of implications for policy change.

I

In the years following World War II, a number of factors provided legitimacy for the welfare state -- the general acceptance of the Keynesian solution to economic ills and state intervention, the surplus provided by an expanding economy, the development of theories of industrial and post-industrial society which saw an inherent need for state intervention, and the desire of some to pursue the social goal of attaining "socialism" through welfare policies.[6] In the 1970's, other circumstances heralded trouble for the policies associated with this position. Welfare states stopped or slowed their postwar expansion. Decreasing rates of economic growth, declining industrial productivity, government deficits, and increasing public demands, exposed social programs to criticism and even doubts about their legitimacy. Public distrust of governments increased while citizen participation in policy-making dropped, curtailing institutionalized channels for voicing discontent and planning responsive social programs.[7] Left-of-center political parties suffered losses in Great Britain, the United States, West Germany, Denmark and Sweden. A resurgent right succeeded in halting the growth of domestic spending. These developments have made further advances in welfare provision problematic and they have increased the importance of public reaction -- do or will we see a "welfare backlash"; do pro-welfare constituencies exist and can they be mobilized?[8]

As a basis for understanding why certain groups in the population differ in evaluating government performance, we derive three models of public reaction to the welfare state based on major views of who supports, who gains and who loses in welfare states. We call these models Individual Slippage (based on Consensus theories), Beneficiary Disillusionment (based on Marxist and Neo-Marxist views) and Benefactor Crunch (deriving from the Neo-conservative critique). The Individual Slippage model of public reactions to welfare policies assumes that the welfare state relies on a consensus among the population. Only through a sharing of attitudes could a welfare state arise in liberal democracies. Its relative stability and continued functioning also depend on this shared agreement. Consensus exists in recognizing modern social problems as well as in formulating policies. Social harmony prevails through a balancing of interests and adapting society's resources to these demands. One version of this perspective is presented by Marshall who accounts for an expanding welfare state as an evolution in citizenship rights.[9] The state responds to the growing needs in industrial society historically by granting rights from political incorporation to social entitlements. Later work stressed the growth of social security developments in response to the demands of modernization. This "logic of industrialization" thesis suggests that changes such as economic development, urbanization, and an aging population require the state to expand its functions to meet the changing requirements of modern societies.[10]

In reviewing why a consensus might exist, Esping-Andersen suggests that the welfare state embodies all citizens as its "client".[11] Everyone benefits -- from minimum levels of financial support for the poor to job mobility for the service workers, professionals and bureaucrats. Even "conservative" political parties have consistently offered support for welfare policies. Following World War II, for example, center and center-right coalitions increased social transfer payments more than left governments.[12] Cross-national reports of relative consensus support the claim of public acceptance of the government responsibility in providing a basic level of economic and social well-being. Coughlin finds the majority of the public across eight nations supporting the government effort in social welfare. Free and Cantril, as early as 1967, showed that two-thirds of the public in a welfare laggard, the United States, believed in the operating assumptions of the welfare state.[13]

Consensus, however, need not be automatic. As Logue argues in this volume, consensus (social solidarity) can lose its persuasive power in justifying the expensive costs of welfare policies. Marshall sees the dilemmas of the welfare state in a similar way: "The trouble is that no way has been found of equating a man's values in the market (capitalist value), his value as a citizen (democratic value), and his value for himself (welfare value)".[14] Under the logic of this position, discontent will be rooted in the state's failure to provide individuals with what the welfare states promised them. This is not a crisis in redistribution, simply particular individuals from various backgrounds "slipping through the cracks" of the system. Public discontent will show up not in group characteristics, say for example the elderly, but for those individuals who personally feel that their lot has not been improved, that the government has performed irresponsibly, or that it has not addressed issues relevant to them. In sum, if a crisis occurs it revolves around a breakdown in consensus and individual dislocations that arise from it. If this model operates, we do not expect socio-economic, political or demographic characteristics of individuals to be significantly related to their evaluations of government performance on welfare state issues.[15] Rather, controlling for these group characteristics, we expect relevant individual perceptions and attitudes to result in different appraisals of the government's effort.[16]

The remaining two models present the views of critics of welfare state policies. Their disapproval is not simply a response to their perceived failure or the current crisis but stems from early debates over their implementation. Even if consensus theorists claim near-universal agreement, the welfare state had no lack of vocal dissenters. Harold Macmillan, recalling the institution and expansion of welfare policies following World War II in Great Britain, fought opposition from two sources:[17]

> There were those who believed that private enterprise, left alone and allowed to operate untramelled, would in the long run produce wealth on a greater scale than any

> other system...On the other side were ranged the Labour and socialist parties who disclaimed all responsibility for all that was wrong by repeating the parrot cry -- "It is the fault of the system". This was supposed to mean that there was nothing that could be done except by revolutionary changes...

So, from both ends of the political spectrum, politicians and scholars decried the advent of the welfare state and, following or instigating the proclaiming of "crisis", they have developed new, more varied and sophisticated attacks of the welfare state. As Wilensky and others point out, these critics share certain similarities -- the denouncing of state intervention; the rejection of the notion that the state is an agent of integration necessary to discourage alienation; the indictment of welfare bureaucrats who act to unduly restrict individual actions and work in their own interest; and, the rejection of the plausibility of a mixed (capitalist and socialist) economy.[18] Yet, these critics offer diverse views of why the welfare state fails, who suffers under it, the degree to which the damage can be repaired and by what methods, and, the future directions to pursue. As such, they provide the basis of two very different models of public reactions to welfare policies.

The orientation of the radical left, Marxist or Neo-Marxist, suggests a model of Beneficiary Disillusionment. This model focuses on the Marxists' skepticism of the ability of the welfare state to improve the lot of its less fortunate citizens. Early on, Marxists like Saville maintained that the government serves the interests of the powerful (of which key government actors are a part). Any reform developed in a capitalist and democratic arena is limited simply but severely by this fact. Reform, necessarily, is a "social bandage" buttressing the weakness of industrial capitalism.[19] Since the goal of the welfare state is, in part, to protect the political status quo favoring owners of the means of production and to provide them with requisite needs (e.g., a fairly docile but efficient labor force), no real distribution of social wealth could be expected.[20] And Marxists do not have to look far for support for their claims. Jackman fails to find welfare programs decreasing overall income inequality. Many studies of public medical care policies claim that middle and upper class groups gain greater benefit and that class differences in health have either stayed the same, or in fact, widened under the welfare state.[21]

Neo-Marxists have refined these ideas into more sophisticated theories of the role of contradiction. The current crisis across welfare states represents the fundamental contradictions (or in Offe's terms the structural dilemmas) inherent in welfare capitalism. The state cannot meet its two basic but contradictory functions: fostering capital accumulation to ensure monopoly sector profits, and maintaining public legitimacy by distributing welfare benefits. Welfare policies are not only a response to functional necessity of capitalism, but a political settlement between workers and employers. Such balancing acts become impossible with slow economic growth and high inflation. Eventually a crisis occurs because of the state's inability to maintain both production costs for industry and social services costs for the citizenry.[22] In the ensuing crisis, great hardships occur for the powerless, those most in need of social welfare -- the unskilled, unemployed, lower classes and the elderly. These groups voice disapproval because of government failure to provide them with promised guarantees of security and equality. Further, what services are provided are administered in an authoritarian or paternalistic fashion.[23]

In sum, a crisis in governmental effectiveness exacerbated by an economic crisis and a crisis in public sector growth make a crisis of redistribution more visible. Poor performance ratings among beneficiary groups result from the government's inability to provide them with what other groups commonly have. Offe's "who benefits" criterion suggests that welfare state policies mean "capitalism for the poor and socialism for the rich."[24] For social reformers as well, the welfare state fails to redistribute income and resources while protecting or advancing the interests of the private sector and administrative bureaucracies. These groups, regardless of their personal perceptions of the government, will react more negatively to what the government does.[25]

The attack on the welfare state from the right targets those who underwrite the costs of the welfare state. Our third model, Benefactor Crunch, stems from the conservative and neo-conservative's claim that welfare policies are contradictory to a capitalist democracy. The welfare state leans heavily on private businesses and absorbs capital necessary for economic growth. At the same time, it decreases productivity by providing disincentives to the surplus labor force (the poor work less because they are paid to do so). As a result, corporate investments decline and technological innovation is slowed. Further, those who administer welfare state policies profit more from the spending than others.

They deflect the goals of policies to their own interests and become their major proponents and beneficiaries.[26]

According to this view, left-leaning governments are the culprits responsible for inflated welfare budgets. They promise handouts to ensure electoral success. The political market has no inherent constraints, and the ever-escalating demands of the citizenry wreak havoc with an economic market marked by finite limits.[27] Whether intended or not, government intervention fails to improve the lot of the "needy," and, to make matters worse, destroys the emotional and financial support provided by the traditional culture of the underprivileged -- a cohesive family, strong ethnic ties, stable neighborhoods, and influential religious institutions.[28] In short, the welfare state rewards the lazy and punishes the hard-working and successful. It creates a false audience for welfare benefits (bureaucrats) while doing little actual good for the targeted population. It denigrates individualism and undermines foundations of the private market economy.

But it is not just the upper strata that bear the burden of the welfare state. We must consider under this model the possibility of a "middle mass" or a "reluctant middle". They benefit neither from "welfare" (public assistance) or "wealthfare" (government aid). Public relief and income maintenance policies provide cash and benefits-in-kind to the poor, disabled and unemployed; tax loopholes and government loans to aid the rich. The middle groups, hit with higher taxes and inflation, are increasingly impoverished.[29] Wilensky suggests that rising taxes for the middle classes caused by increased welfare spending results in a political backlash (e.g., anti-tax movements and disillusionment with the welfare state).[30] In the United States, public opinion polls show a reluctant middle class. Maximum resistance to government guarantees of employment and health care occurs among the middle income respondents with moderate levels of education. In Sweden, the same study points to a "middle mass" that shows more variability for social reforms and equality.[31] Victories at the polls for neo-conservative parties appear to stem from new "middle group" support. In Denmark, for example, traditional working class Social Democrats have defected to anti-welfare political parties. Productive manual workers saw themselves carrying the financial burden of the welfare state. The political victories of the Thatcher government in Britain and the Reagan government in the United States reflect the realignment of these middle groups.[32]

The Benefactor Crunch model suggests two possible sources of negative evaluations. In the most straightforward way, the "elite" version of the model sees more negative evaluations originating among those who control societal resources, that is, among those who assume they are, or in fact are, paying for welfare goods and services: those in upper social classes, income, occupational prestige, education groups and those affiliated with major right political parties (who typically represent more of the interests of the corporate sector). In a more subtle way, however, the Benefactor Crunch may hit middle groups. In the "middle mass" version, socio-economic and demographic middle groups see their polar counterparts (e.g., higher and lower classes, youth and aged) as receiving more benefits from government intervention.[33]

II

We have translated ideological views of who gains and looses from welfare state policies into three models proposing the loci of popular discontent. Two types of factors come out as important considerations: social position and attitudes or perceptions.[34] Our task now is to evaluate these claims empirically. Our examination of the ideologies of crisis ranges over eight advanced industrial democracies (Great Britain, West Germany, the Netherlands, Austria, the United States, Italy, Switzerland and Finland). The analysis is based on Barnes and Kaase's national surveys conducted during the mid-70's. In each country over 1500 individuals were asked a broad range of questions on political attitudes and action.[35] A data set of this size creates both opportunities and constraints. There are great differences in the welfare programs of each country regarding origins, eligibility, benefits (both in levels and duration), growth rates, and administration.[36] But in this very caution lies the strength and additional insight provided by a cross-national approach. A number of ways of characterizing welfare states have been proposed -- they are leaders or laggards; positive, social security or social welfare states; corporatist or non-corporatist; consumption or production oriented.[37] By comparing the results across countries and noting any patterns, we will be able to see whether and how these larger distinctions capture interesting features of the welfare state crisis. The analytic tasks, then, involve both a deductive and inductive component. Within each country, we will examine competing models derived from ideological views of the welfare state and its difficulties. Across countries, patterns in the source of public evaluations suggest the importance of history, timing, and state capacity.[38]

We begin the discussion of the results with an overview. Our analyses suggest the importance of Consensus and, to a more limited extent, the Benefactor Crunch model in European countries. In contrast, in the American case, disapproval among benefactor groups is clear and consistent. Further, the effect of politics is strong in all but two countries. In sum, the public's view of crisis does not neatly conform to the ideological viewpoints we described above. In each country, negative public reactions stem from different sources -- rarely coming from targeted beneficiaries, more often from benefactor groups, and always from individuals at odds with the government and its policies. Differences across countries are not major, but where there is a pattern it suggests the importance of leader/laggard standing and corporatist/non-corporatist forms of political organization. A detailed account of the data, measures and methods used here are presented in the Technical Appendix at the end of this chapter.

Simply looking at the overall levels of negative public reactions, we find that countries fall fairly neatly along the leader/laggard distinction. Italy, Finland and the United States report higher levels of disapproval than any of the other countries in our study.[39] Great Britain comes next followed by the Netherlands and West Germany. Individuals in Switzerland and Austria report the lowest levels of disapproval of government performance on welfare. The United States, among all of the countries included here, is marked by a distinctly different profile. In Table 1, we find overwhelming support for the Benefactor Crunch Model. Following the "elite" version, individuals in upper social classes, those with the higher levels of educational attainment and income, all report more negative evaluations. However, those in middle-aged groups report greater disapproval than their older or younger counterparts. This points to support for the "middle mass" version as well since the old and the young bear less burden for financing the welfare state.[40] There is only weak support for the Beneficiary Disillusionment model since the unemployed are the only targeted group significantly more likely to report negative views.

In the United States we also see the overall importance of politics but with an unexpected twist. People with political "leanings", either Republican or Democrat, are less negative in their views than independents. These results support none of the three models of crisis but suggest rather the importance of institutional power. Both Republicans and Democrats are in power in the United States, and their supporters approve of welfare policies more than do those outside the system. This feature will be seen repeatedly across countries. Several attitudes and perceptions are significant and consistent with the Individual Slippage model. Individuals who distrust the government or who see it run for big interests report more negative evaluations. When actual socio-economic position is taken into account, respondents who perceive a greater discrepancy between what they are entitled to and what they have report more negative evaluations. Finally, in terms of individual self-interest, those who believe welfare issues are important disapprove most.

In sharp contrast to the effect of demographic and socio-economic variables in the United States, the picture in Italy shows only very limited support for the Benefactor Crunch model. Those with higher educational attainment report more negative evaluations. Yet, overall, these factors do not matter while attitudes and perceptions do. These results, taken together, support the Individual Slippage model. Like the United States, we find that individuals in Italy who view welfare issues as important, who see the government run for big interests, and who distrust the government, also report greater disapproval. However, in Italy, those who see the government taking more responsibility for welfare provisions are also more negative contrary to consensus view expectations. We will also see this feature in Finland and the opposite effect in three of the five "leaders" (West Germany, Austria and Switzerland). It appears that where the government has a long history of intervention, seeing the government taking responsibility lessens negative evaluations. In those countries where the government has only recently or in piecemeal fashion been interventionist, individuals who see the government taking new initiatives are disgruntled with this turn of events.

Finally, in Italy individual party affiliation is important. In particular, the members of the Socialist Proletariat Party disapprove more of government performance than do the Italian Socialists, while the Christian Democrats disapprove less. Looking at the signs of all the party identification coefficients, we see a pattern.[41] Both Socialist parties, the Communists and the Neo-Fascists share more negative evaluations, while the Social and Christian Democrats, Republicans and Liberals voice greater support. What this picks up, as we saw in the United States, is not directly in line with the models of crisis, but supports the notion that supporters of parties in power approve while those outside disapprove despite their particular parties' views on the welfare state.

In Finland, we see results fairly similar to Italy. These also are presented in Table 1. Some more educated groups report more negative evaluations weakly supporting the Benefactor Crunch model. In addition, those working full time (the omitted category) give poorer evaluations than the retired and disabled. Overall, however, the support for anything but the Individual Slippage model is weak. As in Italy, greater perception of responsibility, importance, distrust and seeing the government run for big interests, result in more negative evaluations. Individuals supporting all parties (e.g., Social Democrats, Liberals, Centre) report less negative evaluations than those identifying with the National Party. Once again, this reflects the in or out of power distinction.

The German, British, and Austrian cases are presented in Table 2. In Germany, there is mixed and weak support for the Beneficiary Disillusionment and Benefactor Crunch models since the unemployed and educated both report more negative evaluations of government performance. The age effect should be interpreted cautiously. Rather than supporting the Benefactor Crunch model (where the young and middle aged groups express greater disapproval because they apply for services to the old), we may be seeing a foreshadowing of the "Youth Rebellion" that facilitated the formation of the Green Party in the years following the survey.[42]

Regarding the Individual Slippage model, we find consistent effects here as in other countries. Greater discrepancy between actual and entitled worth, distrust of government, and seeing the government run for big interests, result in more negative evaluations. Here, for the first time, individuals who perceive the government taking greater responsibility report more favorable evaluations underscoring the contextual effect of leader/laggard status. West Germany stands apart on another contextual dimension. This is the first country examined (and only one of two) where individuals' political identifications do not matter as a whole or as individual parties. Both West Germany and Austria (the other null case) are considered to be the most corporatistic of the countries we consider.[43] Also, in Austria and in West Germany since 1965, we cannot easily distinguish "in" from "out" parties except in the case of the "Greens".

Great Britain stands as the one country where political party affiliation targets the supporters and opponents of the welfare state rather than the "in power" distinction seen earlier. Both

Conservative and Labour Parties had been in power by the time of survey, yet those who identify with the Labour Party voice greater disapproval while those aligned with the Conservatives report less. This result supports the Beneficiary Disillusionment model; but here again support for the models described in Section One is mixed. Those individuals with high occupational prestige express greater disapproval. Work status as a whole affects evaluations of government performance, and those in any other situation besides working full-time for others (who pay more taxes) are significantly less negative toward government initiatives. Both results support the Benefactor Crunch model. As we have seen in all cases to this point, the support for the Individual Slippage model is clear and consistent; those who perceive greater discrepancy, distrust the government, and see it run for big interests, report more negative evaluations.

In Austria, the Individual Slippage model received support as well. Only one socio-economic variable, education, is significant and it supports the Benefactor Crunch model. However, consistent with the Individual Slippage model in "leaders", perceiving the government taking more responsibility lessens disapproval. And, as in many other countries, individuals who perceive greater discrepancy, distrust the government, and see it run for big interests, report more negative evaluations.

Turning to Table 3, we see that the Individual Slippage model continues to operate in the Netherlands. Those with more education report greater disapproval supporting the Benefactor Crunch model. Again, the pattern of effect for party identification (significant overall) suggests that those in power (e.g., the Catholic People's Party, the Labour Party) evaluate government performance less harshly than those out of power (e.g., the Pacifist Socialists, Radicals, Communists). In line with the Consensus view, those who distrust the government and think it is run for the sake of big interests report more negative evaluations.

Finally, in Switzerland, the only model that receives support is the Individual Slippage model. There are no demographic or socio-economic effects to support the other two ideological perspectives. Again, the influence of politics on public reactions reveals the importance of access to power. Those who belong to the National Union of Independents and the Communist Party express greater disapproval while all others report less.

Looking at Tables 1 through 3, we see a number of patterns. First, no single model adequately explains public reactions to government performance in any country. Individuals do not see the welfare state crisis in strict alignment with the ideological views of scholars and politicians. Second, the importance of individual attitudes and perceptions, regardless of social position, are important factors in an individual's assessment of the welfare state crisis. Third, targeted beneficiaries of welfare state policies across the eight countries rarely give poorer performance ratings. Only in the United States and West Germany do the unemployed voice greater disapproval, and only the Labour Party members do so in Great Britain. Other political party effects reflect the current power of parties rather than their ideological stance. The results suggest that welfare policies have succeeded in quelling the public demand of beneficiary groups. Fourth, the results also suggest that those who pay for welfare programs are consistently (though weakly) the groups most likely to disapprove of the government's performance. Here the case for American exceptionalism is clear. The Benefactor Crunch model operates strongly in the United States. Finally, history and socio-economic organization (leader/laggard, corporatist/non-corporatist) helps us understand differences in the models across countries to some extent.

From the public's viewpoint, the welfare state crisis represents, in a most straightforward way, a crisis of consensus -- individual disagreement with the government about rights and obligations. There is little support here for the position that a crisis in public sector growth or a crisis in redistribution is central to the public's evaluation of government performance as indicated by the failure of the Beneficiary Disillusionment model to predict individual's views. To the extent that the crisis is perceived as an economic one (as in the Benefactor Crunch model), our results suggest that this is a minor component since socio-economic position only weakly affects the public's view. (However, as we saw earlier, this appears to be at the heart of the crisis in the United States.) Finally, the pattern of political party effects suggests that the welfare state crisis is a crisis of government effectiveness stemming directly from their affiliation with the party in power. If their party holds power, there is no perceived crisis; if it does not, there is one. This supports Van Schendelen's notion that the welfare state crisis can be used to mobilize support for or against the government.

III

We are now in a position to describe the behavioral implications of these different perspectives. The policy effects of attitudes depend in part on the willingness of individuals to take political action based on their beliefs. Each of the perspectives outlined in Section One also suggests the type of political action necessary to initiate change, and, in some cases, the direction of policy changes. To adopt, for example, a Marxist view of the welfare state crisis carries with it a very different resolution of the crisis and the public's role in it than does a Conservative view. In this section we will briefly review the forms of political action associated with the consensus, Neo-Marxist and conservative perspectives and then examine the extent to which the expectations align with our data.

The Consensus model implies a pluralist view of politics. The government as the "broker" state mediates between competing interest groups and develops policy "as a near perfect reflection of aggregated individual preferences."[44] Social groups see their interests realized through participation in institutionalized politics. When individuals become dissatisfied with the government action, they work through the system to voice their discontent. Because the system is open to all who wish to compete, regular and orderly change follows the will of the governed. It is, according to Gamson:[45]

> a contest carried out under well-defined rules. The rules prohibit the use of violence or any efforts aimed at permanently removing other contestants from the game.

Access to the state occurs through electoral politics, lobbying and interest bargaining, not through extremist political action.[46] While those with strong interest group representation have a greater chance to change social policy, this reflects apathy among the general public and serves to dampen the potential for conflict. Violent political action is seen as the attempt to use irrational behavior antithetical to the inherent rationality of the political system. Ultimately those who employ "street tactics" will be unsuccessful.[47]

Critics of the pluralist view contend that access to the political system is neither open, nor is the battle equal for the privileged and the powerless. Violence has effects whether it accomplishes basic change or merely gains concessions from those in power. Central to Neo-Marxist arguments about welfare state development is the use of political protest to induce welfare outlays. The institutionalized political routes to redress inequities are generally unavailable or ineffective for those less well-off. Consequently, these groups resort to disruptive actions which threaten the state's legitimacy and the social order. For example, insurgency by blacks in the postwar United States resulted in the expansion of welfare rolls. Labor militancy through the use of strikes is disruptive, threatens political stability because it interrupts capital production, and has been linked to changes in welfare policies as well.[48] At the basis of reform in democratic countries, they argue, is the necessity to gain the worker's approval of the legitimacy of the government and the system of private property. Bismarck's early introduction of social insurance for medical care is widely reported to be a concession to contain unrest and instability. So too in Britain, reformers deliberately set out to use social programs to pacify the disgruntled. Even in the Netherlands, a nation considered to have a low amount of violence, Mulisc points out that:[49]

> official reaction (to protest), is, correspondingly, not geared to isolation and stamping out "dangerous elements" but rather at aiming at coming to terms with a respectable opposition.

Real social change, some Neo-Marxists contend, comes not through protest but revolution. Collective action is limited since inequities come from inherent social and economic contradictions in capitalism. Piecemeal reform to deal with those contradictions simply lead to new ones. The welfare state does not produce basic changes and is not a revolutionary process.[50]

Whether reform or revolution is the answer, Marxists point to the importance of non-institutionalized forms of political action to alter the fate of the underprivileged.[51] Their willingness to take measures outside of the voting arena and the approval of third parties to these means is central. When crisis generated by the action of elites comes to the attention of others through protest, they can form "conscience constituencies" or simply groups wanting to institutionalize the conflict. This argument points to both approval and willingness to participate in "radical" or non-institutional politics such as boycotts, demonstrations, strikes, sit-ins and violence.[52]

The Neo-Conservatives appear to be less concerned with the wishes and rights of the governed than with the implementation of policies they "know" to be best. Because of their professional and social ties, resources and social background, the privileged have disproportionate access to government leaders. Political decisions should be made by a coalition of state managers and a small, restricted elite comprised mainly of big business. According to this typically instrumental view, the great majority of the public is effectively excluded from government decision-making. In this sense, they share assumptions with the Marxists regarding the control of the political system by a few. They differ simply in their reaction to it. The Marxists see a power elite model as harmful; the conservatives see it as beneficial. According to the latter, the elites institute policies which will benefit all in the long run because measures are based on sound economic theories that will reestablish a firm base for industry.[53] Under the welfare state, the conservatives see their agendas interrupted and their interests unserved since welfare state policies undermine corporate interests while state administrators act in relative autonomy. To end the crisis created by the welfare state, policies must call for the state to stop intervening in the market and allow it to operate freely. While these solutions are political in nature and legitimated by political arguments (e.g., the "need" to regain geo-political parity, the "need" to strengthen democratic institutions), the neo-conservatives say virtually nothing about the role of the public.[54] Implicit is a power elite model with "nobless oblige" overtones focusing on the desires, orientations, wisdom, and power of the privileged classes. Since their views are more sound, their vote should count more and it is essential that they act within the system (as well as being willing to take non-institutional means if necessary). As Althuser bluntly states this position regarding blacks in the United States:[55]

> The question for us is more than one of peace, it is on of legitimacy. It is first: how can we sustain the interest of blacks in peaceful compromise -- in sharing laws, institutions and even a common nationality with the white majority? And in the second: how can we pursue this aim effectively within the American political system?

Underlying this view is a desire to restrict the scope of the political arena and to lead the "public" in the pursuit of private gain.

In sum, the pluralist view underlies Consensus theory: If those who have negative views of government take institutional actions, policies will change. Theories of radical mobilization underlie Neo-Marxist theory. Only non-institutionalized forms of political protest can bring about policy change whether it is short term and compromising or revolutionary in nature. Third party support of these means is critical to success. A "nobless oblige" version of the power elite model underlies the Conservative critique. Only the more powerful sectors need and should take institutional action to correct current errors in social policy. This brief summary suggests three different measures of political action to examine: institutional activity; non-institutional activity; and approval of the latter.[56] For each country, then, we present three analyses locating the sources of political action and change.

Tables 4 through 8 present the results. Since we are less interested in understanding the social bases of political action in each country than in the link between our previous findings and the potential for change through political action, we discard a country by country analysis in favor of an overall assessment of the viability of each ideological model. We do this by linking our discussion of the correlates of political action to the loci of negative evaluations of government performance in welfare provision for each theoretical perspective.

In the previous section, we found moderate and consistent support for the Individual Slippage model suggested by the Consensus view. Here, however, we find little evidence for political changes implied by that model. The consistent and strong role of attitudes and perceptions in explaining public reactions to welfare state policies is not paralleled here. For example, individuals who report a distrust of the government and see it run for big interests evaluate government performance more negatively in every country. These people do not express similar consistency in political action. Only in the Netherlands do individuals who see the government run for big interests report that they participate in institutionalized activity. Those who distrust the government approve of non-institutionalized forms of political action in the United States and Switzerland and, in the latter, they also indicate a willingness to engage in strikes, demonstrations, violence, etc. As might be expected, they are significantly less likely to participate through institutional channels; but, again, this is true only in two countries, Finland and Great Britain. The impact of individuals' seeing discrepancies between their actual and deserved material conditions also provides meager and inconsistent results. People who perceive more discrepancy in the United States, West Germany and Great Britain report more negative evaluations of government welfare action; yet, in Great Britain, these individuals do not indicate any significant feelings on political action of any sort. In West Germany, they are <u>less</u> willing to take non-institutional action. Only in the United States do these individuals report both greater institutionalized activity and approval of non-institutional measures, but even here there is no greater willingness to actually engage in these activities.[57]

Only one attitude provides a fairly strong and consistent result. In seven of the eight countries, individuals' evaluations of government performance influence some aspect of political activity. In two, the United States and Italy, those who disapprove are also involved in institutional political activity. In five (the United States, Italy, Finland, Great Britain and Switzerland), they indicate a willingness to take non-institutional action, and in all but Austria they express greater approval of these tactics.[58] What implications do these results have on changes in welfare state policies? Under a pure democratic model where votes are simply aggregated into policy decisions, the fact that those who disapprove of the welfare state are willing to take political action might make a difference. However, even under the pluralist model, organization into interest groups counts. In order to change welfare policies, individuals would have to join together for change. Yet the results indicate no underlying connection to organized bases of support (e.g., class, work status); without these, social mobilization theorists predict little success. If these results showed the strong and consistent influence of general negative attitudes toward the government, mobilization along this broad basis might be easier. So while the consensus view appears to locate the loci of welfare state evaluation in individual slippages, those who disapprove appear to be unwilling to translate their attitudes into action. Unless they mobilize into a single issue movement, more characteristic of the United States, their discontent may be a force against further development of the welfare state but not its retrenchment.

The Neo-Marxist model continues to provide little insight here as it did for predicting the public's view of crisis. Earlier, we found the unemployed in the United States and West Germany expressed greater disapproval. Here too the unemployed express greater approval (not willingness) of non-institutional political action. But, in general, there is a mismatch. In West Germany, Italy, Finland, Austria, the Netherlands and Switzerland, work status has an overall influence on institutional activity (and also, willingness in Finland and West Germany; approval in Switzerland; see Tables 4-8). However, with the exception of West Germany, these are not countries where the work status of individuals significantly affects reactions to government performance. There is evidence to suggest that beneficiary groups are predisposed to non-institutional action, and, in Italy and the Netherlands, approve of it. Yet these groups do not appear likely to mobilize their efforts on welfare issues since they report neither more positive nor more negative views of government action in welfare provision. This is also true with regard to political party affiliation. We do not see the "in" or "out" of power split here as we did on welfare state evaluations. Rather the split is a more traditional left-right one where left parties (in five countries), whether or not they are in power, appear to approve of or are willing to engage in non-institutional activity (see effects of party affiliation in the United States, Italy, Great Britain, the Netherlands and Switzerland). In Switzerland and Great Britain, however, this is limited only to approval (see Tables 6 and 7).[59] Italy stands as an interesting exception, as the Communist and Socialist Proletariat parties are also significantly more likely to engage in politics through the system (closer to the ideal of a Marxist working class movement). Overall, the political prospects suggested by the Neo-Marxists are poor since the left parties are splintered in their reactions to the welfare state. Establishment parties of the left lean toward non-institutional political action but do not disapprove of government welfare provision. The generally smaller and less powerful political parties express both negative evaluation and the tendency to engage in or approve of non-institutional action (e.g., the Socialist Proletariat in Italy, National Party in Finland; see Tables 4 and 5 respectively). Further, third party approval of these means from groups likely to be sympathetic to their views, critical in social mobilization theories, is virtually absent.

Continuing with the importance of political party affiliation but switching to a consideration of the Neo-Conservative view, we can see why political action on welfare state policies has tended toward limited retrenchment. Compared with other parties, parties of the right are much more likely to disapprove of non-institutional action. Only those identifying with the Republican Party in the United States report significantly greater institutional political activity than other parties; but those in the left party, the Democrats, do so as well . Since the overall effect of party is significant and the individual coefficients for right parties is in the expected direction, this indicates greater support for the nobless oblige version of political change suggested by the Neo-conservative view than any other. Further, the most consistent effect on political action, both institutional and non-institutional, is that of education. More highly educated groups report greater participation in institutional politics in six of the eight countries (Switzerland and Finland as exceptions), approval of non-institutional action in six (Switzerland and Italy as exceptions), and willingness to engage in non-institutional politics in three (the United States, West Germany and Great Britain). These groups, except in Finland and Great Britain, also express more negative views of government efforts in welfare provision. This finding is more consistent and, therefore, powerful than any support mustered for the Consensus or Neo-Marxist views. Further, benefactor groups (either high prestige, income or both, the middle-aged) overall report greater institutional activity. So while there is no one-to-one correspondence between the particular characteristics of those who give negative evaluations and who work within the system, some of the action in both sets of analyses revolves around benefactor groups. Still, their impact on changing welfare policy has been limited since only in the United States do both benefactors and those affiliated with right political parties express a propensity toward institutional politics.

There are two general conclusions to be drawn from this discussion. First, none of the ideological models provides a direct insight into how the public evaluates government performance in the area of welfare provision. In no country does the Marxist perspective correspond to the public's view, and only in the United States is the Neo-conservative model helpful. In all countries, individual dislocations suggested by the Consensus perspective find support. But second, even where these models provide an understanding of public evaluations, we do not find support for the type of political action they see as necessary to change policy in the desired directions. Benefactor groups, who disapprove of welfare policies, only weakly report a greater willingness to be involved within the system and to work outside it. An absence of commitment to engage in political action of any sort suggests that negative attitudes will not be translated into political change.

TECHNICAL APPENDIX

DATA. The data used to examine the public evaluation of the welfare crisis are taken from Barnes and Kaase's cross-national survey, "Political Action -- An Eight Nation Study". Though the design and analysis were done collaboratively, separate national research groups executed and financed their survey. National sample surveys were conducted in each of the eight countries from November, 1973 to May, 1976. Multistage probability samples to the dwelling unit were used in each country to select a representative cross-section of the population 16 years of age and over (in Austria people over 70 were excluded; the Swiss survey interviewed no one younger than 20 years old). To insure that each national sample was representative of its population, several variables such as sex, marital status, age, education, and religion were compared with the country's census data. Researchers paid close attention to the problems of data comparability. Overall sample sizes are: Great Britain (N=2345), West Germany (N=3195), Netherlands (N=1800) Austria (N=2493) United States (N=2429) Italy (N=2500); Switzerland (N=1840) Finland (N=1676). We restrict our analysis to the unpaired cross-section of the sample. More detailed descriptions of sampling procedures, interviewer characteristics and comparisons of sample estimates with census characteristics are archived with the Zentralarchiv für Empirische Sozialforschung, University of Cologne. See Barnes and Kaase, cited earlier, for a more detailed description.

ANALYTIC TECHNIQUES. We use ordinary least squares regression to examine the different ideological models of public evaluation of welfare issues. A single linear and additive equation provides an empirical test of the three models (with one exception, discussed below):

(1) Evaluation = f(social position, party affiliation, attitudes and perceptions)

If the Individual Slippage model operates, we expect no significant coefficients for the social position of party affiliation variables but the coefficients of the attitudes and perception factors to be significant. Under the Beneficiary Disillusionment model, given the coding of the variables (see below), we expect the effects of social position to be significant and negative. In addition, the effects of age and left political party should be positive and significant. if a Benefactor Crunch model operates, the expected sign of the coefficients is reversed from those above.

The "middle mass" version of the Benefactor Crunch model calls for additional analyses. The curvilinear relationships predicted require a second specification adding squared terms for age, social class, family income and occupational prestige to the linear and additive equation (1):

(2) Evaluation = f(social position, party affiliation, attitudes and perceptions, social position^2).

We expect the squared terms for age, social class, income and occupational prestige to be significant. Specifically, here, we expect the coefficient for the linear term to be positive while the coefficient for the squared term to be negative.

In order to reduce the complexity of the presentation of results and improve the stability of the final coefficients, we ran preliminary analyses using a number of other variables that might be important (e.g., gender) and all of the squared terms. In the final versions presented, we dropped any variables consistently unrelated to the dependent variables and not influencing the effects of other independent variables. As a result, only one of the squared terms remains in the model (e.g., age). In all tables, we report the unstandardized coefficients and their corresponding significance tests (alpha-level = .05, two-tailed test).

MEASURES.

WELFARE STATE EVALUATION SCALE; Respondents were asked a series of questions on "issues and problems that people often talk about these days". One question asks: "How well do you think the government has been doing in handling this problem?" We combined individual responses (very good, good, bad, very bad) for the following six welfare-state related items into the factor analytic scale:

1. Looking after old people
2. Seeing to it that everyone who wants a job can have one
3. Providing good education
4. Providing good medical care
5. Providing adequate housing
6. Trying to even out differences in wealth between people

For all countries, factor loadings were over .5 (with few exceptions, e.g., the loading on the sixth item often loaded in the .4 range). The reliability coefficients, Cronbach's alpha, are: United States (.76), Italy (.81), Finland (.67), West Germany (.68), Great Britain (.74), Austria (.65), Netherlands (.67) and Switzerland (.70).

A higher score on this scale indicates great disillusionment or disapproval of the government's performance on these issues overall.

AGE: Actual age is reported in years or computed from the date of birth (in the British, Dutch, Austrian and Swiss surveys).

SOCIAL CLASS: This is a three category subjective measure - working class, middle class (Austria and Germany: middle and lower middle class) and upper middle class. Higher score indicates upper social classes.

EDUCATION: In West Germany, Austria, United States, Italy and Switzerland, the highest grade of school or year of college completed is reported and coded from low to high. In Great Britain, the Netherlands and Finland, the type of school or college last attended is reported. In these three countries we construct dummy variables for the educational categories. Both the included and omitted categories are indicated on each table.

OCCUPATIONAL PRESTIGE: This measure is based on Treiman's standard international scale. The 92 point index ranges from -2 (low prestige, "gatherer") to 90 (high prestige, chief of state). See Donald J. Treiman, _Occupational Prestige in Comparative Perspective_ (New York: Academic Press, 1977).

FAMILY INCOME: The total amount of money that the family received from all sources after taxes and deductions is reported. The Italian survey contained no explicit question pertaining to family income. Instead the following two questions were asked: "What monthly figure would your family need to live without worrying financially?" "Which amount is missing?" The second figure was subtracted from the first. In the United States, family income is based on gross income for 1973.

WORK STATUS: A combination of the respondent's present employment status and self-employment status results in the following set of dummy variables: self-employed; works for someone else, part-time; retired or disabled; housewife; and, unemployed. The omitted category is works full-time for someone else.

POLITICAL PARTY AFFILIATION: Respondents in each country were asked: "Which political party do you feel closest to?" We assign dummy variables for each political party in the eight countries. In West Germany and Austria, the question was worded slightly differently: "Many people in your country lean toward a particular party for a long time, although they may occasionally vote for a different party. How about you: do you lean towards a particular party? If so, which one?"

IMPORTANCE OF WELFARE ISSUES: In the same series of questions on current important issues listed under the evaluation measure, respondents were asked: "How important is this problem in your view?" The recoded responses for each of the welfare issues (very important, important, not very important and absolutely unimportant) were combined into a factor scale with a higher score indicating greater importance. Due to the low reliability of this scale in some countries (Italy, Finland and the Netherlands), the results in these countries should be treated with some caution. Details on loadings and reliability coefficients will be provided on request.

GOVERNMENT RESPONSIBILITY FOR WELFARE ISSUES: In the same series, respondents were asked: "How much responsibility do you think the government has for dealing with this problem?" Recoded responses (an essential responsibility, an important responsibility, some responsibility, no responsibility at all) were factor analyzed and combined into a scale with a higher score indicating greater perceived responsibility. Here, both factor loadings and reliability coefficients indicate a strong scale (details on request).

DISCREPANCY, IMPROVEMENT IN MATERIAL SATISFACTION: Three questions based on a measurement technique by Cantril determine the respondents' satisfaction with the material side of their lives. Respondents place themselves on a self-anchoring ladder that is scaled from zero (completely dissatisfied) to ten (completely satisfied). Respondents report their present satisfaction, past satisfaction and their "deserved" satisfaction.

The exact wording is as follows: (1) Present satisfaction: "All things considered, how satisfied or dissatisfied are you overall with the material side of your life today?" (2) Past satisfaction: "Where would you have put yourself five years ago?" (3) "Entitled" satisfaction: "What level of material satisfaction do you feel that people like yourself are entitled to?" Scores of the differences between these various questions on material satisfaction are used to construct measures of improvement and discrepancy. To measure improvement, past satisfaction is subtracted from present satisfaction. Similarly, the measure of discrepancy is derived by subtracting present satisfaction from entitled satisfaction. Both scales range from -10 (low improvement or low discrepancy) to +10 (greater improvement or greater discrepancy).

GOVERNMENT FOR THE PEOPLE: This question asks "Generally speaking, would you say that this country is run by a few big interests looking out for themselves or that it is run for the benefit of all the people?" A dummy variable is scored one if the respondent indicates that the government is run for the benefit of big interests and zero for the benefit of all people.

DISTRUST OF GOVERNMENT: Respondents were asked: "how much do you trust the government to do what is right?" Scores range from 1 (just about always, low distrust) to 4 (almost never, high distrust).

INSTITUTIONALIZED POLITICAL ACTION: Respondents were asked four questions: "How often do you try to convince friends to vote the same as you? How often do you attend a political rally or meeting? How often do you contact public officials or politicians? How often do you spend time working for a political party or candidate?" The recoded responses (ranging from 1=never to 4=often) were factor analyzed and combined into a scale. Factor loadings are over .5 with few exceptions and reliability coefficients are over .75 with the exception of Great Britain (alpha = .69) and the Netherlands (alpha = .71).

NON-INSTITUTIONALIZED PROTEST ORIENTATION AND APPROVAL: These two measures are drawn from a series of questions asked of respondents regarding "some kinds of action that people sometimes take to protest about something or simply make their views known to other people". Of the ten available, we eliminated one (signing a petition) and employed the remaining nine as indicators of non-institutional action. They are:

1. Joining in boycotts
2. Attending lawful demonstrations
3. Refusing to pay rent, taxes, etc.
4. Joining in wildcat strikes
5. Painting slogans on walls
6. Occupying buildings or factories -- "sit-ins"
7. Blocking traffic (with a street demonstration)

8. Damaging things like breaking windows, removing road signs, etc.
9. Using personal violence like fighting with other demonstrators or the police

The protest orientation measure is a simple likert scale. Respondents were handed a list of activities and asked: "...show me, first, whether 1) you have actually done any of these things on the cards during the past ten years; 2) you would do any of these things if it were important to you; 3) you might do it in a particular situation or 4) you would never do it under any circumstances." We added up the number of activities which respondents indicated they would or might do. A higher score indicates a greater willingness to use non-institutional means of political action. Again, in all countries, the reliability analysis showed the scale to be strong (Chronbach's alpha over .7 in all countries except Italy).

Regarding approval, respondents were asked "whether, in a general way, you feel you approve strongly, approve, disapprove or disapprove strongly." Recoded responses, ranging from (1) disagree strongly to (4) agree strongly were factor analyzed and combined into a scale. Loadings were generally over .4 and reliability coefficients over .75. In a number of cases, the violence items (8 and 9 above) had factor loadings in the .3 range but, for theoretical reasons, we left them in the final scale.

Table 1. Regression Analysis of Negative Public Reaction to Government Action in Welfare State Sectors-United States, Italy and Finland.

Independent Variable	United States b	United States t	Italy b	Italy t	Finland b	Finland t
Age	.017*	2.76	.010	.99	.004	.42
Age Squared[1]	-.002*	2.92	-.000	.77	-.000	.17
Social Class	.064*	2.09	.021	.48	.074	1.49
Education[2]	.004*	3.26	.056*	1.96		
Less than Public school					-.037	.32
Elementary and Trade School					.019	.34
Secondary or Public school					.083	.95
Secondary/Public and Trade school					.067	.71
Examination for college admission					.247*	2.04
College exam /trade/upper school					.062	.40
University exams					.009	.06
Occupational Prestige	.001	.60	.000	.04	-.001	.40
Family Income	.013*	2.36	.001	.24	.001	.13
Work Status[3]						
Self-employed	-.096	1.23	-.132	1.67	-.063	.82
Works for other part-time	-.084	.98	-.008	.07	-.186	1.58
Retired, disabled	.006	.08	-.129	1.28	-.226*	2.66
Housewife	-.038	.76	-.119	1.73	.015	.19
Unemployed	.228*	2.04	-.066	.39	.094	.52
Political Party Affiliation[4,5]						
Democratic	-.121*	2.26				
Republican	-.211*	3.49				
Italian Communist Party (PCI)			.085	1.02		
Italian Socialist Party of Proletarian Unity(PSIUP-DPUP)			.549*	2.49		
Social Democratic Party (PSDI)			-.068	.43		
Italian Republican Party (PRI)			-.167	.96		
Christian Democratic Party (DC)			-.221*	2.64		
Italian Liberal Party (PLI)			.075	.40		
Neo-Fascist Italian Social Movement (MSI)			.025	.16		
No difference among the parties			.057	.60		
Social Democratic Party (SDP)					-.201*	3.12
Finnish Rural Party (SMP)					-.284*	2.24
Centre Party (KEK)					-.299*	3.70
Liberal Party (LKP)					-.150	1.31
Swedish People's Party (RKP)					-.184	1.34
Popular Democratic Party (KDK)					-.239*	2.66
Importance of Welfare Issues	.105*	2.21	.222*	3.18	.116*	2.07
Government Responsibility for Welfare Sector	.039	1.30	.108*	2.14	.082*	2.20
Discrepancy in material satisfaction	.034*	3.58	.009	.66	--[6]	--
Improvement in material satisfaction	-.005	.67	-.007	.62	--	--
Government for Big Interests	.179*	4.02	.273*	4.23	.179*	3.91
Distrust of government	.205*	7.51	.282*	7.35	.130*	3.98
Constant	1.10		.69		1.96	
R^2	.20		.36		.15	
S.E.E.	.61		.58		.54	
F	13.9 $p \leq .001$		11.7 $p \leq .001$		4.33 $p \leq .001$	
(N)	(1056)		(547)		(708)	

*$p \leq .05$, two-tailed test.

1 Coefficient is multiplied by 10.

2 In U.S. and Italy, education is coded in years; dummy categories for Finland only (Elementary school completed, omitted).

3 Omitted category: full time, working for others

4 Omitted categories: U.S. (no party preference), Italy (Italian Socialist Party, PSI), Finland (National Party, SKDL).

5 Overall, party preference (as a set of dummy variables) is significant in the U.S., Italy and Finland

6 Discrepancy and improvement variables not available in Finland.

Table 2. Regression Analysis of Negative Public Reactions to Government Action in Welfare State Sectors-West Germany, Great Britain and Austria.

Independent Variables	West Germany b	West Germany t	Great Britain b	Great Britain t	Austria b	Austria t
Age	-.012*	2.71	.005	.82	-.012	1.24
Age Squared[1]	.001	1.93	-.000	.45	.001	1.03
Social Class	.014	.55	-.040	.98	-.008	.18
Education[2]	.028*	3.66			.048*	2.17
Elementary/Primary			-.064	1.17		
Technical School			.198	1.52		
Comprehensive			-.065	.63		
Grammar School			-.020	.29		
Technical/Art			.016	.20		
University			.084	.73		
Commerical/Vocational			.198	1.91		
Public School Only			.156	1.24		
Occupational Prestige	-.000	.33	.006*	3.08	.003	1.28
Family Income	.002	.32	.009	1.10	.011	1.23
Work Status[3]						
Self-employed	-.084	1.59	-.167*	2.05	-.005	.06
Works for others, part time	.005	.09	-.209*	3.39	.125	1.20
Retired, disabled	.019	.36	-.124	1.62	.042	.46
Housewife	.047	1.34	-.184*	3.82	.106	1.72
Unemployed	.321*	2.03	-.112	.64	.234	.88
Political Party Affiliation[4,5]						
Social Democratic Party (SPD)	.051	.82				
Christian Democratic Union/Christian Social Union (CDU/CSU)	.101	1.65				
No Party Preference	.077	1.25				
Conservative			-.151*	2.54		
Labour			.147*	2.54		
Socialist					-.072	.65
Right and Extreme Right					-.275	1.74
Peasant Parties					-.190	1.47
Socialist (SPO)					-.144	.96
Austrian Peoples Party (OVP)					-.062	.42
No Party Preference					-.006	.04
Importance of Welfare Issues	-.030	.83	.022	.37	-.027	.45
Government Responsibility for Welfare Sector	-.101*	3.50	.039	1.07	-.195*	4.25
Discrepancy in Material Satisfaction	.021*	2.67	.036*	3.77	.023	1.68
Improvement in Material Satisfaction	.011	1.70	-.005	.69	-.007	.60
Government for Big Interests	.261*	8.29	.212*	4.96	.236*	4.07
Distruct of Government	.133*	7.03	.204*	7.47	.158*	4.83
Constant	3.31		1.79		3.33	
R^2	.16		.30		.23	
S.E.E.	.54		.56		.53	
F	16.31 $p \leq .001$		15.28 $p \leq .001$		8.55 $p \leq .001$	
(N)	(1723)		(956)		(585)	

*p ≤.05, two-tailed test

[1]Coefficient multiplied by 10.

[2]In West Germany and Austria, education coded in years; dummy categories for Great Britain only (secondary modern, omitted).

[3]Omitted Category: full time, working for others. Overall the set of work status dummies is significant in Great Britain.

[4]Omitted Categories: West Germany (Free Democratic Party, FDP), Great Britain (Liberal), Austria (Liberal Party, FPO)

[5]Overall party affiliation is significant in Great Britain.

Table 3. Regression Analyses of Negative Public Reactions to Government Action in Welfare State Sectors-Netherlands, Switzerland.

Independent Variables	Netherlands b	Netherlands t	Switzerland b	Switzerland t
Age	.007	1.02	.010	1.26
Age Squared[1]	-.001	1.36	-.001	1.52
Social Class	-.032	.87	-.021	.52
Education[2]			.021	1.57
Little or no schooling	.236	1.63		
Elementary	-.048	.76		
Secondary school (< 3 years)	.030	.33		
Lower occupational course	.031	.45		
Secondary school (3-4 years)	-.022	..30		
Secondary school (5-6 years)	.082	.82		
Middle occ./incomplete Undergraduate	.018	.26		
Semi-higher occupational	.096	.96		
Graduate study/higher occupational	.059	.46		
Occupational Prestige	.004*	2.18	-.001	.59
Family Income	-.016	1.61	.012	1.06
Work Status				
Self-employed	-.008	.09	-.090	1.22
Works for others, part-time	-.021	.24	.027	.28
Retired, disabled	.009	.10	.020	.23
Housewife	.034	.68	-.017	.32
Unemployed	-.118	.79	.204	.91
Political Party Affiliation[4,5]				
Pacifist Socialist Party (PSP)	.524*	3.66		
Labor Party (PVD)	-.013	.20		
Party for Freedom and Democracy (VVD)	.106	1.47		
Anti-Revolutionary Party (ARP)	-.114	1.16		
Christian Historical Union (CHU)	-.109	1.10		
Radical Party (PPR)	.119	1.29		
Communist Party (CPN)	.123	.87		
Other Parties	-.023	.19		
CDA (3 Christian Parties)	-.010	.09		
No Party Preference	-.053	.69		
Liberal Parties			-.217*	1.95
No Party Preference			-.240*	2.20
Religious Parties (Christian Democrats)			-.221	1.92
Communist			.105	.61
Socialist			-.072	.65
Right and Extreme Right			-.275	1.74
Peasant Parties			-.190	1.47
Importance of Welfare Issues	-.006	.10	.108*	2.02
Government Responsibility for Welfare Sector	-.059	1.34	-.121*	2.94
Discrepancy in Material Satisfaction	.019	1.56	.019	1.75
Improvement in Material Satisfaction	-.002	.16	.009	.92
Government for Big Interests	.127*	3.03	.134*	2.72
Distrust of Government	.156*	5.65	.155*	4.55
Constant	2.74		2.49	
R^2	.17		.15	
S.E.E.	.51		.53	
F	4.22 $p \leq .001$		4.81 $p \leq .001$	
(N)	(759)		(689)	

*$p \leq .05$, two-tailed test

[1]Coefficient multiplied by 10.

[2]In Switzerland, education coded in years; dummy categories for Netherlands only (extended lower occupational school, omitted).

[3]Omitted category: full-time, working for others.

[4]Omitted categories: Netherlands (Catholic People's Party, KVP) Switzerland (Independents). In Switzerland parties are grouped by type, according to the Swiss research teams designations.

[5]Overall, party affiliation is significant in the Netherlands and Switzerland.

Table 4. Regression Analyses of Political Action and Protest Orientation - the United States and Italy.

Independent Variables	United States Institutionalized Activity b	United States Non-Institutionalized Willingness b	United States Non-Institutionalized Approval b	Italy Institutionalized Activity b	Italy Non-Institutionalized Willingness b	Italy Non-Institutionalized Approval b
Age	.027*	-.065*	-.025*	.007	-.036	-.021*
Age Squared[1]	-.002*	.003[5]	.001*	-.001	.001	.002
Social Class	.094*	.046	-.014	-.015	-.169	-.116*
Education	.006*	.008*	.003*	.130*	-.008	.035
Occupational Prestige	.006*	.003	.000	.003	.003	.002
Family Income	.010	.029*	.000	-.001	.005	.001
Work Status[2]						
Self-employed	.059	.063	.006	-.081	-.332	.054
Works for other, part-time	.039	.137	.076	.046	.192	.186
Retired, disabled	-.054	.096	.101	-.002	.036	.057
Housewife	-.147*	-.209	.043	-.357*	-.070	.086
Unemployed	.042	.086	.164	-.037	.743	.469*
Political Party Affiliation[3]						
Democratic	.257*	.279*	.024			
Republican	.247*	.148	-.132*			
Italian Communist Party (PCI)				.300*	.406	.227*
Italian Socialist Party of Proletarian Unity (PSIUP-PDUP)				.903*	1.414*	1.431*
Social Democratic Party (PSDI				.060	-.710	-.345*
Italian Republican Party (PRI)				.131	-.348	-.211
Christian Democratic Party (DC)				.037	-.543*	-.130
Italian Liberal Party (PLI)				-.154	-1.372*	-.530*
Neo-Fascist Italian Social Movement (MSI)				.185	-.979*	-.339*
No difference among the parties				-.288*	-.371	-.021
Importance of Welfare Issues	-.048	-.006	-.048	.061	.237	-.012
Government Responsibility for Welfare Sector	.040	.023	.036	-.031	-.014	-.002
Discrepancy in Material Satisfaction	-.012	.060*	.021*	.025	-.005	-.010
Improvement in Material Satisfaction	.003	.030	.008	.007	-.022	-.007
Government for Big Interests	.032	.069	.031	.083	.163	.055
Distrust of Government	-.028	.025	.070*	-.072	-.068	.053
Evaluation of Government Performance in Welfare	.087*	.328*	.120*	.123*	.345*	.175*
Constant	.03	1.91	2.48	.71	1.33	1.85
R^2	.18	.22	.24	.27	.24	.37
S.E.E.	.68	1.64	.57	.69	1.62	.55
F[4]	11.4	14.7	16.27	7.33	6.33	11.55
(N)	(1056)	(1056)	(1056)	(547)	(547)	(547)

*$p \leq .05$, two-tailed test.
[1]Coefficient is multiplied by 10.
[2]Omitted Category: full time, working for others. Overall effect significant in Italy for Institutionalized Activity
[3]Omitted Categories: US (no party preference), Italy (Italian Socialist Party,PSI) Overall the effect of party affiliation is significant for Institutionalized activity and approval and for all three in Italy.
[4]p-value always $\leq .001$ unless otherwise indicated.
[5]$p \leq .065$

able 5. Regression Analyses of Political Action and Protest Orientation- Finland and West Germany.

ndependent Variables	Finland Institutionalized Activity	Finland Non-Institutionalized Willingness	Finland Non-Institutionalized Approval	West Germany Institutionalized Activity	West Germany Non-Institutionalized Willingness	West Germany Non-Institutionalized Approval
ge	.019	-.047	-.011	.015*	-.045*	-.026*
ge Squared[1]	-.001	.002	.000	-.002*	.001	.002*
ocial Class	-.006	-.029	-.006	.057	-.192*	-.115*
ducation[2]				.056*	.146*	.053*
Less than public school	.067	-.401	.131			
Elementary & trade school	-.084	.192	.119*			
Secondary or public school	-.063	.174	.095			
Secondary/public and trade school	-.158	.624*	.072			
Examination for college admission	.106	1.45*	.383*			
College exam/trade/upper school	.301	.471	.180			
University exams	.079	.638	.189			
ccupational Prestige	.007*	.012	.002	.001	.003	.001
amily Income	.004	.028	-.004	.024*	.010	-.006
rk Status[3]						
Self-employed	.118	-.298	-.068	.082	-.334	-.136*
Works for other, part-time	-.102	.431	.024	-.347*	-.422*	-.061
Retired, disabled	-.260*	-.158	.019	-.107	-.273	-.088
Housewife	-.186*	-.669*	-.027	-.334*	-.416*	-.083*
Unemployed	-.165	-.300	.013	-.241	.593	.020
litical Party Affiliation[4,5]						
Social Democratic Party (SDP)	-.243*	-.269	-.217*			
Finnish Rural Party (SMP)	-.373*	-.473	-.257*			
Centre Party (KEK)	-.226*	-.898*	-.387*			
Liberal Party (LKP)	-.333*	-.870*	-.287*			
Swedish People's Party (RKP)	-.522*	-1.75*	-.798*			
Popular Democratic Party (KOK)	-.354*	-1.20*	-.521*			
Social Democratic Party (SPD)				.198*	.362	.122[8]
Christian Democratic Union/Christian Social Union (CDU/CSU)				.021	-.490*	-.243*
No Party Preference				-.094	-.250	-.103
portance of Welfare Issues	-.058	.015	-.018	.039	-.273*	-.094*
vernment Responsibility for Welfare Sector	.043	.001	.035	-.034	.028	.029
screpancy in Material Satisfaction				-.009	-.052[8]	.005
provement in material Satisfaction				-.012	-.052*	-.005
vernment for Big Interests	.060	.262	.045	-.038	-.075	.020
strust of government	-.085*	-.136	-.025	-.044[8]	-.045	.006
aluation of Government Performance in Welfare	-.014	.348*	.098*	.067*	.109	.071*
Constant	1.41	2.44	2.94	1.00	5.09	3.00
R^2	.10	.23	.22	.17	.20	.23
S.E.E.	.64	1.86	.55	.68	1.89	.57
F7	2.66	7.33	6.73	17.19	19.98	24.07
(N)	(708)	(708)	(708)	(1723)	(1723)	(1723)

≤.05, two-tailed test.
efficient is multiplied by 10.
West Germany education is coded in years; dummy categories for Finland only (elementary school completed, itted). Overall effect significant for willingness.
itted category: full time, working for others. Overall effect significant in Finland for Institutionalized tivity; in West Germany for this and willingness.
itted categories: Finland (National Party SKDL), West Germany (Free Democratic Party, FDP).
erall, party preference (as a set of dummy variables) is significant in West Germany in all three equations.
screpancy and improvement variables not available in Finland.
≤ .001 unless otherwise indicated
≤ .07

Table 6. Regression Analyses of Political Action and Protest Orientation- Great Britain and Austria.

Independent Variables	Great Britain Institutionalized Activity	Great Britain Non-Institutionalized Willingness	Great Britain Non-Institutionalized Approval	Austria Institutionalized Activity	Austria Non-Institutionalized Willingness	Austria Non-Institutionalized Approval
Age	.008	-.078*	-.020*	.010	-.067*	-.018
Age Squared[1]	-.000	.001*	.001	-.001	.000	.001
Social Class	.061	-.171	-.097*	-.034	-.300*	-.027
Education[2]				.074*	.053	.079*
Elementary/Primary	.032	-.078	-.035			
Technical School	.160	.534	.094			
Comprehensive	.028	.465	-.084			
Grammar School	.158*	.309	.107			
Technical/Art	.026	.557*	.150*			
University	.215*	.843*	.350*			
Commercial/Vocational	.104	.910*	.063			
Public School Only	.377*	-.168	.275*			
Occupational Prestige	.004*	.013*	-.002	-.001	.020*	.003
Family Income	.021*	.111*	-.013	.018	.066*	.002
Work Status[3]						
Self-employed	-.033	.447	.067	.124	-.223	-.032
Works for others, part-time	-.088	-.436	-.106	-.316*	-.175	.065
Retired, disabled	-.094	.143	.063	-.104	.055	.039
Housewife	-.105*	-.212	.004	-.203*	-.243	.018
Unemployed	-.033	.087	-.071	-.225	-1.14	-.655*
Political Party Affiliation[4]						
Conservative	-.064	-.314	-.075			
Labour	.039	-.023	.127*			
Socialist (SPO)				.293	-.373	-.013
Austrian Peoples Party (OVP)				.197	-.283	-.081
No Party Preference				-.037	-.623	-.026
Importance of Welfare Issues	-.037	-.064	-.040	-.015	.067	-.102
Government Responsibility for Welfare Sector	.019	.097	-.002	.051	.027	.018
Discrepancy in Material Satisfaction	.003	.025	.012	.023	.078	.032*
Improvement in Material Satisfaction	-.004	-.025	.002	.006	.008	-.003
Government for Big Interests	.056	.121	.041	.109	.156	-.011
Distrust of Government	-.064*	.008	.017	-.036	-.188	-.027
Evaluation of Government Performance in Welfare	.016	.227*	.097*	-.065	.242	.040
Constant	.92	2.34	3.27	1.12	2.34	2.99
R^2	.09	.23	.21	.10	.11	.11
S.E.E.	.55	1.75	.54	.69	1.80	.64
F	3.48	10.06	9.55	3.01	3.40	3.37
(N)	(956)	(956)	(956)	(585)	(585)	(585)

*p .05, two-tailed test

[1] Coefficient multiplied by 10.

[2] In Austria, education coded in years; dummy categories for Great Britain only (secondary modern, omitted). Overall effect significant for willingness and approval there.

[3] Omitted Category: full time, wroking for others. Over-all effect significant in Austria for Institutionalized activity.

[4] Omitted categories: Great Britain (Liberal), Austria (Liberal Party, FPO). Overall effect significant for approval in Great Britain and Institutionalized-activity in Austria.

[5] p ≤ .001 unless otherwise indicated.

Table 7. Regression Analyses of Political Action and Protest Orientation- the Netherlands and Switzerland.

Independent Variables	Netherlands Institutionalized Activity	Netherlands Non-Institutionalized Willingness	Netherlands Non-Institutionalized Approval	Switzerland Institutionalized Activity	Switzerland Non-Institutionalized Willingness	Switzerland Non-Institutionalized Approval
Age	-.002	-.027	.002	.023*	-.073*	-.020*
Age Squared[1]	.000	-.002	-.001	-.002*	.003	.001
Social Class	.040	-.310*	-.109*	-.007	.009	-.020
Education[2]						
Little or no schooling	-.095	-.922	-.140			
Elementary	-.038	.015	.046			
Secondary School (< 3 years)	-.041	-.166	-.048			
Lower Occupational course	.006	.398	.123			
Secondary School (3-4 years)	.041	.381	.238*			
Secondary School (5-6 years)	.251*	.377	.088			
Middle occ/incomplete undergraduate	.223*	.072	.138			
Semi-higher occupational	.177[8]	.274	.352*			
Graduate study/higher occupational	.175	1.09*	.725*			
ccupational Prestige	.002	.006	.001	.003	.009	.007*
amily Income	.018[8]	.089*	.010	.016	.032	.007
ork Status						
Self-employed	.104	-.142	-.079	.005	.286	.115
Works for others, part-time	-.104	.104	.081	-.195	-.055	.165
Retired, disabled	-.037	.130	.031	-.119	.084	.057
Housewife	-.050	-.202	.067	-.302*	-.094	.039
Unemployed	.392*	-.036	.384*	.065	.855	.788*
olitical Party Affiliation[4,5]						
Pacifist Socialist Party	.174	1.02[6]	.546*			
Labor Party	.124*	.578*	.254*			
Party for Freedom & Democracy	-.014	-.325	-.200*			
Anti-Revolutionary Party	.128	-.084	-.061			
Christian Historical Union	.097	-.282	-.153			
Radical Party	.157	.528	.272*			
Communist Party	.186	1.31*	.611*			
Other Parties	-.085	-.010	-.088			
CDA (3 Christian Parties)	.047	-.053	-.112			
No Party Preference	-.133	-.345	-.002			
Liberal Party				.029	-.745*	-.267*
Religious Parties				.089	-.581	-.274*
Communist Party				-.228	.204	.564*
Socialist Party				.121	-.150	.132
Right Parties				-.054	-.192	-.045
Peasant Parties				.097	-.938*	-.246
No Party Preference				-.421*	-1.10*	-.217
portance of Welfare Issues	-.038	-.127	-.073	-.010	-.127	-.039
vernment Responsibility for Welfare Sector	.050	.407*	.193*	-.020	-.146	.003
screpancy in Material Satisfaction	.002	-.009	.005	-.001	.022	.000
provement in Material Satisfaction	-.336	.046	.001	.017	.022	-.004
vernment for Big Interests	.113*	.122	.074	.014	-.108	.028
strust of Government	-.023	-.087	-.002	-.030	.356*	.163*
aluation of Government Performance in Welfare.	-.014	.247	.161*	.010	.389*	.172*
Constant	1.05	2.03	1.90	1.19	4.15	1.93
R^2	.13	.24	.29	.21	.24	.27
S.E.E.	.51	1.95	.60	.66	1.83	.60
F[5]	2.92	6.38	8.03	6.95	8.34	9.95
(N)	(759)	(759)	(759)	(689)	(689)	(689)

< .05, two-tailed test
oefficient multiplied by 10.
Switzerland, education coded in years; dummy categories for Netherlands only (extended lower occupational
hool, omitted). Overall effect significant for approval.
itted category: full-time, working for others. Overall effect significant for Institutionalized activity
the Netherlands, for this and approval in Switzerland.
itted categories: Netherlands (Catholic People's Party, KVP), Switzerland (Independents), In Switzerland
rties are grouped by type, according to the Swiss research teams designations. Overall effect significant
Switzerland and the Netherlands for all three.
≤ .001 unless otherwise indicated.
≤ .07

NOTES

1. Ramesh Mishra, Society and Social Policy: Theories and Practice of Welfare (New Jersey, Humanities Press, 1981), 169.

2. What results we do have are contradictory. A number of researchers find the majority of the public across nations supporting government efforts in social welfare. On the other hand, Hibbs and Madsen's work finds increasing support for reducing levels of spending in Denmark, Sweden and Great Britain. See Samuel Barnes and Max Kaase, Political Action: Mass Participation in Five Western Democracies (Beverly Hills: Sage, 1979); Alan Marsh, Protest and Political Consensus (Beverly Hills, Sage, 1977); Richard Coughlin, Ideology, Public Opinion and Welfare Policy (Berkeley: Institute of International Studies, 1980); Lloyd Free and Hadley Cantril, The Political Beliefs of Americans (New Jersey: Rutgers University Press, 1976); Douglas Hibbs and Henrik Madsen, "Public reaction to the growth of taxation and government expenditure.", World Politics 33 (1981); Michael Shalev, "The Social Democratic model and beyond: Two 'generations' of comparative research on the welfare state." In Richard F. Tomasson (ed.) Comparative Social Research (Greenwich, Ct.: JAI Press, 1983).

3. Mishra sees the public loss of confidence at the heart of the welfare state crisis. See Ramesh Mishra, The Welfare State in Crisis: Social Thought and Social Change (New York: St. Martin's Press, 1984). Also see M.C.P.M. Van Schendelen, "Crisis of the Dutch Welfare State", Contemporary Crises 7 (1983).

4. Research on the public evaluation of the welfare state has had persistent shortcomings. Studies limited to one country obviate a test of how generally widespread disapproval is and how the socio-political context across nations impacts differently on the public. Further, few studies of public attitudes toward the welfare state consider political action.

5. We recognize the limitations of a cross-sectional analysis, but data over time on attitudes about how well the state performs do not exist. We strike a compromise by examining the determinants of public approval in the unique social context of each country and then comparing these findings across eight countries.

6. Outlined in Mishra, 1984, pp. 1-25.

7. For general discussions of these factors, see Samuel Bowles and Herbert Gintis, "The crisis of liberal democratic capitalism: The case of the

United States.", Politics and Society 11 (1982); Gosta Esping-Andersen, "Comparative social policy and political conflict in advanced welfare states: Denmark and Sweden.", International Journal of Health Services 9 (1979); Walter Korpi, "Social democracy in welfare capitalism -- structural erosion, welfare backlash and incorporation?", Acta Sociological 21 (1978); Seymour M. Lipset and William Schneider, The Confidence Gap (New York: Free Press, 1983); James O'Connor, The Fiscal Crisis of the State (New York, St. Martin's Press, 1973); Richard Rose and Guy Peters, Can Government Go Bankrupt? (New York: Basic Books, 1978); Deborah A. Stone, The Disabled State (Philadelphia: Temple University Press, 1984); Jeffrey D. Straussman, "Spending more and enjoying it less: On the political economy of advanced capitalism.", Contemporary Politics 13 (1981); and, Harold Wilensky, The Welfare State and Equality (Berkeley: University of California Press, 1975).

8. Any and all of these problems can constitute a "crisis" for welfare states and the term "crisis" is neither self-evident nor neutral. Van Schendelen has provided a useful taxonomy of the "crises" of the welfare state. A crisis of consensus occurs when the government and its citizens suddenly and fundamentally disagree about each other's obligations and rights. An economic crisis results from a sharp decrease in a nation's wealth. A crisis of the public sector's growth entails the stagnation of formerly expanding social programs. A crisis of redistribution targets the failure of government intervention to affect set goals of equity. Finally, a crisis of governmental effectiveness follows the government's failure to demonstrate the efficacy of its chosen policies (e.g., the production of public goods for which there is no demand). These dimensions of crisis are not independent, often provoking or aggravating each other. Where politicians or analysts of the political system choose to lay major blame forms a critical part of their ideological stance. And which problems of those cited above become the targets reveal not only a clash of values regarding the most critical features of welfare state problems but also leads to rationales to gather support for future social policy. In the Netherlands, Van Schendelen claims that the "official" reading of the current crisis focuses on the weaknesses of the international economy and provides a mask for political instabilities in the Dutch political and welfare systems. O'Connor and Van Schendelen only see the state as having the necessity to "manipulate the word 'crisis' with the purpose of building support for new

interventionist policies." James O'Connor, "Accumulation crisis: the problem and its setting", Contemporary Crisis 5(1981), pp. 121; Van Schendelen, 1983.

9. Of course, total agreement is unnecessary. As Marshall puts it, "Total consensus with regard to them (altruistic values) is unthinkable, outside a devout religious community, but without a foundation of near-consensus, no general social welfare policy would be possible." T.H. Marshall, The Right to Welfare (New York: The Free Press), pp. 109 (parenthetical insert added). See also T. H. Marshall. Class, Citizenship and Social Development (Garden City, N.Y.: Doubleday, 1965). In 1972, even Neo-Marxists, like Offe conceded, "By this time even the taxpaying man on the street has accepted features of the welfare state as at least necessary evils." Claus Offe, "Advanced capitalism and the welfare state.", Politics and Society 2 (1972), p. 479.

10. See Wilensky, 1975; also Robert Jackman, Politics and Social Equality (New York: John Wiley and Sons, 1975). Of course citizenship and industrialization theories differ on many counts but they share an inevitable tone about the development of the welfare state. See Mishra's discussion of these theories, 1981, Pp. 27-65.

11. Esping-Andersen, 1979.

12. See Jackman, 1975; Offe, 1972; Wilensky, 1975 and Flora and Heidenheimer (eds.), The Development of Welfare States in Europe and America (New Jersey: Transaction Books, 1981).

13. Coughlin, 1980; Free and Cantril, 1967.

14. Marshall, 1981, pp. 119. See also Mishra, 1984, pp.25ff.

15. Here, specifically, we consider the effects of indicators of social position (e.g., family income, age, social class, occupational prestige, work status and education) and political party affiliation will be insignificant.

16. These are measured here through feelings of relative deprivation, political distrust, government irresponsibility and the salience of social policies.

17. Harold Macmillan, Winds of Change, 1914-1939 (New York: Harper and Row, 1966), pp. 456 and 458 respectively.

18. Wilensky, 1975. p. xv; see also Mishra, 1984, p. 25. Titmuss provides a full discussion of the welfare state's role in discouraging alienation. Richard Titmuss, The Gift Relationship (Harmondsworth: Penguin Books, 1973), pp. 199ff.

19. John Saville, "The Welfare State: An historical approach.", New Reasoner 3(1957-8).

20. See also, William G. Domhoff, The Higher Circles: The Governing Class in America (New York: Random House, 1970) and Ralph Miliband, The State in Capitalist Society (New York: Basic Books, 1969).

21. Robert Jackman, "Socialist parties and income inequality in western industrial societies.", Journal of Politics 42 (1980). On the medical issue, see Robin Badgley, Robin Hetherington, V.L. Matthews and Majorie Schulte, "The Impact of Medicare in Wheatville, Saskatchewan, 1960-1965." Canadian Journal of Public Health 58 (1967); R. Beck, "Economic class and access to physician services and public medical care insurance.", International Journal of Health Services 3 (1973); R. Beck and J. Horne, "Economic class and risk avoidance: Experience under public medical care insurance.", The Journal of Risk and Insurance 43 (1976); Norman Furniss and Timothy Tilton, The Case for the Welfare State (Bloomington: Indiana University Press, 1977); Richard Titmuss, Commitment to Welfare (London: George Allen and Unwin Ltd., 1968).

Of course, the evidence is not clear-cut. Studies reporting "success" include Hewitt's findings that more developed welfare programs produce greater equality in capitalist nations. On governmental medical care policies, the evidence is also mixed. In the United States and Great Britain, a number of researchers find that welfare state policies decrease class differentials in the use of services. See Hewitt, "The effect of political democracy on equality in industrial societies." American Sociological Review 42 (1977). On medical care, see LuAnn Aday, Ronald Andersen and Gretchen Fleming, Health Care in the United States (Beverly Hills: Sage, 1980); Thomas Brice, Robert Eichorn and Peter Fox, "Socio-economic status and use of physician services: A reconsideration", Medical Care 10 (1972); Martin Rein, "Social class and the utilization of medical care services: A study of British experience in the National Health Service.", Hospitals 43 (1969); William Stewart and Philip Enterline, "Effects of the National Health Service on physician utilization and health in England and Wales.", New England Journal of Medicine 265 (1961).

22. See O'Connor, 1973, and Offe, 1972. Also, see Frances Fox Piven and Richard Cloward, Regulating the Poor (New York: Pantheon, 1971) and Ian Gough, "Theories of the welfare state: A Critique", International Journal of Health Services 8 (1978).

23. See Offe, 1972, and Dorothy Buckton James, "The limits of liberal reform.", Politics and Society 2 (1972). Even Marshall concedes that "...it would be dishonest to pretend that there is not about

welfare policy decisions something authoritarian or to use a less loaded but rather horrible word, paternalistic." Marshall, 1981, pp. 109.

24. Offe, 1972.

25. Here specifically, we expect the following groups to more negatively evaluate the government's role: the unemployed, disabled and retired; the aged; those affiliated with left political parties; the lowest social classes; the lowest income, occupational, and education groups. Affiliation with a left political party is important both because left parties tend to draw their constituencies from lower socio-economic groups and hold supporters of reform for targeted groups. See Douglas Hibbs, "Political parties and macroeconomic parties and macroeconomic policy.", _American Political Science Review_ 71 (1977).

26. Milton Friedman, "The line we dare not cross: The fragility of freedom at '60' percent.", _Encounter_ 47 (1976). Research, albeit from a different ideological camp, fuels the fire of the conservative argument. State managers, according to Block, act in relative autonomy and pursue their own interest. See Fred Block, "The ruling class does not rule: Notes on the Marxist theory of the State." _Socialist Revolution_ 33 (1977).

27. For example, opinion polls repeatedly show that individuals are inconsistent in their demands. While they want reduced taxes, they express strong sentiments to retain or expand more social services.

28. Nathan Glazer, "The limits of social policy." In Paul E. Weinberger (ed.) _Perspectives on Social Welfare_ (New York: Macmillan, 1974). See also Mishra's, 1984, excellent discussion of the neo-conservative view, Chapter 2.

29. See A. Dale Tussing's distinction, "The dual welfare system.", _Society_ 9 (1974).

30. Wilensky, 1975.

31. Coughlin, 1980.

32. Esping-Andersen, 1979; Hibbs and Madsen, 1981.

33. Specifically, under the "elite" version of this model, controlling for attitudes and perceptions, we expect social class, income, occupational prestige, and education to be positive and significant. Under the "middle mass" version, both the linear and squared terms for the demographic and socio-economic variables will be significant. We expect the linear term to be negative while the squared term is positive.

34. An individuals' status (e.g., age, income, work status) allows us to identify whether they are benefactors or recipients of welfare state programs. In addition, factors such as political affiliation

permit an examination of groups generally thought to be ideological supporters or opponents of welfare policies. Attitudes permit us to examine how individuals' subjective views of the government and their fate under welfare policies affect their evaluation of government intervention.

35. Methodological details on the study, measures and analytic techniques are provided in the Technical Appendix.

36. The exact meaning of negative evaluations given these differences may vary from country to country. What specific disgruntlements the survey may be tapping cannot be understood through this analysis. It may be that individuals in one country decry retrenchment while those in another are outraged by expansion. Both may, however, report strong negative evaluations and the temptation to say why this is so need be avoided.

37. See a complete discussion of these typologies in Norman S. Furniss, "European Welfare States in Transition." Paper presented at the "Germany in the European Community" Conference, St. Louis, 1985.

38. In our previous study on public reactions to government intervention in the medical sector, we found the leader/laggard distinction paralleling important differences in the significance and direction of effects across countries. See Bernice A. Pescosolido, Carol A. Boyer and Wai Ying Tsui, "Medical Care in the Welfare State: A cross-national study of public evaluations", _Journal of Health and Social Behavior_ 26 (1985).

39. The means and standard deviations (in parentheses, respectively) for the evaluation scale are, in descending order: Italy (3.69, .71), Finland (3.26, .57), the United States (3.10, .68), Great Britain (3.05, .65), the Netherlands (3.03, .54), West Germany (3.03, .58), Switzerland (2.94, .56) and Austria (2.75, .59).

40. However, support for the "middle mass" version of the conservative critique remains meager. This is the only factor and the only country in which this version finds support.

41. Since the overall F-test indicates the significance of party identification as a group, relying solely on significant individual coefficients is inaccurate and misleading.

42. See Albrecht Rothacher, "The Green Party in German Politics.", _West European Politics_ 7 (1984); Eva Kolinsky, "The Greens in Germany.", _Parliamentary Affairs_ (Autumn, 1984).

43. See Gerhard Lehmbruch, "Liberal corporatism and party government." In Berhard Lehmbruch and Philippe C. Schmitter (eds.) _Trends Toward_

Corporatist intermediation (Beverly Hills: Sage, 1979).

44. Larry Isaac and William R. Kelly, "Racial insurgency, the state, and welfare expansion: Local and national level evidence from the postwar United States.", American Journal of Sociology 86 (1981), p. 1353. See also Larry Isaac, Elizabeth Mutran and Sheldon Stryker, "Political protest orientations among Black and White adults.", American Sociological Review 45 (1980).

45. William A. Gamson, The Strategy of Social Protest (Illinois: The Dorsey Press, 1975), p. 9.

46. This may work better in Western Europe than in the United States where Jenkins claims that proportional representation and parliamentary governments allow ideological parties a more stable basis of support. Craig Jenkins, "Resource mobilization theory and the study of social movements." Annual Review of Sociology 9 (1983).

47. Jeffrey M. Berry, The Interest Group Society (Boston: Little, Brown and Company, 1984), p. 66. This book has a good general discussion and critique of the pluralist model as does Gamson, 1975. See also Ira Katznelson, "Antagonistic ambiguity: Notes on reformism and decentralization.", Politics and Society 2 (Spring, 1972) for a critique of the pluralist view.

48. Larry J. Griffin, Joel Devine and Michael Wallace, "On the economic and political determinants of welfare spending in the Post-World War II Era.", Politics and Society 3 (1983); Larry J. Griffin, Michael Wallace and Joel Devine, "The political economy of military spending: Evidence from the United States.", Cambridge Journal of Economics 6 (1982); Frances Fox Piven and Richard Cloward, Regulating the Poor (New York: Vintage Books, 1973); and Poor People's Movements: Why They Succeed, How They Fail (New York: Vintage, 1977); see also Isaac and Kelly, 1981.

49. Harry Mulisc, "Editorial.", Contemporary Crises 7 (1983), P. 93. Parenthetical insert added. Also, see the discussion of the Marxist view in Stone, 1984, p. 188ff and Mishra, 1981, p. 76ff.

50. See Offe, 1972, p. 481. Early on, Marxists often saw the welfare state as a "back door" to socialism or as a real way for the working class to redress inequities in the capitalist system.

51. Offe (1972, p. 481) questions the ability of the "permanent welfare class" to become an active force since the state must "suppress, control or fragment, for it cannot allow it to become an independent, organized political force." Even Piven and Cloward, 1977, question their earlier claim of

the real gains of violence they espoused in 1972.

52. See Jenkins', 1983, complete review of studies on the role of third party support. See also Isaac et al., 1980; Gamson, 1975, pp. 111ff; Jack Goldstone, "The weakness of organization: A new look at The Strategy of Social Protest." American Journal of Sociology 85 (1980).

53. This paternalistic view also underlay many of the notions of consensus theorists, like Marshall, who saw welfare state policy as eventually "creating" a standard and "promoting consensus". See Marshall, 1981, p. 109.

54. See O'Connor, 1981, for a concise discussion of the neo-conservative political argument.

55. Quoted in Katznelson, 1972, p. 329.

56. Because the Eight Nation Study focused on political action, we had a wealth of indicators to choose from for our analysis. We actually analyzed over 10 different measures and found the results for the ones reported to be fairly consistent with others of the same class. In the end, we chose three scales. First, we constructed and used a scale of four items of respondents' "usual" activities within the political system (e.g., working for political candidates). We did this in favor of voting in the last national election because the very high participation rates in Europe made this more obvious measure for the United States less relevant. Second, we used a scale of "willingness" to engage in non-institutional activity (e.g., demonstrations) rather than actual past activity since the latter appeared to tap the historical experience of certain age cohorts e.g., those who were young during the 1960's. Third, we used a scale of "approval" of non-institutional activities (the same as in the second) to tap third party support. Full detail on items, questions and scale construction are presented in the Technical Appendix.

57. In Austria, individuals who perceive greater discrepancy indicate greater approval of non-institutional activity but this is not paralleled in their evaluation of government intervention in welfare sectors (see Table 6).

58. It is critical to note that the importance of welfare state evaluations and the concomitant irrelevance of other attitudes and perception variables is not connected. We ran each of these models with and without welfare state evaluation to check this possibility. Of all of the coefficients in the 24 equations, only one changed. Without welfare state evaluation in the model, those who distrust the government report greater approval of non-institutional activity in Italy. Given the

number of coefficients involved here, this could have occurred solely by chance.

59. In Italy, Finland, West Germany, the Netherlands and Switzerland, party affiliation, overall, is significant for all three political action variables. In the United States, it significantly influences institutionalization and approval; in Great Britain, approval; in Austria, institutionalized politics.

IX.

John Logue

Scandinavian Welfare States between Solidarity and Self-Interest

TROUBLES IN THE LAB

For more than half a century, Denmark, Norway and Sweden have been a place of pilgrimage for British and American social scientists, commentators and reformers seeking to determine whether the problems of modern industrial society not solved at home had been solved in the Scandinavian "social laboratory."[1] Some went home convinced that the Scandinavian solutions worked; others judged the solutions worse than the problems. The titles of their reports -- from Howe's _Denmark--A Cooperative Commonwealth_ (1921) and Childs' _Sweden: The Middle Way_ (1936) to Furniss and Tilton's _Case for the Welfare State_ (1977) and Huntford's _New Totalitarians_ (1972)[2] -- read like a litany of our hopes and fears. Perhaps their pictures of Scandinavia say as much about what they came looking for than about what the Scandinavians had actually achieved; social progress, like beauty, may be in the eye of the beholder. Still, whether the Scandinavian achievements are a subject of approbation or opprobrium, they epitomize the welfare state. And they epitomize the accomplishments of Social Democracy, for only in Scandinavia have the Social Democrats achieved political hegemony sufficient to permit them to restructure society. During their long tenure in office, many of the norms of the labor movement were embodied in the state. As a consequence, Scandinavian welfare systems bear little resemblance to the poorhouse systems that preceded them and which continue, in modernized form, to shape many welfare programs elsewhere, including those in the United States.

Though the Scandinavian countries are not the social paradise sometimes imagined by their less realistic admirers, they have used the public sector to abolish the kind of abject poverty and economic insecurity that continue to characterize life for significant minorities in other advanced industrial democracies, including Britain and the United States. They are decent societies not only in the sense that the weakest members of society -- the elderly, sick, disabled, unemployed -- live materially decent lives but also in the fundamental moral sense that the prosperity and happiness of the materially and psychologically prosperous are not purchased at the price of the misery of others.

Until 1974, the Scandinavian democracies seemed to have found a way to combine increasing economic security, expanding social services, and raising the relative income of the worst off through the public sector with steady economic growth in a capitalistic market economy. That is no mean accomplishment. Moreover, the Scandinavian Social Democrats succeeded in developing a consensus far beyond their own ranks in support of their key programs. Social services and income transfer programs were developed and expanded with broad domestic support. Governmental outlays in general and social welfare spending in particular expanded rapidly, particularly in the late 1960s and early 1970s, as benefit levels were raised, coverage expanded, and new programs initiated. Public sector employment grew with equal haste. Economic growth was stimulated by labor market measures that increased labor mobility. The development of consultation between government and interests groups, particularly trade unions and employers' organizations, on making economic policy and implementing it afterwards permitted an informal, consensual incomes policy over a number of years. The long post-war economic expansion, assisted by governmental policies both orthodox and innovative, provided the wherewithal for transforming what had been among the poorer and more backward countries of Europe in the last quarter of the nineteenth century into the richest and most progressive in the last quarter of the twentieth.

But the halcyon days of expansion came to an abrupt halt in 1973. The international economic crisis that followed demonstrated the worth of the welfare state everywhere in the West in permitting levels of unemployment not seen since the 1930s without the misery and political extremism that followed in the wake of sharp declines in the past. In Scandinavia it did more: a wide range of countercyclical programs cushioned the impact of the downturn on the economy[3] and the high levels of income replacement for the unemployed minimized economic hardship for the individual. Without the expanding oil wealth of Norway, Denmark and Sweden still came through the crisis without the homeless, the soup lines, and the cheese giveaways that characterized life in the United States in the winter of 1982-83.

The crisis also revealed serious structural problems in the design of the welfare state in Denmark and Sweden. The most obvious was the explosive development of the budget deficit. The self-equilibriating features of Scandinavian welfare states under conditions of sharp but temporary downturns -- massive countercyclical transfer payments and special programs -- induce major budgetary disequilibriums when an upturn does not follow fairly quickly. The Swedes and Danes adopted different strategies for dealing with the international downturn, but the results were the same. The Swedes struggled to bridge the crisis by maintaining production and employment, spending heavily on labor market measures, public works and industrial subsidies, and sent their budget deficit spiraling. The Danes left correction to the market with a sharp rise in open employment as a result, triggering large transfer payments with similar consequences for public expenditures and the deficit. By the early 1980s, budget deficits had exploded to double digit percentages of the GDP in both countries,[4] apparently squeezing business investment.[5] Moreover, rates of gross savings and capital formation, which had previously been at or above the OECD average, plunged both in absolute terms and relative to competitors. By 1980, Denmark's gross savings rate was at the bottom of the OECD list, and Sweden stood little better. Danish net savings, which had been a respectable 17.3% of the GDP in 1973, plummeted to a catastrophic 2.9% in 1981.[6] None of this boded well for the future.

Less obvious but more disturbing, at least to this admirer of Scandinavian Social Democratic achievements, was the gradual disclosure of what seems to be a fundamental change in attitudes toward utilization of programs that calls some of the premises of the Scandinavian welfare state model into question.

The model has always been characterized by the fact that though the Social Democratic architects of the Scandinavian welfare states were pragmatists, they also aimed to create a society that embodied class-specific and, they were convinced, higher values than those of bourgeois society. Thus, for example, K.K. Steincke, who as Social Democratic Minister for Social Affairs laid the foundations for the modern welfare state in Denmark with the Social Reform Act of 1933, defined what he called "the special ethics" of the working class to include "a feeling of solidarity, a willingness to sacrifice, a subordination to common economic and political goals" which gave promise of a better social order based on "cooperation and reciprocal aid."[7]

Steincke may have been something of an idealist, but like other Social Democrats, his faith in the solidaristic norms of the working class rested not on belief in working class altruism but upon a firm commitment to the rationality of class action. The only route to economic security for individual workingmen and their families was through collective measures. It is not surprising that solidaristic norms came to characterize the welfare state wherever the Social Democrats were able to shape it. Generalized benefits, universalistic criteria, and the elimination of the stigma attached to using public programs reflected the extension of the concept of solidarity from the trade union benefit fund to the entire society.

What has become increasingly apparent during the crisis is what was previously concealed by economic growth: the solidaristic values of the generation that built the welfare state are giving way to far more egotistical values in the generation that grew up with it. There seems to be a long-term rise in the use of social welfare benefits that is independent of objective need. And, over time, the prevalence of high income tax rates for average people has promoted a speculation in tax deductions and tax-free income -- the tax expenditure side of the welfare state -- that characterizes only the wealthy elsewhere. There is a good bit of evidence, in short, that the structure of material incentives in the Scandinavian welfare states is undermining the norms that made them work well in the past. Perhaps the welfare state in its attractive, solidaristic Scandinavian variant can only be a one-generational phenomenon.

OVERLOADING AND UNDERMINING THE WELFARE STATE

Eat green, vote red, and work black.
--Anonymous graffiti, Copenhagen 1982

To explain the nature of public attitudes toward the welfare state, Hans Zetterberg, Swedish sociologist and pollster, recently invoked the medieval cult of the Virgin with her infinite compassion. "The Protestant industrial countries have secularized...this vision of a helping hand which, through all life's changes, is available to the good and the bad, the happy and the unhappy, those who can express themselves and those who mumble."[8] The analogy is a good one, for however it began, the welfare state now provides help for the well-to-do as well as the impoverished, the successful as well as the failures.

The strain on the welfare state today is not occasioned primarily by countercyclical expenditures, high levels of benefits for the worst off or even the oft-cited growth in transfer payments to the elderly and the rising costs of treating the sick. These costs _have_ increased. But countercyclical expenditures have the virtue of declining when the economic cycle turns up, and taking care of the poor, the old, and the sick is at the very heart of the welfare state.

My concern is with a change in attitudes toward the utilization of programs more voluntary than those for the elderly and the hospitalized. Much of the growth in social welfare outlays in the last fifteen years has been a consequence of the generalization of benefits originally intended for the disadvantaged to the advantaged as well, and the rapid expansion of tax expenditures has dwarfed the growth in social programs. High marginal tax rates over the years, have led families with means to reshape their economic behavior to fit the contours of the tax code. As a consequence, the benefits provided to the unemployed single mother, say, have increasingly been eclipsed by those accruing to people far better off.

Attitudes toward welfare programs have changed, shifting rates of utilization upward. I am not alleging cheating. In fact, as far as I can judge, there is very little abuse in the sense of getting benefits one is not legally entitled to, despite the generosity of benefits and the laxity of safeguards in Scandinavia. What I am suggesting is that the Social Democratic success in eliminating the stigma once attached to receiving welfare benefits has not been without costs. Now that benefits are a matter of _right_, there has been a generational change in the attitudes of the middle class toward using them.

THE CHANGING DEFINITION OF NEED

There is generally an inverse relationship between levels of benefits and demand for them. Countries with high unemployment rates, for example, typically pay low rates of unemployment compensation; those with full employment can afford higher rates. The Scandinavians have managed their economies well enough to pay the very high rates already cited. Such rates are obviously beneficial for the individual unemployed and, in normal times, no particular burden for the society. While it has been estimated that the annual costs per 100,000 unemployed run about $285 million in the United

States, $585 million in West Germany and $780 million in Denmark,[9] Danish unemployment rates in the 1960s and early 1970s were typically less than a third of the American, holding costs below the American _despite_ much higher benefits.[10]

There is, however, a good bit of fragmentary evidence that high benefit levels over time change citizen perception of need. Let us explore the impact of this changing concept of need in Denmark in terms of the excellent sick-pay and unemployment compensation systems which replace up to 90% of lost earnings.

After the implementation of the 1976 Social Reform Act, the Danish Social Research Institute undertook a survey of citizen use of social benefits and institutions; a comparable study had been made in 1966. The 1977 study found, startlingly, that the incidence of of illness was notably greater among the young than among the old. In the three month period studied, more than a quarter of employed workers between 20 and 29 were sufficiently ill to draw sick pay; only half that proportion between 60 and 66 did. From age 20 up, the incidence of illness among the employed dropped in each age category. Older workers were sick for longer periods, but far less often.[11]

One could attribute this counterintuitive finding to the success of the health care system: the longer one lives, the more exposure one has to it, and the healthier one becomes. Unfortunately this optimistic explanation does not stand up. Between 1966 and 1977, "the number of periods of sickness a little more than doubled, and almost all the increase occurred in sickness of less than eight days' length."[12] (And the 1966 figures included those who went to work despite being sick under the less generous sick-pay rules of the time. Longer illness were equally frequent in both years.

Are Danes really sicker? Part of the increase is accounted for by the larger proportion of mothers of small children in the labor force in 1977; they call in sick when their children are ill. That and maternity leave account for part of the discrepancy between sick rates in different age categories. However, after we control for both maternity and use of sick days to take care of sick children -- and men take some for the latter -- _the young still have a higher incidence of sickness than the old_. I know of no objective evidence for increased malingering. In fact, after the sick-pay system was improved by raising benefits and dropping the unpaid three-day waiting period in 1973, the number of people calling in sick actually fell in some firms, much to the amazement of employers; apparently people who were willing to call in "sick" at their own expense were not willing to do so when they got paid for it. What seems to be happening is that the threshold for considering oneself sick, at least as far as going to work is concerned, has been progressively lowered. Ailments ignored in the past (and hence not registered in the 1966 survey as "going to work despite being ill") have become grounds for staying home. Sickness, at this level, is voluntary. Effective April 1,1983, Danish sick pay rules were changed so that both blue- and white-collar employees paid for the first day of each period of illness themselves, except when caused by accident, chronic ailment, or need to care for sick children. The consequences of this change are worth reporting. A study of municipal employees indicates that the number of one-day illnesses was more than halved and the number of sick calls was reduced by almost one fifth in the first year after the policy was changed. The total number of sick <u>days</u>, however did not decline at all. Sick days attributed to chronic illness rose by almost 500% over the previous year while days attributed to accidents more than doubled and those attributed to care for sick children increased 50%.[13]

PART-TIME WORK OR PART-TIME UNEMPLOYMENT?

Unemployment, at least during economic crises, has traditionally been as involuntary as death or taxes. That remains true today. But there are some quirks in Danish unemployment statistics that suggest that good unemployment compensation (and Danes can draw 90% of wages up to a ceiling of about $235 a week for 2 1/2 years) may change the definition of unemployment.

Consider the impact of supplemental unemployment compensation paid to those employed part-time but seeking full-time work. This admirable system not only protects those dependent on the weather, such as construction workers, and on intermittent or seasonal work, such as longshoremen and workers in fish packing plants, but has also encouraged firms to maintain their full labor force on short hours (with supplemental unemployment compensation) during the downturn.

But what is also striking is that unemployment rates by marital status reveal a curious sexual difference. While single, divorced, and widowed women all have lower unemployment rates than their male counterparts, married women have <u>higher</u> unemployment rates than married men.[14] The best explanation for the discrepancy is that married women have a higher tendency than others to hold part-time jobs while seeking full-time work.

Precisely the same situation pertains in a number of university-educated groups where extended periods of part-time work were once considered part of a normal career pattern. A part-time university instructor, for example, who draws a very good hourly wage in Denmark will now generally draw supplemental unemployment compensation in addition, and it is not difficult to find examples of university-trained professionals who make more money working part-time than industrial workers make for full-time, yet who top their wages off with unemployment compensation. Unemployment records, in fact, show supplemental payments to be more common among the university-trained than among any group of blue collar workers except those most affected by the weather, like bricklayers, and those for whom full-time jobs are rarities, like musicians. This pattern is not only legal but, in a sense, just: after all, why should professionals who can only find half-time work be treated worse than dockworkers who aren't paid when there are no ships to unload? Still, supplemental unemployment compensation was not intended to provide an income increment for already reasonably paid professionals. As in the case of the sick-pay system, what we are discussing is not abuse but a change in attitudes. A university teaching assistantship, while still a step on a career ladder, now also represents a failure to find a full-time university job. The spouse's half-time position, which used to be a welcome supplement to the family income, is now a bigger supplement because it is only half a full-time job.

A final testimony on changing attitudes: despite increased eligibility for unemployment compensation payments, the elimination of the unpaid quarantine period, and a doubling of real benefits between 1966 and 1977 -- which is reflected in the fact that only about a quarter of the unemployed in 1977 reported drawing down family savings while unemployed -- the proportion of the unemployed seeking emergency aid from the social relief office almost doubled between 1966 and 1977 from 12 1/2% to 23%.[15] And that occurred in spite of the fact that the unemployed of 1966 were more likely to be blue collar workers and the sole support of their families than those of 1977.

IN LOCO FAMILIAS

Among the most expensive new programs initiated in the last two decades in Denmark and Sweden have been those in which the public sector has assumed some of the traditional responsibilities of the family toward care of children and the elderly. The most notable have been the development of excellent systems of home assistance for the elderly and day-care (and after-school care) for children. The development of these programs reflected not only the traditional Social Democratic concern with conditions of working class families -- mothers forced by economic necessity into the factories, toddlers abandoned to the tender mercies of slightly older siblings -- but also all parties' responsiveness to the new women's movement, for these family roles were, of course, women's responsibilities.

If current conservative proposals to reduce unemployment by driving women out of the labor market and back into the kitchen are motivated more by an innate discomfort with sexual equality than by concern for the family, it is still true that the open-ended commitment to public sector provision of some of what were the housewife's roles has proven expensive. Again a major reason is the increased demand for services stimulated in the middle class when programs initially designed for working class mothers proved successful.

Consider day-care. The provision of a superb, heavily subsidized day care system has, in a single generation, changed the middle class ideal. Mothers no longer give up paid employment until their youngest child reaches nursery school age, but instead take only the paid months of maternity leave and consign infants to day-care from the age of 6 months. Other factors, of course, also contribute: consumption plays a bigger role in personal identity; the tax structure adds special incentives for wives to enter the labor market;[16] and once there, unemployment compensation rules require that unemployed mothers keep their kids in day-care so they remain "available for the labor market" and hence eligible for unemployment compensation. But the professionalization of the mother's role has also promoted a kind of day-care ideology which holds that only professionals are fit to raise small children, as only certified teachers are fit to teach bigger ones. Official Danish day-care statistics categorize children as "taken care of in day-care institutions," "taken care of by [approved] day-nurses," and "not taken care of," i.e., left to their mothers.[17]

The result has been an explosion in demand for day-care. Although the number of day care places in Denmark increased by 150% between 1971 and 1981 and the number of under-twos in day-care doubled (from 20% to more than 40% of children) between 1976 and 1981,[18] waiting lists in many places have lengthened. The situation seems analogous to the American urban freeway problem: when we build more, more people drive to work. The traffic jam remains. The major beneficiaries of the public subsidy to day care (which in Denmark is now larger than the cost of higher education) are higher income families, which is not surprising since they have two incomes; more surprisingly, white collar families get about 50% more benefits than blue collar families.[19]

Over time, successful public provision of services formerly provided by the family tends to crowd out the provision of such services between family, friends, and neighbors. Should you really insist on helping old Mrs. Hansen next door with her shopping if the city will provide her with home assistance? Your help is irregular; the public sector does it better. And why impose on Grandma to keep the baby when excellent day-care is available? The logic, over time, becomes compelling; the demand for public services, greater.

The traditional ties of obligation in civil society -- of family, neighbors, workmates, and friends -- depended on reciprocity. As a matter of fact, they demanded reciprocity. Freeloaders had to be very charming indeed if they were not to be ostracized. But the public sector makes no similarly direct demands on the individual. Your obligation is to pay your taxes. And taxes, among rational people, were made to be minimized.

THE TAX EXPENDITURE AS ENTITLEMENT

New Year's Eve is a holiday in Denmark. Grocery stores have token open hours in the morning, but most of the rest of the country shuts down tight. One exception on December 31, 1982, was the leasing companies; they stayed open late doing a land office business in selling shares of ships, dairy equipment, fork lifts and almost anything else that could be imagined. The point was not acquiring part of a dairy to toast as you popped the champagne cork that evening: it was getting a tax break before the witching hour.

The most spectacular tax shelter sold between Christmas and New Year's was the Dana Anglia, a luxurious modern ferry that was the flagship of the DFDS shipping line. Danish shipbuilding was in the slough of despondency; the closing of the Helsingør shipyard had just been announced because neither the state nor private interests had the funds to contract for the ferries that had been the yard's specialty. Yet it took less than 48 hours to find 6,000 Danes willing to put up 50,000 Dkr. apiece (about $6,000 at the then-current rate of exchange) almost entirely in borrowed money to buy the Dana Anglia for some 300 million Dkr from DFDS...in order to lease it back to the same company. The reason? The leasing arrangement offered a lucrative tax shelter for investors: 1500 Dkr. in cash in 1982 bought a tax reduction of 7650 for those paying a marginal rate of 60%. Over 10 years a 75 million Dkr cash investment by the 6,000 share leasers -- the rest was borrowed

-- should yield 200 million kr. in tax reductions.[20] But many, perhaps most, of the purchasers faced a marginal tax rate of 70%, so the tax reductions were even greater. By the close of business December 31, 1982, Danes had committed 2 billion kr. to tax leasing arrangements;[21] by comparison, figures for the last year available show that total net savings in Denmark was slightly under 12 billion kr. (1981) and net industrial investment in machinery and tools was about 4 1/2 billion kr. (1980).[22]

Far from stifling initiative, as conservative journalists allege, high marginal income tax rates have stimulated ingenuity in diverting taxable income into tax-sheltered forms. But reshaping individual economic behavior to fit the contours of the tax code has depressing long-term consequences. What concerns me here in particular is the fact that, at Scandinavian marginal tax levels, tax expenditures -- deductions from normal taxable income and the tax-privileged status accorded certain forms of income -- become open-ended entitlement programs for all who choose to participate at whatever level they cut themselves in.

In the past, tax considerations motivated the well-to-do. Today they are an increasingly common preoccupation. The reason is simple: marginal tax rates for the middle class have been pushed up to levels previously applied only to the very rich. In 1970 in Sweden, for example, it required a taxable income equivalent to 500,000 Skr. in 1981 kronor -- about $100,000 -- to reach the marginal tax rate of 70%; in 1981 you could achieve the same distinction with an income under 100,000 Skr, or less than $20,000. The development was comparable in Denmark.

Despite the notoriety of Mogens Glistrup's tax resisters' party in Denmark, political support for high tax levels in Scandinavia has been impressive. Even at the individual level, willingness to pay was startlingly high. In the last decade while support for taxes in the abstract -- recognized as vital to support popular public sector programs -- remained high, individual willingness to pay declined sharply. The rush to buy the Dana Anglia was merely one of the more noticeable demonstrations of that fact.

Again we face the problem of additional change occasioned by public policies. In 1960 Danes and Swedes were no more heavily taxed than Americans. However the rapid growth of the public sector of the last two decades sent revenue needs soaring. Today taxes absorb half or more of the GDP in Denmark and Sweden as compared to a third in the United States. As a consequence Danes and Swedes pay taxes on practically everything: necessities as well as luxuries, virtues as well as vices. They even pay taxes on taxes: the exorbitant excise taxes on gasoline, cigarettes and alcohol are, by some Kafkaesque sleight of hand, considered to be added value for the purpose of assessing the value-added tax (VAT). Above all else, they pay taxes on income. Danes and Swedes have the dubious distinction of ranking first and second, respectively, in individual income tax burdens among the OECD countries.[23]

Sales and excise taxes affect consumption patterns. But so long as they are concentrated on those necessities without which life is impossible and on those vices without which it is unbearable, their ultimate effect on behavior is limited. That, unfortunately, is not true of high income tax rates. We may not be as quick as Pavlov's dogs, but the learning process is just as certain. When your marginal tax rate (that is, the tax paid on your last dollar earned) hits 70% as it does in Denmark at about $20,000 in taxable income, much less 85% as it did for many in Sweden prior to January, 1983 you learn to run for the nearest tax shelter. At these rates, _every_ loophole acquires a constituency of users that extends beyond corporate lawyers, society surgeons, and the rich to include carpenters with a bit of overtime and nurses who work inconvenient hours.

Tax expenditures have become the major welfare program for the employed. While there is a good bit of justice in providing benefits for the productive as well as for the sick, unemployed, children, and elderly, the current structure of tax expenditures is ill-designed for this purpose. Not only do benefits rise with income, tax expenditures channel family financial decisions toward increased debt-financed consumption, which stretches family budgets to the breaking point and sometimes beyond, thereby increasing demands on welfare programs. There is evidence as well that tax expenditures have reduced productive investment, and it is indisputable that they have undercut government revenues and raised deficits. Worst, they have grown with a dynamism lacking elsewhere in the economy during the recession.

Tax expenditures constitute welfare for the better off. Deductions from taxable income rise a good bit more quickly than income. The importance of tax-free income derived from perquisites and capital gains probably rises even more sharply with income levels, but hard data are lacking since tax-free income need not be reported.[24] The result is that the individual income tax is notably less progressive in actuality than in theory. But what is socially demoralizing is that benefits accrue to those who actively pursue them, like the buyers of the Dana Anglia, and that these benefits outweigh the rewards of months of productive labor. If you want to improve your standard of living, the most obvious strategy is not to increase your income but to cut your taxes. On occasion even Social Democratic ministers have succumbed to the temptation.

The complexities of tax strategies in common use in Scandinavia defy simple explanation. They range from convoluted combinations of using tax-privileged savings to guarantee loans (and the interest deduction) to buy machinery currently in use and lease it back to the sellers while drawing tax benefits from depreciation to straightforward creation of capital gains (untaxed in Denmark and taxed at very low rates in Sweden) through the purchase of discounted bonds. The latter has become so standard in Denmark that even state paper is regularly issued at discount to attract tax-paying buyers.[25] In 1981, for example, coupon rates on Danish state notes and bonds averaged about 60% of the real market interest rate. Thus some 45 billion Dkr. in state bonds at nominal value in that year yielded only 29 billion Dkr. cash to the state and 16 billion Dkr. in tax-free <u>and</u> <u>risk-free</u> capital gains to the purchasers.[26] The nominal value of all bonds issued in Denmark in 1981 was 68 billion Dkr., but borrowers realized only 42 billion. The remaining 26 billion represented future capital gains and 6.8% of the GDP. That was no exception. In 1980 the figures were 33.6 billion realized on 62.3 billion nominal value with future capital gains of 28.7 billion or 7.7% of the GDP.[27] Macroeconomic distortions are serious.

The pattern of distortion reaches the family budget as well. The deductibility of interest on private debt, a feature common to American, Danish and Swedish tax systems but rare in other industrial countries, has led to an explosion in household indebtedness, stretching family budgets to the breaking point. The consequence of overindebtedness is that even brief periods of unemployment force families to appeal for emergency relief payments, despite the very high unemployment compensation levels. This is part of the explanation why demands for emergency relief have risen at the same time as the welfare net has been improved. The deductibility of interest has also fueled a boom in real estate prices that has pushed housing costs from some 13% of net disposable family income in Denmark in 1966 to 21% in 1976 and about 25% in 1981 (though the 1976 and 1981 figures were not completely comparable). Danes are house happy, but even so it would be remarkable that housing costs as a proportion of family income rise sharply with income in every category of family size,[28] were it not for the simple fact that buying housing represents a major chance for middle and upper-middle income families to save using tax leverage and pass the tax bill on to lower income renters.

The combination of high marginal tax rates and deductible interest means that household borrowing ceases to be sensitive to interest rates. Though interest rates in Denmark doubled from 9% in 1971 to an apparently prohibitive 18% in 1980, the post-tax rate for those at the 70% marginal level went only from 2.7% to 5.4%, lagging far behind the rate of inflation. During the last decade, the post-tax post-inflation interest rates for the majority of middle class Danes and Swedes have always been negative in real terms. In the long run given sufficiently high tax rates even those imbued with the strictest Puritan values concerning savings succumb to the lure of borrowing instead. Interest payments thus increased from 3% to 8 1/2% of household disposable income (i.e., post-tax income) in Sweden between 1970 and 1982 and amounted to an incredible 16% of household disposable income in Denmark in 1979 and 17 1/2% in 1982.[29]

Unfortunately for employment, however, industrial investment _is_ interest sensitive. The maximum corporate tax rate is lower than the household rate, while depreciation rules and other deductions are generous in sheltering profits. Idle industrial equipment neither appreciates in value as real estate does with the passing of time, nor is it of the same value to a businessman that a house is to a family. Thus high interest rates deter business borrowing for investment, but not household borrowing for consumption. So Danes and Swedes find themselves in the anomalous situation where the captain of industry not only declines to borrow money for investment but places his company's available funds in state paper, which over the last five years has yielded a better rate of return than the average return on net corporate assets -- financial investments of Swedish industrial corporations yielded 30% of industrial profits at the beginning of the 1970s and 50 to 60% at the end of the 1970s[30] -- while borrowing heavily as an individual to build a new house, buy a new car, and go on vacation.

The other side of the coin is that the return on savings has also been negative. It pays households to borrow, not to save, and that is what they have done. Sweden has the lowest net household savings rate of the 16 OECD countries for which comparable figures are available, and Swedish household savings have declined from about three-fifths of the OECD-Europe average at the beginning of the 1960s to about one-third of the OECD-Europe average in the latter half of the 1970s.[31] Danish figures are not directly comparable (and not included in the OECD data), but household surveys indicate savings on roughly the

Swedish level and show a decline in savings among blue and white collar employees from about 8% of disposable income in 1966 to 5% in 1976.[32]

The typical policy response in Denmark and Sweden to negative post-tax, post-inflation rates of return on savings has been to embark on new tax expenditures to encourage savings for a variety of purposes including pensions, children, investment, establishment of independent business, and, most recently, stock purchases. To the extent that these forms allow individual choice -- and all except collective pension funds do -- their primary impact apparently has been to channel savings away from taxable forms, not to increase the overall rate of household savings. (Conceivably the rate of savings would have been lower without the additional tax expenditures.) No doubt these are worthy purposes for savings, and one can certainly think of other worthy private goals for which the state might want to subsidize savings. The dilemma is that, with tax rates as they are, either the state has to subsidize savings for <u>every</u> useful purpose or run the risk of underfunding the unsubsidized activities if it attempts to see that tax-privileged savings are used for their intended purposes; alternatively, it can permit the market to operate by ignoring use of the accounts for other than their intended purposes with the deterioration of civic morality that that encourages. In the worst and most likely case, the state pursues both policies simultaneously, giving full rein to the caprice of all those who administer the programs, including financial institutions and tax authorities.

Thus the long-term effect of high marginal income tax rates is to increase tax planning. At the Scandinavian rates, deductions and tax-privileged income have risen far more quickly than taxable income because tax expenditures amount to voluntary, open-ended entitlement programs. Unlike other welfare state programs which have some relation to need, the only qualification for a tax expenditure is having taxable income. Worse, differences in taxes actually paid among normal income families depend on their willingness to "exploit" the tax system, and the difference in living standards that results is clearly visible. Tax statistics provide eloquent testimony to citizens' adaptation of their behavior to the contours of the tax code. Between 1971 and 1981, deductions rose steadily from 13% to 23% of taxable income in Denmark despite some tightening of tax provisions. Needless to say, the principal beneficiaries were the well-to-do: among the top 5% of households, deductions jumped from 17% to 37% in the same period.[33]

VISION IN AN ERA OF MORAL AMBIGUITY

There's a lot of talk about lack of vision. But what does a politician get out of vision if the voters throw him out in the next election?

-- Ole Borre[34]

Vision is not the first attribute one associates with politicians, but many Scandinavians would share election expert Ole Borre's sense that it has become less common than it was in the past. Nostalgia? Probably. But I also suspect that it reflects reality, for the vision of the welfare state that was the beacon of Social Democratic politics in Scandinavia for half a century has been realized. What we see now are the problems of its success.

Through the intermittent hard times since 1973, Danish and Swedish welfare states have proved their worth from their countercyclical employment and income transfer policies to their care for the old, sick, and handicapped. But the greater expenditures imposed by countercyclical policies, demographic trends, and rising rates of program utilization have stretched resources to the breaking point, especially as tax expenditures erode revenues. The resumption of steady economic growth would help, but will not, by itself, eliminate the strain, for it will reduce only cyclical expenditures. In the long run it is going to be difficult to avoid marked changes in the Scandinavian welfare state model. The question is whether they will take the form of the general benefit cuts that conservatives advocate, which will hit the worst off hardest, or whether the Social Democrats can develop and implement more equitable alternatives.

The cost of increased countercyclical spending (principally for unemployment compensation, emergency employment programs, and emergency welfare payments) has been heavy. During the economic crisis, the price tag for direct subsidies to workers and business in Sweden has ranged between 3 and 5% of the GDP; in Denmark the direct costs for countercyclical programs -- and here our definition is a bit broader -- have risen steadily from 3 to 7% of the GDP, as contrasted to 1% of the GDP in the pre-1973 period.[35] These costs are dwarfed by pension and medical costs. Public sector expenditures for pensions, care for the aged, and all medical programs in Denmark stood at 13.8% of the GDP in 1978, up from 12.0% of the GDP in 1970, and the cost of these programs will continue to rise as the population ages. But these are core areas of the welfare state, and not susceptible to easy cuts. The only obvious socially equitable way to reduce pension costs markedly, for example --

postponing the pension age for healthy elderly -- is impractical as long as unemployment remains substantial. And to cut countercyclical programs during a recession entitles one to the Herbert Hoover prize for economic policy.

The rising rates of utilization of more voluntary welfare state programs - including sick pay, supplemental unemployment compensation, day-care, home assistance for the elderly, rent subsidies and a variety of other programs - are expensive. Much of the increase is an unmitigated good, filling unmet needs; one major welfare state improvement in the 1970s was making social services previously available primarily in the cities, like day-care and home assistance, available in small towns and rural areas, and that, of course, increases utilization rates. Though supplemental unemployment compensation was not designed to encourage employers to hold inventory down by shortening the workday or workweek rather than laying people off, that is an advantage as well. And one hopes that the pride that led fathers to keep their kids in shoes that were two sizes too small rather than seek aid has gone by the boards in these days when every tenth Danish family receives emergency welfare payments. Separating the cost of meeting real needs like these from the price of the generational change in attitudes toward utilization of welfare programs requires heroic assumptions. But though the data do not provide an adequate basis for a cost estimate, they do seem to confirm a clear generational change in attitudes that will push program costs higher in the future in those areas where beneficiaries define their own need.

The most egregious examples of the consequences of beneficiaries determining need are to be found in the area of tax expenditures. Here cost estimates are possible. If we limit concern to tax expenditures that (1) are freely chosen and (2) are not associated with earned income, the specific tax benefits for interest on debt unrelated to employment, the tax benefits of tax-privileged savings excluding collective pension funds, and the tax-free status of realized capital gains on stocks, bonds, and mortgage notes, amount to between 6 to 10% of the GDP in Denmark in 1980. Unlike attitudes toward sickness and unemployment, there is no question of changing social definitions here: this is exclusively a matter of economic incentives. Moreover, there are good reasons to believe that these tax expenditures have created substantial economic dislocations, particularly in Denmark, that probably reduce the efficiency of the managed market economy as a basis for the welfare state.

The obvious interim measure to deal with the fiscal crisis of the Danish and Swedish welfare states is to curtail tax expenditures. During the last three years there has been a serious attempt to deal with the deductibility of interest on private debt, which is the most disruptive tax expenditure at high marginal tax rates because it makes borrowing to finance private consumption much more attractive than private savings. In Sweden the tax reform agreement between the Social Democratic opposition and the Liberal and Center parties (which caused the collapse of the bourgeois coalition government in 1981) roughly halved the deduction of interest on private debt while cutting marginal tax rates so that, by 1985, 90% of taxpayers would face marginal rates of 50% or less while only 5% would have marginal rates over 55%. As a consequence, the tax advantages of borrowing will decline sharply. In Denmark the conservative coalition government and Social Democratic opposition agreed in 1985 on a package of measures which, if passed in the fall 1985 session of parliament, will go even further in cutting the advantages according tax planning. The package provides, effective 1987, for a flat 50% tax on interest income and identical credit for interest payment; this will raise the after-tax return on savings for top income bracket taxpayers (who faced a marginal tax of 73% of 1985) by 100% and cut the tax break accorded borrowing by one third, doubling the effective post-tax interest rate on loans. The package also imposes a capital gains tax generally for the first time. As a result, the more elaborate strategies used currently to convert taxable earned income into capital gains will cease to be profitable. There is little pretense of egalitarianism in either reform -- both benefit those who save relative to those who borrow, and savers have traditionally been well-to-do -- but current tax expenditures are probably more inegalitarian and, worse, impose tax penalties on those who don't speculate in the tax code. Still, with high marginal tax rates, tax planning is likely to crop up in other areas, unless there is a cultural transformation.

POLITICAL BARRIERS

Four political problems of an institutional and ideological nature make the task of adapting the welfare state difficult. Taken together, perhaps they explain the general failure to do so despite the exigencies of the crisis. The first is the obvious one: governmental stability and, with it, consistency in policy have declined dramatically. From 1929 to 1973, the Social Democrats governed Denmark for all but 10 years; from 1932 to 1976, their Swedish colleagues held office continually except for a few months in 1936. But since the 1973 election plunged Denmark into something approaching parliamentary chaos, Denmark has had a succession of weak minority governments and frequent elections, and after 1976, Sweden's non-socialist parties ran through four governments in six years before losing office to the Social Democrats in 1982. Coherent policy is difficult under these circumstances.

The second problem exists no matter which party is in office: while budget and tax expenditures are pushed up without decision by or even consent from the political authorities, political factors militate against any cuts. The public sector has become a mass employer in its own right. More people are employed in Denmark in day-care alone than in the textile, garment and shoe industries put together. The biggest union in Sweden today is no longer the metal workers but the municipal employees. We know the clout that American public employee unions have in municipal politics, and in Denmark and Sweden the tie between public sector unions and the Social Democrats rivals that of the firemen's benevolent association and the party in machine-run cities in the United States. Likewise, every tax expenditure is stoutly defended by those with a vested interest in it. The trouble is known elsewhere: while every loophole has its well-organized defenders, there is no lobby at all for general tax reform. The curiosity is that the Social Democrats come closer than any other group in having an interest in the general health of the capitalist economy. But even its voters are so tied to their tax expenditures that efforts to go it alone with reforms in this area threaten electoral disaster; it is worth noting that in both Denmark and Sweden the most successful attacks on tax expenditures have been carried out by bourgeois governments.

The third problem is closely related: the corporatist structure of the Scandinavian political systems. Programs are put into place not by simple political decision but by agreement among interest groups and the state with all the bargaining and horse-trading that that implies. These programs come with a built-in constituency. Interest organizations see "their" programs as similar to contractual agreements between organizations and the state which the state cannot abrogate unilaterally. The state has that right legally, of course, but in those sectors where corporatism is strong,[36] its hands are tied, if not by moral obligation, then by the need for continuing corporatist relations in the future.

Finally, there is the ideological problem: the Social Democrats are ill-equipped ideologically to deal with retrenchment in the public sector, while the non-socialists lack the political credibility to do so. The welfare state in Scandinavia is, after all, a Social Democratic creation. The Party sees it as the "strong society" that takes care of the weak, if not as a surrogate for socialism, and defends it with the same vigor that Congressman Pepper brings to dealing with the critics of Social Security. Social Democratic identification with the public sector runs deep precisely because the public sector has been structured to embody worthy Social Democratic principles: benefits as rights, no stigma attached to beneficiaries, no means tests, equal treatment regardless of class.

That public sector expansion has so changed incentives that many of the strong now see more opportunity in the "strong society" than in the private sector is often difficult for Scandinavian Social Democrats to accept. In my experience the typical Social Democratic response has been either to deny the existence of the problem or to regard it as cheating, to be dealt with as harshly as one deals with economic criminality, with the increased coercion and unpleasant consequences that that entails. But it is not cheating, and it does exist. And it is generated by what are otherwise virtues of the public sector.

MORAL DILEMMAS

To discuss politics in terms of moral choices strikes a chord of unworldly idealism. Yet the Scandinavian welfare states rest on a clear moral premise: the obligation of society to protect its weakest members not only against thieves, murderers and foreign enemies but also against economic catastrophe. It is this economic security that provides a basis for individual liberty. The society in which "the strongest shoulders bear the heaviest burdens," as the Danish phrase has it, is implicitly judged morally superior to societies in which burdens are otherwise distributed.

This ethical view reflects not altruism but a fundamental sense of group solidarity. It is symptomatic that most basic Scandinavian welfare programs, including unemployment compensation and the national health system, had their origins in local benefit societies organized by union locals, farmers' organizations, or on a neighborhood basis. In their original form, these benefit societies owed their existence to the clear connection between obligation and rights. The right to benefits was premised on the obligation to contribute; without the latter, the former could not have existed.

If there is a common root for the current ills of the Scandinavian welfare states, it is that in the eagerness to see benefits generalized and minimum levels raised, the ties of reciprocal obligation have been lessened. While the connection between benefits and obligations remains at a societal level, it is far more abstract than the concrete individual obligation of the past. The sense of social solidarity remains ingrained as a cultural norm and continues to be invoked to justify paying the heavy costs of social programs, but its force has diminished, and the limits it puts on the pursuit of individual interest are increasingly nebulous.

Breaking the link between benefits and obligations has encouraged the use of the former and avoidance of the latter. The general availability of high benefits prompted increased utilization. Your tax money pays for them, so why not use them? The state found itself expanding social services that have tended to crowd out civil society's obligations between family and friends. The aim has been the admirable one of protecting the weakest, which the networks of family and friendship had failed to do. But the effect has frequently also been to accelerate the atomization of society, creating need for greater state aid.

In the small group there is a natural limit to individual overuse and avoidance of obligation in the censure of one's friends, if not in ostracism from the group. That seems to have been internalized as a class-specific cultural norm. A homily endlessly repeated in the 19th century Social Democratic press was the moral superiority of the trade unionist who accepted his duty to his fellows over the egotism that characterized the members of the bourgeoisie. There is no reason to be nostalgic about the 19th century. The appearance of solidarity in the labor movement may have reflected more a lack of opportunity to act egotistically than solidaristic values, and the frequent expressions of solidarity may be no more than evidence of the effectiveness of group pressure when one lived one's life in a working class neighborhood and within the organizations that made up the labor movement. But when the nexus between obligation and benefit dissolves, when group ties are loosened, and when the citizen deals not with his workmates or neighbors but with the state, the stigma attached to "using" the system is much diminished. One no longer victimizes friends and colleagues but cleverly fools some distant opponent. Mogens Glistrup's celebrated characterization of the tax resister -- and he was thinking of himself -- as the modern equivalent of the Resistance fighter during World War II is the perfect rationalization of egotism.

The American welfare state, such as it is, has rested on a self-limiting combination of altruism and self-insurance: altruism toward the worst off, self-insurance for oneself. Altruism was sufficient to prevent starvation, and collective self-insurance cut risks of catastrophe, but neither offered a basis for more far-reaching programs. By contrast, the Social Democratic concept of reciprocal obligation contained no intrinsic limits; programs could be extended into any area in which citizens agreed to accept obligation. It was not altruism toward the weak nor rational choice of the best form of self-insurance; rather it reflected, to use Steincke's words again, the special working class ethics of "solidarity, a willingness to sacrifice, a subordination to common economic and political goals" and, above all else, a sense of "cooperation and reciprocal aid." But the close group ties of the past that had shaped these ethics have dissolved.

And so the situation today in Scandinavia resembles the old problem of the common village grazing lands. Everyone has a right to use them -- and should. It is to each individual's advantage to run every cow on them that he can, but if everyone does that, the common lands will quickly be overgrazed and cease to support village herds. The success of the welfare state -- like that of the commons -- depends on restraint in utilization. Individual self-deprivation is not the answer, any more than the problem of the commons can be solved by the widow voluntarily removing her cow from the common pasture. What is necessary is general restraint. When that is no longer automatic, even Social Democrats who draft blueprints of the future social welfare system have to talk less of "cooperation and reciprocal aid" and more about manipulating individual incentives and disincentives to encourage self-restraint.

NOTES

1. The "social laboratory" metaphor dates at least to Peter Manniche's volume _Denmark: A Social Laboratory_ (Oxford: Oxford University Press, 1939); his principal theme was the development of cooperatives, hardly our first interest in the Scandinavian laboratory results today. Walter Galenson put it succinctly a decade later, "The small nations that comprise the Scandinavian area constitute a social laboratory for the Western world." _Labor in Norway_ (Cambridge: Harvard University Press, 1949), p. 1, as he took up those modern themes -- labor and Social Democracy -- that have subsequently been the focus of foreign interest in laboratory results.

2. The references are to Frederic C. Howe, _Denmark - A Cooperative Commonwealth_ (New York: Harcourt, Brace, 1921); Marquis Childs, _Sweden: The Middle Way_ (New Haven: Yale University Press, 1936); Norman Furniss and Timothy Tilton, _The Case for the Welfare State_ (Bloomington: Indiana University Press, 1977); and Roland Huntford, _The New Totalitarians_ (New York: Stein and Day, 1972).

3. The very size of the public sector, which is unaffected by market forces, cushioned downturns in the market. A number of transfer payments are specifically countercyclical; unemployment compensation is the most notable, but other income-related transfer payments, including rent subsidies, also act in the same fashion. A number of programs have been specifically designed to provide countercyclical stimulation, including pump-priming public works projects and the Swedish relief employment program. Further, the Swedes have pioneered new techniques for counteracting the market cycle from their investment fund scheme, put into place in 1938, to the production for inventory program that was developed in the 1970s; first introduced on a small scale in 1972, this stockpiling subsidy scheme was used as a major countercyclical tool in 1975-76. (For discussions of these innovations, see Gunnar Eliasson, _Investment Funds in Operation_ (Stockholm: Konjunkturinstitutet, 1965) and Karin Rudberg and Christer Öhman, _Investment funds -- The Release of 1967_ (Stockholm: Konjunkturinstitutet, 1971) on the countercyclical impact of the funds, and OECD, _Economic Surveys: Sweden_, 1976-80, for descriptions of the stockbuilding program and analyses of its impact.

4. Under the impact of recession, central government annual budget deficits grew between 1975 and 1982 from 1.4% to 11.9% of the GDP in Denmark and from 3.9% to 12.3% in Sweden. The cumulative net debt grew from a small _surplus_ in Denmark to 60% of

the GDP and from 21% to 52% of the GDP in Sweden in the same time period. (Figures exclude social security funds.) By comparison, the Reagan deficits that panicked American credit markets were less than half the relative size of the Scandinavian annual deficits.

5. Cf. OECD, Economic Surveys: Sweden, 1982, pp. 46-48, and Ministry of Economic Affairs, The Revised Economic Policy and Budget Statements 1982 (April 1982), pp. 23-24. "Crowding out" was of less concern at the time in Denmark, because of the weak credit demand in the private sector and heavy foreign borrowing, though governmental borrowing emptied the Danish credit market.

6. Danmarks Statistik, Statistisk Tiarsoversigt 1982 (Copenhagen: Danmarks Statistik, 1982), p. 114.

7. K. K. Steincke, Fremtidens Forsorgelsesvaesen: Oversigt over og Kritik af den samlede Forsørgelseslovgivning samt Betaenkning og motiverede Forslag til en systematisk Nyordning (Copenhagen: Schultz, 1920), pp. 9 and 5.

8. Hans L. Zetterberg, "Hur väderingarna förändras i välfärdsstaten," in Nordal Akerman, Välfärd --och sedan? Teorier och experiment for ett alternativt samhälle (Stockholm: Rabén & Sjögren 1981), p. 107.

9. The German and American figures come from the Wall Street Journal, December 3, 1982, and may be based on comparable definitions. The Danish figure is derived by dividing 1981 unemployment compensation payments (16.1 billion Dkr) by the most inclusive unemployment figure which includes the uninsured and the part-time unemployed for 1981 (243,000) and converting to US$ at the rate current in December 1982 (8.5 Dkr = $1).

10. High benefit rates become a fiscal burden, however, when unemployment goes up and stays up. Thus the Danes topped the OECD tabulations for unemployment compensation as a percentage of GDP in 1979, coming in with a figure (2.8% of GDP) about seven times the American one (0.4%) despite the fact that unemployment rates were roughly comparable. (OECD Observer, no. 115 (March 1982), p. 11.) As K.K. Steincke put it while defending the social reform act as Minister for Social Affairs in the Danish parliament in 1934, "The expenditures of any social welfare law, even the pure poor law...rise more than proportionally with unemployment. So the crucial problem remains, after as well as before the social reform, not whether this or that in the reform can be changed -- because that doesn't make any difference -- but: How can we bring unemployment down sharply?....{N}o law on support payments can, in the long run, replace loss of work either for the unemployed or from the point of view of the society's

economy." (November 8, 1934), Steincke's speech was reprinted in pamphlet form as Stormen paa Social-Reformen (Copenhagen: Schultz, 1934), pp. 20, 22.)

11. Mogens Kjaer Jensen, Sociale problemer og ydelser 1966-1977 (Copenhagen: Socialforsknings-instituttet, 1980), p. 15.

12. Kjaer Jensen, op.cit., p. 57.

13. Kommunernes Landsforening, "Landsforeningens undersogelse vedrorende karendsdagslovens okonomiske virkninger," typescript, March 22, 1985. In the private sector, the number of sick days initially dropped by about 20%, and it seems to have stabalized about 10% under the previous level. (Dansk Arbejdsgiverforening, fourth quarter, 1982-84, supplement to Arbejdsgiveren, June 10, 1983, and ne 20, 1985.) See also, Jon Sundbo, Annemarie Knigge, Susanne Dalsgaard Nielsen, and David Bunnage, Arbejdsfravaer (Copenhagen: Socialforsknings-instituttet, 1982), pp. 100-107. A portion of the official sickpay data compiled by the Danish Employers' Confederation is reported in a form that permits control for age, sex, and reason for sickpay (sickness, accident, and maternity are the causes specifically listed). This material confirms the survey findings that the young are sick more frequently than the old. Cf. Dansk Arbejdsgiverforening, Statistisk afdeling, MLM - Fravaersstatistik (Copenhagen, quarterly).

14. Arbejdsløshedsstatistik, 1982: 9 (December 8, 1982) and Statistiske Efterretninger. Arbejdsmarked 1983:1 (February 2, 1983).

15. Kjaer Jensen, op. cit., pp. 45, 54-55.

16. The marginal tax rate for additional family income in Sweden was 68% in 1978 for production workers if the husband doubled the household income but only 37% if the wife achieved the same result by taking a job; the Danish figures were 63% and 44%. (Organization for Economic Cooperation and Development, Economic Surveys: Sweden, 1981, Table 12.)

Bent Rold Andersen stresses the role played by the rapid increase in housing costs as well as the decline in the provision of social services by the extended family in an excellent book Kan vi bevare velfaerdsstaten? (Copenhagen: AKF, 1984) which draws on his experience and frustration as Social Democratic minister of social affairs. Cf. also Bent Rold Andersen, "Ratinality and Irrationality of the Nordic Welfare State," Daedalus, v. 113, no. 1 (winter 1984), pp. 109-139.

17. Statistiske Efterretninger, A1982 no. 12, p. 376.

18. Ibid., p. 374.

19. Ibid., A1980 no. 26, pp. 884, 890.

20. Revisions og Forvaltnings Institutet, Arhus, cited in *Politiken,* December 12, 1982.

21. Estimate by C.C. Sandberg, director of DMK leasing, the dominant concern in the field, *Politiken,* December 29, 1982.

22. Danmarks Statistik, *Statistisk Tiarsoversigt 1982* (Copenhagen: Danmarks Statistik, 1982), pp. 111 and 66, respectively.

23. Cf. OECD, *Long-Term Trends in Tax Revenues of OECD Member Countries, 1955-1980* (Paris: OECD, 1981).

24. An indication is provided, however, by Danish wealth tax returns. In 1978, the last year in which those with low assets were asked to specify what assets they held, the national survey of wealth tax returns indicated that about half the financial assets that yield capital gains -- bonds issues at discount, private mortgage notes (always issued at great discount), and stocks (stock dividends are standard practice) -- were owned by the top 10% of taxpayers ranked by taxable income and, hence, by marginal tax rates.

25. The advantage for the buyer is easy to see: he realizes the equivalent of interest without the pain of taxes. This is an important consideration. A state bond carrying a 20% interest rate (the market rate on state paper in 1981) would have yielded 6% after taxes to an individual with a marginal tax rate of 70%; a bond carrying a 10% coupon would yield 12% after taxes. The advantage to the seller -- the state -- is the ability to market its paper to taxpaying buyers, for interest on bonds carrying market rates (i.e., without the built-in capital gains provision) would have been *negative* every year of the last decade after marginal taxes and inflation. Without the capital gains provision, 1981 state paper would have had to carry an interest rate of 40% for the return after taxes to match inflation. Cf. Michael Møller and Niels Chr. Nielsen, "Statsgaeldens finansiering og de private investeringer," *Samfundsøkonomen*, v.l, no. 1 (1983), pp. 15-20.

26. Danmarks Nationalbank, *Kvartalsoversigt,*, November 1982, pp. 36-37.

27. *Ibid.*, p. 36

28. "Forbrugsundersøgelsen 1976," *Statistiske Efterretninger*, A1980 no.l. pp. 6, 10. The 1981 figures are from *Statistik Fiarsovesigt 1984* (Copenhagen: Danmarks Statistik, 1984), p. 49.

29. Swedish Figures, OECD, *Economic Surveys: Sweden* 1982. p. 39. Danish figures calculated on the basis of national account figures on income (*Statistisk Tiarsoversigt 1981*, p. 113) and on personal tax deductions for interest (*Statistisk Arbog 1982,* Table 392). The astonishing Danish figure reflects the combination of very high interest

rates with the fact that most interest payments are derived from the tax deductible nature of interest, and do not come out of what otherwise would have been net income. For further information on the interest problem, see Den Skattemaessige behandling af renter og andet Kapital afkast (Betaenkning no. 949 {April 1982}).

30. OECD, Economic Surveys: Sweden, 1982, p. 48.

31. OECD, Historical Statistics 1960-1980, Table 6.16.

32. "Forbrugsundersøgelsen 1976, Statistiske Efterretninger, A1980 no. 1, p. 16.

33. Calculated from Danmarks Statistik, Statistisk Arbog, 1973-82, various tables and Denmarks Statistik, Skatter og Afgifter: Oversigt 1983, Table 5.13.

34. Interview in Politiken (Copenhagen), September 5, 1982.

35. Swedish figures include labor market measures, inventory support, and direct industrial subsidies. Danish figures include all labor market measures, emergence relief payments, and the early pension program implemented in 1979 principally to reduce unemployment.

36. Cf. Jacob Buksti's argument that what exists in Denmark is "sectoral corporatism"; "Organisationer og offentlig politik," paper, Stockholm, April 1982.

PART THREE

Future Potentialities

X.

Harrell Rodgers

The American Welfare System in Transition

America has always been the laggard welfare state. Of the major western industrial nations, America's welfare programs are the most recent in origin, and the most limited in design, coverage, and cost.[1] Despite their modesty, they rest on very tentative and reluctant public support.[2]

THE POSITIVE STATE

In a recent article, Furniss and Mitchell analyzed how social welfare provisions differ among western industrial nations, and related these differences to the public philosophies that guide the economic and political systems of each nation.[3] Their analysis revealed that each of the major western nations has a complex public philosophy which sets limits on, and defines the role of, the state in the economic and political systems. To isolate the similarities and differences between the nations, Furniss and Mitchell elaborated a framework for analyzing social welfare systems based on three major criteria: (1) the design and goals of the programs, (2) the political, economic and social priorities reflected by them; and (3) the impact of the programs on recipients and the political and economic systems. This analytical framework produced four state types: the Positive state, the Social Security state, the Democratic Corporatist state, and the Social Welfare state. Furniss and Mitchell argue that the American system approximates the Positive state -- the least developed form. In the Positive state, welfare policy is primarily a means of social control based on "free market" principles. Social welfare programs are designed to protect holders of property from the difficulties of unregulated markets and from demands for redistribution of income. The poor, in Wilensky's words, are given just enough to "defang the revolutionary tiger."[4] The resistance of the American philosophy to social welfare programs is so strong, in fact, that only acute crisis has prompted the establishment and expansion of such programs.

THE "BIG BANG"

While all the other major western industrial nations had been evolving welfare programs for decades, the United States first established very limited and modest programs only in response to the economic collapse of 1929 brought about by the Great Depression.[5] The collapse of the economy was so massive that by 1933 one-fourth of the nation's adult men were unemployed,[6] millions of families were losing their homes, and thousands stood in breadlines each day. Millions of those who suffered from the economic crisis were registered voters, increasingly willing to support radical remedies.[7] Still, the government's response was slow. Between 1933 and 1935 President Roosevelt centered his attention on emergency measures such as public works projects and prevention of bank closures.

By 1935 the crisis had deepened. The Works Project Administration (WPA) had provided jobs for millions of U.S. citizens, but some 8 million males were still unemployed. It has been estimated that WPA provided jobs to only one of every four applicants.[8] Those millions who could not find work, along with the aged, handicapped, and orphans, turned to state and local governments for assistance. Many of the states could not handle the burden. Some cut the size of the grants so that more of the needy could receive some assistance. Others abolished all assistance. The state of New Jersey offered the indigent licenses to beg.[9]

The continuing hardship spawned more and more radical critics of the Roosevelt administration. Under these pressures, Roosevelt launched what historians refer to as the "Second New Deal." This New Deal had two primary thrusts. First, the government would use Keynesian economics to stimulate and, hopefully, regulate the economy, and increased assistance to business to promote an economic recovery. Second, the government would establish through the Social Security Act of 1935 assistance programs for those who were outside the labor force.

The Social Security Act consisted of five major titles. Title I provided grants to the states for assistance to the aged. Title II established the Social Security system. Title III provided grants to the states for the administration of unemployment compensation. Title IV established the Aid to Dependent Children (ADC) program. Title V provided grants to the states for aid to the blind. The

Social Security Act represented a radical new role for the federal government. Congress previously had enacted programs to subsidize state and local assistance programs, but this was the first time that programs had been established which would be run by the federal government (social security) or in partnership with the states (ADC).

As radical a departure as the Social Security Act was, its benefits were originally quite modest. Benefits under social security were extended only to those aged who worked in certain occupations and industries, and benefits were delayed until 1942. It was not until 1950 that half the aged received any benefits under the program. Until 1950 only orphans and poor children received any assistance from the ADC program, and benefits were extended very slowly. In 1950 the program was changed to Aid to Families with Dependent Children (AFDC), allowing benefits to one parent (usually the mother) in a family with eligible children.

With the passage of the Social Security Act of 1935, the United States became the last of the major industrial nations to develop national welfare programs, which by European standards were quite modest. In addition to its modesty, the Social Security Act contained three features which had long-term and significant consequences for U.S. social welfare programs. First, benefits under the various social security titles were designed for only a select category of the needy. Even as social welfare programs expanded greatly in the 1960s and early 1970s, they continued to be categorical, rather than universal as they are in many other nations.

Second, some of the social security titles allowed the states to determine who would receive assistance and how much they would receive. As AFDC expanded to become the nation's primary cash assistance program for the needy, this feature remained. Variations in state benefits under AFDC are huge, with some states being much more generous than others. Titles I and V also allowed a great deal of local autonomy in funding assistance to the aged and blind. Until these titles were superseded by the Supplemental Security Income (SSI) program in 1974, funding variations by state were substantial.

Last, the Social Security Act did not include health insurance. Most of the other western industrial nations already had health insurance programs by 1935. Roosevelt considered including health insurance in the Social Security Act, but opposition from the American Medical Association and southern congressmen was so intense he eliminated it.

State control over the benefit levels under Titles I, II, IV, and V of the Social Security Act substantially limited growth in these programs through the 1950s. In 1960 there were only 803,000 families receiving benefits under AFDC, and only 144,000 blind or disabled citizens were receiving assistance under Title V.[10] Thus, by 1960, 25 years after the original act, U.S. welfare programs were still very limited and, as events would prove, poverty was still severe.

Just as the Great Depression had served as the catalyst for the nation's first major social welfare programs, the civil rights movement and the ghetto riots of the 1960s served as the stimulus for the next substantial expansion of the welfare state. The civil rights movement, which developed in the late 1950s and early 1960s, centered attention on the economic conditions of millions of U.S. citizens. Civil rights workers often charged that many U.S. citizens of all races were ill-housed, ill-clothed, medically neglected, malnourished, and even suffering from hunger. Most of the nation's public leaders simply dismissed the suggestion that any significant number of U.S. citizens were suffering from hunger. But slowly the evidence of acute poverty, malnutrition, poverty-related disease, and even starvation began to be documented.

In 1967 the Senate Subcommittee on Employment, Manpower and Poverty held hearings on U.S. poverty. The testimony of many civil rights leaders contained graphic allegations of acute hunger in the south. This testimony stimulated two liberal members of the subcommittee -- Robert Kennedy (D., N.Y.) and Joseph Clark (D., Penn.) -- to conduct a personal tour of the Mississippi delta. They returned to Washington to testify to the presence of severe hunger and malnutrition in the areas they visited.

The subcommittee's initial investigation also had encouraged the Field Foundation to send a team of doctors to Mississippi to investigate the health of children in Head Start programs. The team issued a report entitled "Children in Mississippi." The report documented extensive poverty, poverty-related diseases, and malnutrition among the children and their families.[11]

The most dramatic documentation of U.S. poverty was yet to come. In the mid-1960s the Field Foundation and the Citizens' Crusade against Poverty formed the Citizens's Board of Inquiry into Hunger and Malnutrition in the United States. The Citizen's Board conducted investigations, held hearings, and reported its findings in late 1967 and 1968. The findings confirmed the worse suspicions of welfare reform advocates. They discovered within the general population of the United States a population that might best be described as an underdeveloped nation. They reported "concrete evidence of chronic hunger and malnutrition in every part of the United States where we have held hearings or conducted field trips."12

These findings contributed to the pressures on Congress for improvements in and expansion of welfare programs. The leaders of the civil rights movement continued to demand new programs for the poor, and between 1965 and 1968 literally hundreds of riots erupted in U.S. cities. Many conservatives saw the riots as evidence of a breakdown of morals in U.S. society and an attack on the nation's institutions.[13] In the final analysis, however, most conservative members of Congress agreed with liberal members that social programs had to be expanded. Both conservatives and liberals agreed that expanding social programs would at least help restore order. Thus, with the cities on fire, and media attention focused on the struggles of the black population and the poverty of millions of U.S. citizens, Congress passed a number of new civil rights laws and welfare provisions during the 1960s.

Major civil rights acts were passed in 1964, 1965, and 1968. Also, in the 1960s and early 1970s Congress expanded existing welfare programs and created other major welfare programs. In 1961 an amendment to the AFDC title allowed states to provide benefits to two-parent families where both parents were unemployed. Less than half the states adopted this option. In 1963 a bill providing maternal and child care planning was passed. In 1964 Congress formally established the Food Stamp program, which twenty-two states initially opted to participate in. In 1965 both the Medicare and Medicaid programs were enacted by Congress, and federal funding for the AFDC program was increased substantially. In 1971 Congress adopted national standards for the Food Stamp program, but it was not extended to all the states until 1974. The Supplemental Security Income (SSI) program was passed in 1972 and went into effect in 1974. By 1975 a total of five new titles had been added to the original Social Security Act, and all the original titles had been expanded through amendments. The 1960s and early 1970s, then, saw the second significant installment in the development of American social welfare programs. It is doubtful that anything short of serious civil strife could have produced such drastic changes.

SYSTEM AND PHILOSOPHICAL LIMITATIONS ON THE WELFARE STATE: FURTHER EXPLORATIONS OF THE POSITIVE STATE

Why is America the laggard in welfare programs? It is certainly not because America lacks adequate finances, because its tax rate is too high, or because public needs are less. America is rich, comparatively its rate of taxation is low, and the rate of poverty is high.[14] There are at least three major differences between America and its major western allies which yield some insights. The first is philosophical. America has a stronger commitment to individualism and free enterprise. Both of the nation's two major parties basically support these principles and there are no significant third parties which promote other principles.

Second, America's fragmented power structure makes the passage of non-traditional and non-incremental public policies very difficult. In the parliamentary systems of Europe the executive's party or coalition is in control of the legislative branch, and disciplined parties generally ensure support for the executive's policies. In the United States power is split between the Executive and Congress, Congress is divided into two competing branches, and party membership does not indicate support for the party. The result is that a consensus can rarely be reached on major policy objectives. Public policy in the United States then is generally a short-term compromise between competing interest groups to meet only limited, sometimes conflicting, and almost always incremental goals. Power is so fragmented that small entrenched groups can often veto even modest, incremental policies. Thus, only some perceived crisis can promote major change -- even significant incremental change.

Third, working class and poorer citizens have less influence in the American political system than do similar citizens in Europe. They have less influence because they are less politically mobilized. The traditional institutions that play such an important role in mobilizing the working class electorate in Europe, such as unions and third parties, are very weak in the United States. The result is what Burnham has called the "hole in the electorate" -- the absence of those voters who support social welfare programs and left wing movements in other western nations.[15]

Fragmented political power and an immobilized working class give the economic elite a great deal of power in the American political process.[16] While political administrations change, the economic elite is enduring, rich and mobilized. Thus, the economic elite, through its agents in public office and its influence with other public figures, can generally veto public policies that deviate too radically from the status quo, conflict too drastically with capitalist principles, or impose costs on business. The business elite particularly dislikes welfare programs because they raise the tax burden, reduce financial incentives or other imperatives to work (especially for low wages), and sometimes mobilize the poor.

CHARACTERISTICS OF THE AMERICAN WELFARE SYSTEM

These systemic and philosophical factors have obvious impacts on the design of American welfare programs. Basically, welfare programs in the American system are viewed as a necessary evil. They are required to control disorder,[17] and as a testimonial to the fundamental decency of American society and capitalism. Thus, assistance is given grudgingly, in a form that makes clear that it is charity, and only to those citizens who are considered the legitimate poor -- the aged, unemployed parents and their children (the great majority of these families are female-headed), and the handicapped and disabled. Aid to these groups is means-tested, and designed to be modest, and, if possible, temporary. Assistance even to groups such as mothers and their children is not designed to end poverty. It is designed only as temporary, transitory aid to see the family through a rough period. The conditions that make the mother poor -- lack of job skills or a job, transportation, or child care -- receive only scant attention.[18] Only limited attention is given to these matters because it is generally believed that the American economy is viable enough to take care of everyone's needs unless they are aged, disabled, or a dependent minority. Assistance to select others is necessary only to allow them a period in which to personally resolve some individual shortcoming.

Since poverty is generally thought to result from personal, rather than systemic malfunctions, the state of poverty is essentially an illegitimate condition even for those who obtain assistance. A poor person is suspected of sloth, moral corruption, or personal shortsightedness and thus it is feared that aiding those who become poor only encourages such behavior. Since the economy is thought to be basically viable and dynamic enough to meet the needs of all but the most disabilitated of citizens, aid to the healthy poor and their offspring only burdens the economy and keeps it from being as profitable and prosperous as it could be. Thus, welfare assistance is essentially seen as parasitic on the economy, and when economic conditions are particularly bad -- unemployment and poverty are quite high -- welfare assistance is thought to be something that cannot be afforded. Thus, when poverty is highest, many public officials will demand that assistance be lowered or that benefits to some be terminated so that the economy can recover.

The results of such an approach to welfare are obvious. Aid is kept categorical (only specific groups among the poor are given aid), assistance is given only to the poor as charity (rather than in the universal forms that are common in Europe), and poverty remains quite high. Even when benefits increase, as they did in the 1960s and 1970s, poverty remains high and may even increase. There are three reasons why poverty persists: (1) the conditions that make people poor are often not addressed. High rates of unemployment and subemployment, for example, may be tolerated or even encouraged in an effort to lower inflation; (2) those who obtain aid often receive too little to push them over the poverty line; and (3) many of the poor receive no assistance.[19]

None of this should be understood to say that American welfare programs do not benefit recipients. The evidence shows that the programs play a very large role in reducing the incidence of poverty in the United States. According to the government's measure of poverty, without social welfare expenditures the number of poor would almost double, leaving about one U.S. citizen in five in poverty.[20] But even though the programs substantially reduce the incidence of poverty (primarily among the aged), a legitimate argument might be made that the programs could be better designed. We will return to this point below.

REAGAN'S APPROACH TO WELFARE

During a long career as an advocate of individualism and free enterprise, Ronald Reagan preached that welfare programs were riddled with fraud, excessively generous, detrimental to individual initiative, and a drag on the economy. In the American context these were hardly radical ideas. The economic problems which began in the early 1970s and extended through the last two years of the Nixon administration and the entirety of the Ford and Carter administrations, created an atmosphere in which Reagan could, however, advance some basically radical ideas about the causes of the nation's economic problems and the solutions that should be pursued.

Reagan's basic argument was that government, rather than being a solver of economic and social problems, had become the problem. His solution, not surprisingly, was to significantly reduce the role of government. Thus, he advocated less government regulation, lower taxes (especially for corporations and the wealthy), and reductions in social welfare expenditures. Reagan's approach represented a major retreat from the egalitarian values that the national government had promoted in limited ways since the "Second New Deal."

Reagan's efforts to reduce the coverage and costs of social welfare programs were guided by several principles.[21] One of the most important was his argument that programs should not deliberately attempt to redistribute income. Social welfare programs, Reagan argued, should serve only as a temporary safety net with limited purposes, benefits, and beneficiaries. Reagan convinced Congress that aid to the working poor or near poor often constituted illegitimate assistance. For example, he argued that the food stamp program had "moved toward a generalized income transfer program, regardless of nutritional need."[21] Thus, Reagan convinced Congress to pass new regulations which removed or reduced food stamp benefits to millions of individuals.

Second, Reagan argued that limited benefits should be extended only to the legitimate poor, not those who choose to be poor. Reagan often referred to the "deserving poor" and the "truly needy" as those who deserved temporary assistance. Reagan's definition of the deserving poor was "those who through no fault of their own became poor." The deserving poor were nonworking single mothers and their children, the aged and the disabled. The nondeserving poor were students, able-bodied males, strikers and employed individuals and families that fell below the poverty line.

Reagan's resistance to assisting the able-bodied unemployed reflects his belief that regardless of how high the official unemployment rate is, anyone who really wants to find work can do so. During the 1980 elections Reagan often referred to unemployment compensation as a paid vacation. Additionally, Reagan believes that assistance to the unemployed only discourages them from diligently searching for employment. Reagan's administrators tinkered with eligibility criteria and benefit formulas to remove or reduce the benefits of millions of those families and individuals considered illegitimate. Third, Reagan argued that any able-bodied citizen receiving assistance (e.g., AFDC or food stamps) should be required to provide labor in return. This is not a new idea. Several administrations since the New Deal have developed limited work programs, but administrative costs, lack of child care facilities, and participant problems have always kept such programs very small.[23]

Fourth, Reagan wanted to turn welfare programs over to state and local governments. Reagan devised a "New Federalism" plan in which the Federal government would take over full costs of the Medicaid program, while the states, in return, would take over the costs and administration of the food stamp and AFDC programs. The states often argue that federal programs should be turned over to them, but this proposal met with little real enthusiasm. The states were basically concerned that they would be saddled with additional welfare costs, costs they could ill-afford.

Examining the impact of the Reagan administration on welfare programs is instructive for understanding both the role and future of welfare programs in the American political system. Clearly, Reagan has had a significant impact on welfare programs. Reductions in program funding and a tightening of eligibility standards have removed or reduced benefits to millions of individuals and families. By late 1983 some one million families had lost their eligibility for food stamps, while 95 percent of all recipients have had their benefits reduced -- including those recipients below the poverty line.[24] Another three million school children had lost their eligibility for a free or partially subsidized lunch. Some 350,000 families had been dropped from the AFDC program, including about 1.5 million children. Those dropped have primarily been working mothers, even when their earnings have been quite low. For example, 23 states dropped mothers of three earning $5,000 or more, while an additional 13 states dropped families of this size if they earned as little as $3,000 a year. In 1983 the average benefits to a child receiving AFDC was $107 a month. In inflation adjusted dollars, this was less than the average child received in 1967. Another 725,000 people, mostly women and children, have lost their coverage under the Medicaid program. Some 239 community health centers have also been closed.[25]

The program cuts that Congress has agreed to have been a great deal smaller than those recommended to it by President Reagan. His budget recommendations would have cut program costs by about 20 percent. The actual cuts have reduced benefits by about 7 percent.[26] Actual cuts have been below budget requests in part because both Republican and Democratic members of Congress have often believed that Reagan's proposals would have hurt too many people. These suspicions were reinforced by new charges that hunger is again becoming a serious problem,[27] and by official government figures showing large increases in poverty during the first Reagan Administration.

After years of decline, poverty increased from 1979 through 1983 by over ten million individuals.[28] In 1983 the poverty count was the largest since 1966, and represented 15.2 percent of the total population. Given this increase in poverty, it is both surprising and insightful that President Reagan was as successful as he was in convincing Congress to cut social welfare benefits. Cuts in the face of increases in poverty reflect the tenuous support that welfare programs enjoy in the United States. However, the fact that Congress (including many

Republican members of Congress) refused to make additional major cuts is also insightful. The reluctance to make even more substantial cuts suggests that the majority of the members of Congress believe that basically the programs are necessary, and that they can be trimmed but not eliminated or drastically reduced. In fact, Congress on a number of occasions added supplements to programs when faced with evidence of unmet needs in the community.

WELFARE REFORM IN THE 1980S

In this last section we will discuss the prospects of welfare reform in the 1980s. Every administration since the Nixon years has been interested in seriously altering the American welfare system. Presidents Nixon, Ford and Carter all recommended major welfare reforms to Congress. Interestingly, all the reform proposals involved substituting a negative income tax and/or guaranteed income for most of the nation's current welfare programs. None of the proposals sought to emphasize family policy, and none placed major emphasis on policies to improve the economy. While the reform proposals were seriously debated during both the Nixon and Carter administrations, they eventually failed in Congress. Perhaps the most interesting feature of the long reform effort is that for some 10 years both conservatives and liberals pursued basically the same types of reform.

The first attempt to establish a Negative Income Tax (NIT) plan as a substitute for the traditional welfare approach was the Family Assistant Plan (FAP) recommended to Congress by President Nixon in 1969.[29] Although the FAP was twice passed by the House of Representatives, it was finally rejected by Congress in 1972. The demise of FAP led to a more sophisticated and comprehensive NIT proposal developed by the Joint Economic Committee of Congress.[30] In 1974 the Committee proposed a NIT plan based on cash grants, tax reform and tax credits. The plan was entitled Allowances for Basic Living Expenses (ABLE) and was estimated to cost about $15.4 billion if fully operational in 1976, with about half the cost in the form of tax relief to low-income working families.

Shortly after the Joint Economic Committee put forth the ABLE proposal, the Ford Administration formulated a plan entitled the Income Supplement Program (ISP). Like ABLE, ISP proposed an NIT program, consolidation of some programs and tax breaks. Like ABLE, the plan provided $3,600.00 in cash assistance to a penniless family of four. However, because of high inflation and unemployment during Ford's administration, all reform proposals were set aside. In the fall of 1977, President Carter forwarded to Congress a major welfare reform proposal.[31] Carter's plan emphasized a dual strategy: the poor would have been divided into those who could work and those who could not. Those designated as capable of work were expected to accept a public-or-private-sector job, which the government would have supplemented through the use of a NIT program if wages fell below levels established for varying family sizes. Many workers also would have received some tax relief (the cutoff point for a family of four would have been $15,600.00). Those unable to work would have been eligible for a guaranteed income based on family size. The income programs and the job programs would have covered all the poor, including two-parent families, single persons and childless couples.

To provide employment for the poor, the plan proposed the creation of 1.4 million public-sector jobs, some 300,000 of which were part-time. The jobs would have paid the minimum wage. To qualify for one of the public-sector jobs, an individual would have had to be unemployed for five weeks. All holders of the newly created jobs were required once every twelve months to engage in a thorough search for private-sector employment.

Those required to work would have included parents with children above fourteen and those healthy, nonelderly adults with no children. Single parents with children aged seven to fourteen were expected to work full-time if child-care facilities were available, part-time if they were not. Single parents with preschool children were exempt from the work requirement. Some 42 percent of the public-sector jobs were reserved for heads of AFDC families. Additionally, many low-income workers (the major exceptions being those holding the public-sector jobs created under the plan and families without children) would have received some tax breaks. Families with children could have claimed a 10 percent tax credit on earnings up to $4,000.00. Above $4,000.00 in earnings an additional credit of 5 percent could have been claimed up to a cutoff point at which the family would have ceased to be eligible for cash assistance. The various supplements were designed to make employment more attractive than welfare and to encourage workers to earn above the threshold point. The denial of the tax credit to those holding the public-sector jobs was designed to encourage them to obtain employment in the private sector.

Those who could not work would have received a cash grant under a guaranteed income plan. The grant would have replaced the AFDC, SSI and food-stamp programs. The cash grants would have been small and would have varied by family size. A family of four would have received a total grant of $4,200.00, about $1,615.00 less than the poverty threshold for a nonfarm family of four in 1977. (In 1977 only twelve states, mostly in the South, paid less than $4,200.00 a year to a four-person family.) An aged, blind or disabled individual would have received only $1,100.00; a couple without children $2,200.00. The cash grants were modest for two reasons. Most obviously they were meant to force as many adults as possible to work. Second, the low grants were designed to encourage state supplements. The federal government would have paid 75 percent of the first $500.00 in supplements for a family of four, and 25 percent of all additional supplements.

For a variety of reasons, Congress rejected Carter's reform plan. Critics pointed out that benefits to non-workers under the plan were quite low, that the jobs it would have created were only minimum-wage jobs, that there was little emphasis on quality child care, and that it was not based on a strategy to improve the overall performance of the economy.[32] Many members of Congress also feared that during periods of high unemployment, Carter's welfare plan would have greatly raised welfare costs. And, as we will detail below, many members of Congress have severe reservations about the efficacy and impact of NIT plans.

THE FAILURE OF REFORM

Both conservative and liberal scholars often argue that welfare reform has been stymied because it must meet a number of seemingly conflicting goals. Martin Anderson, for example, argues that "to become a political reality the plan must provide a decent level of support for those on welfare, it must contain strong incentives to work, and it must have a reasonable cost. And it must do all three at the same time."[33] Anderson, and two other prominent conservative scholars, Milton Friedman and George Gilder, all argue that it would be impossible for any plan to achieve all the necessary conditions.[34] All the major welfare reform proposals discussed above scared off some supporters because it was feared that the new plan would be more expensive than the old system.[35] Many moderates, and even some liberals, also refused to support the various plans because benefits to many recipients would have been lower under the substitute plan.[36]

Liberals, in addition, raise other objections. They often argue that the reform dilemma discussed above occurred for two reasons. First, the cost problems occurred because the reform proposals were not comprehensive enough. They argue that if a reform proposal included Social Security, social welfare costs could be reduced. The Social Security program, many liberals argue, should be turned into a genuine insurance program based on a guaranteed income concept. Only those elderly persons with resources or incomes below a guaranteed level would receive any benefits. A guaranteed income for the elderly would be considerably less expensive than Social Security, and the saving here would significantly reduce social welfare expenditures.[37]

Second, liberals argue that the reform proposals failed because too little attention was paid to the economy. They suggest that the reform plans might very well have expanded the welfare rolls because the unemployment rate was high and growing throughout the 1970s and early 1980s. Liberals believe that genuine reform can occur only if it is coordinated with a market strategy designed to greatly reduce the unemployment rate and improve the overall performance of the economy.[38]

The major welfare reform efforts failed for one reason not included in the reform dilemma discussed above. They failed in part because many members of Congress are skeptical about the Negative Income Tax proposal. The fear of many members of Congress is that the NIT would encourage millions of poor Americans to quit their jobs and stay at home. Although the NIT is not an untested proposal, most would agree that it has not been adequately tested. The Institute for the Study of Poverty did conduct a number of experiments in urban and rural areas to determine how well the NIT concept would work.[39] Selected families were enrolled in a NIT program and their work habits and other social behavior were studied for the duration of the experiment.

The studies showed that male heads of households reduced their work efforts very little (about 5%). Female heads of households also reduced their work efforts very little (about 8%). Wives dropped out of the job market at a rather high rate -- reducing their work effort by 22 percent. Children in the families reduced their work role by some 46 percent. Interpretation of these findings is to some extent a matter of value judgment. Reduction of work effort by wives and children might be considered positive if it promoted the family or improved the educational performance of the children. But the reductions in work effort by heads of households clearly worried many policy makers. This may seem puzzling since the work reductions were small. But the concern of many policy makers grows out of the fact that the NIT recipients were aware that they were part of a closely observed experiment. Each family was interviewed 22 times a year. Many policy makers feared that a less closely observed set of recipients would reduce their work effort much more substantially.[40] The experiments were clearly not extensive enough to address these fears. As a result, many members of Congress, including conservatives, moderates and even some liberals, simply are not convinced that the NIT is a viable reform alternative.

CONSERVATIVE AND LIBERAL REFORM PROPOSALS

Many conservatives are convinced that our present welfare system is reasonably effective and that it should be reformed in only minor ways. Martin Anderson, a policy advisor to both Presidents Nixon and Reagan, provides the following assessment:

> There may be great inefficiencies in our welfare programs, the level of fraud may be very high, the quality of management may be terrible, the programs may overlap, inequities may abound, and the financial incentives to work may be virtually non-existent. But if we step back and judge a vast array of welfare programs...by two basic criteria -- the completeness of coverage for those who really need help, and the adequacy of the amount of help they do receive-- the picture changes dramatically. Judged by these standards our welfare system has been a brilliant success.[41]

Anderson believes that the idea of substantially reforming our welfare system should be abandoned and that we should try instead to make the current system work better.

Another prominent conservative, George Gilder, basically agrees. Gilder argues that the NIT would be a disastrous substitute for the nation's current welfare programs. He argues that the poor can escape poverty only through work, family and faith. Gilder argues that many poor Americans simply do not work hard enough. He believes that this is true because many poor families (especially those headed by a women) often live better on welfare than on the incomes they can earn in the market. He believes that an NIT would only enhance this problem. Gilder does not believe that women will ever do very well in the job market because their family responsibilities always will keep them from devoting full attention to their jobs. Women, he believes, should stay home and let the men work.[42]

Gilder believes that the welfare system drives fathers away from their families because they often cannot support them as well as they can be supported by the welfare system or even by the wife. This is a particularly critical problem for black families. Young black males are discouraged from working because they have been denied the opportunity to support their families. Steps must be taken so that young males learn to accept their responsibilities and work harder. Gilder would have women stay home so that the husband could have the psychological satisfaction of fulfilling his need to be the breadwinner. Welfare support would be lowered, aimed primarily at emergencies, and limited to in-kind aid (like food stamps) rather than cash. To keep Medicaid from being a work disincentive, a fee system would be established to make the program less desirable, and working mothers would not have their benefits reduced or taken away.

Since Gilder believes that the families of poor citizens must be strengthened if poverty is to be overcome, he supports the adoption of a universal system of family allowances.[43] He believes that the evidence shows that family allowances have greatly aided families in Europe and have spared the countries that employ them many of the social problems that plague this nation. The allowances would be universal so that people will not have to be poor or stay poor to receive them. Last, Gilder argues that the poor must be given faith in their ability to improve their lot. Faith in one's ability to improve one's future through hard work, often lacking among the poor, is important to all people. It is wrong, he says, for the message to be spread that racism, for example, holds back black citizens. Gilder argues that there is almost no racism in America today and that to lead blacks to believe that there is only discourages them.[44]

Other conservatives, such as Milton Friedman, still believe that the best alternative would be to adopt the NIT proposal. Friedman believes that the NIT experiments vindicated the proposal, and that there is still a good chance that the NIT concept will be adopted. The benefits under the NIT must be lower than under current welfare programs, Friedman believes, to keep program costs down and to encourage work.[45]

Liberals tend to be critical of many of the conservative assumptions and proposals, but there are areas of agreement. First, they tend to believe that a guaranteed income for the aged and disabled is both necessary and humane. It is necessary to replace the Social Security system -- which they view as an outdated and unnecessarily expensive program -- in order to fund other social welfare programs. Liberals are divided over the NIT proposal. Some believe that it would be best to give AFDC a uniform benefit level and extend it to all poor families, regardless of whether they are headed by a male or female. Others would prefer to give the NIT proposal a national trial.[46]

A fundamental flaw that most liberals find in the conservative critiques and proposals is that they pay little attention to the economy. Most liberals feel that many poor citizens are inadequately integrated into the job market because there are no decent jobs for them, because they cannot get needed job training, or because they cannot obtain or afford the child care services they require. It will be necessary, they argue, to establish job training programs to teach the poor the skills they need, and perhaps even for the government to become the employer of last resort.[47]

Many liberals also contend that a national family policy that included universal maternity leaves, pre-natal and post-natal child care, family planning and child care could play a large role in preventing poverty. They note that the largest group of welfare recipients in America is single women and their dependent children. Over 3.9 million women and about 7.1 million children constitute the major recipient group of the AFDC program. In recent years some 99 percent of all AFDC families also have received Medicaid services, and about 80 percent have received food stamps. Mothers and their children are, then, the largest and most expensive group of welfare recipients in America.

Many liberals note that family policies could be designed to serve the needs of all families. The intent would be to promote women's equality, prevent families from falling into poverty, and provide the poor with the support they need to achieve independence. A universal system of child care, for example, would free parents to work, or obtain the education and job training they need for work. A system of child care that addressed the educational, nutritional and health needs of poor children would help to break the cycle of poverty by ensuring that the poor start life without many of the typical poverty-related handicaps. Most liberals would be quite sympathetic to Gilder's family allowance proposal.[48]

Liberals do not agree with Gilder's call for women to quit the job market and professions and return to the home. The entry of women into the job market reflects healthy and inevitable alterations in life styles and family structures, a lowering of discriminatory barriers, and outright economic necessity. They feel the evidence indicates that most women, including those who are married, work out of compelling economic necessity.[49] Liberals do not accept the argument that some men always will be discouraged from working as long as women are in the job market. The type of man that Gilder refers to will accept family responsibilities when our society provides him with opportunities to earn a decent living in the job market.

Liberals do not accept Gilder's argument that racism is a thing of the past in America. They do, in fact, argue that current and past racism accounts for many of the problems that continue to plague minorities and women in America. True, racism is a much less severe problem now than it once was, and in a few cases being a minority can increase opportunities. But liberals believe that discrimination is still a significant problem. They are sympathetic to Gilder's argument that faith is an important motivation, and that many poor people have less faith in their abilities and future than they should have. But there are many features of the political and economic system that serve to discourage the poor. Until job opportunities, housing and many other conditions in our society are improved, many people will have good reason to doubt their ability to join the great American dream. Liberals, then, believe that ending poverty in America means designing better welfare programs and providing certain services such as good housing, equal educational opportunities, health care and child care to all citizens. They also believe that these programs must be based upon, and backed up by, a healthy economy that meets the needs of all citizens.

IMMEDIATE PROSPECTS FOR WELFARE REFORM

The prospects for significant welfare reform in the immediate future do not look good. The Reagan administration has no interest in major innovations. Its primary interest is in limiting and further reducing benefits and beneficiaries. Reagan can always use the huge deficits his administration has run up as a reason for holding down the cost of welfare programs. Even if the Democrats could win in 1988, the new administration would be saddled with the huge deficits that Reagan's tax cuts, military expenditures, and high rates of unemployment have caused. Thus, even a Democratic administration is likely to only restore some of the benefits that were cut during the Reagan years. Reagan's impact on the American welfare system, then, is likely to be substantial. At the least, the status quo is likely to be maintained for a considerable period of time.

Of course, even in the absence of the financial problems that the Reagan administration will most likely leave behind, the Democratic party will probably not propose major alternatives to current welfare programs unless the system is in crisis. Civil strife or major financial crisis could stimulate an administration to pursue major changes in the nation's approach to welfare assistance. There is no guarantee, however, that the changes would be egalitarian in nature.

The welfare state that has evolved in America reflects quite well the principles that underlie the public philosophy of the nation. Most scholars, policy makers, and much of the public believe that the current welfare system is less efficient and effective than it should be, but few seem to appreciate the role that the public philosophy and entrenched power play in limiting the nation's ability to design better, more effective policies. As this chapter has shown, there is no genuine consensus among or between the two major parties about the specific reforms or alternatives that should be pursued, and efforts to radically reform the welfare system under both Republican and Democratic administrations have failed. It is perhaps of some importance, however, that all major political groups in America now believe that the nation is obligated at least to assist its less fortunate citizens. Some conservative welfare reform proposals, such as Milton Friedman's Negative Income Tax proposal and George Gilder's family allowance proposal, even have a distinctly radical ring to them. But, even so, both proposals build upon the nation's commitment to individualism and free enterprise.

There are some fundamental areas of agreement between liberals and conservatives. Both conservatives and liberals tend to believe that most of the able-bodied poor must be moved into the job market, and that the welfare system should strengthen the family. Conservatives tend to put more stress on designing programs to encourage the poor to develop self-reliance, on keeping programs and their costs as modest as possible, and allowing state and local governments as much participation as possible. Liberals place more stress on reforming the economy so that there will be better job opportunities, and on more universal social welfare programs to provide all citizens with child care, housing assistance and other basic services.

Thus, while the policy differences between conservatives and liberals concerning the issue of poverty have narrowed over the last couple of decades, the differences between them are hardly trivial. The differences reflect divergent philosophies about the obligations of society to its citizens, and the impact of government on individual freedom and growth. And these, of course, are the fundamental differences that have always divided conservatives and liberals.

The structural resistance of the American political system to change, the power of vested interest groups, and the financial problems that are likely to face the nation for years to come, bode poorly for major alternations in the nation's welfare programs. The poor may not be with us always, but it is a safe bet that poverty will remain high in America for a long time to come.

NOTES

1. See, for example, Harold Wilensky, The Welfare State and Equality (Berkeley: University of California Press, 1975), p. 11; and Public Expenditure on Income Maintenance Programmes (Paris: OECD, 1976), p. 17.

2. For an excellent overview see Joe R. Feagin, Subordinating the Poor: Welfare and American Beliefs (Englewood Cliffs, New Jersey: Prentice-Hall, Inc., 1975), Chapter 4.

3. Norman Furniss and Neil Mitchell, "Social Welfare Provisions in Western Europe: Current Status and Future Possibilities," in Harrell R. Rodgers, Jr. (ed.), Public Policy and Social Institutions (Greenwich, Connecticut: JAI Press, Inc., 1984), 15-54.

4. Wilensky, The Welfare State and Equality, p. 109.

5. See Frances Fox Piven and Richard A. Coward, Poor People's Movements: Why They Succeed, How They Fail (New York: Random House, 1979), Chapter 2; and Frances Fox Piven and Richard A. Cloward, Regulating the Poor: The Functions of Public Welfare (New York: Vintage Books, 1971).

6. Piven and Cloward, Regulating the Poor, p. 49.

7. Harrell R. Rodgers, Jr., Poverty Amid Plenty: A Political and Economic Analysis (Reading, Mass.: Addison-Wesley Publishing Col., 1979), pp. 43-72.

8. Piven and Cloward, Regulating the Poor, p. 98.

9. Ibid, p. 109.

10. There is some evidence that the differences between the states are narrowing. The gap has been closing because those states that once provided the most generous benefits (mostly midwestern and eastern states) have in recent years suffered economically. Thus, these states have stopped increasing benefits, bringing them closer to the lower paying states. See Russell L. Hanson, "Federalism and Nonuniform Policies: The Case of AFDC," prepared for delivery at the Southern Political Science Association Meetings, November 3-5, 1983; and Russell L. Hanson, "The Content of Welfare Policy: The States and Aid to Families with Dependent Children," The Journal of

Politics, Volume 45, Number 3, August, 1983, pp. 771-785.

11. See Nick Koltz, Let Them Eat Promises: The Politics of Hunger in America (New York: Doubleday, 1971), pp. 8-9.

12. Hunger, USA: A Report by the Citizen's Board of Inquiry into Hunger and Malnutrition in the United States (Boston: Beacon Press, 1968).

13. Harlan Hahn and Joe R. Feagin, "Rank-And-File Versus Congressional Percentions of Ghetto Riots," Social Science Quarterly, 51 (September, 1970), pp. 361-73.

14. See Harrell R. Rodgers, Jr., The Cost of Human Neglect: America's Welfare Failure (Armonk, New York: M.E. Sharpe, Inc.: 1982), pp. 1-13.

15. Walter Dean Burnham, "American Politics in the 1980s," Dissent (Spring, 1980), pp. 152-157.

16. This is a typical structural argument. For a discussion of structuralism see Robert R. Alford, "Paradigms of Relations Between State and Society," in Leon Lindberg et al., (eds.) Stress and Contradiction in Modern Capitalism (Lexington, Mass.: Heath, 1975).

17. The best discussion of this point is Piven and Cloward, Regulating the Poor.

18. For a review and critique of support services see Rodgers, Poverty Amid Plenty, pp. 93-102.

19. U.S. Bureau of the Census, Characteristics of Households and Persons Receiving Noncash Benefits, Current Population Reports, series P-32, no. 110, March 1981, p. 20. See also Harrell R. Rodgers, Jr., "Hiding Versus Ending Poverty," Politics and Society, 8 (1978), pp. 253-66.

20. "Money Income and Poverty Status of Families and Persons in the United States: 1982," Current Population Reports, Series P-60, No. 140, p. 2.

21. See Malcolm L. Goggin, "Social Policy As Theory: Reagan's Public Philosophy," in Harrell R. Rodgers, Jr. (ed.), Public Policy and Social Institutions (Greenwich, Conn., JAI Press, Inc., 1984), 55-96.

22. Executive Office of the President, Office of Management and Budget. Budget of the United States Government, Fiscal Year 1984 (Washington, D.C.: U.S. Government Printing Office, March 1983), p. 33.

23. Eli Ginsberg, (ed.,), Employing the Unemployed (New York: Basic Books, 1980).

24. Sheldon Danziger and Robert Haveman, "The Reagan Administration's Budget Cuts: Their Impact on the Poor," Challenge, 24 (May-June 1981), 5-13; Danziger, "Children in Poverty: The Truly Needy Who Fall Through the Safety Net," Children and Youth Services, 4 (1982), 35-51; P. Gottschalk, "Transfer Scenarios and Projections of Poverty into the 1980s," Journal of Human Resources, 16 (1981), 41-60.

25. Robert Pear, "Reagan's Social Impact," *The New York Times*, Wednesday, August 25, 1982, p. 14.

26. Congressional Budget Office, "Major Legislative Changes in Human Resources Programs Since January 1981," Staff Memorandum, August 1983, p. vii.

27. For an overview see "Congress, Administration Debate Need for More Help to Fight Hunger in America," *Congressional Quarterly Weekly Report*, May 7, 1983, pp. 881-886.

28. "Money Income and Poverty Status of Families and Persons in the United States: 1982," *Current Population Reports*, Series P-60, No. 140, p.l.

29. For an outline of the plan see U.S. Congress, House, "Welfare Reform: A Message from the President of the United States," House Document No. 91-146, Congressional Record 115, No. 135, 91st Congress, 1st Session, H7239-7241.

30. U.S. Congress, Joint Economic Committee, Subcommittee on Fiscal Policy, *Income Security for Americans: Recommendations of the Public Welfare Study* (Washington, D.C.: Government Printing Office, 1974).

31. See Lawrence E. Lynn, Jr. and David de F. Whitman, *The President As Policymaker: Jimmy Carter and Welfare Reform* (Philadelphia: Temple University Press, 1981).

32. For a discussion of debate within the Carter administration on this point see *Ibid*, pp. 90-116.

33. Martin Anderson, *Welfare* (Palo Alto, California: Hoover Institute Press, 1978), p. 135; and Henry J. Aaron, *Why Is Welfare So Hard to Reform?* (Washington, D.C.: The Brookings Institute, 1973).

34. Milton Friedman and Rose Friedman, *Free To Choose* (New York: Avon), pp. 116-117; George Gilder, *Wealth and Poverty* (New York: Bantam Books, 1981, p. 153.

35. See Daniel Patrick Moynihan, *The Politics of a Guaranteed Income* (New York: Random House, 1973).

36. Lynn and Whitman, *The President as Policymaker*, pp. 227-261.

37. Rodgers, *The Cost of Human Neglect: America's Welfare Failure* (White Plains, New York: M.E. Sharpe, 1982), Chapter 8.

38. *Ibid*.

39. For an overview see Anderson, *Welfare*, pp. 87-151.

40. *Ibid*, pp. 105-108.

41. *Ibid*, p. 39; See Friedman's critical reaction, *Free to Choose*, pp. 98-100.

42. Gilder, *Wealth and Poverty*, pp. 88-171. For a critical analysis of Gilder's data, see Norman Waitzman, "A Sorcerer in Search of Sources," *Dissent*, Fall 1983, pp. 505-508.

43. *Ibid*, p. 153.

44. *Ibid*, p. 86.

45. Friedman and Friedman, _Free to Choose_, pp. 110-117.

46. Rodgers, _The Cost of Human Neglect_, Chapter 8.

47. See Lester T. Thurow, _The Zero-Sum Society_ (New York: Basic Books, Inc., 1980), pp. 204-205.

48. See Alfred J. Kahn and Shelia B. Kamerman, _Not for the Poor Alone: European Social Services_ (New York: Harper and Row, 1975); Alfred J. Kahn and Shelia B. Kamerman (eds.), _Family Policies in Fourteen Countries_ (New York: Columbia University Press, 1978); Carolyn Teich Adams and Kathryn Teich Winston, _Mothers at Work: Public Policies in the United States, Sweden and China_ (New York: Longman, 1980).

49. Hearing before the Subcommittee on Equal Opportunities of the Committee on Education and Labor, part 5, March 1976, p. 167; Bureau of the Census, "A Statistical Portrait of Women in the U.S.," U.S. Department of Commerce, _Current Population Reports_, Special Studies, Series P-23, No. 58.

XI.

Larry J. Griffin
Kevin T. Leicht

Politicizing Welfare Expenditures in the United States

There is an emerging consensus in the social sciences that the state budget of the U.S. is both a "politicized" and a "politicizing" document and not simply a formal administrative statement reflecting predominantly technocratic rationality or even bureaucratic haggling.[1] Theoretical explanations for the politicization of the budget vary: the politics of pluralism; the cynical and self-interested nature of government officials; the structural dependence of the democratic state on the imperatives of large capitalists; and the vulnerability of the electoral-representative system to protest from below. In this essay, we develop conceptually the idea of the politicization of the state budget and discuss the most salient political mechanisms used by actors to affect budgetary policy. We then empirically test our notions with observed patterns of welfare spending in the U.S. during the period 1949-1980. Of importance to our empirical analyses are assessments of the temporal stability of our statistical estimates of the budgetary processes since this allows us to gauge whether the U.S. budget has become more politicized in the recent past. Through our examination of the politicization of U.S. welfare spending, we attempt more generally to elucidate the contradictory roles performed by the democratic state embedded in capitalist society and speculate on how both socio-political change and continuity is affected by the state and its policies.

CONCEPTUALIZATION

The "politicization" of taxation and expenditure policies refers to the attempt to use public authority over economic activities to secure the private wants of a multitude of competing individuals and groups which strive to maintain or improve their absolute or relative standing in a structure of privilege and domination.[2] A state budget therefore is "politicized" when politico-economic actors (e.g; classes, industries, racial minorities, women's groups. etc.) target certain programs as potentially beneficial to them and then apply pressure -- overtly political or otherwise -- on elected officials and appointed bureaucrats to manipulate the budget in ways favorable to their desires. Likewise, it is "politicizing" because popular perceptions of just such a redistributive outcome may awaken actors to the political usages to which the budget may be put, mobilize them to join or organize political constituencies, and to participate in one way or another in "politics" (broadly defined) in an attempt to maintain their socioeconomic position and achievements.

The politicization of budgetary processes is possible only if the state and its policies are both accessible to the general populace as arenas within which private interests may be expressed and managed by an elite with at least some minimum understanding of the behavior of the macro-economy and a willingness to pursue interventionist economic strategies. It is economically relevant to the well-being of the bulk of the population only if a non-trivial portion of the national product is funneled through the state as it attempts to direct aggregate production and consumption. Below we elaborate briefly on these points within the context of budgetary politicization processes occurring generally in liberal capitalist democracies and specifically in the U.S.

SIZE AND SCOPE OF STATE ACTIVITY

For reasons which we will discuss below, the state in the U.S., though proportionately smaller than many of its counterparts in Western Europe, has nevertheless grown dramatically in recent decades at all administrative levels of government and is now "large" by any criterion. Growth in size has, of course, been accompanied by growth in scope; during the last 50 years public authority, again for reasons to be more fully discussed, has become increasingly responsible for (and implicated in) the production and distribution of the national product. This extension of state size and control over economic matters was necessitated by the breakdown of private enterprise and its subsequent inability to make good the American Dream during the Great Depression, by wartime contingencies, and by the increasingly "social" character of production in the economy's growing industrial core (i.e., an elaborate and interdependent division of labor, reliance on new forms of federally subsidized capital such as human capital, science, and technology, high overhead costs, and long lag-times between investment and profit). It was facilitated by the Keynesian macro-economic "revolution" of the 1930's, which was implemented, however faint-heartedly, in the years 1937-1949.[3] If the Depression and the war provided the impetus for the initiation of massive state intervention, and the post-war growth in the large firms in the most advanced economic sectors for its continuance, Keynes' General Theory of Employment Interest and Money[4] afforded, for the first time, the theoretical justification and the tools necessary for conscious (if flawed) political management of the economy and of the structure of social inequality.[5]

ACCESSIBILITY OF THE STATE

The electoral-representative form of government and the existence of the institutionalized political party system are specific features of liberal democratic capitalist societies which account for the structural accessibility of state. Political parties appeal to, mobilize, or even organize constituencies with particular -- but still relatively diverse -- socio-economic interests in the hope of defeating the opposition at the polls. The budgetary platforms of competing parties[6] and the actual fiscal programs of parties in power[7] then, reflect or represent loosely the preferences (or the perceived, "feasible" preferences) of partisan constituencies[8] Politicization processes of this sort take the form of a common-sensible, intuitive "political" sort, such as the use of educational campaigns, lobbying, and, if all else fails, threats of electoral reward or punishment. These are examples of the use of "institutionalized" political apparatuses, a concept we employ to refer to the relatively formal and routine forms of political participation used most effectively (or perhaps only) by those groups who have the ability to act legitimately in a pluralist polity, e.g., labor unions, business associations, women's, civil rights, and consumer organizations, political action committees, etc.[9] Institutionalized electoral-representative politics therefore provide at least some actors an avenue to the state and to state policy.

This rather conventional pluralist interpretation of public policy formation needs to be complemented with, or balanced by, recent theoretical developments which suggest that the politicization of budgetary processes is due to the self-interestedness of those who manage the state. This perspective -- known as "political business cycle theory" -- argues that political elites, faced with a myopic and gullible electorate, may cynically manipulate budgetary policy during crucial periods of the electoral cycle, not so much in response to the expressed interests or preferences of organized or vocal constituencies, but simply to increase their (or their party's) political popularity and re-election chances.[10] The U.S. is argued to have experienced two types of political business cycles: a two-year cycle of acceleration and deceleration in real personal income and a four year presidential cycle of unemployment fluctuations.[11] Typically, for example, unemployment is relatively high a year or two preceding an election, begins to decline as the election approaches due to expansionary fiscal policy and is relatively low at election times. The reason for the timing of the unemployment cycle, of course, is to improve the re-election chances of the incumbent president or his party.[12] Safely re-elected, the president then turns his attention to reducing federal outlays and inflation, which increased during the period of tight labor markets and economic growth induced by the fiscal stimulant, and he does this by means of budgetary contraction. Unemployment eventually rises again, thus starting the cycle anew.[13]

By linking fiscal policy to the rhythms of election politics, political business cycle theory has much in common with pluralist interpretations of policy. But there is an important distinction: pluralists emphasize the role of elections specifically and democratic politics generally in translating the wishes of voters into policy; aspects of the budget are construed to be political debts paid to interest groups by elected representatives beholden to their constituents. One implication that can be gleaned from political business cycle literature, however, is that budgetary manipulation is severed from the preferences of organized constituencies; that it is not at all a reflection of "representation." Indeed, an extreme reading of this theory would suggest that state managers represent a "class-for-themselves" with their own group interests; and that they, at least in budgetary terms, represent, if anyone, only themselves. Therefore, they politicize fiscal policy in an attempt to realize their "class" interests.[14]

We have thus far attempted to delineate some of the rather obvious ways in which the electoral-representative system and political parties provide access to the reigns of policy formation. There are, however, two other -- possibly less obvious -- mechanisms through which some segments of the populace can affect state policy in capitalist democracies; one rests upon the structural centrality of capitalists in large firms in the economy; the other, on the social protest or collective violence of political insurgents. Both stem from the (possibly contradictory) functions performed by the liberal democratic state embedded in advanced capitalist society: accumulation (i.e., extended reproduction of private capital) and legitimation (i.e., the maintenance or re-creation of the conditions of social harmony, which may involve the concealment or justification of state accumulation policies).

The accumulation functions of the state result from the inability of private capital to insure the production or reproduction of conditions facilitating the realization of profit.[15] Future profit depends on current investment, and capitalists will not invest in a particular venture (or in a particular region, industry, or nation) if alternative investment decisions (including the option of not investing at all) appear more profitable (or less costly). Perceptions of potential profitability, in turn, are influenced by, among other factors, political stability, relatively harmonious labor relations, adequate infrastructural development to produce and market commodities, sufficient consumer demand, and the availability of a plentiful and adequately trained labor force. Some of these "needs" require the continued expansion of "social capital" (social investment and social consumption) since they are financially prohibitive, or entail too much risk for even the largest firms to undertake.[16] Others are simply beyond the purview of the private sector entirely. Only the state has the necessary economic and political entitlement to ignore short-run profitability criteria for such massive expenditures; only the state can insure political stability and the legitimacy of capitalist relations of production. Hence continued productivity and profit-taking depend on the socialization of production costs; i.e., the assumption of some of these expenses by the state, and on the socialization of consumption.[17] These are the accumulation functions of the state and are partially responsible for the growth of the state sector in the last half-century.

What does all of this have to do with the politicization of budgetary processes and the accessibility of the liberal democratic state? The answer hinges on the profound importance of private investment. General economic prosperity in contemporary capitalist nations rests on the willingness of capitalists -- especially those controlling huge multi-billion dollar enterprises -- to invest in new plants and equipment, in inventories, in raw materials, and in the purchase of labor power [18] Continued production, jobs for the vast bulk of the population who are not capitalists, the wages and salaries of workers (and hence the prime component of their standards of living), and even government revenue in the form of taxes on corporate and individual income and sales, are all therefore fundamentally a function of private investment. There is, literally by definition, no alternative to this within the confines of the capitalist system. Because social stability also rests ultimately on the avoidance of sustained economic crises, it too is determined partially, if indirectly, by investment decisions. Even state expenditures designed to improve the material conditions of the elderly, the poor, etc. (e.g., social security, subsidized schooling), which must be financed out of past, current, or projected revenue,[19] are economically feasible only if capitalists invest in income-generating enterprises.

The investment decisions of large firms, then, are of unparalleled importance to the national economy and to the social order of capitalist society generally. The state is, as a consequence, deeply dependent on private investment patterns and this structural dependence gives large capitalists enormous political leverage in clashes over state programs, including, of course, budgetary policy. If "tax rates" are excessively steep, they are likely to be lowered;[20] if an interstate highway system needs to be built, it is likely to happen;[21] if a boost in expenditures for military purposes is needed to protect U.S. capital and counter ideological opponents abroad and to increase markets domestically, Congress will probably grant it;[22] if outlays for basic research and technological development is necessary to compete more effectively in the world market, we are apt to see solicitous response from policymakers.[23] Thus is the liberal democratic state accessible to large capitalists and thus is the budget politicized.

This is not an "instrumentalist" conception of the capitalist state, which often theorizes that state policy is congruent with the needs of capital because of the similar social origins, values, and narrow economic interests of business and government elites[24] Nor is it a "liberal corporate" view of the state,[25] which argues that a liberal, progressive and far-sighted corporate elite understands the "necessity of stepped-up state intervention and will use their great resources and prestige to persuade many capitalists to go along and to pressure politicians to implement needed programs"[26] to rationalize capitalism. Undoubtedly, the capitalist class does generally have greater input into policy formation than does the working class for these and other reasons having to do with pluralist politics (e.g.; superior financial and organizational resources). However, this argument is essentially independent of those. It instead revolves around the structure of capitalism itself, especially the "veto power" of elite capitalists in investment decisions and the embeddedness of the liberal democratic state in capitalist society.[27] In any battle over the state budget, big capital thus has decided structural advantages because of the possibility of a "capital strike"; i.e., the decision not to invest, and the immediately wrenching economic, social, and political consequences of such a decision.

So the state must aid large corporations to grow and to realize profit. But, successful accumulation may engender specific contradictions.[28] These are: (a) surplus productive capacity (i.e., potential industrial output outpaces demand for products and, therefore, plants are not fully utilized); and (b) an expanding pool of surplus labor (i.e., the displacement of large sectors of the population, both workers and petit-bourgeoisie, due to the increasing capital intensiveness of production techniques and the liquidation of small capital respectively.[29] Both surplus productive capacity and an expanding pool of surplus labor generate pressures which tend to politicize state policy, but it is the existence of a more-or-less permanent underclass which is most important for our discussion of the political determinants of welfare outlays. These "redundant" members of capitalist society generally are unable to find full-time work, due to internal labor markets within firms, union restrictions, and the lack of the "right" skills and work histories, and "increasingly become(s) dependent on the state."[30]

An underclass in liberal capitalist democracies poses simultaneous economic and political challenges to state managers. Those disaffected or alienated by successful capital accumulation, or those simply forgotten in the celebration of "national" prosperity, must be economically subsidized[31] and socially controlled.[32] Neither starvation nor violent repression generally is the optimal or preferred solution of elites governing democratic regimes, especially those characterized by political liberality and extensive citizenship rights.[33] The state, instead, seeks, by showing itself to be economically humane and politically accessible, to elicit from the underclass, and the citizenry generally, a belief in the moral worthiness, the essential correctness, of liberal democratic society. It attempts therefore to legitimate its accumulation policies, the capitalist relations of production, and the electoral-representative political system by making symbolic, organizational, and material concessions to the marginal and to the disenfranchised.

One objection to this view of the state could take the form of the following question: "how can the state be used as a means of reform by those without substantial economic and political power if the state is, in fact, dependent on the investment decisions of large capitalists?" This is less of a paradox than it may seem: we claimed only that the state is dependent on the "business confidence" of the capitalist class, not that it, or its policies, is determined precisely by capitalists' "veto power". The liberal democratic state is relatively autonomous from direct corporate dominance due to intra-class competition among capitalists, to the past and continuing struggles of oppressed groups or classes, to the reality of pluralist elements, and to the political struggles among politicians and state managers themselves.[34] To be sure, this relative autonomy may be thought to be "functional" to the long term survival requirements of capital, in that it allows the state to absorb the economic and social dislocations which accompany capitalist accumulation. But, it may also be occasionally "dysfunctional" because it gives state managers room to maneuver and makes the state vulnerable to protest from below, especially during major electoral and economic upheavals.[35]

But recourse to "relative autonomy" only partially resolves the apparent paradox. Another part of the resolution is straightforward and lies in the logic of commodity production. Income transfer programs designed to provide or augment the buying power of the poor and the un- and under-employed, those with the highest marginal propensity to consume, increase aggregate demand and bolster domestic markets.[36] A "safety net" therefore may be in the interests of capitalists since it is one solution to both the "realization" problem; i.e., the potential profit embedded in a commodity is not realized until it is purchased, and the problem of surplus productive capacity. Many federal programs which subsidize the consumption of the surplus population are now institutionalized as "entitlements" (e.g., social security) and some, in fact, function as automatic countercyclical stabilizers, increasing during slumps and decreasing during booms (e.g., unemployment insurance).[37]

The rest of the resolution to the apparent paradox, however, is more complicated and is at least as much a consequence of the politics of capitalist democracies as it is of their economics. We discussed above "institutionalized" politics within the context of a pluralist polity and argued that it provided interest groups with representation in the state. But, these mechanisms are less effective in pressing the concerns of the underclass and the poor since these groups generally are unorganized (or, if organized, deemed "illegitimate") or are structurally peripheral to core institutions, or only minimally represented (if at all) in the two-party system:38

> Politically powerless and economically marginal, poor people do not have the institutionalized opportunities to voice their political grievances and even their protest is denied political content, thought "irrational" and "deviant". In a word the mechanisms of electoral interest group politics are inaccessible to these groups. If, in fact, collectivities cannot participate effectively in the electoral-representative system, then the only means available to them as they seek redress from the state may be non-institutionalized politics, of which collective protest, mass insurgency, and social disruption are primary mechanisms.

Hence, the underclass resort to the only political resource they possess, the withholding of "accustomed cooperation" which can create "institutional disruptions" in the routine of civil society, in governments, and in the economy.39 If collective violence or disruption is severe enough, or prolonged enough, the smooth and regular functioning of society is jeopardized and state managers must act; they then are more likely to grant (possibly temporary) economic and political "concessions in an attempt to alleviate some of the grievances of the mobilized insurgent groups and, thereby, re-legitimate electoral-representative politics generally and state policies particularly."40 They do this not as advocates or representatives of the poor or of the protestors, but rather to acquire the consent of the governed to govern, "which may occasionally require efforts by political elites, first, to quiet the protestors by some legitimating activity and, at a later stage, to institutionalize the conflict in order to integrate both the issue and the insurgents into (or back into) electoral-interest group politics."41

Not every riot, demonstration, or strike is "politically" motivated, of course, but many are consciously so.42 More important, it is not the explicit motivation of the participants which is of the utmost importance to any form of non-institutionalized political activity, it is whether state managers perceive the disruption to be a political problem and believe that a political response would diminish the insurgency and lead to a return of societal quietude and "normalcy". This reaction to mass protest, insurgency, and collective action -- indeed this structural accessibility of the machinery of the state -- is most likely to occur in one of two periods. During economic crises, when capital is disorganized, defensive, and demoralized, searching for a new "social structure of accumulation,"[43] the state's autonomy from capital's veto power is at its height and significant pro-working class reforms are possible.[44] Likewise, during times of electoral instability, when traditional political coalitions and alignments are no longer effective in turning out the vote and winning elections, governing elites may attempt to mobilize support by organizing new electoral constituencies, again occasionally through significant reform of the political economy.[45] Piven and Cloward best summarize this view:[46]

> (C)oncessions were won by protestors only when political leaders were finally forced, out of concern for their own survival, to act in ways that aroused the fierce opposition of economic elites. In short, under conditions of severe electoral instability, the alliance of public and private power is sometimes weakened, if only briefly, and at these points a defiant poor may make gains.

Legitimating activities of the state, then, politicize the budget. Welfare programs, in particular, thus may be thought of as a political response to the presence of a surplus population of economically redundant members of society. Transfers can be used more-or-less ordinarily to augment the "citizen" or "social" wage and continually to legitimate capitalist productive relations by providing for a "safety net" for the "truly needy".[47] Transfers may be used only extraordinarily -- as apparently are some direct relief outlays, such as Aid to Families with Dependent Children -- to control politically a visibly restive or disruptive underclass.[48] Finally, they may be used by state managers as one of a number of strategies to forge new political coalitions and realignments during critical election periods.[49] Regardless of the intent of the programs, however, or of the motivations of those who implement them, transfer payments and welfare outlays are monetary expressions of the politicization of public policy, of the systemic tie between the state's budget and electoral-representative politics in capitalist society.

Our basic argument, therefore, is that budgetary policy in the U.S. is developed, implemented, and executed not by politically- or class- neutral technicians responding to the "public need" or to the "good of the commonweal," but rather by an elite, itself politicized, which must function within the economic and political constraints imposed by liberal democratic capitalism. This effectively means that state managers must simultaneously attempt to (1) insure "business confidence," an adequate level of private investment, and thereby economic growth; (2) legitimate the entire system to those who are redundant in that system and dampen the potentiality or fact of periodic collective outbursts by this group; and (3) maintain or create the allegiance of a fickle electorate notorious for short memories and heads easily turned, an electorate with power, in principle, to "turn the rascals out" every two or four years. Budgetary processes, therefore, are politicized precisely because all of these properties define an institutionalized arena within which private actors -- some permanently organized, others only temporarily mobilized -- collide, where they take their competing and even occasionally contradictory <u>private</u> wants and grievances for satisfaction or redress by <u>public</u> authority.

<u>THE PRESENT RESEARCH</u>

We believe that budgetary processes are politicized in the U.S., and we have attempted to delineate some of the political mechanisms implicated in that process. There is ample evidence suggesting that politicization of state policy -- as we have conceptualized it -- extends back into the U.S. of the nineteenth century,[50] though it has gained prominence as a mode of public resource allocation since Roosevelt's first term[51] and particularly so since World War II.[52] Using the insights and analytic strategies of much of this past research, we analyze in this section aggregated and program-specific transfer outlays since 1949 to illustrate our notions about budget-making processes.

Throughout these analyses, we use five indicators of transfer or welfare outlays. All are expressed as percentages of nominal GNP, the conventional measure of a nation's "welfare effort".[53] The first is the simple summation of all governmental transfer payments, as these are defined by the National Income and Product Accounts, and consists of benefits from state and federal social insurance funds, from state and local direct relief programs, and all other miscellaneous transfers. The other four measures, which are specific federal or state transfer programs or are limited aggregations of specific programs, are

(1) federal Old Age and Survivors Disability Insurance (OASDI) and (2) federal Unemployment Insurance (UI), (3) Aid to Families with Dependent Children (AFDC), administered at the state level, and (4) other direct relief (ODR), which includes food stamps (federal) and other categorical public assistance and general assistance (state).

We use indicators of varying levels of aggregation because of our desire to assess both general and program-specific budgetary processes. On the one hand, the all-inclusive transfer indicator represents the best summary measure of the U.S.'s monetary commitment to redistributive fiscal policy; as such, it is the single most appropriate indicator to use in rather general evaluations of the politicization of the welfare policy in the post-War period. On the other hand, the very inclusiveness of the aggregate transfer measure presents analytic difficulties; each specific social insurance and direct relief program is directed toward different targeted populations, is administered differentially, has different eligibility criteria, etc.. Each series also has a different trend (see Table 1). Past research has shown, moreover, that specific expenditure categories -- or aggregations of several categories -- are differentially affected by economic and political processes.[54] All of this suggests that the use of aggregate transfers may mask or average out program-specific politicization processes. Analysis of the specific expenditure categories are not subject to these problems.

We construct models of the politicization of transfer outlays based on our conceptualization discussed above and estimate a number of time-series equations using annual economic and political data for the U.S. for the period 1949-1980. In our regression equations, we control initially for four budgetary constraints on transfer outlays: (1) the current rate of inflation, which may depress some expenditures but may also stimulate the federal programs since OASDI was officially pegged to increases in the cost of living in 1972; (2) current revenue, which generally should increase outlays (see above discussion); (3) current defense spending, which is expected to reduce spending due to the tradeoff between "guns" and "butter," and (4) anticipated budgetary deficits or surpluses, which should decrease outlays since state managers generally set this year's funding partially in response to their expectations as to its consequences on next year's budget.[55] Defense spending, revenue, and the anticipated deficit are expressed as percentages of GNP. In several of the specific program outlays (OASDI, ODR) we control also for the percentage of population aged 65 or older. Finally, we include lagged values of the dependent variables (i.e., the values of the expenditures for the previous year). These serve as global controls for a host of otherwise unspecified effects, including "bureaucratic momentum" and budgetary incrementa-incrementalism.[56]

Table 2 presents the hypothesized conceptual mechanisms we argued to be responsible for politicizing transfers and their operationalizations in this analysis. Our operationalizations of these concepts and the specification of the equations more generally (including the exact lag structures assumed for the independent variables) is based on Griffin, et al.,[57] who provide the theoretical rationale for these models and the industrial-or occupational-specific forms of the wage and unemployment measures.

Our earlier theoretical discussions lead us to expect that transfers should increase as (a) the surplus labor force increases,[58] as (b) political insurgency and civil disruption increases, and (c) in years immediately preceding presidential elections. The effects of indicators of economic "subsistence" may vary, however. On the one hand, decreases in the need to subsidize the buying power of the "working poor" (and decreases in surplus capital) should reduce welfare outlays since state aid is less likely to be needed during periods of heavy capital utilization and relatively higher market wages of the most economically disadvantaged workers. On the other hand, transfers may be pegged in some fashion to competitive wages and the standard of living (and aggregate demand) afforded by income levels or by other definitions of subsistence, such as the legal minimum wage. This reasoning then would lead us to expect competitive sector wages and/or the minimum wage to stimulate welfare outlays, since either could, in effect, establish a floor below which income (earned or transferred) should not fall. We also have no strong expectations as to the potential impact of Democratic party domination of either the executive or the legislative branches of the federal government. The Democratic party generally has been thought to be more ready to aid the poor through welfare expansion, perhaps particularly so since during the "Great Society" era. Democratic control, then, might increase social security and income maintenance payments. But the upward trend in most transfer outlays throughout most administrations, Democratic and Republican alike, during the entire post-War period suggests that partisan politics may have only marginal effects on welfare expansion. Moreover, it should be remembered that we are effectively analyzing changes in transfers, not levels (see note 56); this means that the positive zero-order relationships between, particularly, the percentage of Democrats in the House of Representatives and the levels of the expenditures of most of the specific transfer programs has no necessary implication for assessments of changes in outlays.[59]

Our analyses are bounded by the years 1949 and 1980 for historical, theoretical, and pragmatic reasons. Historically, the U.S. did not even develop a "mature" welfare apparatus until after World War II.[60] Theoretically, the linkages assumed by most theorists between economic and political processes and state expenditures appear particularly important for the post-war era.[61] There is little reason to assume that the structure of the U.S. political economy and the state's fiscal response to economic organization and fluctuations and to political events were identical in the pre- and post-war periods.[62] Pragmatically, 1949 represents the first year for which we have data and 1980 the last. Regression results presented in the next five tables were derived in the following manner. First, we initially estimated the coefficients of all budgetary constraints, the lagged endogenous variable, and those variables deemed theoretically appropriate for each expenditure category. Only in the aggregate transfer equation did we initially include all regressors shown in Table 2 and the proportion of the population 65 years or older; we used this "saturated" specification here because overall transfer payments are a combination of many specific program outlays, each possibly subject to rather specific processes. We then excluded statistically irrelevant variables or regressors with unstable or seemingly artifactual coefficients (i.e., a statistically significant coefficient which appeared to result from multicolinearity) and re-estimated each equation. The coefficients derived from the "second" stage estimation of the now "trimmed" statistical models are reported in Tables 3-7, where we present regression results for the years 1949-76, -78, -79, -80.

Consider first the patterns of determination of the aggregate transfer equation in Table 3. The lagged endogenous variable is positive in all equations, becomes and remains statistically significant after year 1977 is added to the series, and becomes increasingly larger as each additional year is added. The increasing significance and size of this coefficient suggests that transfers were increasingly subject to budgetary incrementalism and bureaucratic inertia; that is, the proportion of GNP allocated to overall transfers at any given year was increasingly a function of the prior year's proportion. Revenue, too, is seen increasingly to stimulate transfer outlays, though its coefficients are statistically significant only with the addition of 1979 to the series. Military expenditures and anticipated budget deficits retard, as expected, increases in aggregate transfers; and, like revenue and the lagged endogenous variable, defense outlays exert an increasingly significant impact over time. Neither inflation nor proportion "elderly" significantly affected transfers during this period.

Among variables of theoretical interest, unskilled occupational unemployment, detrended competitive wages, and racial riots stimulate, and Democratic administrations depress, transfers (as a percent of GNP). The unemployment and riot coefficients are consistent with our earlier arguments about the need for state managers both to subsidize economically the "surplus population" (the unemployment effect) and to respond to mass disruption, here in major urban centers by rioting blacks, by the expansion of transfer outlays. The positive wages coefficient suggests that the summary transfer measure (but, as we will see, not the specific programs constituting this index) is responsive to an income floor generated, in this case, in the private sector. The negative influence of Democratic presidents may seem at first sight to be puzzling, but it should be remembered that we are assessing the impact of political parties on <u>changes</u> in the levels of transfers, rather than on the levels per se; the depressant influence of Democratic administrations, therefore, is observed after controlling for "bureaucratic momentum" (in the form of the lagged endogenous variables), including that induced by earlier Democratic control (see also notes 56 and 59).[63] Finally, we find no consistent evidence that labor militancy,[64] election year,[65] or industrial utilization significantly affected overall transfers.

What are we to conclude from the findings shown in Table 3? First, there are bureaucratic and fiscal limitations on the degree to which transfers can be politicized. Yet there is evidence, too, of politicization stemming from a variety of sources; e.g.; racial insurgency, the presence of low-paid, economically marginal, and/or unemployed workers, and partisan budgetary manipulation. And, importantly, there is suggestive evidence that some of these effects, i.e., racial insurgency and political party differences, have become more pronounced since 1976. In sum, the percentage of GNP devoted broadly to income redistribution does, in fact, appear to be governed partially by a variety of political influences, each reflecting claims made on the state or responsibilities assumed by the state in the context of the structural weakness of the private sector.

We argued above that the use of summary transfer measures, while quite useful for some purposes, may nonetheless lead to incomplete or imprecise inferences for a variety of reasons. In Tables 4 through 7, we address this possibility by examining the determinants of four specific transfer programs, OASDI, unemployment insurance, AFDC, and non-AFDC direct relief. The regression coefficients presented in these tables were derived in an identical manner to those presented in Table 3; that is, insignificant or unstable regressors were deleted and the "trimmed" equations were then estimated. For all expenditures considered we see again a general mix of budgetary constraints and budgetary politicization. We see also some commonalities and some divergencies in processes determining changes in outlays of these programs.

First, the commonalities. Defense spending does not depress any program outlay, suggesting that no single program (studied here) is significantly adversely affected by the militarization of the budget (though monies allocated to all transfer programs -- as indexed by the summary transfer measure -- is reduced by defense outlays; see Table 3). Revenue is a constraint on three of the four programs; the sole exception is OASDI (see Table 4), which is the single most institutionalized "entitlement" program extant and, additionally, is complicated by legal considerations about financing. With the exception of unemployment insurance (Table 5), all expenditures are rather strongly determined by their prior years's values, suggesting again the relevance of budgetary incrementalism. (The absence of an effect of the lagged endogenous variable for UI is not surprising; unemployment, and hence UI, is cyclical and exhibits no appreciable trend throughout most of the post-War years). Of variables indexing politicization processes, as we have defined those in this paper, Democratic administrations appear to decrease outlays for all programs. This, of course, is consistent with the results obtained with overall transfers. Unskilled occupational unemployment (a measure of the prevalence of the surplus labor force), increases, as expected, expenditures of all programs except OASDI. Again, this latter null result is not surprising.

There are also several divergences from these general patterns which appear important. Percent of the population 65 years or older naturally increases OASDI expenditures and also increases other direct relief as well.[66] The two federal programs, OASDI and UI, are stimulated by inflation (see Tables 4 and 5), suggesting the "pegging" process discussed above, but the other programs, AFDC and ODR (Tables 6 and 7), are not (indeed, inflationary pressures seem to depress significantly outlays of ODR). This probably reflects the centralized versus decentralized nature of these programs. Another difference between these two types of programs, and one of major theoretical importance to this study, is their differential sensitivity to mass insurgency and civil disobedience. Outlays for the state programs are increased either by racial violence (AFDC) or by racial and labor insurgency (ODR); the two federal programs appear impervious to both. This implies that annual variations in federal transfers are somewhat insulated from distributional struggles within cities and a states or among classes.[67] The AFDC and ODR findings also support the hypothesis of Friedland, Piven and Alford who argue that local governments are often the "loci for popular political participation because they are structurally accessible" to mobilized insurgents.[68] The heightened politicization of the state-level relief programs vis-a-vis the federal programs is also suggested by the stimulative impact of presidential elections on AFDC payments; indeed, only AFDC appears sensitive to the electoral cycle, providing limited and quite specific support of political business cycle theories.

Hypotheses predicting an effect on welfare outlays of an "income floor" also receive some support; as their negative coefficients indicate both minimum wages (in the OASDI equation; see Table 4) and cyclical variation in competitive-sector wages (in the UI equation; see Table 5) appear to operate as substitutes for public subsidization of those caught on the economy's fringes. Finally, the hypotheses that the existence of surplus capital directly exerts pressure for welfare expansion is only weakly supported. Reduction in utilization of industrial structures do appear to stimulate OASDI expenditures, but the coefficients on Table 4 are of marginal and variable significance. This, coupled with the peculiarities of the OASDI equation (see note 65), and the fact that capacity utilization failed to increase significantly any other welfare outlay, leads us to advance this interpretation quite cautiously. However, the notion that surplus capital indirectly governs welfare state expansion is amply supported by the strong and rather general stimulative influence on most transfers of the unemployment rates of the surplus working population; that is, surplus capital generates surplus workers who, in turn, require state relief.

In general, then, analyses of these four specific programs (or, in the case of non-AFDC direct relief, limited aggregations of programs) suggest that they are, in fact, politicized in that macro-economic fluctuations and the use of institutionalized and non-institutionalized politics increase or decrease expenditures over and above what would be predicted from budgetary incrementalism, fiscal constraints, and demographic pressures. But, importantly, the impact of specific politico-economic variables is also often limited to specific programs, suggesting to us that annual variations in program outlays are not equally politicized. Less institutionalized (and more controversial) state-level relief programs appear substantially more sensitive to a variety of political influences than do the more "routine", bureaucratically-entrenched federal entitlement programs.[69]

HAS TRANSFER POLICY BECOME MORE POLITICIZED?

We have thus far assumed that the politicization processes we have discussed have operated more or less constantly throughout the entire post-War period. There is some impressionistic evidence, however, indicating that the political-economic structure of U.S. capitalism altered in the mid-1960's.[70] If this has indeed happened, politicization processes may be different, or may be more pronounced or less, in the two sub-periods. Thus, the estimates above, which of course pertain to the entire post-War period, may be somewhat misleading. It seems to us that a plausible case can be made for the belief that budgetary processes have become more politicized since the mid-1960's than earlier in the post-War period. Manifestations of this, while too numerous to catalogue here, include the Kennedy-Johnson tax cut of 1964, the inflationary financing of the Vietnam War, the increasing restiveness of the black community and the corresponding strategic shift among some blacks from non-violent civil disobedience to violence, and the birth of the Great Society programs, which increased sharply transfer outlays.

Our speculations are easily tested. We simply re-estimated the equations presented in Tables 3-7 for the period 1949-63. Our expectations are that these coefficients should be smaller than those discussed above since the entire post-War period coefficients are estimated over presumably more politicized years; i.e., 1964-1980. The results of this analysis are presented in Table 8.

Comparisons of these coefficients with those for the entire 1949-1980 period (the last column in Tables 3-7) suggest that the evidence is mixed. Macro-economic determinants do not appear to be less influential in the pre-1964 years (if anything, the opposite is the case); the more overtly "political" influences, however, do appear to have greater salience when the post-1963 years are added to the analysis. This is true for all dimensions of "political" activity: partisan policy differences, as reflected by the depressant influences of Democratic presidents across all welfare outcomes; political definitions of economic subsistence as reflected by the minimum wage effect in the OASDI equation; political insurgency by, especially, blacks, and, possibly, labor, as reflected by the positive riot coefficient in the AFDC equation and both the riot and strike coefficients in the AFDC and ODR equations; and the stimulative impact of presidential elections in the AFDC equation.

We interpret the party and electoral timing influences to mean that state managers in the executive branch have become more explicitly "political" actors, more willing (and able) to manipulate transfers in order to realize their own politico-economic interests.The noninstitutionalized political influences suggest possibly that the liberal capitalist state has become more accessible to the surplus population, <u>if they disrupt social order</u>, and to insurgents generally or that state policy has become more democratized. It may also mean little more than that politicians were simply frightened by the black uprising of the 1960's and understood that fiscal concessions could represent a political bandaid to hide the crisis of the ghetto. Since the vast bulk of the racial riots which have occurred since the end of the War erupted in the mid- and late 1960's we simply do not know which interpretation is correct. Regardless of the "accuracy" of these competing interpretations, however, we can conclude from a comparison of the results presented in Table 8 with those presented in previous tables that, while welfare policy is not generally more politicized, particular transfers have become (at least until Ronald Reagan's election in 1980) increasingly sensitive in the last 15 to 20 years to partisan party agendas, to rhythms of the electoral cycle, and to the use of noninstitutionalized politics by political and, possibly, economic insurgents.

CONCLUSION

Less than three months into his Presidency, Ronald Reagan submitted to Congress the Administration's proposed fiscal year 1982 budget, a document reflecting in a number of particulars the conservatism of the President, his Cabinet officers, Congress, and (presumably) a large segment of the electorate. At the heart of the FY82 budget were unprecedented, perhaps "historic," reductions in a broad range of social service expenditure categories. Admirers of the Administration argued that the welfare reductions, in particular, were necessary to control the growth of the federal government and the federal debt; in a word, they were a welcome first step along a political path culminating ultimately-at least in the eyes of administrative spokespersons-in a return to "fiscal responsibility" and "individual incentive." Critics of budget director David Stockman's "budget ax," of course, paint a different scenario: that the Reagan Administration does not simply wish to reduce federal spending but also desires to redistribute wealth and income from the working class and middle income groups to the (already) richest segments of American society and to the corporate sector. This redistribution would occur both by dismantling the social programs which characterized the Democratically-dominated period from Roosevelt's New Deal through Johnson's Great Society, and by reducing the "tax burden" on the wealthy.

Regardless of political allegiance or ideological hue, however, most White House and Congressional observers agree that the Reagan Administration, desirous of reducing the roles and responsibilities of the federal government, is using fiscal policy, in particular the allocation of monies to so-called "entitlement" programs, as an instrument of social and economic change. We are witnessing, then, a general recognition that the state, through its budgetary policy, is itself a dynamic actor in the political economy of the U.S. and that it is, moreover, "a product, an object, and a determinant of class struggle."71

Ronald Reagan's budgets may represent, quantitatively, a heightened degree of politicization when compared to the policies of his immediate predecessors and undoubtedly they are more explicitly and visibly advantageous for the rich than previous budgets. But, in our opinion, his contributions to budgetary politicization do not represent a fundamental break with traditions established by the time of the New Deal and more-or-less faithfully perpetuated by every administration since then. The empirical results presented in this paper demonstrate that welfare expenditure policy since World War II is, in fact, a highly politicized vehicle used by state managers in the U.S. as they try to: insure capital accumulation; placate or encourage competing classes and political actors; and acquiesce to or rebuff demands of mass insurgents. All of this is done within the context of tenuously legitimate electoral institutions. This is particularly true, we believe, for state-level relief programs, such as AFDC, but it is also characterizes, though less dramatically so, such institutionalized federal social insurance programs as OASDI. Moreover, while there is little evidence to suggest that purely economic influences have become more heavily implicated in determining welfare policy since the mid-1960's than earlier, we did find that more overtly political factors, especially those revolving around partisan party politics and the use of noninstitutionalized collective action and mass disruption, indeed even violence, by, particularly, urban blacks, have increasingly governed relief outlays. This is consistent with the notion that redistributive expenditures have become more politicized, that selective actors have stepped-up the use of their political resources in order to acquire public redress of private wants.

We should reiterate here that these effects are observed to be independent of the influences of our previously described budgetary constraints of societal demographics, and of bureaucratic momentum and budgetary incrementalism. Beyond what we would predict from these factors, then, annual variations in all transfers, and in important disaggregated transfer programs, are affected appreciably by the economic and political variables we have identified. We should also emphasize that the budgetary controls which we considered exogenous, revenue,[72] inflation,[73] military expenditures,[74] and budget deficits[75] have selective, class-discriminating causes and consequences and are themselves a function of past and continuing politico-economic struggles, of the politicization of the state. In all likelihood then, our statistical analyses probably underestimate the prevalence of budgetary politicization more generally.

It could be argued, of course, that some of the structural linkages which we have interpreted as evidence of politization, especially those describing the relationships between employment and wage fluctuations, on the one hand, and transfers, on the other, are evidence only of the efficacy of Keynesian stewardship, of technocratic monitoring of the economy. We agree that they do in fact represent Keynesian-style macroeconomic intervention, but we also believe the concept of "politicization" explains why, among an array of possible policy responses to electoral pressure and economic crisis, political elites in virtually every advanced capitalist democracy came to perceive the utility and "wisdom" of Keynesian theory, however distorted or incomplete its actual implementation. The very adoption of Keynesian economics is itself perhaps the hallmark of the politicized economy.[76]

The budget is not completely elastic; it cannot be politicized infinitely. In the U.S., as in any advanced capitalist democracy, processes of politicization are bounded at the extremes by the structural imperatives of capitalism, on the one hand, and by electoral-representative politics, on the other. Faced with capitalist hegemony at home and abroad, political elites could not, for example, increase transfers to the point where government subsidization of consumption allowed most of the populace to choose not to participate in the labor market, however politically popular or politically self-serving such a redistributive strategy may have appeared initially. Even a serious attempt to do so would create economically damning profit losses, disinvestment and capital flight, a shrinking tax base, and, subsequently, a general deterioration in the living standards of all.77 Its political appeal at that point would be conspicuously absent, even among those once favoring the program. Likewise, the complete elimination of the welfare state, however profitable in the short run and however "efficient" according to the calculus of capital, would entail tremendous political struggle and, possibly, nearly insurmountable obstacles, at least as those could be handled within the confines of liberal democracy. Such a move would be defined as "illegitimate", a violation of the "rules of the game," and quickly scrapped as angry masses mobilized to use the machinery of democracy to replace the "executive arm of the bourgeoise" with elites more attuned to the wishes of the majority. These, therefore, are the limits of budgetary politicization.

But within these constraints the degree of politicization is variable and depends on the institutional, organizational, intellectual, and economic resources of politico-economic actors, on their ability and willingness to use those resources to affect fiscal policy, and on the perceptiveness and willingness of state managers to manipulate budgetary policy for political objectives. And we believe the budget will continue to be politicized as long as the coupling of electoral-representative politics and the inherent stratification induced by the dynamic of capital accumulation leaves the state exposed to discriminatory political and economic payoffs of fiscal manipulation by either its own agents or unequally rewarded and resourceful actors in civil society.

Table 1

Descriptive Statistics on the Growth of Post-World War II Government Spending

Years	Total Government Expenditures $\overline{X}$ (Nominal)	$\overline{X}$ (Real)	% GNP	Transfers $\overline{X}$ (Nominal)	$\overline{X}$ (Real)	% GNP
1949-1955	87025.1	1115.38	25.6	13444.7	173.85	4.[illegible]
1956-1960	135618.2	1579.46	29.3	22781.4	264.94	4.[illegible]
1961-1965	186493.2	2027.99	31.1	33643.6	365.89	5.[illegible]
1966-1970	289930.6	2735.7	33.3	57239.8	537.78	6.[illegible]
1971-1975	468446.4	3386.35	36.1	121266.6	869.28	9.[illegible]
1976-1980	795930.0	3939.78	37.4	225052.2	1109.32	10.[illegible]

All dollar figures in millions

Table 2

Theoretical Concept and Hypothesized Mechanism	Operationalization of Concept
1. Increases in surplus labor force	1. Unskilled occupational unemployment
2. Decreases in need to subsidize buying power of the "working" poor	2a. De-trended competitive sector wages b. Legal minimum wage
3. Decreases in surplus capital/ renewed accumulation	3. Utilization of existing industrial structure
4. Increases in mass insurgency and mobilization of working class and other dependent populations	4a. % of total potential working time lost due to strikes b. frequency of racial riots
5. Political party partisanship	5. Democratic control of legislative/executive
6. Rhythms of electoral cycle	6. Presidential election year

Table 3

Economic and Political Determinants of Government Transfers as a Percentage of GNP: Various Years (OLS Estimates).

Independent Variables	1949-76	1949-77	1949-78	1949-79	1949-80
TRANSFERS/GNP (t-1)	.179[a] (1.22)	.227 (1.50)*	.241 (1.52)*	.378 (2.64)**	.395 (3.32)**
DEFENSE/GNP (t)	-.083 (1.60)*	-.095 (1.77)**	-.120 (2.29)**	-.136 (2.52)**	-.139 (2.78)**
REVENUE/GNP (t)	.034 (.525)	.041 (.620)	.069 (1.06)	.116 (1.92)**	.133 (2.78)**
BUDGET SURPLUS-DEFICIT/GNP $_{(t+1)}$	-.126 (3.54)**	-.144 (3.78)**	-.138 (3.49)**	-.136 (3.28)**	-.131 (3.45)**
UNSKILLED OCCUPATIONAL UNEMPLOYMENT (t)	.237 (5.81)**	.230 (5.40)**	.228 (5.20)**	.220 (4.84)**	.218 (5.15)**
DETRENDED COMPETITIVE WAGES $_{(t)}$	.575[b] (4.07)**	.483[b] (3.47)**	.437[b] (3.03)**	.281[b] (2.40)**	.261[b] (3.52)**
RIOT FREQUENCY $_{(t-1)}$	.431[b] (1.76)**	.472[b] (1.94)**	.492[b] (1.97)**	.531[b] (2.05)**	.539[b] (2.16)**
DEMOCRATIC PRESIDENT $_{(t)}$	-.169 (1.47)*	-.252 (2.31)**	-.289 (2.69)**	-.332 (3.04)**	-.338 (3.19)**
$\bar{R}^2$	.986	.986	.986	.986	.987
DURBIN'S H	.218	.474	1.18	.655	.360

[a] metric coefficient (t-statistic)
[b] coefficient multiplied by 100
*$p \leq .10$ (one-tailed test)
**$p \leq .05$ (one-tailed test)

Table 4

Economic and Political Determinants of Old Age, Survivors, and Disability Insurance as a Percentage of GNP: Various Years

Independent Variables	1949-76[a]	1949-77[b]	1949-78[c]	1949-79[c]	1949-80[b]
OASDI/GNP (t-1)	.251[d] (1.90)**	.639 (6.05)**	.927 (12.17)**	.951 (19.14)**	.864 (14.82)**
INFLATION (t)	.033 (4.72)**	.033 (5.22)**	.028 (4.02)**	.027 (4.11)**	.033 (4.73)**
BUDGET SURPLUS-DEFICIT/GNP$_{(t+1)}$	-.021 (2.23)**	-.019 (2.15)**	-.013 (1.14)	-.012 (1.14)	-.012 (1.35)*
INDUSTRIAL UTILIZATION$_{(t-1)}$	-.011 (3.91)**	-.006 (2.71)**	-.002 (1.26)*	-.002 (1.25)	-.003 (1.57)*
DEMOCRATIC PRESIDENT$_{(t)}$	.032 (.920)	-.055 (2.18)**	-.117 (5.88)**	-.122 (7.96)**	-.103 (5.03)**
PERCENT OF POPULATION >65 YEARS OLD$_{(t)}$	1.54 (6.03)**	.847 (3.88)**	.295 (1.60)*	.241 (1.80)**	.436 (2.86)**
MINIMUM WAGE (t)	-.541 (4.49)**	-.509 (4.48)**	-.400 (3.26)**	-.379 (3.39)**	-.477 (3.75)**
$\bar{R}^2$	.998	.999	.999	.999	.999
DURBIN'S H	-.875	-.686	.225	.114	1.13

[a]OLS estimates
[b]GLS estimates
[c]second order autoregressive process
[d]metric coefficient (t-statistic)
*p < .10 (one-tailed test)
**p < .05 (one-tailed test)

Table 5

Economic and Political Determinants of Unemployment Insurance as a Percentage of GNP: Various Years (OLS Estimates)

Independent Variables	1949-76	1949-77	1949-78	1949-79	1949-80
REVENUE/GNP (t)	.025[a] (2.56)**	.023 (2.43)**	.023 (2.38)**	.025 (2.47)**	.031 (3.06)**
INFLATION (t)	.017 (2.36)**	.017 (2.51)**	.018 (2.48)**	.016 (2.12)**	.014 (1.92)**
BUDGET SURPLUS-DEFICIT/GNP$_{(t+1)}$	-.030 (3.31)**	-.029 (3.21)**	-.029 (3.01)**	-.027 (2.64)**	-.025 (2.67)**
UNSKILLED OCCUPATIONAL UNEMPLOYMENT$_{(t)}$	.145 (14.46)**	.146 (14.81)**	.147 (14.23)**	.148 (13.60)**	.146 (13.82)**
DETRENDED COMPETITIVE WAGES$_{(t)}$	-.038[b] (2.69)**	-.039[b] (3.02)**	-.047[b] (3.46)**	-.051[b] (3.66)**	-.050[b] (3.72)**
DEMOCRATIC PRESIDENT$_{(t)}$	-.041 (1.46)*	-.038 (1.47)*	-.047 (1.76)**	-.055 (1.99)**	-.057 (2.12)**
$\bar{R}^2$	.913	.914	.902	.889	.891
DURBIN-WATSON	1.82	1.83	1.75	1.51	1.50

[a]metric coefficient (t-statistic)
[b]coefficient multiplied by 100
*p < .10 (one-tailed test)
**p < .05 (one-tailed test)

Table 6

Economic and Political Determinants of Aid to Families with Dependent Children as a Percentage of GNP: Various Years (OLS Estimates)

Independent Variables	1949-76	1949-77	1949-78	1949-79	1979-80
AFDC/GNP (t-1)	.936[a] (31.36)**	.934 (32.45)**	.918 (28.17)**	.918 (26.78)**	.922 (27.70)**
REVENUE/GNP (t)	.004 (2.21)**	.003 (1.84)**	.003 (1.16)	.001 (.535)	.003 (1.23)
BUDGET SURPLUS-DEFICIT/GNP $_{(t+1)}$	-.011 (5.33)**	-.011 (5.63)**	-.012 (5.02)**	-.011 (4.62)**	-.011 (4.92)**
UNSKILLED OCCUPATIONAL UNEMPLOYMENT $_{(t)}$	.008 (3.91)**	.008 (3.93)**	.008 (3.32)**	.008 (3.21)**	.009 (3.58)*
RIOT FREQUENCY (t-1)	.108[b] (7.47)**	.105[b] (7.81)**	.107[b] (6.97)**	.112[b] (7.15)**	.115[b] (7.54)*
DEMOCRATIC PRESIDENT $_{(t)}$	-.014 (2.04)**	-.013 (2.27)**	-.018 (2.78)**	-.021 (3.19)**	-.020 (3.21)*
ELECTION YEAR (t-1)	.016 (2.30)**	.015 (2.18)**	.015 (2.00)**	.010 (1.37)*	.012 (1.59)*
$\overline{R}^2$	.992	.992	.990	.989	.989
DURBIN'S H	-.207	-.202	-.797	.285	.155

[a] metric coefficient (t-statistic)
[b] coefficient multiplied by 100
*p < .10 (one-tailed test)
**p < .05 (one-tailed test)

Table 7

Economic and Political Determinants of Other Direct Relief[a] as a Percentage of GNP: Various Years (GLS Estimates)

Independent Variables	1949-76	1949-77	1949-78	1949-79	1949-80
OTHER DIRECT RELIEF/GNP$_{(t-1)}$	.825[b] (14.64)**	.841 (14.82)**	.839 (14.11)**	.789 (11.77)**	.736 (9.83)**
INFLATION (t)	-.007 (4.53)**	-.006 (4.30)**	-.006 (3.86)**	-.005 (2.87)**	-.004 (2.12)**
BUDGET SURPLUS-DEFICIT/GNP$_{(t+1)}$	-.028 (10.71)**	-.027 (10.49)**	-.026 (10.14)**	-.028 (9.42)**	-.029 (9.29)**
UNSKILLED OCCUPATIONAL UNEMPLOYMENT$_{(t)}$	.009 (4.15)**	.010 (4.60)**	.010 (4.63)**	.010 (3.79)**	.010 (3.46)**
PERCENTAGE OF TIME LOST DUE TO STRIKES$_{(t-1)}$	.108 (2.96)**	.119 (3.27)**	.132 (3.64)**	.168 (4.17)**	.167 (3.86)**
RIOT FREQUENCY (t-1)	.091[c] (6.37)**	.083[c] (5.94)**	.076[c] (5.40)**	.057[c] (3.79)**	.056[c] (3.39)**
DEMOCRATIC PRESIDENT$_{(t)}$	-.034 (6.58)**	-.030 (6.14)**	-.026 (5.45)**	-.022 (4.10)**	-.024 (3.85)**
PERCENT OF POPULATION >65 YEARS OLD$_{(t)}$	.040 (3.72)**	.027 (2.82)**	.020 (2.15)**	.022 (2.10)**	.036 (2.80)**
$\bar{R}^2$	.969	.970	.964	.953	.931
DURBIN'S H	-.528	-.317	-.255	.093	-.008

[a]other direct relief includes food stamps and non-AFDC direct relief.
[b]metric coefficient (t-statistic)
[c]coefficient multiplied by 100
*p < .10 (one-tailed test)
**p < .05 (one-tailed test)

Table 8

Economic and Political Determinants of Overall Transfers and Specific Transfe[r]
Programs as a Percentage of GNP: 1949-63

	Transfers[c]	AFDC[d]	Unemployment Insurance[d]	OASDI[c]	Other Direct Relief[d]
DEPENDENT VARIABLES/ $GNP_{(t-1)}$	.034[a] (.121)	.834 (6.54)**	--	.429 (5.16)**	.059 (.617)
$DEFENSE/GNP_{(t)}$	-.070 (1.22)	--	.041 (3.76)**	--	--
$REVENUE/GNP_{(t)}$	.062 (.638)	.001 (1.47)**	--	--	--
$INFLATION_{(t)}$	--	--	.019 (2.58)**	.026 (5.68)**	.001 (.947)
BUDGET SURPLUS-DEFICIT/$GNP_{(t+1)}$	-.005 (.008)	-.004 (2.73)**	-.034 (2.82)**	-.021 (2.81)**	-.010 (3.77)**
UNSKILLED OCCUPATIONAL $UNEMPLOYMENT_{(t)}$	.332 (6.02)**	.010 (10.82)**	.151 (10.20)**	--	.022 (10.69)**
DETRENDED COMPETITIVE $WAGES_{(t)}$	3.41[b] (1.27)	--	-.833 (2.63)**	--	--
RIOT FREQUENCY (t-1)	-1.78[b] (.901)	-.023[b] (.568)	--	--	-.017[b] (.232)
POLITICAL PARTY OF $PRESIDENT_{(t)}$	.117 (.699)	.002 (.422)	-.010 (.364)	.012 (.465)	-.014 (4.81)**
ELECTION YEAR (t-1)	--	-.009 (2.53)**	--	--	--
INDUSTRIAL $UTILIZATION_{(t-1)}$	--	--	--	-.009 (5.42)**	--
PERCENTAGE OF POPULATION >65 YEARS $OLD_{(t)}$	--	--	--	1.15 (7.12)**	-.141 (7.22)**
MINIMUM $WAGE_{(t)}$	--	--	--	-.342 (3.61)**	--
PERCENTAGE OF TIME LOST DUE TO STRIKES (t-1)	--	--	--	--	.099 (4.68)**
$\bar{R}^2$	.956	.993	.946	.999	.933
Durbin's H (Durbin-Watson)	(2.16)	-.825	(1.71)	-.247	1.13

[a]Metric coefficient (t-statistic)
[b]Coefficient multiplied by 100

[c]OLS estimates
[d]GLS estimates
*p < .10 (one-tailed test)
**p < .05 (one-tailed test)

NOTES

1. David Stockman's comments to William Greider candidly demonstrate an insider's view of the politicization of federal budgetary policy in the Reagan administration; see Greider's "The Education of David Stockman." Atlantic 248-6: pp. 27-54. Daniel Patrick Moynihan's famous essay "The Professionalization of Reform" (Public Interest, 1 (1965), pp. 6-16) is indicative of technocratic explanations of social policy, as are the now exceedingly optimistic assessments of the utility of the "New Economics" of the 1960's contained in Walter Heller's New Dimensions of Political Economy (Cambridge: Harvard University Press, 1967) and Arthur Okun's The Political Economy of Prosperity (Washington, D.C.: Brookings, 1970). The classic statement arguing for the importance of bureaucratic micro-politics is Aaron Wildavsky's The Politics of the Budgetary Process (Boston: Little, Brown, 1964).

2. Daniel Bell, The Cultural Contradictions of Capitalism. (New York: Harper Colophon, 1978.)

3. See E. Cory Brown, "Fiscal Policy in the Thirties: a Reappraisal." American Economic Review, 66 (1956), pp. 857-79; see also Charles Kindleberger, The World in Depression. Berkeley: University of California Press, 1973; David Gold, "The Rise and Decline of the Keynesian Coalition." Kapitalistate, 6 (1977), pp. 129-61; and Samuel Bowles, "The Post-Keynesian Capital-Labor Stalemate." Socialist Review, 65 (1982), pp. 45-72.

4. London: Macmillan, 1936.

5. A large interventionist capitalist state armed with Keynesian precepts has replaced neither the market allocation of resources nor private negotiations among private economic actors, of course, but it does introduce the principle that the shape of the stratification system and of the positioning of individuals therein is subject to public authority, to political determination. That principle has in turn become a structural characteristic of all democratic capitalist nations, the U.S. included.

6. Benjamin Ginsberg, "Elections and Public Policy." American Political Science Review, 70 (1976), pp. 41-49.

7. Douglas Hibbs, "Political Parties and Macroeconomic Policy." American Political Science Review, 71 (1977), pp. 1467-87.

8. Douglas Hibbs, "On the Demand for Economic Outcomes: Macroeconomic Performance and Mass Political Support in the United States, Great Britain, and Germany." Journal of Politics, 44 (1982), pp. 426-63.

9. Larry Isaac and William Kelly, "Racial Insurgency, the State,and Welfare Expansion: Local and National Level Evidence from the Post-War United States." American Journal of Sociology, 86 (1981), pp. 1341-86.

10. Edward Tufte, Political Control of the Economy. (Princeton: Princeton University Press, 1978); Bruno Frey and Freidrich Schneider, An Empirical Study of Politico-Economic Interaction in the United States." Review of Economics and Statistics, 60 (1978), pp. 174-83.

11. Tufte, op. cit.

12. Ibid.

13. Examples of fiscal instruments which appear to respond to the electoral cycles include military spending (see Larry Griffin, Joel Devine, and Michael Wallace, Monopoly Capital, Organized Labor, and Military Spending in the United States, 1949-1976," in Michael Burroway and Theda Skocpol, eds., Marxist Inquiries: Studies of Labor, Class, and States (a special supplement to the American Journal of Sociology 1982), pp. A113-A153, and Griffin, Wallace, and Devine, "The Political Economy of Military Spending: Evidence from the United States," Cambridge Journal of Economics, 6 (1982), pp. 1-14), agricultural appropriations (Gavin Wright, "The Political Economy of New Deal Spending: An Econometric Analysis", Review of Economics and Statistics, 56 (1974), pp. 30-38), civilian outlays and public sector jobs (Frey and Schneider, op. cit.), and social security outlays (Tufte, op. cit.).

14. Fred Block, "The Ruling Class Does not Rule: Notes on the Marxist Theory of the State." Socialist Review, 33 (1977), pp. 6-28; Griffin, Devine, and Wallace, 1982, op. cit.; Theda Skocpol, "Political Response to Capitalist Crisis: Neo-Marxist Theories of the State and the Case of the New Deal." Politics and Society, 10 (1980), pp. 155-201; Francis Fox Piven, "The Great Society as Political Strategy," in Richard Cloward and Francis Fox Piven, eds., The Politics of Turmoil: Poverty, Race, and the Urban Crisis. (New York: Vintage, 1975). We do not want to imply that political elites can do just anything they wish with the budget. There are a number of constraints on discretionary spending, all of which restrict the latitude of state managers to play politics with the budget (see our concluding comments). We discuss most of them in the course of this paper. We will add one additional limitation -- a lack of information about precisely which mix of budgetary outlays would maximize the political opportunities of state managers. A serious examination of this issue is beyond the scope of this paper, so we must simply note its importance.

15. James O'Conner, _The Fiscal Crisis of the State_. (New York: St. Martin's Press, 1973).

16. Ibid.

17. Ibid.; see also John Kenneth Galbraith, _The New Industrial State_. (New York: Houghton-Mifflin, 1973.)

18. O'Connor, op. cit.; Block, op. cit.; Griffin, Devine, and Wallace, 1982, op. cit.

19. Any given expenditure is financed out of revenue. Deficit financing is of course a very real possibility for state managers desirous of expanding outlays without increasing revenue, say, through additional taxes. But even deficit spending has its limits, as we are currently witnessing in the Reagan administration's attempts to explain its defense "requirements." But increases in the national debt are possible only if creditors believe that the debt will be serviced promptly and, in time, retired. Both debt service and retirement, in turn, depend on future revenues, so outlays are ultimately limited (to a degree) by revenue and by past and projected deficits and increments to the national debt (see Larry Griffin, Joel Devine, and Michael Wallace, "On the Economic and Political Determinants of Welfare Spending in the Post-World War Two Era". _Politics and Society_, 12 (1983), pp. 331-372).

20. Ronald King, "From Redistributive to Hegemonic Logic: The Transformation of American Tax Policies, 1894-1963." _Politics and Society_, 12 (1983), pp. 1-52.

21. Joel Devine, "Capitalist Development, State Expenditures, and Economic Inequality: Historical and Quantitative Analysis of the United States." Ph.D. Dissertation, Department of Sociology, Indiana University, 1981.

22. Griffin, Devine, and Wallace, 1982, op. cit.; Griffin, Wallace, and Devine, 1982, op. cit.

23. David Noble, _America by Design: Science, Technology and the Rise of Corporate Capitalism_. (New York: Knopf, 1977.)

24. Ralph Miliband, _The Capitalist State_. (New York: Basic, 1969.)

25. James Weinstein, _The Corporate Ideal in the Liberal State, 1900-1918_. (Boston: Beacon Press, 1968.)

26. Skocpol, op. cit., p. 162.

27. We do not want to exaggerate the power of large capital to dominate budgetary processes. The state's response to this "veto power" is not automatic; it does involve struggle with competing elites, with the rank-and-file, with insurgents, and it does require lobbying, political pressure, and organization. The outcome of democratic politics is always problematic: capitalists have lost, their preferences or structural requirements have been

implemented in a distorted fashion, and even the "victories" have not proved as functional as hoped. See, e.g., Leonard Berkowitz and Kim McQuaid, Creating the Welfare State: The Political Economy of Twentieth Century Reform. (New York: Praeger, 1980); Skocpol, op. cit.; Colin Crouch, "The State, Capital, and Liberal Democracy," in C. Crouch, ed., State and Economy in Contemporary Capitalism. (New York: St. Martin's Press, 1979); Gold, op. cit.; Samuel Bowles, "The Post-Keynsian Capital-Labor Stalemate." Socialist Review, 65 (1982), pp. 45-72; Block, op. cit.

28. O'Conner, op. cit.

29. Griffin, Devine, and Wallace, 1983, op. cit., p. 11.

30. O'Connor, op. cit., p. 161.

31. O'Connor, op. cit.

32. Francis Fox Piven and Richard Cloward, Poor People's Movements: Why They Succeed, How They Fail. (New York: Pantheon, 1977); Piven and Cloward, Regulating the Poor: The Functions of Public Welfare. (New York: Vintage, 1971.)

33. T. H. Marshall, Citizenship and Social Class. (Cambridge: Cambridge University Press, 1950.) This is not to say that repression or complete neglect has never been employed by agents of capital or the state to control oppressed classes. It has and continues to be used: histories of the labor movement and of the continuing struggles of racial minorities are replete with examples of this.

34. Block, op. cit.; Crouch, op. cit.; Charles Lindblom, Politics and Markets. (New York: Basic Books, 1977); Skocpol, op. cit.

35. Piven and Cloward, 1977, op. cit.

36. O'Conner, op. cit.; Griffin, Devine, and Wallace, 1983, op. cit.

37. E.g., unemployment insurance. See Griffin, Devine, and Wallace, 1983, op. cit. However "routine" such programs as OASDI and unemployment compensation appear today, their very existence as programs aiding millions of Americans resulted from past political struggles over the budget. See Berkowitz and McQuaid, op. cit.

38. Griffin, Devine, and Wallace, 1983, op. cit.

39. The quotation is from Piven and Cloward, 1977, op. cit., p. 24.

40. Griffin, Devine, and Wallace, 1983, op. cit., p. 18.

41. Ibid. Adam Przeworski has argued that before class struggle per se is possible, struggle about class must occur. That is, some movements by protestors represent conflicts about the rights of insurgents to be recognized as legitimate political actors with definable boundaries and interests. This may be beneficial to elites attempting to control

protestors, since state managers can now deal with class or interest group organizations -- with perhaps their own centralized concerns -- rather than with a disparate mass of individuals, all with different motivations and objectives. See his "Proletariat into Class: The Process of Class Formation from Karl Kautsky's *The Class Struggle* to Recent Controversies." *Politics and Society*, 7 (1977), pp. 343-401.

42. David Snyder and Charles Tilly, "Hardships and Collective Violence in France, 1830-1960." *American Sociological Review*, 37 (1972), pp. 520-32; E. Shorter and Charles Tilly. *Strikes in France, 1830-1968*. (Cambridge: Cambridge University Press, 1974.)

43. David Gordon, Richard Edwards, and Michael Reich, *Segmented work, Divided Workers: the Historical Transformation of Labor in the U.S.* (Cambridge: Cambridge University Press, 1982.)

44. Skocpol, op. cit.; Beth Rubin, Larry Griffin, and Michael Wallace, " `Provided Only that their Voice was Strong': Insurgency and Organization of American Labor from NRA to Taft-Hartley." *Work and Occupations*, 10 (1983), pp. 325-47; Block, op.cit.

45. Skocpol, op. cit.; Devine, op. cit.

46. Pivin and Cloward, 1977, op. cit., pp 29-30.

47. O'Conner, op. cit.; Bowles, op. cit.

48. Piven and Cloward, 1971, op. cit.; Isaac and Kelly, op. cit.; Griffin, Devine, and Wallace, 1983, op. cit.

49. Pivin, op. cit; Skocpol, op. cit.

50. Ann Orloff and Theda Skocpol, "Why not Equal Protection? Explaining the Politics of Public Social Spending in Britain, 1900-1911, and the United States, 1880s-1920." *American Sociological Review*, 49 (1984), pp. 726-50.

51. Wright, 1974, op. cit.; Skocpol, op. cit.

52. Paul Baran and Paul Sweezy, *Monopoly Capitalism*. (New York: Monthly Review Press, 1966); Block, op. cit.; Isaac and Kelly, op. cit.; Griffin, Devine, and Wallace, 1983, op. cit.; Alexander Hicks, "Elections, Keynes, Bureaucracy, and Class: Explaining U.S. Budget Deficits, 1961-1978." *American Sociological Review*, 49 (1984), pp. 165-181.

53. Harold Wilensky, *The Welfare State and Equality*. (Berkeley: University of California Press, 1975.)

54. Isaac and Kelly, op. cit.; Griffin, Devine, and Wallace, 1983, op. cit.

55. William Greider, "The Education of David Stockman." *Atlantic*, 248-6 (1981), pp. 27-54; Griffin, Devine, and Wallace, 1983, op. cit. The index is computed as follows: we estimated the predicted values (i.e., at t + 1) of both revenue and total expenditure by regressing current levels on the lagged levels (the correlations between the levels at

t and t - 1 were over .98 for both variables). We then subtracted expected revenue from expected expenditures; the difference, therefore, is the anticipated deficit or surplus. We then divided it by GNP. An alternative measure of the deficit constraint on expenditure, anticipated surplus/deficit as a percentage of the anticipated budget, correlated with the GNP-based measure at .98 and produced almost identical results.

56. Wilensky, op. cit.; Griffin, Devine, and Wallace, 1982, op. cit. The use of the lagged endogenous variable also generally reduces autocorrelation of the error terms and removes the time trend from the dependent variable. An additional property of an equation containing the lagged endogenous variable has a very important substantive implication: by lagging the dependent variable one year, we effectively residualize the dependent variable in question against its prior level and, thereby, create change scores. So we are actually analyzing changes in, rather than levels of, welfare outlays.

57. Griffin, Devine, and Wallace, 1983, op. cit.

58. A precise operationalization of the "surplus population" back to the 1940's is not possible with the extant data. O'Connor, loc. cit., argues that the employment and economic vitality of workers in jobs in firms and industries characterized by low levels of unionization, of wages, and of skills are most likely to be adversely affected by successful accumulation in firms in the economy's large, capital-intensive core. We experimented with a variety of indicators designed to measure the extent of this population, and found that the unemployment of labor in predominantly (and relatively) unskilled occupations (see appendix) proved empirically superior. One of the measures used but discarded was the percentage of the U.S. population officially declared "poor." Similarly, we used the detrended wages of workers in industries containing the generally smallest, least-capitalized firms, those with the smallest levels of profits and the highest risk of organizational extinction, to measure cyclical variations in earned income of economically insecure and marginal workers.

59. The zero-order correlations between our indicators of welfare outlays and percent Democrat in the House at time t are .557 (overall transfers), .401 (AFDC), .556 (OASDI), .314 (UI), and -.326 (ODR). Zero-order correlations between Democratic President at time t and these outlays, on the other hand, are all negative, ranging from -.041 (OASDI) to -.244 (ODR).

60. Berkowitz and McQuaid, op. cit.; Norman Furniss and Timothy Tilton, _The Case for the Welfare State_. (Bloomington: Indiana University Press.)

61. O'Conner, op. cit.; Gold, op. cit.

62. Griffin, Devine, and Wallace, 1982, op. cit.; H.G. Vattner, "Perspectives on the Forty-sixth Anniversary of the U.S. Mixed Economy." _Explorations in Economic History_, 16 (1979), pp. 297-330.

63. Quite similar results were obtained when the variable measuring Democratic administrations was lagged one year and two years. Democratic domination of the House also reduced transfers, but not significantly so.

64. We did find that strikes stimulated transfers, but the coefficients varied considerably over the five periods, each differing from the other only by the addition of a single year, and depended excessively on the precise combination of other variables included in the equation and on the procedure used to estimate the equations. We conclude, then, that there is weak but inconsistent and unstable evidence supporting the view that transfers -- a component of the "social wage" -- represent fiscal concessions to striking workers throughout the entire post-war period.

65. We experimented with a variety of indicators of Presidential popularity in lieu of the use of the election year variable and found generally that decreased popularity _depressed_ transfers. This result was unstable and contrary to our expectations that reductions in popularity should stimulate transfers as state managers expend legitimation expenses in an attempt to woo the electorate. We believe these results to be more a reflection of the inability of the popularity indicators to measure adequately this argument's central concept -- administration legitimacy -- than reliable empirical evidence about political business cycles.

66. Estimates of the OASDI equation are somewhat suspect. We experimented with a variety of plausible specifications, but the estimated equations were plagued by auto-correlation and excessive levels of multicollinearity. Moreover, unless minimum wages are included in the equation, virtually nothing (_including_ percent of population 65 years old or older) exerts significant influences. Since there are extremely strong logical reasons for OASDI to reflect partially the demographic composition of the population, we present the estimates of the equation containing minimum wages.

67. The lack of "class conflict" or "political struggle" influences on the federal programs should be interpreted cautiously. In particular, it does not imply that such struggles do not evoke some federal concessions in the form, say, of the

implementation of a particular transfer program. It indicates only that annual changes in already existing federal programs are relatively insensitive to annual variation in labor militancy and racial insurgency.

68. Roger Friedland, Francis Fox Piven, and Robert Alford, "Political Conflict, Urban Structure, and the Fiscal Crisis." Paper Presented at the American Sociological Association meetings.

69. We addressed the possibility that our results were simply artifacts of the GNP-based expenditure and revenue measures by examining the performance of measures converted into their logged levels. The general patterning of results is quite comparable to those presented in Tables 3-7, though the significance of coefficients in logged-level equations were generally reduced (e.g., election year proved insignificant, anticipated deficit was of variable significance, etc.). The unemployment, industrial capacity, and riot measures, however, were strongly significant, and in the predicted direction. Use of logged-level metrics produced only two sign changes.

70. Gold, op. cit.; David Gordon, "Up and Down the Long Roller Coaster," in Fred Hirch and John Goldthorpe, eds., The Political Economy of Inflation. (Cambridge: Harvard University Press, 1978); Eric Olin Wright, Class, Crisis, and State. (London: New Left Books, 1978); Manuel Castells, The Economic Crisis and American Society. (Princeton: Princeton University Press, 1980); Griffin, Devine, and Wallace, 1982, op. cit.

71. Gosta Esping-Anderson, Roger Friedland, and Eric Olin Wright, "Modes of Class Struggle and the Capitalist State." Kapitalistate 4/5 (1976), p. 106.

72. King, op. cit.

73. Alan Blinder and Howard Esaki, "Macroeconomic Activity and Income Distribution in the Post War United States." Review of Economics and Statistics, 60 (1978), pp. 604-08; Goldthorpe, op. cit.

74. Griffin, Devine, and Wallace, 1982, op. cit.; Griffin, Wallace, and Devine, 1982, op. cit.

75. Hicks, op. cit.

76. Adam Przeworski, "Social Democracy as a Historical Phenomenon." New Left Review, 122 (1980), pp. 27-58.

77. Ibid.

XII.

Uriel Rosenthal

The Welfare State
Sticks, No Carrots

INTRODUCTION

Although in some countries of the Western World the tax-welfare backlash has, until now, not materialized, there is no doubt about the potential impact of anti-welfare sentiments. As we have seen documented in the paper by Bernice Pescosolido, we are facing a public mood that has become highly critical of the "evils of the welfare state." Political science offers a rich variety of sinister characterizations for what is called "the crisis of the welfare state": nongovernability, overload, bankruptcy, impotence, over-regulation.[1] Unfortunately, such labels refer to different problems. More importantly, the careless use of such labels makes it possible to shift the responsibility for "the crisis of the welfare state" onto actors or factors beyond one's own sphere of influence.[2]

'Nongovernability' suggests that society lacks the capacity and the will to comply with prudent governmental policies. Public authorities must cope with Hobbesian turbulence, it is argued, and should not be blamed for being unable to perform their impossible task of managing the *bellum omnium contra omnes*. When "the crisis of the welfare state" is pictured in terms of 'overload,' the major focus is on political actors and factors that put such tremendous pressure on the machinery of government: "government is an organization bearing many of the burdens of contemporary society."[3] Here political scientists point to the malfunctioning of intermediary structures; pressure groups and political parties seem to increase rather than reduce the load upon government.

In contrast, the telling phrase of 'bankruptcy' is usually reserved for the state or for government. Governments can go bankrupt. Explanations which suggest social or political causes are treated with suspicion. State institutions and state officials appear as incompetent or irresponsible controllers of the national treasury. Turning to 'impotence,' we see a state which, in spite of its physical, legal and financial resources, seems to have insufficient steering capacity. In particular, we are struck by the lack of leadership and will power on the part of the political authorities. Finally, 'over-regulation' is bound to stir widespread emotions against the excesses of governmental bureaucracy. In the struggle against bureaucracy the left and the right, liberals and conservatives, all unite.[4]

The solutions offered for the "crisis of the welfare state" differ accordingly. Some analysts advocate a re-orientation regarding the fundamentals of social order. People should lower their aspiration levels and reconsider the value of social arrangements in securing collective goods. They should take more seriously the principles of political obligation and put somewhat more trust in the prudence of governmental authorities. Representatives of intermediary groups and institutions should be aware of the limits of government. They should be "realistic."[5]

But what should be the contribution of the state in solving the "crisis of the welfare state?" Popular answers vary from advocating a reassumption of its authoritative position in the political system (the revitalization of leadership) to weeding out counter-productive bureaucratic rules and regulations. Without acknowledging it, we have moved from a focus on society to the political system; and the state turns out to be made up of a political stratum and the bureaucratic apparatus. We have not yet considered the state bureaucracy itself which would appear to be a complex conglomerate of organizations.

The rhetoric of these debates obscures some important questions about the crisis of the welfare state. These questions deal with the proper limits of state activity and the basic functions and essential activities of the state. In the few instances when such questions are raised explicitly, too often they threaten to lead to fruitless disputes as to what is proper, basic or essential. We are reminded of the 1960's when the democratic debate caused similar polemics on genuine versus manipulative participation and real versus pseudo-democracy. Yet, by avoiding basic questions about the state, political scientists are in danger of losing contact with contemporary political reality.

They should keep up with the currents in society, politics and the state itself, where people are discussing questions about the basic functions and -- _a contrario_ -- luxurious and unnecessary activities of the modern state.

In addition, political scientists should recognize that their own conceptualizations and analyses of the role of the welfare state are deficient. We should blame ourselves for confounding the welfare state with welfare society. And we have not taken seriously the differences between states and polities. We have not given sufficient consideration to the shortcomings of a monolithic state concept. At least in some countries, a basic distinction should be made between the political authorities and governmental bureaucracy. And there is no country where the state bureaucracy does not consist of a myriad of ministries, departments, agencies, bureaus, and indeed people -- with their own interests, values, and norms. We should, for instance, remember that some parts of the state bureaucracy engage in the provision of social services and that others do not. If there is a crisis of the welfare state, some parts of the state might find themselves in a fairly awkward position, while other parts could be successful in defending or expanding their position.

One purpose of this paper will be to draw attention to the welfare state rather than to a state of welfare.[6] If there is something "statelike" to the welfare state, it is remarkable that there is almost no discussion concerning the odd relation between the repressive and welfare tasks of this type of state. In this paper we shall, first, discuss the link between the original concept of the state and the concept of the welfare state, as it is used in present-day political theory and political practice. We shall emphasize the distinction between the instrumental and functional perspectives of the state.

Next, we shall develop a conceptual framework based on two dimensions: repression versus welfare and instrumental versus functional aspects of the state. This conceptual framework will illuminate the predicament of the welfare complex in the modern state. Such a framework also proves useful for a systematic examination of several knotty questions about the welfare functions of the state.

Subsequently, we look at the political relevance of the repression-welfare distinction. While political scientists may doubt that such a distinction is valid, public opinion, politicians and bureaucrats indeed see a split "welfare state." The analysis will bring us, finally, to some rather speculative remarks on the role of the state. Some well-known answers -- such as those of public choice theory -- offer a highly promising but insufficient explanation. For proper answers we need to know more about individual orientations to the state. People do not read public choice literature.

THE STATE AND THE WELFARE STATE

Some sixty years ago Robert MacIver wrote: "It may seem curious that so great and obvious a fact as the state should be the object of quite conflicting definitions, yet such is certainly the case. Some writers define the state as essentially a class structure. . .; others regard it as the one organization that transcends class and stands for the whole community. Some interpret it as a power-system, others as a welfare-system."[7] MacIver argued that we must distinguish the state from society. Further, we must understand that if the state has a particular fitness for some function, it may be unqualified for other tasks: "Certain tasks the instrument can perform, but badly and clumsily -- we do not sharpen pencils with an ax. Other tasks it cannot perform at all and when it is directed upon them it only ruins the material."[8] According to MacIver, "we must definitely declare it to be an association belonging to the same category as the family or the church. Like these it consists essentially of a group of members organized in a definite way and therefore for limited ends."[9]

In contrast to many contemporary political scientists, MacIver was very clear in distinguishing between instrumental and functional perspectives of the state.[10] Indeed, he was so anxious to hammer this point home that he did not really discuss the question of why there should always be a perfect correspondence between instruments and functions. For MacIver the state was a specific organization fit for specific purposes.

MacIver's analysis is a fruitful starting point. By distinguishing between instrumental and functional aspects, we may elucidate the conceptual link between the original idea of the state and that of the welfare state.[11] The ambiguity of the modern welfare state concept is rather obvious; but there are also some complications with regard to the original concept of the state.

THE CONCEPT OF THE STATE

Whether they like it or not, political scientists cannot evade the concept of the state. They may call it by different names or they may claim that their approach to political life is not limited to the role of the state; but in the end they have to give in.

By now, not only the concept but also the term is used widely in political science.[12]

The dominant concept of the state, which goes back to the origins of modern political science, was developed by Max Weber. The Weberian state concept stresses the importance of the monopoly of the legitimate(d) use of physical violence in society. In Weber's conceptual framework, the state belongs to the category of territorially-based political associations. The empirical concept of the state is separated from the Staatsidee.

The Weberian state concept looks instrumental: "It is not possible to define a political corporate group, including the state, in terms of the end to which its corporate action is devoted. All the way from provision for subsistence to the patronage of art, there is no conceivable end which some political corporation has not at some time pursued. And from the protection of personal security to the administration of justice, there is none which all have recognized. Thus it is possible to define the 'political' character of a corporate group only in terms of the means peculiar to it, the use of force."[13] It should be also noted that Weber warns against the reification of the state. But this does not mean that people cannot develop orientations toward it: "One of the important aspects of the 'existence' of a modern state....consists in the fact that the action of various individuals is oriented to the belief that it exists or should exist, thus that it acts."[14]

Weber's concept of the state is not, however, a purely instrumental one. The (threatened) use of physical force is related to the function of maintaining public order.[15] The emphasis upon the legitimation of the infliction of physical sanctions makes it clear that Weber sees a link between the instrument of physical force and the enforcement of order. If there were any doubt about this function, it would be better not to speak of the legitimate use of physical force. This would amount to saying that as yet there are state contenders rather than a state.

Further, Weber does not suggest that the instruments of the state be limited to physical means. State authorities have a variety of means at their disposal: "The definition put forward here is only a more precise formulation of what is meant in everyday usage in that it gives sharp emphasis to what is the most characteristic of those means, the actual or threatened use of force."[16]

Both in political theory and in political practice the Weberian notion of the state is still very much alive. This includes the apparently self-evident connection between the availability of means of physical power and the preservation of order. It involves the protection of "life, liberty and estate" against internal and external aggression. In positive terms, the state is supposed to provide a satisfactory level of physical security and, in upholding the legal system, to create the conditions necessary for orderly economic processes. The close connection between the instruments of physical force and the order-preserving function would become a bit strained were the instruments of the state to be used for more ambitious purposes. People would be forced to be happy, for example. Although Weber did not exclude the possibility of the state taking on that kind of mission, he certainly would have supported an extensive analysis of instruments suited for the purpose.

THE WELFARE STATE

Richard Titmuss has called the welfare state an "indefinable abstraction."[17] This should not lead us to accept too easily the conceptual mess which is characteristic of most analyses of the modern welfare state. Many scholars mix up the welfare state and welfare society, as if there could not be any tension between society and the state. Quite often, the wish is the father to the thought.[18] Facing the welfare backlash, we should not -- it is said -- insist upon this "intellectual" distinction. We should defend the welfare state by declaring it to be a shared societal value.[19] In other words, the welfare state should be elevated to a post-industrial version of the *Staatsidee*.

The welfare state should be distinguished from the polity as a whole. It may happen, even in a democratic polity, that preferences and performances of state officials and state agencies diverge from those in other parts of the political system. The welfare state can be an autonomous state.[20] There is no reason to deny the usefulness of Wilensky's reference to "government-protected minimum standards of income, nutrition, health, housing, and education, assured to every citizen as a political right, not as charity."[21] But this should not be mistaken for a polity-wide consensus on the principles, and definitely not on the content of specific programs. Again, the wish may be the father to the thought. If the welfare state has been a result of an ideological compromise, it could very well be that by now it lacks this sort of political support. Or, to note another possibility, there might be more support for the welfare state among certain political groups than in certain parts of the (welfare) state itself. Even the most complete agreement among political groups regarding the future of the welfare state would not be sufficient without the cooperation of state agencies and state officials. One should be aware, for instance, of the need for some sort of *modus vivendi* between welfare-oriented and their repression-oriented counterparts within the state system.

In most analyses of the welfare state there is an almost exclusive orientation to the welfare functions of the state and to the substantive content of specific welfare programs. It sometimes looks as if the state had substituted welfare for repression. Conceptually, this would be an easy way out of the uncomfortable link between the original notion of the state and the notion of the modern welfare state.

One should not give in to this temptation. The tensions are too important to reason them away. First, contrary to the original state concept, the standard concept of the welfare state focuses on state functions rather than on specific instruments. Second, the traditional functions of the state seem to be of minor importance. A wide range of values is being covered from social and economic security to equality, positive freedom and solidarity. Paradoxically, basic values such as physical security from internal and external aggression are taken for granted. The welfare state should not be charged with the sort of tasks which would compel it to use sordid instruments. Third, the jump to a definition in terms of specific programs may only add to the confusion. The current conceptualizations of welfare instruments leave much to be desired. Detailed analyses of rules and regulations cannot compensate for the lack of attention to the ways by which welfare can best be promoted.[22]

If the term 'welfare state' is usually reserved for the welfare complex of the state, this does not preclude us from developing a view of the welfare state that includes the repressive complex as well. This kind of perspective provides a parsimonious resolution to the unfortunate divergence of the original state concept and the concept of the welfare state. Besides, it enables us to throw more light on the awkward situation of the welfare complex in the so-called welfare state.

THE PREDICAMENT OF THE WELFARE COMPLEX

The preceding analysis allows for the construction of a conceptual framework based on two dimensions: repression versus welfare and instrumental versus functional aspects of the state. The quadrant is depicted on the following page.

Repression and Welfare

	Repression	Welfare
Instrumental	I	II
Functional	III	IV

In cell I we may place the Weberian state concept, but we should then bracket Weber's suggestions about the intrinsic relation between the use of physical force and the enforcement of public order. Cell I may also include instruments backed up by the threat of physical force: taxation, legal instruments, bureaucratic rules and regulations. It is no accident that these instruments were analyzed extensively by Weber. Their close relation to the instrument of physical force is symbolized by the circular notion of the Rechtsstaat: The state is based on law and limited by law, yet physical force is necessary to remove unyielding state officials offending the law.[23]

Cell II is a highly problematic one. Abstractly and theoretically, we may discuss the advantages of such instruments as incentives, rewards and rational persuasion. We may even draw on the results of learning psychology and make a convincing case for the superiority of incentives and rewards. However, we lack a comprehensive understanding about such welfare instruments. One thing which is clear is that they are costly: "It is characteristic of all these instruments that they avoid the direct coercion of individual private decisions, and that most of them do so by substituting government expenditures for direct behavior control. In its permissiveness, therefore, the welfare state is necessarily expensive in terms of its demands on the fiscal resources of the state."[24]

Cell III refers to those functions which are usually associated with the traditional state concept: the protection against internal and external aggression and, if desired, the protection of property rights. Although these functions are often labeled minimal, they are definitely complex; and their association with the traditional state concept should not be viewed as an indication of unchanging contexts of physical security.25 In addition, the relation between internal and external order may take on various forms: one may be independent, complement, or provide a substitute for the other.

There remains much confusion about the basic values to which Cell III refers. Should we interpret the value of physical security as identical to physical integrity? Does protection against internal and external aggression imply a responsibility for the physical integrity of the individuals protected by the state? If we were to relate physical integrity to the basic function of upholding individual property rights, would not this imply, by analogy, some sort of state responsibility for a property structure which would not endanger the physical integrity of individual citizens? Finally, should we accept arguments concerning subjective contexts of physical security? People are not always both safe and sound.

Such questions suggest that even traditional state functions may not be uncomplicated. Let us accept for the sake of argument that at one time there existed a night-watchman state, "doing no more than protecting its citizens from force and fraud and such like, leaving them free to pursue their individual projects."26 We would, then, have to ask ourselves whether these tasks were ever really simple. In any case, nowadays they are extraordinarily complicated and require equally complex instruments.

In Cell IV is found the standard version of the welfare state. It brings together two perspectives. First, there is the provision of minimum benefits for all. Basic values -- such as social and economic security -- and basic needs are at stake. At first, the state is supposed to guarantee minimum standards of income, nutrition, and health. Minimum standards are set "at a level commensurate with the minimum expectations of society."27 Such expectations may rise and they may fall.28 Second, the function of promoting welfare is linked to the values of equality and solidarity. Here the state is supposed to pursue re-distributive goals. To the extent that not everybody will embrace the values of equality and solidarity, the realization of the "social welfare state" and the increase in collective welfare means conflict and redistribution. Collective welfare must be pursued -- if necessary at the expense of the welfare of some of us who happen to be better off. In other words, welfare becomes collectivized.

The major points of this discussion are presented below. With this conceptualization we have been able to move from a sole concern with traditional repressive instruments to a consideration of both repressive and welfare instruments and collective welfare. As we shall see, the paradoxical fact is that there is an intimate connection between the repressive instruments and collective welfare. This connection appears to be counter-productive to the realization of welfare.

Repression and Welfare:
From Repressive Instruments
to Collective Welfare

	Repression	Welfare
	I	II
Instrumental	Physical Force Threat of physical force Taxation Legal system Bureaucracy	Rewards, incentives Welfare programs
	III	IV
Functional	Protection from physical agres-sion Protection of property rights	Social and economic security Collective welfare

With this figure we move from analyzing each cell separately to exploring the most relevant relations between the four aspects: I-III, II-IV, II-III and I-IV.[29] We begin with I-III.

This pattern of relations fits in with the usual interpretation of the Weberian state concept. We have argued that this is due to the emphasis upon the legitimation of physical force rather than to a self-evident connection between repressive instruments and the preservation of public order. In itself, the use of repressive means may, of course, be effective as a mode of direct control, and the threatened use of physical force may have a broad scope. But there are situations where the (threatened) use of physical force causes disorder and turmoil instead of public order.[30]

It should also be recognized that the protection from foreign aggression by the state has taken on new dimensions. By now, no state -- the nuclear powers included -- can ever give a rock-bottom guarantee to its people that their territory is immune from foreign weapons. States with a nuclear defense force are dependent on the effectiveness of deterrence. The overwhelming majority in the world community of states is compelled to believe in the assistance of its nuclear friends as well. Nowadays, no state is self-sufficient in securing protection from foreign aggression.[31]

Turning to the relationship between welfare instruments and welfare functions (II-IV), we note several problems. We do not know much about the qualities of incentives and rewards, and the more we move beyond social and economic security, the more fuzzy the notion of welfare becomes. Thus, welfare functions tend to be viewed as normative conceptions rather than as observable and measurable effects of the use of specific instruments.

In specific welfare programs, incentives are of minor importance. Such programs often boil down to rules and regulations regarding payments and re-payments, on rewards for future services (subsidies) and punishments, on allowances and control. Clients do not always feel they get what they have a right to. They may rather feel humiliated by state charity.[32]

As we move in the direction of collective welfare and redistribution, the emphasis on incentives and rewards becomes increasingly dubious. Any state activity requires some expenditure of revenues, revenue which is usually generated through taxation. In the case of re-distribution policies, then, we enter "the most conflict-laden realm, the realm of winners and losers, of haves and have-nots."[33] If they do not value social justice, the haves must be forced. Nozick might be one of them: "There are only individual people, different individual people, with their own individual lives. Using one of these people for the benefit of others, uses him and benefits the others. Nothing more. What happens is that something is done to him for the sake of others. Talk of an overall social good covers this up."[34]

Consideration of relation II-IV provides support for the thesis that the ideology of the welfare society is eclectic. It could be argued that there is an intrinsic contradiction in the welfare state project. Could one ever demand of state officials and state agencies that they develop the sets of instruments described as welfare instruments? If this is too much to expect, would not this imply that, in the absence of adequate means, the welfare state has been charged with an impossible task? In times of economic growth, this task, perhaps, can be broughtoff.[35] Even redistributive aims were pursued with apparent success in this way. But when (as now) money is short, there does not seem to be either moral (persuasion) or intellectual (imagination substitutes.)

Welfare instruments, including various kinds of welfare programs, can be used as a means to secure internal order. This perspective (II-III) has been the subject of the warfare-welfare debate. It also underlies the discussion on the relation between welfare expenditures and the degree of conflict in society. Titmuss' residual welfare model refers to the disciplinary effects of welfare programs.

Our conceptual framework helps to systematize this kind of discussion and, possibly, helps to place some of the empirical findings into a proper perspective. First, the connection II-III deals with the application of welfare instruments; it does not involve considerations with regard to the promotion of welfare (cell IV). The focus is on the preservation of public order (cell III). If there are still other considerations, these involve the limited effectiveness of repressive instruments in securing public order (cell I).

Second, let us accept for the sake of argument the conclusions of some empirical studies that under certain circumstances welfare programs can buy off public order.[36] This implies that such programs may be more effective as a supplement or substitute to repressive instruments (cell I) than as a part of the symbiotic relation II-IV. This only emphasizes the point raised before that many welfare programs appear to include various repressive elements. Gradually, the welfare functions of the state (Cell IV) become surrounded by repressive factors.

Our conceptual framework can illuminate as well some aspects of the redistributive state. As soon as there are people who do not cherish the value of social justice, welfare becomes the subject of conflict and coercion, the most extreme form of coercion being the infliction of physical harm or expropriation.[37] Relation I-IV stands for welfare by repression.

Having noticed the problems of relation II-IV, we should now explore relation I-IV. Our conceptual analysis, then, leads to the conclusion that we can see a manifest penetration of repressive instruments into the welfare sphere. At first sight, one might welcome this as an indication of a successful step towards integration: "In our fragmented, interdependent world, the justice of the princely sector must not be merely juridical; it must be largely _social_ justice...Just as all societies need regulation of conduct, so all need a just principle of allocation. The first, in our world, belongs properly to the 'new corporations'; the other, to what one ought perhaps to call the 'new State'."[38]

But it seems more appropriate to stand with both feet on the ground and confess that here, instead, we face evidence of a new Staatsidee. And any Staatsidee -- whether old or new -- is synonymous with repression and aggression. "Collective welfare" (IV) may ultimately be enforced at the expense of internal and external order and social and economic security alike. In fact, what looks like the integration of the welfare function of the state may actually be the ultimate push into isolation. Collective welfare invites conflict and instability. Consequently, it gives an impulse to the repressive complex. The welfare complex may perish from its own pretensions. I show this possibility in schematic form.

THE PREDICAMENT OF THE WELFARE COMPLEX

	Repression	Welfare
Instrumental	I Physical force	II Welfare programs
Functional	Public order III	Collective welfare IV

REPRESSION VERSUS WELFARE: THE SPLIT WELFARE STATE

Several objections could be raised regarding the distinction between repression and welfare. In intellectual debates we see the relativity of a strict separation of repressive and welfare-oriented activities. What is a "positive" action in our eyes may be considered a highly "negative" action by others. In discussions on the role of the state, the repression-welfare distinction may be considered obvious, or even trite. Everybody knows that the state is not a monolith. Consequently, we should not be surprised that the instruments and functions of the state are rather diverse and could indeed be difficult to combine.

On the other hand, the distinction between repression and welfare has always been one of the most important yardsticks for political judgment and action. With regard to the activities of the state, this distinction falls back on the differentiation between traditional and modern functions. For some time this interpretation lent itself admirably to the proposition that the repressive functions of the state should give way to a modern emphasis on welfare. At present, however, there is a tendency to embrace the "old" functions of the state and to denounce the welfare functions as modish products of an affluent era.

In the preceding sections, we have suggested a perspective on the welfare state that includes both sides: repression and welfare. This should not be regarded as an affirmation of the objections to the repression-welfare distinction. On the contrary, our view of the welfare state differentiates very sharply between the two complexes. The welfare state is a split state. If intellectual objections are raised to this perspective, it should not be forgotten that the split welfare state is a fundamental factor in daily politics. Public opinion, politicians and bureaucrats see a split "welfare state".

PUBLIC OPINION

It is unfortunate that mass surveys, which take stock of value orientations among people, seldom delve into the subject of mass attitudes towards the state. There is a lot of information on the attitudes of people to social and political problems. But seldom do we find specific data on whether people want the state or other political actors to solve such problems. Usually there is a significant gap between cataloging value preferences and collecting specific information on what the state should or should not do.

Let us, however, follow this road in order to assess the relevance to mass publics of the repression-welfare dimension of state action. We can begin with Ronald Inglehart's Materialist/Post-Materialist value construct.[39] First, people are asked: "If you had to choose among the following things, which are the <u>two</u> that seem most desirable to you? Maintaining order in the nation. Giving the people more to say in important political decisions. Fighting rising prices. Protecting freedom of speech."[40] The first and third items refer to materialist values; the second and fourth to post-materialist values. As Inglehart states, the two materialist items reflect a concern with physical safety and economic stability respectively -- which happen to be closely related to the repressive functions of the state (see section III).

Subsequently, Inglehart introduces a more broadly based value index. Materialist values come to include: strong defense forces; fighting crime; maintaining order; a stable economy; economic growth;

and fighting rising prices. Post-materialist values pertain to: beautiful cities/nature; the importance of ideas; free speech; less impersonal society; more say on the job; and more say in government.[41] This Materialist/Post-Materialist value index corresponds to some extent to our repression-welfare distinction. But there is more clarity on the repressive than on the welfare side. In addition, as yet there is no perspective of mass orientations to the functions of the state. We can only guess that those favoring strong defense forces and the preservation of order would like the state to take part in this effort. And, upon further reflection, it is not clear whether these materialists might not prefer private protective associations for the maintenance of internal order.

We need, then, to try to collect more information on two matters: the relation between the "Post-Materialism" categories and our concept of welfare, and the relation of his index to people's orientations to the state. As regards the relation between post-materialist and welfare values, Inglehart himself indicates that these two value categories should correspond. Indeed, his empirical research shows that, for instance, post-materialists "are substantially more apt to view a more equal distribution of wealth as 'very important'." They also tend to rate "equal rights for men and women" as highly important.[42]

Our second point is brought nearer to a resolution by Klingemann's research on the political importance of social equality.[43] The political importance of social equality is supposed to depend upon the priority people attribute to questions of social equality, and upon the extent to which people stress state responsibility for handling such questions. It is shown that post-materialists score high on the index of the political importance of social equality. This result is reinforced by the fact that post-materialists locate themselves at the left side of the left-right dimension-- this, again, implies support for an active role of the state in promoting welfare.[44]

Finally, there are data on the relation of Materialism/Post-materialism to behavioral orientations. Post-materialists would be more inclined to participate in protest activities (petitions, demonstrations, boycotts, rent strikes, unofficial strikes, and blockades).[45] For our purpose, it is particularly interesting to note that they would also tend to denounce repressive responses by the state: severe sentences by the courts; police force against demonstrators; military force against strikers; or legislation against political demonstrations.[46] It is fairly obvious that the repression-welfare dimension of state action is, indeed, relevant to mass publics.

A reconstruction of the argument brings us back to Inglehart's Materialism/Post-Materialism value index and to the data on the distribution of these value categories among mass publics. For instance, during the 1970s the percentages of pure post-materialists and materialists did not change very much in the Netherlands: from 17 to 19% and from 30 to 28% respectively.[47] Compared to other Western countries, the Netherlands had and has a large contingent of post-materialists. And, they had the highest levels of protest potential and the lowest levels of support for repressive responses by the state. But there have always been pure materialists too -- up to about 30% of the population.[48] If we correctly interpret the dramatic changes in the public mood over the last few years of severe depression, we may safely assume that pure Materialism and "law and order" will grow much more important. Perhaps Inglehart is right in his appreciation of the rise of a new class of post-materialists during the 1970's.[49] In that case, the split welfare state might, after all, have its roots in a split welfare society.

POLITICIANS AND BUREAUCRATS

Both politicians and bureaucrats accept the notion of the split welfare state; and they act upon it. Whether we like it or not, they are prone to interpret the repression-welfare distinction in increasingly straightforward terms. The repressive complex of the state provides the *sine qua non* activities of the state. These tasks are performed by Foreign Affairs, Defense, the Interior, Justice and Finance -- the old or traditional Ministries. In contrast, the welfare complex is viewed as a residual.

Of course, some politicians may consider welfare activities as a vital part of the functioning of the modern state. Post-materialists can certainly be found among the political elites.[50] But, nevertheless, they are constantly put on the defensive. Being unable to deny the centrality of the repressive complex, at most they can call for a reduction of state expenditures in this sphere. furthermore, the elimination of the repressive complex would not serve their interests. Without taxation, there would be no welfare state; without rules and regulations, there would be no welfare programs. But without welfare there could and would still be a state. In short, welfare politicians are no exception to the rule; they, too, accept the notion of the split welfare state.

Within the civil service, the notion of the split welfare state has found acceptance in spite of the myth of the one-and-united public interest. In terms of bureaucratic politics, we may take it for granted that civil servants in the old departments will stress, and indeed believe in, the distinction between their activities and the remaining tasks of the state. For their part, welfare bureaucrats are in an awkward position. They work in relatively new agencies. They owe whatever prestige they have to the huge growth of their budgets. But, again, they have to admit that their position is dependent on the effectiveness of the other departments. They cannot but recognize the qualitative differences between the repressive and welfare complexes of the state: the state can survive without welfare, but the welfare state cannot live from and for welfare alone. Welfare bureaucrats, too, must accept the notion of the split welfare state, even if it is increasingly advantageous for them to stress the linkages and similarities between the two spheres.

In this connection it is interesting to note the differences in the style and pattern of decision-making between the repressive and welfare agencies of the state. The repressive agencies are much more inner-oriented than their counterparts in the welfare complex.[51] Welfare agencies are significantly more involved with the social and political environment. This orientation of the welfare agencies is certainly related to the influence of pressure groups on welfare politics. But it also attests to the necessity for welfare agencies to mobilize support outside the state system. In the Netherlands, for example, the relation between the welfare complex and its social and political environment has always operated on an explicit _quid pro quo_ basis. Private or semi-public organizations spend the money which state agencies belonging to the welfare complex have wrung, with growing difficulties, from the Treasury.

The relevance of the repression-welfare cleavage in the Netherlands can also be seen in recent efforts to reorganize central government as well as in the substance of the Government Memoranda on the Reconsideration of Public Expenditures discussed in the contribution of Percy Lehning, to this volume.[52] These two items -- the reorganization of the central government machinery and the reappraisal of public expenditures -- dominate the public debate and the political discussions on the role of the state. Implicitly, and sometimes explicitly, the repression-welfare distinction functions as one of the guiding principles.

In May 1979, the Under-Secretary of the Interior established a Committee on the Central Government Structure. The Committee was asked to present, among other things, recommendations on the number and the substantive tasks of the Ministries. By then there were fourteen Ministries which perhaps can best be described as a monarchy of fourteen disunited departments.[53] As a solution to the problem of stagnation and segmentation, the interim reports and the final proposals of the Committee -- issued in 1981 -- suggested the restructuring of the policy process into five "main policy areas": administrative and legal affairs; international and military affairs; physical and environmental planning; socio-economic affairs; and socio-cultural affairs. Policy coordination in these five areas would become the responsibility of the secretaries of the Interior, Foreign Affairs, Physical Planning, Commerce, and Cultural Affairs respectively. Although the Committee did not propose a corresponding reduction of the number of Ministries -- Dutch coalition politics would not allow it --, it did recommend a rearrangement of the bureaucratic structures in accordance with the policy areas just mentioned.[54] Further, it was recommended that the structures of external advisory bodies be tuned to this design. The Committee proposals met with much criticism. Objections varied from the supposed arbitrary and artificial nature of the scheme to the supposed lack of sound argumentation, insufficient conceptualization and a deficient sense of political reality. The Committee was also accused of being obsessed with finding the administrative philosopher's stone.[55]

Let us now consider the response of the Committee to its critics. First, the Committee argued that in the public sector any pattern of organization has its arbitrary aspects. This would apply to the present structure as well as to any proposal for reorganization. Nevertheless, the Committee stressed that the five policy areas reflect the crucial aspects of public policy and that there be a broad consensus on the proposed design. Indeed, the Committee insisted that it had followed the existing administrative patterns which, in turn, fit in with prevailing political preferences.

It is clear that one of the principles taken for granted by the Committee pertained to the repression-welfare cleavage. The discussion thus far reveals that the Committee felt confident of the arrangements it had proposed. The policy areas for administrative-legal and international-military affairs hardly needed any comment. In contradistinction to the other policy areas, they seemed to have clear boundaries. The only complication involved the activities of some sections of the Ministry of Justice. Child protection, probation and even confinement policies might be conceived in socio-cultural terms. But, except for child protection, this kind of activity should eventually be allocated to the administrative-legal area. As the Committee suggested, this revealed the responsibility of the authorities in the administrative-legal area for the administrative infrastructure of society. As to confinement policies it should be understood that a state without prisons is not a state anymore. To relinquish child protection to the welfare complex might already be seen as a concession. Insofar as child protection was to be considered as a response to maltreatment, the state should be nearby for its own sake -- crushing the illegitimate infliction of physical harm upon people.

A second, equally important illustration of the relevance of the repression-welfare split has been the reappraisal of public expenditures which has been underway since 1980.[56] Nearly all programs in the welfare complex have been hit hard: public education, arts and sciences, health, social work, and social assistance. Meanwhile, the repressive complex has presented its case. As far as military defense is concerned, commitments to NATO set limits to the possibilities of budget cuts. The military can also point to the fact that their share in the governmental budget has fallen from 13.7% in 1970 to 11.6% in 1980. However, limited cutbacks have been achieved. Here it should be understood that efficiency could lead to highly counterproductive procurement policies; no compensating orders, no employment.[57]

With regard to law and order, it is tempting to anticipate the consequences of the economic depression and of the accompanying reduction of welfare: "the socio-economic problems and the measures to get them under control will lead to more social instability. Naturally, this calls for prudence with regard to such stabilizing factors as the police." One should also take into account that public cuts in the budget for law and order might undermine people's feelings of security. Basic policing functions, such as patrol work, would be affected adversely.[58]

The repressive tasks of the state concerning crime and detention require a very careful approach too. The social costs of severe cuts in probation programs could easily exceed the savings in direct costs. Possible savings in the penal system might also prove to be counterproductive. For instance, it would seem quite simple to accommodate two detainees in one cell. This would yield substantial savings. However, even if there were no legal impediments to this measure, it would have tremendous organizational implications. It would impair human relations within prisons: "It would make it more difficult for the management to keep the situation under control."[59] No state that respects itself will allow such things.

The Memoranda on the Re-consideration of Public Expenditures is clearly based on the repression-welfare distinction. Nobody wants the repressive complex to be threatened -- especially because the repressive complex may indeed be a sine qua non in times of severe depression and mass unemployment. Officials in the repressive complex of the state are well aware of this trend. By now one can say that the police are among the very few public institutions which have not been subjected to significant budget and personnel cuts. The police forces of the four big cities in the Netherlands are considered understaffed and have recently received extra funds. After some spectacular cases of criminal policies involving the release of criminals from over-crowded prisons, the expansion of confinement capacity could rely on a broad consensus in Parliament.

For their part, officials and agencies in the welfare complex have tended to redefine their position. There are many indications that welfare bureaucrats will take a repressive stand. Confronted with the rise of welfare crime, they may consider it in their own interest to yield to the popular call for harsh measures and, in spirit, they seem ready to join the repressive complex. They tend to welcome the far-reaching investigative and controlling powers laid down in an increasing number of special provisions in welfare laws. Within welfare bureaucracies, special branches are found which differ from the regular police in only their tenacity and missionary persecution of various kinds of welfare crime. Interestingly, the legal powers of the special branches go far beyond those provided for in general laws.[60]

This new kind of linkage between the welfare and repressive complexes of the state is quite questionable. It is not clear that this trend will strengthen the position of the welfare sector in the state. It could very well contribute to a further curtailment of the welfare complex, with the special branches crossing the line to the repressive side of the state.

WHAT SHOULD BE DONE BY THE STATE

In the preceding sections we have stressed the multi-dimensionality of the state. Our analysis appears to imply that it is very difficult to give adequate prescriptions on the role of the state. What should be done by the state? The answer may be much more complex than some theoretical approaches suggest. For instance, public choice theory seems to offer very elegant, parsimonious prescriptions. Such devices as joint consumption and exclusion would go a long way toward resolving troublesome questions about proper activities of the state. And we would seem to have an adequate prescriptive theory, if we took into account that there may be different arrangements for providing public services: "Collective action is by no means synonymous with government action."[61] But from the preceding sections we can draw the tentative conclusion that we need to know much more for an adequate prescriptive theory of the state. A discussion about the particular qualities of specific goods and services will not do. Economy and efficiency may be important yet insufficient considerations -- theoretically as well as empirically.

As we have discussed previously, one of the most intriguing questions regarding the role of the state concerns the stability and content of people's orientations to the state. If we have referred to the wide acceptance of the notion of the split welfare state, we have only taken the first step toward a more basic understanding of the intricate relations of people to the state. We can expect different people to have diverse orientations to the state. It can be assumed that elites, sub-elites and mass publics have divergent perspectives of the state as well. How do they conceptualize the state? Do they see the state in the French way: *L'etat c'est moi*? Or do they rather conceive of the state in terms of a complex institutional framework? Would they, then, share Miliband's idea of the scope of the state: the chief executive, the civil service, the armed forces and the police, the courts, but also the representative bodies and the sub-national levels of government?[62] Or do they adhere to a more restrictive orientation -- which many empirical studies tend to reserve for the first stages of political socialization: The President (or the Queen) and the men-in-uniform? Would a cynical attitude towards politics ("one big mess") imply a negative orientation to both the polity at large and the state? Would such an attitude imply a negative orientation to the chief executive as well as to bureaucracy? Usually, empirical research does not extend to this level of theoretical and conceptual sophistication. It may include questions on pride in "governmental, political institutions" and may, at best, suggest that "a more discriminating series of questions would no doubt have produced a more complex pattern and more reliable body of information."[63]

Let us now reflect and speculate on what an adequate prescriptive theory of the state might look like. First, a prescriptive theory on the role of the state should consider the possibility that people have internalized the Weberian concept of the state. It is easily forgotten that this concept was meant to give expression to a long-term historical process and, to this day, constitutes the point of orientation for both rulers and revolutionaries.[64] Perhaps the continental tradition of the state has taken root not only in parts of Western political thought, but also in the minds of common people.[65]

If there is some truth to this suggestion, one should be very careful in accepting the rational yardsticks of public choice. Take for instance the question of private versus public policing. A public choice analyst may state: "The duties of private and public police are vastly different, in the aggregate, but for the narrow function of deterrence by patrol they can be compared, at least with respect to cost if not effectiveness. In 1976, in New York City, contract guards could be procured at a total cost of $4 to $7 per hour, whereas the remuneration alone of a regular police officer, including all fringe benefits but not including any overhead costs, was about $15 per hour."[66] But this kind of comparison may be misleading. Even if, beside being more efficient and effective, private policemen were to treat people equally and according to all standards of equity, this would not be sufficient evidence in favor of private policing. People may have intrinsic expectations with regard to public versus private arrangements for maintaining internal order. They may want the state to perform this function -- even at some extra cost. Protective associations may be efficient, quite effective and even rather equitable. Yet it could be that, after all, people would prefer the state to protect them.

It could be argued that in contrast to the repressive state concept, people may not have internalized the concept of the welfare state. This applies to the redistributive functions of the state in particular. The Weberian concept of the state can be traced through centuries. On the other hand, while redistributive state functions may have been propagated by various ideological currents, they lack both the historical and consensual foundation of the repressive functions. The privatization of welfare -- for instance the reintroduction of private insurance schemes -- might, then, enjoy warm support. Criteria of efficiency and effectiveness might prevail and collective arrangements instead of state measures could be quite acceptable. Public choice theory has more to say about collective than about public goods and services -- and more about the private sector than about the state.

Second, in answering the question about what the state should do, we should keep in mind the possibility that people orient themselves to the state as an integrative symbol. Their perception of a split welfare state may lead them to attack what they see as luxurious and unnecessary activities of the state. To a certain degree, the opposition to the welfare role of the state may be an expression of people's aversion to a multi-functional state.

Viewed that way, the broad disappointment with the state -- and with state bureaucracy in particular -- could be explained in terms of unrealistic expectations regarding this highly complex organization. Being familiar with the sometimes messy social process and being aware of the tough dimensions of political conflict, many people expect the state to be the last resort of the public interest -- the common good. What they do not expect is a mixture of as many interests as there are bureaus and officials. Seen in this light, the antipathy to bureaucracy and bureaucrats becomes more understandable. In their encounters with bureaucracy people come to recognize that the image of a public service does not entirely fit reality. On a certain level of comprehension they understand that bureaucrats may be politicians in disguise or very ordinary people. The servants of the state turn out to be public officials pursuing (quasi-) private interests.

Third, considerations of this kind have some interesting consequences for the discussion of state activities on various governmental levels. How can a focus on the state as a symbol of nationwide unity be reconciled to the idea of a multi-tier governmental system? Should we accept Miliband's concept of the state which includes all levels of government?[67]

It can be assumed that different arrangements of centralization and decentralization are closely related to different conceptions of the state.[68] Some arrangements will be of particular importance. For instance, the degree of decentralization of authority and control over the police is highly indicative of the relative significance of a unitary versus multi-tier conception of the state. In the Netherlands, where the issue of the authority over the police is labeled "the police question," this perspective has hardly been examined. The various options (centralization; regional police; or municipal forces) are based on the weighing of such factors as effectiveness, efficiency, democratic control and communal concern. In this example we can see that the orientations of people to the state and to its functions have been left out of the discussion.

In no way are we suggesting that this perspective be used on behalf of some sort of national police -- or on behalf of the centralization of any other institution or task. Our intention has been to stress the relevance of these kinds of issues. As we have said before, we do not know much about people's orientations to the state. Here we add that we hardly know anything about the intrinsic importance people attach to the role of the state on the central, regional and local level. Insofar as "the integrity of the state" is a relevant category in the minds of the people, we should not hesitate to ask relevant questions about it.[69] In this connection competing interpretations of decentralization come to the fore: Does the state relinquish power to other public institutions; or does it penetrate the periphery through sub-central units of government? Indeed, one wonders if any state would ever voluntarily give up authority. Let us not forget that some people may indeed take the "integrity of the state" in its moral sense. A coalition between state morality and state interest is easy to forge.[70]

CONCLUSIONS

We have investigated several conceptual and empirical questions regarding the crisis and the future of the welfare state. Conceptually, our perspectives are based on a distinction between the state, the polity and society. Whether the welfare state is autonomous or not, the conceptual distinction between the state and other categories of political and social organization is crucial to a sound analysis of the programs of the welfare state.

From this conceptual starting point we proceeded to develop a conceptual framework based on two dimensions which are present implicitly in most analyses of the welfare state. The first dimension involves the orientation to repression versus welfare; it is related to the transition from traditional to more contemporary perspectives on state activity. The second dimension refers to instrumental versus functional aspects of the state. The conceptual framework makes it possible to draw a clear picture of the critical position of the welfare complex in the contemporary state. On the repressive side, state instruments and state functions definitely raise difficult questions, yet appear to match to a certain degree. On the welfare side, however, effective instruments are lacking and one of the functions -- the promotion of collective welfare -- is highly disputed. Indeed, in its efforts to increase collective welfare the state may turn to the repressive instruments it has at its disposal: welfare by repression. The welfare complex of the state gets squeezed.

This conclusion is also drawn from the analysis of the empirical relevance of the repression-welfare distinction. It appears that the public and the political elites act upon this distinction -- to the disadvantage of the welfare complex. The welfare state is perceived as a split state. If reorganization is in the offing, the "natural" point of departure appears to be the repression-welfare distinction. Plans for cutbacks in public expenditures "naturally" set the repressive against the welfare complex. Welfare bureaucrats are well-advised to emphasize their more repressive aspects. Considering the explosive growth of special branches for the struggle against welfare crime, we can conclude that many welfare agencies and welfare officials have taken this advice to heart. As a matter of fact, this development tends to contribute to a further curtailment of the welfare complex and thus may ultimately work against them: no welfare, no welfare crime.

There are, then, many dimensions to the state. The state represents complex distinctions and linkages, connections and disconnections. Because of the multi-dimensionality of the state, it is clear that prescriptions regarding the role of the state are very difficult to give. Until we know more about the orientations of various categories of people to the state -- to the *Staat* or *L'etat* as against a conglomerate of organizational units and elected and bureaucratic officials -- we should be very careful about converting rational designs into political reality. Public choice theory may be very helpful, but it cannot replace public psychology and political history.

It is not merely a commonplace observation to note that sound prescriptions with regard to the role of the modern state depend on our capacity to raise the relevant questions. Our pre-occupation with the financial and economic state of the nation must not prevent us from emphasizing the importance of psychological and historical considerations. There is more to the state than the allocation and distribution of collective goods.

NOTES

1. Jeffrey D. Strausmann, "Spending More and Enjoying It Less", in: _Comparative Politics_, 13 (1981), pp. 235-252.

2. See John Logue, "The Welfare State: Victim of Its Success," in: _Daedalus_, 1979, pp. 69-87.

3. Richard Rose, "The Nature of the Challenge," in: Richard Rose (ed.), _Challenge to Governance_ (London: Sage, 1980), p. 6.

4. The "struggle against bureaucracy" is one of the declared aims of nearly every political party in The Netherlands.

5. The chairman of the Dutch Labor Party asked for a "new realism" in 1981. By then, he was considered one of the champions of the activist wing in the party.

6. See too Uriel Rosenthal, "Welfare State or State of Welfare," in: _Comparative Social Research_, 6 (1982).

7. Robert Maclver, _The Modern State_ (London: Oxford University Press, 1926), p. 2.

8. Maclver, _op. cit._, p. 149.

9. Maclver, _op. cit._, p. 7.

10. An exception among contemporary political scientists is Nordlinger. See Eric Nordlinger, _On the Autonomy of the Democratic State_ (Cambridge Mass.: Harvard University Press, 1981).

11. See, too, John G. Ruggie, "Complexity, Planning, and Public Order," in: Todd R. La Porte (ed.), _Organized Social Complexity_ (Princeton N.J.: Princeton University Press, 1975), pp. 147-148.

12. Compare David Easton, "The Political System Besieged by the State," in: _Political Theory_, 9 (1981), pp. 303-325.

13. Max Weber, _The Theory of Social and Economic Organization_, trans.. A.M. Henderson and Talcott Parsons (New York: Oxford University Press, 1947), p. 155.

14. Weber, _op. cit.,_ p. 102. See also Kenneth H.F. Dyson, _The State Tradition in Western Europe_ (Oxford: Martin Robertson, 1980), p. 12.

15. See also Harry Eckstein, "On the Science of the State," in: _Daedalus_, 1979, pp. 1-20.

16. Weber, _op. cit._, p. 155

17. Richard Titmuss, _Commitment to Welfare_ (London: Allen and Unwin, 1968), p. 2.

18. See for instance Piet Thoenes, _The Elite in the Welfare State_ (London: Faber, 1966).

19. On this pattern of reasoning see Norman Furniss and Timothy Tilton, _The Case for the Welfare State_ (Bloomington: Indiana University Press, 1979), p. 25.

20. See Nordlinger, _op. cit._

21. Harold L. Wilensky, The Welfare State and Equality: Structural and Ideological Roots of Public Expenditures (Berkeley: California University Press,1975), p. 1.

22. Let us not forget that the Western European welfare states are, to some extent, a combination of social-democratic goals and capitalist-liberal means.

23. See Otto Kirchheimer, "The Rechtsstaat as Magic Wall," in: Kurt Wolff and Barrington Moore, Jr. (eds.), The Critical Spirit: Essays in Honor of Herbert Marcuse (Boston: Houghton Mifflin, 1967), pp. 287-312.

24. Fritz W. Scharpf, "Public Organization and the Waning of the Welfare State: A Research Perspective," in: European Journal of Political Research, 5 (1977), p. 341.

25. Nozick's "minimal state" is very complex indeed. Robert Nozick, Anarchy, State, and Utopia (Oxford: Basil Blackwell, 1974).

26. Bernard Williams, "The Minimal State," in: Jeffrey Paul (ed). Reading Nozick: Essays on Anarchy, State, and Utopia (Totawa N.J.:Rowman, 1981), p. 29.

27. Furniss and Tilton, op. cit., p.17.

28. Richard Rose, "Ordinarily People in Extraordinary Economic Circumstances," in: Rose (ed.), op. cit., pp. 151-174. Also Hugh Heclo, "Toward a New Welfare State?" in: Peter Flora and Arnold Heidenheimer (eds.), The Development of Welfare States in Europe and America (New Brunswick, N.J., 1981), pp. 383-406.

29. The relations I-II and III-IV may be interesting, but they are less important for our purpose. Regarding I-II one could discuss the relativity of the conceptual distinction between I and II (the baseline concept). Relation III-IV invites questions on the linkages between, for instance, physical and social and economic security: should the state extend its physical power to matters of (personal) health?

30. Uriel Rosenthal, Political Order: Rewards, Punishments, and Political Stability (Alphen a/d Rijn: Sijthoff and Noordhoff, 1978), pp. 156-192. See also Dennis Wrong, Power: Its Forms, Bases and Uses (Oxford: Basil Blackwell 1979), pp. 41-44.

31. Hedley Bull, The Anarchical Society: A Study of Order in World Politics (London: Macmillan, 1977), pp. 233-256.

32. See for instance Michael Hill, The State, Administration and the Individual (Glasgow: Fontana, 1976); D. Grunow et al., Burger und Verwaltung (Frankfurt: Campus, 1978); Jeffrey M. Protas, People-Processing (Lexington Mass.: Health, 1979); Uriel Rosenthal, "Communalism and Clientele Bureaucracy,"

in: The Netherlands' Journal of Sociology, 12 (1976), pp. 79-88.

33. Eckstein, op. cit., p. 17-18.

34. Nozick, op. cit., p. 33.

35. Scharpf, op. cit., p. 336.

36. See for instance Duahe H. Swank, Does Crime Really Pay? (New York: APSP Convention 1981).

37. Nozick, op. cit., Also F.A. Hayek, The Political Order of a Free People (Chicago: Chicago University Press, 1979), pp. 54-56.

38. Eckstein, op. cit., p. 18.

39. Ronald Inglehart, The Silent Revolution: Changing Values and Political Styles Among Western Publics (Princeton: Princeton University Press, 1977); Samuel Barnes and others, Political Action: Mass Participation in Five Western Democracies (London: Sage, 1979), part II; Ronald Inglehart, "Post-Materialism in an Environment of Insecurity, in American Political Science Review 75 (1981), pp. 880-900.

40. Inglehart, The Silent Revolution, op. cit., pp.28.

41. Ibidem, pp. 39-53. Also Ronald Inglehart, "Value Priorities and Economic Change," in: Barnes and others, op. cit., pp. 305-342.

42. Inglehart, "Value Priorities," op. cit., pp. 322-323.

43. Hans D. Klingemann, "Ideological Conceptualization and Political Action," in: Barnes and others, op. cit., pp. 279-303.

44. Ibidem, p. 287. See also Hans D. Klingemann, "Measuring Ideological Conceptualizations," in: Barnes and others, op. cit., pp. 227-233.

45. Alan Marsh and Max Kaase, "Measuring Political Action," in: Barnes and others, op. cit., pp. 57-96; Klingemann, "Measuring Ideological Conceptualizations," op. cit., p. 294.

46. Ibidem.

47. Inglehart, "Post-Materialism," op. cit., p. 888.

48. Marsh and Kaase, "Measuring Political Action," op. cit. Note that in 1974, when the Netherlands were still affluent, a mass survey presented the prevention of crime and the increase of security on the street as the primary task for the state (SMO, Scheveningen, 1975), p. 185.

49. Inglehart, "Post-Materialism," op.cit., p. 880. See too Bernard Cazes, "L'Avenir de l'Etat Protecteur," in: Public and Private: The Crisis of the Western State Model (Rome: Institute for Philosophic Studies, 1979), pp. 85-98.

50. See also Inglehart, "Post-Materialism," op.cit.

51. See Joel D. Aberbach and others, Bureaucrats

and Politicians in Western Democracies (Cambridge Mass.:Harvard University Press, 1981),pp. 224-227.

52. Reports of the Committee on the Central Government Structure (The Hague: State Printing Office, 1979-1981); Memoranda on the Reconsideration of Public Expenditures, Parliamentary Reports, 1980-1981 and 1981-82, 16625.

53. After the glorious Republic of the Seven United Netherlands.

54.On the political complications see for instance Samuel Eldersveld and others, The World of Dutch Elites: Images of MPs and Higher Civil Servants (Ann Arbor: Michigan University Press, 1981).

55. In this respect, the Committee appears to adhere to the rational kind of approach which many experts have turned down. See Harold Seidman, Politics, Position, and Power (New York: Oxford University Press, 3rd. edition, 1980), chapter 1.

56.Memorandum on the Reconsideration, 1981-82, op.cit., p. 29.

57.Memorandum on the Reconsideration, 1980-81, op.cit., pp. 52-58.

58. Ibidem, pp. 70-80.

59. Memorandum on the Reconsideration, 1981-82, op.cit., pp. 113-128.

60. See G.P. A. Aler, Police Powers in Investigative and Controlling Activities (Zwolle: Tjeenk Willink, 1982), pp. 299-305. In Dutch.

61. E.S. Savas, Privatizing the Public Sector: How to Shrink Government (Chatham, N.J.: Chatham); and Vincent Ostrom and Elinor Ostrom, "Public Goods and Public Choices," in E.S. Savas (ed.), Alternatives for Delivering Public Services: Toward Improved Performance (Boulder: Westview Press, 1977), pp. 7-49.

62. Ralph Miliband, The State in Capitalist Society (London: Weidenfeld and Nicholson, 1969), pp. 46-51.

63. Gabriel A. Almond and Sidney Verba, The Civic Culture Revisited (Boston: Little Brown, 1980), pp. 64-71. Easton's analysis of objects of support comes close to this theme, yet does not lead to a thorough examination of the institutional and structural aspects of the "black box of government:" David Easton, A Systems Analysis of Political Life (Chicago: Chicago University Press, 2nd edition, 1979).

64. J.D.B. Miller, The World of States (London: Croom Helm, 1981), pp. 143-160.

65. Dyson, The State Tradition, op.cit., pp. 48-78.

66. Savas, op. cit., p. 105.

67.Miliband is realistic enough to draw the consequences of a complex pattern of intra-state relations. Sub-central units may be "channels of communication and administration from the center to the periphery, but also the voice of the periphery, or of particular interests at the periphery" (Miliband, *op. cit.*, p. 49.)

68. See for instance Tarrow's introduction to Sidney Tarrow and others (eds.) *Territorial Politics in Industrial Nations* (New York: Praeger, 1978), pp. 1-27.

69. Roger Benjamin, *The Limits of Politics* (Chicago: Chicago University Press, 1980), p. 93.

70. Nordlinger, *op. cit.*, pp. 35-38.

XIII.

Norman Furniss

The Welfare State between 'State' and 'Civil Society'

Any consideration of where welfare states might be going should have some link to how they have developed. We can identify four major types of explanations for the origin and development of welfare states. The first focuses on the concept of modernization in general and on the needs of industrial society in particular. The second emphasizes conflict and contradiction arising from the operation of the economic system or the modes of production; welfare institutions are created in response. The third locates the key impetus for change in the shifting balance of power between capital and labor in civil society, with the latter usually given the positive task of establishing welfare provisions. The fourth highlights the relatively autonomous actions of the state; independent roles are assigned to state officials, political parties and political institutions.

The first two explanations tend to see all welfare states as fundamentally the same or at least as on the same path. They are nonpolitical in the straight-forward sense that they reject the importance of political variables or political action. A critique of these explanations has been a common feature of the chapters in Part One of this volume. As Griffin and Associates show, "no 'general' trans-national, trans-temporal determination of transfer outlays exists." The second two explanations do allow for political variables or political action at least in the weak sense that they are consistent with a political analysis of the policy process.[1] They also have the merit of stressing the importance of historical experiences and policy variety.

Unfortunately, however, because the monocausal nature of welfare state development cannot be assumed, in discussing possible future directions it is not enough to determine somehow which of these explanations seems most compelling and then to extrapolate the logic of the argument. This point is acknowledged in much of the recent literature, but its implications are drawn out far less frequently. In their instructive discussion of "The Politics of Public Social Spending in Britain 1900-1911 and the United States 1880s-1920," for example, Orloff and Skocpol remark that "the politics of social-welfare provision are just as much grounded in the processes of statebuilding and the organization and reorganization of political life as in those socioeconomic processes. . . that have traditionally been seen as basic to the development of the welfare state."[2] This phrase, "just as much grounded in," fails to capture the interaction between state and groups in civil society.[3] Nor are we shown theoretically why "socioeconomic processes" are important at all. Nor does the rough equivalence one infers appear especially helpful. Another difficulty can be extracted from the insightful work of Jens Alber who argues that some explanations seem more useful in understanding some periods of welfare state development than others.[4] How can this be? What is the underlying relationship?

PATTERNS OF WELFARE POLICY

As a very preliminary way of looking at welfare provision in advanced capitalist democracies, I will suggest that a key to understanding both determinants and possible futures is found in the dynamic interaction between "state" and "civil society." It is necessary before proceeding to define these two terms. For the former we will adopt the basic Weberian position developed by Uriel Rosenthal in the previous chapter that a "state" exists when the legitimate use of force over a territory is monopolized by a legal and administrative order. A "civil society" will be defined by "citizens dwelling together in a community."[5] Framed in this way, "state" and "civil society" are not coterminous. In the European experience states arose after civil societies in a far from harmonious fashion. Indeed, the aim of early state theorists (Bodin, Hobbes, Pufendorf) was to secure the integrity of the sovereign from what they saw as the unbridled passions of civil society. From the other side, the aim of early nineteenth constitutional documents was to keep the state from unwarranted intrusions into the affairs of society.

All parties, in short, agreed that the relationship between "state" and "civil society" was essentially adversarial and unstable -- the proper functioning of each was threatened fundamentally by the other. It is in this context that the uniqueness of systematic public welfare provisions, or, more broadly, of the "welfare state" can be seen. Recognizing that state and civil society must interact, the "welfare state" offers the framework to organize the relationship in mutually productive ways. This theme is advanced by Douglas Ashford both in this volume and elsewhere: "The welfare state has come of age politically, and in doing so has fundamentally changed the parameters of democratic politics."[6] The results of this accomplishment can be viewed from two directions. From the perspective of civil society, those groups that formerly lost out in the battle for economic and social resources (the elderly, the sick, the "poor", the unemployed, the uneducated) were accorded protection and assistance by the state. At the same time state functions were altered radically. To the elaboration of "police powers" was added the concern for individual social and economic development among the citizenry. Again, the implications of adding the "welfare functions" have been developed in the contribution of Uriel Rosenthal.

We should not conclude from the discussion thus far that the nature of the accommodation between state and civil society is the same in all cases. In considering determinants, a concern with interactions produces in theory, and can be seen to have produced in practice, varying policy outcomes depending on which side was more successful in impressing its values on the other. This process is more subtle than I can develop in this chapter. As a first, crude effort I will suggest which welfare states emerged _primarily_ as a consequence of purposeful state action and which were structured _primarily_ by dominant groups in civil society. The former case is typified in the historical experiences of Britain and France. The latter broadly describes the experience of the United States and Sweden. To pair the last two countries especially is to indicate that dominant groups in civil society can vary.

Of all the contemporary welfare states Britain best exemplifies the imposition of state norms on civil society. Welfare provision is widely and correctly identified not with a particular political party but with a civil servant's report. In his report on "Social Insurance and Allied Services" William Beveridge established the principles that have governed British policy since. The state should "establish a national minimum"; beyond that "it should leave room and encouragement for voluntary action by each individual to provide more for himself and his family." From this policy pattern, which in an earlier work we have termed typical of social security states,[7] we can draw two relevant implications. First, there is a deliberate inattention to the economic system. Second, there is a deliberate inattention to the interests of groups. To be sure, in the actual establishment and implementation of welfare policies, it might be necessary to reach some accord with doctors, Friendly Societies and the like, but these compromises from the perspective of state officials are considered unfortunate deviations. By this comment I do not intend to make a normative judgment. The establishment of a national minimum may well be a worthy policy goal, the most "fair" and "just" welfare principle around.[8] But, as T.H. Marshall makes clear, it is a very unlikely outcome of "pluralistic" bargaining within civil society. The "ethos of the normal process of political and industrial democracy is out of harmony with the spirit of welfare" because the duty of the welfare principle "_is to provide not what the majority wants but what minorities need_."[9] A more concise justification for state imposition would be hard to find.

The French case is more complex. On the one hand, statist rhetoric is more intense. Only a French leader could record such sentiments as "I do not need an 'idea' of France. I live France. I have a deep instinctive awareness of France, of physical France, and a passion for her geography, her living body. For it is there that my roots have grown. There is no need for me to seek the soul of France -- it lives in me."[10] And the French state has long manifested a deep distrust of interest groups epitomized by the outlawing of mutual-aid societies in the "Loi Le Chapelier" in 1791, a measure that was not repealed formally for over eighty years. When we study actual welfare provision, however, we see a "system" not oriented around a coherent policy principle as in Britain but rather a myriad of programs so complex that one expert declares it "practically impossible for the uninitiated to understand anything about it."[11] Still, take the example of pensions, if one turns from the details of the 120 basic and 600 complementary retirement schemes to a consideration of who broadly benefits, a pattern begins to emerge.[12] We find, to cite a government report, that the winners are those groups deemed "indispensable to the national effort." In Britain, the state undertakes welfare provision almost as a matter of public charity. In France, the concern is as much for the state to help itself.

In their policy patterns our other two cases reflect much more the aspirations of the "dominant" group in civil society. For Sweden I accept the description, albeit not the reasoning, of Social Democratic Theorists--Swedish welfare provision broadly reflects the aspirations of the organized interest of the working class. In America the dominant group in civil society was organized business.[13] What is central to an understanding of the American experience is the acceptance among public officials that business could and should be the source of social policies that the public sector was already providing abroad. This triumph of business ideology was based in part on the actions of businessmen who did institute a range of social policies which provided the policy experience on which state policymakers later would draw.[14] When finally it was instituted, public welfare policy took a form broadly consistent with the hegemony of business in civil society. Again, I should emphasize that "capitalists" do not have free reign in America, nor do "social democrats" govern all areas of Swedish life. (In both countries, for example, there have been major concessions to agrarian interests.)[15] What I intend to identify is the primarily policy thrust. Moreover, although this consideration cannot be reconciled easily with the distinctions advanced in this chapter, I would be remiss not to note that within the international economic order outlined in the introduction to this volume, the hegemony of business in civil society gives to welfare policy a pervasiveness that the hegemony of labor cannot provide.

PERSPECTIVES ON WELFARE STATES "IN CRISIS"

To depict welfare states as the potentially fruitful and always changing outcome of the interaction between the interests of state and civil society implies an orientation toward the nature of any crisis different from those commonly advanced. Particularly in this period of welfare state bashing, many commentators have not felt the need to analyze the structural properties of the welfare state before declaring its policies bankrupt and its influence deleterious--like the devil, the welfare state is said to have compiled a record of almost unrelieved failure, and yet somehow it still emits a strange and corrupting attraction. Setting aside more extensive jeremiads, it is claimed that the welfare state, or sometimes more generally "democracy", fosters uncontrollable citizen demands,which then lead to uncontrolled social spending, which then produces government "overload" and crisis. Or, if citizen demands are not the motivating force, then demographic features are said to impel ever increasing levels of social spending leading to the same result. Or, if social spending need not necessarily increase, still beyond a certain threshold it leads to ruin. We will discuss briefly each of these arguments in turn.

The claim that citizen demands produce government responses which produce further demands which yield crisis and overload has become a staple of neoconservative argument.[16] Resting on assumptions of "economic man" and overlaid with notions of "rationality" and "public choice", this idea is not liable to hold over theoretical interest for long. This is not to say that its influence is therefore negligible:[17] "Unless the economic theory of democracy is swept away, we risk being caught in a dangerous web. 'Overload' will then seem to be the problem, excess of democracy its cause, and authoritarian institutions a solution waiting in the wings." But since specific theoretical refutation has been attempted elsewhere, most recently and elegantly in the article by Bennett and Sharpe quoted above, I will restrict myself to its empirical dimension.

If we look at welfare spending as a percentage of gross national product, we see increases at varying rates among all advanced capitalist democracies until the mid 1970s. Then from the mid 1970s to the early 1980s in most but not in all states the rate of spending slowed. And in Germany, during the time it should be recalled of Social Democratic government, the growth rate stopped. Social protection expenditure was 29.8 percent of gross domestic product in 1975 and 29.4 percent in 1981.[18] When we consider particular sectors we find the same pattern. Health care costs, for example, continue for different reasons to rise as a percentage of gross domestic product much more rapidly in Sweden and the United States than in France, Germany, Belgium, and the Netherlands.[19] How can this be? Aren't these still welfare states with demanding voters, self-aggrandizing bureaucrats, and politicians who "compete in the market-place for the votes of an extensive electorate in the same way that oilmen bid for oil or salesmen bid for customers"?[20]

Structural explanations experience similar difficulties. Offered primarily by government officials and social security professionals, these have a distinctly Malthusian tone.[21] Adverse demographic trends are said to place an intolerable burden on the social security system. The Germans even have come up with a specific term -- the "Rentenberg" or pension mountain. In Germany the ratio of workers to pensioners is expected to decline from 2.2 in 1980 to 1.1 in 2030. In some states projections are even gloomier; in Denmark there are fears of major population declines. What can one say about such fears other than mention that in the past demographic projections have proven continually inaccurate? First, the extent of the problem varies considerably. In Germany the figures could be seen as troubling, but in France dependency ratios were worse from 1955-75 than they are expected to be from 1975-2000. Second, from the discovery that France surmounted its demographic challenge without fiscal breakdown, indeed in a better fiscal position than it now enjoys, one can infer that effective policy responses are feasible. This point can be extended to other sectors. In health care, for example, it is correct that health costs increase tremendously for the "very aged," the population over age 80. And this cohort in most advanced capitalist states is growing more rapidly than any other. On the other hand, it also should be noted that even for this age group most people are healthy. A distinct minority absorbs a majority of expenses. Moreover, most of these expenses occur within the last six months of These figures point to difficult policy and personal choices; they do not point to inevitable collapse of welfare provisions.

The third reason why demographic changes need not lead to fiscal crisis lies in differing patterns of social security finance. Under pay as you go systems such as exist in the United States and Britain, there could be a threat to savings rates. "Funded" systems like those in Germany and Switzerland depend more on the maintenance of capital profit than on increasing contributions. And once again there are examples of effective policy response. In Austria, where the federal government is legally obligated to make-up any shortfalls between expenditure and income, the share of central government financing of pension expenditure rose from under 29 percent of the total in the early 1970s to 35 percent in 1977. The government responded by increasing contributions and modifying downward some pension benefits with the result that its share fell to 22 percent in 1982.[22] Finally, it should be emphasized that the principal threat to all funding schemes lies in the general economic situation. "The slow-down in economic activity and the resultant rise in unemployment constitute the main immediate reason for the problems which the social security schemes are now experiencing[23] To combat this slow-down, not to bewail the number of elderly, then becomes the main challenge.

We come now to the argument that regardless of why it occurs a large amount of social or government spending leads inevitably to catastrophe. This claim is most commonly disseminated by political commentators with "academic" pretensions, but it receives some mainstream support as well, as in the contribution by Milton Friedman, "The Line We Dare Not Cross." Writing in 1976, Friedman found in the Allende government in Chile a terrible lesson for all democratic countries. When there is "an expansion in the role of government over the lives of people", the basis of a free society is threatened. Britain is in immediate danger. "The UK is going down the same path as Chile and, I fear, is headed for the same end. . . The odds are at least 50-50 that within the next five years British freedom and democracy, as we have seen it, will be destroyed." So is New York City. "New York City displays precisely the same trends as Chile and the United Kingdom." First comes uncontrolled inflation, then loss of freedom from either the left or right. Why? Because "nobody spends somebody else's money as carefully as he spends his own. That is why trying to do good at someone else's expense leads to financial crisis." And furthermore, "if you are going to do good at somebody else's expense, you have to take the money away from him. So force, coercion, destruction of freedom is at the very bottom, at the very source, of the attempts to do good at somebody else's expense." And although any taxation has this property, beyond a certain level freedom cannot survive at all.[24]

What can we make of this argument? First, like most social scientists Friedman is not good at prognostication. In advanced capitalist democracies the inflation rate has been slowed dramatically without overturning constitutional guarantees of civil liberties. New York City was "bailed out." Mrs. Thatcher may be an "iron lady", but she is no General Pinochet, and so on. The general lesson is that the relationship between politics and economics is much more complex than this or the "overload" perspective can entertain. Second, there is no evidence that national economic efficiency must be undermined by the presence of a large or relatively large government sector. Indeed, as Donald Schwerin reports in his contribution to this volume, advanced Scandinavian welfare states in general have coped with the international economic downturn more effectively than have states with smaller welfare sectors. The dictum that trying to do good at someone else's expense yields financial crisis must be challenged. More fundamentally, we must question once again the psychological assumption that individuals strive only to maximize their own utility defined in economic terms, and that any diminution in their income thus constitutes for them a loss of freedom. The premises of social insurance and of solidarity are different. And if, as we have described in this volume, they are under attack, they are far from nonexistent or impossible to refurbish. Our conclusion for this claim as for the others is that while difficulties may have been identified these are far from constituting a "crisis" in Paul Valery's sense of "the passage of one particular mode of functioning to another."[25] More significant, albeit less apocalyptical, threats to the operation of welfare state institutions must be sought elsewhere.

FUTURE UNCERTAINTIES

As Timothy Tilton argues in chapter one, in one important respect the "industrialization" approach to the study of welfare states is correct: Welfare states were structured in relation to industrial society. Their policies are designed to relieve the casualties of the industrial order and through the actuarial myth of "social insurance" to redistribute resources to those unable to work because they are sick, injured, unemployed, or too old. Politically (a consideration the industrialism approach has trouble incorporating), welfare goals often were articulated and gains achieved through mobilized working class power in civil society. This mobilization in Northern Europe was performed by social democratic parties and trade union organizations. Their policy proposals were based on the assumptions that capital would continue to be consolidated, that firms would grow larger, that cities would expand--in brief, that increasingly centralizing problems mandated centralized solutions.

What now is happening in advanced capitalist democracies is that public intervention designed to meet the "negative externalities" of industrialism is incomplete. In a society that is predominately urban _and_ that is oriented (in life-style if not necessarily in numbers) around industrial work, the policy thrust is clear. It is less so as the goods producing sector of the economy declines and as its composition changes toward smaller manufacturing establishments. It is still less so with the identification of a new class of people needing help, the "new poor", whose problems do not arise from direct contact with industrial work but rather from family disintegration, drug abuse, mental illness, or from never having been in the labor force at all. These problems need specialized social services not necessarily organized most effectively in centralized welfare systems or by corporate groups.[26] All this is fairly well recognized as is the emergence of new political issues outside the traditional welfare state debate--issues concerning women's rights, ecological preservation, nuclear power, nuclear war, neighborhood development. These issues are not only new, they call for different organizational styles and appeals. "Citizens initiatives" fit uneasily with the traditional tenets of social democracy. Thus we see the pertinence of Alain Touraine's question, "What is the movement that will occupy in post-industrial society the central role of the workers' movement in industrial society. . .?"[27]

I do not mean to argue that the "workers' movement" is to be consigned to the dust bin of history. The challenge is to the dynamics of reform. This challenge is developed in another way in one of the last essays by the Herbert Marcuse.[28] With some exaggeration (viz the "new poor") he argues that in many respects, including similar life styles, it is useful to collapse all groups (say 98% of the population) not owning significant amounts of productive property. "Worker" becomes "the people." But "the people" are not a class in any traditional sense. There is nothing corresponding to class consciousness. Politically "the people" are all over the place. If, however, the "working class" is reextracted, then Marcuse notes, following the work of Rudolf Bahro, that it cannot itself constitute a dominant class. It rests on too narrow a base to transform society. And more: Marcuse proceeds to wonder whether this extracted working class plays a fundamentally conservative role, concerned above all to protect previous gains, to preserve as much as possible of the status quo. In an era of Reagan and Thatcher, this is not an unworthy goal. But it does abandon the search for systematic welfare policy development. And it becomes more difficult to regard social democracy, in the words of the Swedish Prime Minister, Olof Palme, as "a movement for the liberation of man."[29]

For those seeking to expand or defend given levels of welfare provision, adverse socio-economic changes are made worse by developments within the international political economy. As I attempted to argue briefly in the introduction to this book, the key problem is not that welfare states are facing "hard times." Welfare provisions were instituted and developed in times far harder than these. The international political economy is constraining because of the nature of policy linkages. Not only is there an absence of "political space" which has been proposed as a necessary or at least useful condition for welfare state development.[30] Alignment with the American pattern, while it need not result in the Dutch concern described by Percy Lehning over how to retrench, at least impells government decision makers toward a reexamination of welfare commitments.

The final set of uncertainties arises from the interaction between the interests of state and civil society outlined earlier in this chapter. Even to note that this interaction produces different policy outcomes is to suggest that the debate over what futures welfare states have and which welfare state types normatively are to be preferred should be intense. The stability of each of the four cases we have identified above rests on different types of self-restraint or conceptions of public interest. State instituted welfare programs that aim to provide "not what majorities want but what minorities need" are viable only if the majority, which derives minimal benefits and pays most of the costs, agrees that the establishment of a "national minimum" is morally warranted. William Beveridge presented the key psychological condition:31 "In the war all of us with incomes above the average have lowered our standards of comfort. . . Is peace so different from war? For my part, I would gladly go on with a lowered standard in peace--if that were necessary--to ensure that no sick or injured or old person, and no child in Britain need to be in want or avoidable sickness. . . The appeal is to our sense of national unity and our feeling of Christian brotherhood." Evidence on the continuing force of this appeal among the British public is mixed.32 So is evidence on the actual effects of Mrs. Thatcher's social policies. But there can be no doubt that her government marks a major break with the political (state centered) consensus since the war that the national minimum should be retained because morally it was the proper thing to do.

The stability of state instituted welfare programs that aim to put the interests of the state first rests on the premise that public officials represent the "national will." Legitimacy in the Weberian sense is an essential prerequisite. And not surprisingly the search for legitimacy is a recurring feature of French political life. All French political leaders have bemoaned what they see as the grumbling and surliness of the population. None has managed to construct long-term working relations with relevant groups in civil society. And the problem may be getting worse. Under the Mitterrand regime, when privileges seem in the least endangered, groups (doctors, lawyers, teachers in Catholic schools) have not hesitated to take the streets or to denounce proposals as efforts to instigate another "Auschwitz." On the other side, when, for example, a compromise on educational reform is painstakingly negotiated, it is undermined by "secularists" within the Socialist Party itself. And labor organizations, the focus of government "affirmative action" policy, have shown more interest in competing among themselves for dwindling worker allegiance than in representing at the state level the general interests of the working class.33 The substitution of dialogue for command remains on elusive ground.

In situations where the primary policy thrust results from the penetration of the state by civil society, the key stabilizing condition is not a feeling of noblesse oblige among those better off or a feeling among the citizenry that state actions are "legitimate." The criterion is a feeling of reciprocity and self-restraint among beneficiaries. When policy is directed toward fulfilling the goals of social democracy, restraint must be manifested by members of social democratic organizations and voters for social democratic parties. It is this restraint that in this book John Logue argues is in danger of being lost. In the case where the penetration of the state is by corporate-business interests, the need for self-restraint is as great and as problematic. Fleix Rohatyn, New York investment banker, former Chairman of the Municipal Assistance Corporation for the City of New York, and a prominent figure in the search for "new ideas" to reanimate the Democratic Party, has posed the question starkly: "Will the middle class sacrifice to keep black mothers on welfare?"34 The 1984 Presidential election again has given the answer. Impetus for self-restraint is further dampened by the difficulties f[illegible]potential opposition groups in civ[illegible]cline in trade union power, a[illegible]e in the goods producing sec[illegible]he shift toward smaller ent[illegible]en more telling in the Unit[illegible]d be in Scandinavia because[illegible]tion of unions has been the [illegible]eeds of "the poor" have reach[illegible] agenda. Meanwhile, of course[illegible] groups for greater public la[illegible]ations have continued unabat[illegible]ny feeling of solidarity or even [illegible]nsibility among dominant groups could be the most important legacy of the Reagan era.

*****

From this discussion we can draw two types of conclusions regarding futures for the welfare state. One one level the policy responses of all welfare states have been and probably will continue to be roughly what they are now. All can be expected to search for financial savings at the margins: to defer cost of living adjustments; to raise contribution levels, and so on. These measures do not alter the basic structure of welfare provision. They do not even preclude continued efforts at consolidation. In Germany, for example, at the same time as qualifying conditions were being tightened in the unemployment insurance plan, the social insurance system itself was being expanded to include artists and free-lance writers, and pension benefits were expanded to include non-Germans residing abroad. (This last reform, to be sure, was made to conform to a decision of the Federal Constitutional Court.) The presence of right-wing governments seems to have little impact. Nor do zealous right-wing politicians aspiring to office appear likely to push through drastic changes. In France, the most important immediate case, "opposition leaders come to a halt at the frontiers of the welfare state . . . There would be no political or sociological majority for an opposition leader who dared to question the reduced working week and extended holidays brought in by the left. . ."[35] In this sense we can agree with Piven and Cloward that even more or less in the United States "the cyclical pattern of providing subsistence resources by the state has been replaced by a variety of permanent income-maintenance entitlements."[36] We also have noted that all welfare states are experiencing similar patterns of socio-economic change, in particular the shift from larger to smaller enterprises, which is likely to continue, and which reinforces Marcuse's previously cited proposition that the "working class" will be concerned above all with protecting its position in the economy. When we associate this socio-economic change with the political entrenchment of "income-maintenance entitlements", we can project for welfare states a continuation of the particular status quo in each country. Under right-wing governments benefits might be given in a meaner fashion, but still they would be provided.

I hope that this chapter also helps show how this bland, albeit rather distasteful, picture is incomplete. The "welfare state" represents more than the provision of a given level of services. In Ashford's terms it encapsulates democratic governance. As I develop the term in this chapter, the welfare state aims to overcome the adversarial relationship between state and civil society, channelling the interaction in ways that promote the best values of each. That one can speak also of different types of welfare states adds to the importance of value concerns. No type of welfare state has a claim to the future, but some types are to be preferred. As we have seen, there is no evidence that current international economic constraints are causing more difficulties for advanced welfare states than for states with less inclusive benefits or with lower rates of taxation. There is no reason to suppose that the policy pattern in social welfare states is less secure than it is in social security states. But this finding offers scant comfort to those who see Scandinavian welfare states as a "model" which must go forward lest the values they promote unravel. It is not the welfare state as a set of policies that is in danger, it is the welfare state as an ideal.

NOTES

1. This formulation is taken from an unpublished paper by Keith Fitzgerald, "Politics, Power, Interests, and the State" (1985).

2. Ann Orloff and Theda Skocpol, "Why Not Equal Protection? Explaining the Politics of Public Social Spending in Britain 1900-1911 and the United States, 1880s-1920," _American Sociological Review_ 49 (1984), p. 732.

3. As Stephen Valocchi concludes, to consider either economic interests or state structures in isolation "purges the historical record of the interactive quality that seems to be necessary in explanations of welfare policymaking." From "Welfare Policy and Stratification Outcomes: A Comparison of Three Social Democracies" (Unpublished Paper: 1985), p. 42.

4. Jens Alber, _Vom Armenhaus zum Wohlfahrstaat_ (Campus Verlag: 1982).

5. In "Reflections on Modern Western States and Civil Societies" (Unpublished Paper: 1985), Reinhard Bendix, John Bendix and I attempt to revolve some of the ambiguities in these definitions which must remain unexplored here.

6. Douglas Ashford, "Differentiating the Welfare State" (Paris: 1984), p. 53.

7. For a more complete discussion see Norman Furniss and Neil Mitchell, "Social Welfare Provisions in Western Europe." In Harrell Rodgers (ed) _Public Policy and Social Institutions_ (JAI Press: 1984). Beveridge's plan was of course but the culmination of decades of work and debate among the British higher civil service and political class in which Beveridge himself played a major role.

8. See David L. Miller, _Social Justice_ (Oxford: Clarendon Press, 1976) for a valuable discussion.

9. Quoted in Furniss and Mitchell, p. 31.

10. Francois Mitterrand, _The Wheat and the Chaff_ (New York: Seaver Books, 1982), p. 269.

11. Quoted in Furniss and Mitchell, p. 19. Again see this account for a further description.

12. The French "system" is so complex that there is even a dispute over how many plans in fact exist. These figures are from the Association des Ages, _Quel avenir pour les retraites?_ (Plon: 1981).

13. Neil Mitchell and I pursue this argument in "American 'Exceptionalism' in Comparative Perspective" (Washington, D.C.: 1985).

14. For a discussion of corporate social policies and ideology that concentrates on the period before the New Deal, See Neil Mitchell, "U.S. Corporate Self-Images and Social Policy" (Ph.D. Dissertation: Indiana University, 1983).

15. See Margaret Weir and Theda Skocpol, "Responses to the Great Depression in Sweden and the United States," International Journal of Contemporary Sociology XXIV, 1-2 (1983), pp. 4-29.

16. See The Crisis of Democracy: Report on the Governability of Democracies to the Trilateral Commission (New York University Press: 1978). Representative academic accounts are provided by Richard Rose and Guy Peters, Can Government Go Bankrupt? (Basic Books: 1978) and Aaron Wildavsky, How to Limit Government Spending (University of California Press: 1978).

17. Douglas C. Bennett and Kenneth E. Sharpe, "Is there a Democracy 'Overload'?" Dissent (Summer 1974), p. 326.

18. Figures from "Social Protection Statistics - ESSPROS-", Statistical Bulletin 1-1984 (Eurostat: March 30, 1984), table 1. These figures have been standardized in accordance with the European System of Integrated Social Protection Statistics.

19. For an overview see Brian Abel-Smith, "Economic Efficiency in Health Care Delivery," International Social Security Review (2/83), pp. 165-179. Abel-Smith points again to the amazing differences among health care delivery systems.

20. The quotation is from Samuel Brittan. From Bennett and Sharpe, "Is There a Democracy 'Overload'"?, p. 319.

21. For a good example see Jean-Jacques Rosa (ed). The World Crisis in Social Security. (San Francisco: Institute for Contemporary Studies:" 1982).

22. See Ramier Münz and Helmut Wintersberger, "The Austrian Welfare State," International Social Security Review 37(1984), pp. 297-314.

23. Commission for the European Communities, Document 5-284 (1984), p. 31.

24. Milton Friedman, "The Line We Dare Not Cross: The fragility of Freedom at 60%," Encounter (November 1976), pp. 8-14. We might take the occasion to note that statements that Friedman was an apologist for the Pinochet regime in Chile are not supported here. Friedman states that the "military junta. . .too is an authoritarian society which denies the liberties and freedoms of the people in the sense in which Anglo-Saxon democrats conceive of them," p. 9.

25. Paul Valéry, The Outlook for Intelligence (Harper: 1962), p. 72.

26. See Ashford, "Differentiating the Welfare State."

27. Alain Touraine, La Voix et le regard (Seuil: 1978), p. 48.

28. Herbert Marcuse, "Protosialisme et Capitalisme Avancée, Les Temps Modernes 394 (1979), pp. 1705-1730.

29. Olof Palme, "Social Justice and Individual Freedom" (The Jackson H. Ralston Lectures in International Law: Stanford University, 1977), p. 8.

30. See Theda Skocpol, "Political Responses to Capitalist Crises," Politics and Society 10(1981), p. 198.

31. William Beveridge, "Beveridge on Beveridge" (London: Social Security League, 1943), p. 16.

32. For a further discussion see Furniss and Mitchell, "American 'Exceptionalism' in Comparative Perspective." The volatility of public attitudes is shown in opinion surveys. In 1977 33% of the voters said that if people were poor their own lack of effort was the primary reason, 30% said "circumstances"; in March, 1985 21% said poverty was the fault of the poor, 49% said "circumstances." In the latter survey 73% of respondents agreed with the proposition that money and wealth should be more equally distributed. And the percentage of Britons wanting "government services extended even if it means some increases in taxes" has risen from 37 in May 1979 to 63 in February 1985.

33. See Martin Schain, "Trade Union Resistance to Radical Reform: The Limits of Corporatism" (Paper presented at the Council for European Studies Meetings, Washington D.C.: 1985).

34. Quoted in Richard Reeves, American Journey: Traveling with Tocqueville in Search of Democracy in America (Simon and Schuster: 1982), p. 72.

35. "L'état c'est eux," a special survey in The Economist (9-15 February 1985), pp. 4, 5.

36. Francis Fox Piven and Richard Cloward, The New Class War (Basic Books: 1981), p.xi.

Elizabeth Trousdell
Neil Mitchell
Stephen Valocchi

Bibliographical Essay

Organizing Principles and Issues in the Welfare State Literature

The purpose of this essay is to provide a general overview of welfare state literature indicating the types of problems and issues that occupy scholars in this field. In our first section we survey descriptions and comparisons of social welfare policy. We highlight studies of: single policies in single countries; cross-national comparisons within single policy areas; multiple policies in single countries; cross-national comparisons across multiple policy areas; the effects of social welfare policies; and finally, basic reference works.

In the second, larger section, we review several perspectives on what social welfare policies actually signify. We survey three major types of explanations of social welfare policy, attempt to identify the conceptions of the role of the state that we argue underlie each type of explanation, and finally, review perspectives about the recent "crisis" of the welfare state.

SOCIAL WELFARE POLICIES DESCRIBED AND COMPARED

We should begin with some words on this subtitle. First, the term "social policy" has escaped a generally acceptable definition. Of course the term "policy" itself is amorphous so we would not expect the adjective to delineate firm boundaries. In general the literature appears to be content to link the term to specific policies -- like pornography one knows social policy when one sees it -- rather than to reach common agreement on a coherent definition. Users of the term often refer to income maintenance policies of one sort or another, housing policies, and health care. Richard Titmuss argues that taxation systems should also be considered social policy, and a good case could be made for including other economic policies, possibly job assistance and training programs or government investment grants for depressed regions.[1] Second, to describe is seldom a non-analytical activity. That is, descriptions often presume a particular analytic approach, be it historical, interpretative, or quantitative. Thus what is considered important to describe varies. For some researchers, including Harold Wilensky, expenditures on social policies capture their essence.[2] Others, such as P.R. Kaim-Caudle, focus more on who is covered, who benefits, who pays, on the values that inform policy and the intentions that guide it.[3] Third, what is to be compared, and how, is contested: as many countries as possible, rich countries alone, perhaps market economies alone, or the experience of single countries over time. Again the conception of comparison is dependent on the analytic approach taken. The central issue is whether comparison is seen as a method of control with the goal of cross-national, cross-cultural generalization, or as a means of illustrating policy choice. So, description and comparison of social policy may range from one country/one policy studies to multi-country/multi-policy studies.

This effort to categorize what is described and what is compared is methodologically indifferent in the sense that the categories may include more than one identifiable methodological approach. We distinguish six categories of description and comparison. In the first category are studies of single policies in single countries. An historical perspective is common. Martha Derthick in her book _Policymaking for Social Security_,[4] describes the origin and institutionalization of the the U.S. social security program. She is particularly interested in the question why, in the past at least, there has been a lack of conflict over social security in the United States. She suggests that important factors contributing to policy consensus have been that social security policy making has been the preserve of a limited number of experts whose concerns have traditionally focused on program maintenance and enlargement rather than considering alternatives, and that the beneficiaries of social security have received far more than they have paid. The present debate over the program is healthy, according to Derthick. Within this first category there also is a tendency to select distinctive or singular policies, like the British National Health Service for example, and place them within the context of a distinctive national experience.[5] The studies in this category describe the fine detail of policy process and content and can provide some basis for inferential statements about the workings of national politics.

A number of studies have attempted cross-national comparisons within single policy areas. These comprise our second category. Arnold Heidenheimer, Hugh Heclo, and Carolyn Adams include in their book Comparative Public Policy,[6] separate studies of housing, education, health care, income maintenance, taxation, and transportation policies in various national settings. A problem underlying their discussion is why the United States lags behind many European countries in social policy development. Differences in political structures, ideology, and social conditions are influential, they argue. A second edition updates the material, provides discussion of policy areas and emphasizes the types of choices open to social policy makers. Bruce Headey in his book Housing Policy in the Developed Economy, has investigated housing policy in Sweden, Britain, and the United States.[7] He argues that these countries represent examples of distinctive approaches to policy making in this area and are illustrative of the policy choices available within market economies. He is interested in why particular choices are made and with what effect. Housing policy is also the subject of a book by Roger Duclaud-Williams, The Politics of Housing in Britain and France.[8] He contrasts the British and French experiences and is particularly concerned with whether there are inherent characteristics of the policy area which might affect the way policy evolves.

The third category comprises descriptions of welfare provision in terms of a range of social policies in a single country. Examples are numerous. Bentley Gilbert in The Evolution of National Insurance, looks at British social policy making in the early twentieth century.[9] He examines six policy areas (school meals, school medical inspection, health, pensions, unemployment insurance, labor exchanges) in his narrative of how Britain avoided socialism and maintained a market system. John F. Sleeman, in The Welfare State: Its Aims, Benefits and Costs, carries the story up to the period in which British welfare provision achieved its contemporary form.[10] Peter A. Kohler and Hans F. Zacher's edited volume, The Evolution of Social Insurance 1881-1981, provides accounts of the historical evolution of social policies in Germany, France, Great Britain, Austria, and Switzerland.[11] It is an interesting collection if only because it includes France, Austria, and Switzerland, whose social policy experiences are less familiar than those of Britain, the Federal Republic of Germany, or Sweden. While Western scholars of social policy have tended to favor Northern Europe over Southern Europe (not without some justification given that Sweden, Germany, and Britain were welfare policy pioneers)

Germany, and Britain were welfare policy pioneers) they have paid even less attention to the Eastern European or Soviet cases. These would be significant cases to consider in addressing, say, the links between modernization and social policy development, the importance of economic system or ideology or even the influence of past policies. Neil Mitchell's article "Ideology or the Iron Laws of Industrialization" is one attempt to deal with some of these issues.[12] More work in this area would be worthwhile. One interesting possibility would be to compare East and West Germany in the light of their common Bismarckian social policy beginnings.

There are two useful studies in English that fit our third category on Soviet social policies: Robert Osborn, _Soviet Social Policies: Welfare, Equality, and Community_; and Bernice Madison, _Social Welfare in the Soviet Union_.[13] Finally, within this category fall studies that analyze data on social policies over time in a single country. The purpose of these studies is more explicitly theoretical than historical/descriptive. Some of these studies, as for example "On the Economic and Political Determinants of Welfare Spending in the Post World War II Era", by Larry Griffin, Joel Devine and Michael Wallace are quantitative. Others, such as the early work by Francis Fox Piven and Richard A. Cloward are nonquantitative.[14]

Efforts to compare several policy areas cross-nationally, our fourth category, also display a variety of research objectives. A similar systems approach is often the basis for country selection. In an attempt to hold constant all dimensions except those of direct interest, the analysis may be restricted to Western Europe, to Scandinavia, or even more narrowly to North America.[15] An alternative strategy is to seek persistent regularities irrespective of particular national characteristics. Harold Wilensky in _The Welfare State and Equality: Structural and Ideological Roots of Public Expenditures_ compares expenditures on social welfare provision in 64 countries. He attempts to isolate significant factors in welfare spending patterns.[16] Given the interest in level of economic development, a cross-nationally common variable, a methodological goal of this type of study is to continue to expand the number of countries considered.[17] In contrast, Norman Furniss and Timothy Tilton in _The Case for the Welfare State_ compare just three countries; Sweden, Britain, and the United States. These countries are chosen as representative of the political possibilities open to advanced Western societies. Government intervention is assumed, the interesting question is its nature and intent.[18] P.R. Kaim-Caudle, in his study of ten West European and North

American countries provides information on the nature and content of social policies in each country. His discussion includes some analysis of the differences between countries in terms of social policies and a comparison of benefit standards.[19] Within this category fall works like Gaston Rimlinger's historical treatment of comparative social policy development. Rimlinger is interested in the types of political structures and ideas historically influential in social policy development.[20] And Hugh Heclo, focusing only on Britain and Sweden, compares the historical development of social welfare provision in these countries with the aim of evaluating the importance of democratic politics in that development. He concludes that "non-democratic" factors like the bureaucracies, the legacies of past policies, and individual reformers and bureaucrats are most significant.[21]

Our fifth category in this section comprises studies that focus on the effect of social policies. Since the 1950s there has been an interest in Britain in systematically examining the effect of social policies on social and economic inequalities. A study edited by Nick Bosanquet and Peter Townsend reviews the performance of the last two Labour Governments (1974-79) in terms of their success in redistributing income, wealth, rights and resources to the poorer sections of society.[22] In _Poverty and Social Security in Britain Since 1961_, Wilfred Beckerman and Stephen Clark examine the impact of British social policies on levels of poverty between 1961 and 1976.[23] A study of the Eastern European experience has provided some very instructive findings on the effect of social policies on inequality in non-market economies. Primarily using data on housing allocation, Ivan Szelenyi claims, for example, that state redistributive mechanisms "add to the privileges of already privileged."[24]

The last category in this section comprises basic reference works. The International Labour Organisation's _The Cost of Social Security_ is a valuable source of statistical information on social policies around the world. It covers a range of policies showing the way they are financed, total expenditures, the distribution of expenditures among the different policies, among other things.[25] Other useful sources of information include _Basic Statistics of the European Community_ and _Yearbook of Nordic Statistics_.[26] The U.S. Department of Health and Social Security's _Social Security Throughout the World_ provides information on the content of pension, sickness and maternity, work injury, unemployment and family allowance policies, with discussions about methods of finance, coverage, and benefit levels.[27] (See also for information on single policy areas the work by Brian Abel-Smith and Alan Maynard, and the President's Commission on Pension Policy.)28

THE MEANING OF SOCIAL WELFARE POLICIES: EXPLANATIONS, THEORIES OF THE STATE AND "CRISIS"

We identify three general approaches to explaining social welfare policies. The first has a major focus on socioeconomic variables. Indicators of large-scale processes connected with industrialization are of particular interest. In the second, the major focus is on the class-related consequences of capitalist industrialization. The third approach gives priority to political, ideological, and historical factors. With this approach policy is viewed more a matter of "design" than as an "output." The first task of this section is to elucidate these three general approaches and to discuss some of the major scholarly work within each.

Discernible in most attempts to explain the development of welfare states and social welfare policy are conceptions about the role of the state in industrial societies. These conceptions vary in both their degree of explicitness and their explanatory focus. We argue that for each of the three explanatory approaches a corresponding theory of the state can be identified. The first group, which focuses on large-scale socioeconomic factors, does not usually explicitly consider the state. These writers sometimes seem to view the state as acting much like the classical "invisible hand," without making any perceptible impact of its own on the policy outcomes. The second group views the capitalist state as working to advance the objectives of specific economic interests. Finally, the third group sees a state as a possible counterweight to private economic power.

The second task of this section thus will be to clarify the various conceptions of the state, a task which we argue is important to an understanding of what is emphasized or ignored in the different explanations of social welfare policy. How causal factors are chosen and measured, _what_ is considered social welfare policy, and, finally, which dimensions of this policy are deemed most important, flow from some notion of the role of the state in industrial societies.[29]

Much of the recent work on social welfare policy in Europe and American converges around the topic of the current "crisis" of the welfare state. The evidence of such a crisis in the United States and Great Britain has been straightforward. Since 1981, twenty percent of U.S. income maintenance programs have been eliminated. Similarly, in Great Britain, social welfare programs have come under severe attack. In other West European nations, signs and symptoms of welfare backlash and fiscal crisis have been seen; however a full-fledged attack on the welfare state has not occurred. Many writers on the welfare state, such as Albert Hirschman and Maurice Rustant, have concentrated their energies on explaining the causes and consequences of this welfare state crisis.[30] Perhaps even more importantly, this current crisis has led some authors to question the very purpose and meaning of the welfare state in terms of its own stated goals, and in terms of the capacities and inherent limits of state structures to realize these values.[31]

Our third task in this section will be to review the various conceptions of crisis. We hope to show that this task is inseparable from our task of making explicit the theories of the welfare state embedded in most descriptions and causal accounts. The tasks are inseparable because in the welfare state literature there is often an implied conception as to the proper functioning of the state according to certain criteria (say, acceptance of welfare programs, efficiency of programs or the 'health' of the economy). Understandings of crisis derive from an identification and analysis of crisis symptoms (e.g., backlash, fiscal crisis, inefficient service delivery, and inflation) in light of a theoretical conception of the role of the modern state in industrial societies.

SOCIAL WELFARE POLICIES EXPLAINED: PROCESSES OF INDUSTRIALIZATION

The first approach to explaining social welfare policies emphasizes the role of demographic and economic characteristics of a society in the development and maintenance of social welfare services. This approach tends to downplay the importance of ideology, insurgency or power balances, and politics in general. The basic idea is that with industrialization and related demographic shifts, there are new needs which are seen as being best met through public intervention. Harold L. Wilensky, in *The Welfare State and Equality* argues that the root cause of welfare state development is economic level of development, and that the effects of economic development level are manifested in demographic changes and the momentum of the social welfare programs once established.[32] The pivotal importance of socioeconomic factors has also been emphasized by Phillips Cutright, Robert Jackman and Frederick Pryor.[33]

With this type of explanation there is a focus on intervention into the society *per se*, and less discussion of the consequences of policies on individual lives. Policy tends to be defined in terms of expenditures, which are relatively easy to compare. The issue of the precise mechanism which causes the positive correlations between certain economic, demographic or bureaucratic characteristics and welfare expenditures is less salient. There is a focus on processes which can be identified cross-nationally, a stress on the convergence of situations in industrialized countries, and attempts to isolate specific indicators (mainly aggregate expenditures on welfare services) and compare them across a large number of countries.

There is a recognition that divergences do exist, but again, the major interest is in understanding the shared characteristics of nations. Wilensky, for example, argues that divergences among the richest countries can be explained with reference to factors such as: the degree of centralization of government; the shape of the stratification order and related mobility rates; the organization of the working class; and the position of the military.[34] Cutright argues that when economic development is controlled for, characteristics of political structures such as the representativeness of a government, are important.[35]

Authors within this approach view welfare policy as the political outcome of some demographic or economic process. These authors see welfare policy as meeting societal needs that are generated by the process of industrialization. Precisely _how_ these needs are registered within the state is not explicitly dealt with in this approach. We assert, however, that insofar as a theory of the state can be discerned within these works, it is pluralist in nature.

A pluralist model ascribes to the state the basic characteristic of openness. The state is seen as a legal-administrative shell where a plurality of interest groups vie for political advantage; the state does not inherently ally itself with any particular interest but seeks to adjudicate in every policy instance among a shifting coalition of interest groups. The state effects policy outcomes, not due to internal processes of party, or structural biases of ensuring business confidence, but because it is, as Larry Isaac and William Kelley argue, the "near perfect reflection of aggregated individual preferences as expressed through interest representation in the polity."[36] The pluralist state thus promotes the general interest as it responds automatically to societal needs and dislocations.[37]

According to this view, industrialization brings population growth and urbanization, a finely graded division of labor, and a stratification system where movement is based on achievement, and economic rewards are distributed on a more equal basis. These developments cause new and varied interests among citizens: occupational, social, familial and political interests. The state coordinates these interests through the democratization and bureaucratization of government institutions. Industrialization, however, is not without its dysfunctions: frictional and cyclical unemployment, industrial accidents, public health problems, and an aging population with no family base of support. These problems are resolved in the state through the creation of centralized structures of welfare policy. Social welfare policy thus manages the tensions of an essentially homeostatic system: it brings into balance societal needs with societal resources.[38]

A minimalist view of the state in this pluralist tradition emphasizes the advantages of the free market in maintaining societal well-being, and, alternatively, views government intervention as an unwarranted intrusion on individual freedom. Milton Friedman in Capitalism and Freedom, for example, specifies the proper role of government as preserving law and order, enforcing private contracts, and fostering competitive markets. In this view, then, all those policies typically associated with the welfare state are economically inefficient intrusions on individual freedom and curtail individual initiative and entrepreneurial spirit, which, it is argued, are crucial for economic growth and prosperity.[39]

A maximalist view of the state within the pluralist tradition recognizes the limited competence of markets. Two proponents of this type of view are John Galbraith and Charles Lindblom.[40] The market, in this view, fails to take unaccounted costs of production into consideration (e.g., costs of water and air pollution). Further, its oligopolistic modern form distorts the equilibrium levels of prices, wages and output. Lastly, the market provides no solution for the provision of public goods. In light of this limited competence, organized actors exercise compensatory power to direct and complement market forces. One manifestation of this compensatory power is social welfare policy.

Just as neo-classical economic theory recognizes problems in achieving and maintaining equilibrium levels of supply and demand (embodied in concepts of stickiness and differing elasticities of demand), so too does this model of political processes recognize what we refer to as the "asymptotic" nature of this pluralist polity; the notion that the state can absorb only a limited number of competing interest groups. It is in this "asymptotic" nature that the normative component of this theory locks horns with empirical reality in a phenomenon called political overload.

When these authors analyze "the crisis of the welfare state" we get a better idea of the nature of the state that remains implicit in their analyses of the "normal" workings of the welfare state. It seems that the state is not always invisible, unproblematically responding to societal needs. The state can indeed make a difference, albeit a negative one. It can, via policy, generate economic problems (e.g., inflation, economic inefficiency) and social problems (welfare backlash, tax revolts). The state, it is argued, causes these problems when it encroaches on the functions of the private marketplace.

Michel Crozier et al., and Samuel Brittan, while acknowledging the basic validity of a pluralist model, emphasize in their analyses of U.S. and West European democracies this "asymptotic" nature.[41] When a wide range of social groups becomes organized and active, the relationship between government and interest groups becomes taut and strained. Colin Crouch states the basic thesis of overloaded government in this way: "That liberal democratic governments have become overloaded by excessive demands from their citizenry."[42]

Two broad interrelated themes lie at the heart of the political overload argument. First, it is the imperative of industrialization and its concomitant social and cultural developments which have raised expectations of the citizenry and have, at the same time, made it possible for a great many more groups to coalesce. Second, the ability of democracies to maintain and develop proper regulations in the face of these developments has broken down. This is due to the nature of political competition. An excessive burden is placed on the 'sharing out' function of government,[43] and the political voter operates in the political arena without a budget constraint. The problem, then, is both systemic and political; systemic in the sense that the nature of growth in industrial societies generates increased needs for improvements in private consumption and public services, political in the sense that the nature of political competition inflates these needs in excess of their equilibrium level.

The difficulties that social democratic and labor parties have faced in some countries have been taken by these theorists as representing one of the consequences of overloaded governments. Emmett Tyrell, for example, cites the state expansionist ideology of social democracy as responsible for capitalist decline in Great Britain. The solutions for what Tyrell regards as manifestations of overloaded government -- unceasing welfare demands, inefficient health care delivery, spiralling inflation coupled with increasing levels of unemployment -- lie primarily with the state's ability to balance the budget, to insulate monetary policy from political pressure, and to impose regulations on powerful interest groups exerting disproportionate influence on a basically pluralist state.[44]

SOCIAL WELFARE POLICIES EXPLAINED II: GROUP AND CLASS CONFLICT

A second major grouping of works explains the onset and continuation of social welfare policies essentially as a function of the need to insure the development or survival of capitalism and as an outcome of social conflict. For these writers, industrialization has not been a class-neutral phenomenon but a process that adversely affects the working class.

Ralph Miliband, in *The State in Capitalist Society: An Analysis of the Western System of Power*, makes the argument that capitalist interests determine the parameters and strongly influence the characteristics of public interventions. Capital's interests are disproportionately represented both inside and outside government. The interests of capital are well served from inside government, in part because the leaders in government do not challenge the basic validity of capitalist prerogatives, either because they believe in the virtues of capitalism or because they accept it as superior to any other social and economic system.[45] Public intervention can be understood as simply a pro-capital activity or as necessary 'ransom' to protect the long-term interests of capital. These interests are well served from outside of government because of capitalists' ability to launch strong effective pressure in support of their favored measures.

Nicos Poulantzas, in *Political Power and Social Classes,* argues that state intervention will of necessity act so as to create, maintain and improve the conditions for capitalist economic activity. Social welfare concessions may be made but they function to keep the working class in a peaceful mood and subordinate condition.[46] Edward Greenberg makes a similar argument in his book *Serving the Few: Corporate Capitalism and the Bias of Government Policy*. He argues that government in capitalist society is not a neutral institution, but an instrument of the corporate capitalists. The government helps to create or maintain an environment in which capital can grow and capitalists can reap profits. With structural changes in the economy and the emergence of the large corporation, requirements of stability, predictability, order and rationality become crucial to the well-being of capital. Social welfare services, in this view, are seen as attempts to keep aggregate demand equal to productive capacity; to assist the profit picture of large corporations; and to buy off lower-class discontent and threats to property.47

James O'Connor, Alan Wolfe, and Francis Fox Piven and Richard A. Cloward argue that social welfare provisions are to be understood as an attempt to buy off the discontented masses while maintaining a supportive environment for capital. In *The Fiscal Crisis of the State*, James O'Connor argues that the expansion of the monopoly sector in advanced industrial capitalism generates a number of problems which require state intervention. State intervention in effect helps to reduce the onerous impact of the problems. If the working class had to directly absorb the costs, the legitimacy of government would be undermined. Thus, social welfare provisions can be understood as a security measure to deal with problems generated by economic conditions.48

Alan Wolfe makes a similar argument. Government is seen as trying to tread carefully so as to help sustain an environment conducive to capitalists' success and to sooth the working class to the extent that the particular political parties can hope to retain their offices.49 Frances Fox Piven and Richard A. Cloward in *Regulating the Poor: The Functions of Public Welfare*, argue that relief measures can be best understood as a governmental measure to stem the tide of civil disorder and to manipulate the behavior of the workforce. When civil disorder occurs on a large-scale, expansive relief measures are made available, and as civil stability is restored, there is a general contraction of relief measures. The attempts to 'buy off' can backfire, as Piven and Cloward suggest in their most recent work, *The New Class War: Reagan's Attack on the Welfare State and Its Consequences*. People's economic security may be increased enough by government social welfare programs so that they are not so easily intimidated by the prospect of being laid off, and are not so eager to grab the first unpleasant job that is offered them. The people also may be able to defend the programs once they have been started.50

Within this second approach there has been some movement away from instrumental and functionalist explanations of social welfare policy patterns. In these newer versions, welfare policy may indeed represent political victories for the working class. But, the structural dependence of the state on business confidence transforms any radical political demands into, at worst, cooptive policy designed to quell discontent or, at best, reformist policy designed to improve the absolute (but not the relative) position of the working class. Fred Block in his article "The Ruling Class Does Not Rule: Notes on the Marxist Theories of the State," makes such an argument. How generous welfare policy is toward the working class depends on the historically and nationally variant strengths of capital, labor and the state. Walter Korpi in his recent book The Democratic Class Struggle, also emphasises the importance of the distribution of power resources to working class gains.[51]

Similar to the works which explain social welfare policies as somehow functional to the continued 'health' of capitalism are works which argue from a slightly different angle that one should not expect public provisions which challenge the distributional principles of a capitalist economy to make much headway in a capitalist economy. John Westergaard in "Social Policy and Class Inequality: Some Notes on Welfare State Limits," sketches out five conceptions of equality, notes that three of them, general minimum, equality of opportunity, and individually graduated 'risk reduction', can be quite easily accommodated within a capitalist economy. The final two conceptions, selective equality of conditions, and diffuse redistribution, face a far more difficult task and rarely would gain real legitimacy within a capitalist society.[52]

While the first approach begs the question of a theory of the state, the second is clearly based on a marxist (or neo-marxist) theory of the state. Marxists devote their analytic energies to describing how the modern state actually operates in a class-based capitalist society. In this sense, it is predominately an empirical theory of society. Normative considerations of how the state "ought" to act or the proper functioning of the state are irrelevant in the sense that there can be no proper functioning of a capitalist state which must, by definition, participate to some degree in the reproduction of a class-based economic order. The ideal normative order upon which Marxists implicitly base their empirical analyses is socialism. What this order would look like is many times left unstated or is expressed in broad values the meaning of which may vary greatly among authors.[53]

The welfare state in the marxist literature is seen as a highly contradictory form of modern capitalism because it introduces "non-economic" elements into the labor and goods markets. By introducing these presumably democratic components, it throws into sharp relief the mutual dependence and yet mutual incompatibility of a structure premised on democracy and a structure premised on private property. Samuel Bowles and Herbert Gintis in "The Crisis of Liberal Democratic Capitalism: The Case of the United States" and James O'Connor in *The Fiscal Crisis of the State* make this type of argument.[54] This literature characterizes the current crisis of the welfare state as rooted in the structural contradictions of the democratic state in capitalist society, that is, the assumption by the state of the investment, consumption and expense-related functions of capital accumulation, while the fruits of that accumulation continue to be privately appropriated. We specify below the exact nature of these contradictions.

The modern democratic state, according to marxist theory, must perform two contradictory functions in a capitalist society; it must assure favorable conditions of capital accumulation; yet, at the same time, must maintain the social peace, disturbed at several critical junctures because of the class-based nature of the accumulation process. This first function derives from the realization that state managers' continued power is dependent on a reasonable level of economic activity in order to provide an economic basis for social stability, and in order to finance the state apparatus through taxation and borrowing.[55] Capital, therefore, because of its privileged position in the economic order, has an implicit veto power over state policies. Capital's failure to invest at adequate levels or to employ sufficient numbers of workers can create major economic problems (e.g., slowed growth, unemployment, balance of payments deficit) as well as political problems (e.g., fiscal crisis, and/or loss of popular legitimacy). So there is a policy bias in favor of capital because the state must use its power to facilitate investment, investment which means profit, employment (possibly) and economic growth. The dynamics of ensuring this business confidence is a major constraint on state policy.

The second function of the capitalist state derives from the class-based nature of the accumulation process. Because of this, it is in workers' interests to support movements that decrease their subordination to capitalists. Thus, in its struggles to protect itself from the adverse consequences of the market economy, the working class has "entered" the state apparatus and has played a role in the regulation of the economy and in the provision of services.[56] The state, of course, cannot ignore these demands yet the state's responsiveness must not damage business confidence. The state remains responsive to labor because of the structural relationship between a democratic state and a capitalist economy; the size of the working class (broadly speaking in terms of wage-earners) gives it importance in electoral politics. Particular state managers must court the working class to support their continuation in office. In addition, the long-term viability of the economic order is premised on a healthy, well-trained workforce with the ability to consume the goods that it produces, a condition which has become the state's responsibility to ensure. However, the state's financial ability to respond to popular demands is dependent on conditions of economic progress, progress defined and directed by private capital. Thus, the structure of state policies in response to popular demands cannot damage business confidence for any appreciable length of time without serious economic and political repercussions.

Implicit in this double-edged situation lies the basis of welfare crisis. The welfare state in capitalist societies does not wholly represent cooptation of working class movements, nor does it provide a complete rationalization or legitimization of capitalism. It is, however, a structure which embodies an insurmountable contradiction for democratic capitalist societies -- that democratic pressures favor increased state spending and a revenue structure which is unproductive or only indirectly productive according to the needs of capital accumulation. This increased public spending acts as a fiscal drain on capital resources. Welfare spending, specifically, serves to lessen the disciplinary effect of the competitive labor market.

Using a variety of economic and social indicators from post World War II U.S. and West European countries, Thomas Weisskopf in "Marxian Crisis Theory and the Rate of Profit in the Postwar U.S. Economy," and Samuel Bowles and Herbert Gintis in their work on the "The Crisis of Liberal Democratic Capitalism" cite the development of the welfare state as a crucial impediment to continued accumulation and thus a component of the current economic crisis.[57] The modern welfare state, for these writers, is one of the by-products of a postwar capital-labor accord, where most working classes relinquished their claims for control over production, investment and international economic policy in return for relatively high levels of employment, the institutionalization of union-management bargaining structures, and a secure claim over distributional gains.

The rapid growth rates and benefit coverage extensions of most postwar welfare states resulted in what Bowles and Gintis refer to as the expansion of the citizen wage (i.e., that part of the person's consumption supplied by the state). This expansion has consequently led, according to Thomas Weisskopf, to a redistribution of the social product away from capital and a lessening of the disciplinary impact of low-wage employment.[58] William D. Nordhaus, in "The Falling Share of Profits," argues that profits, and thus investment, started to shrink beginning in the mid-sixties in the United States and later in Western Europe.[59] Additionally, the remaining productive investment was subject to a variety of state and union regulations over hiring and firing, over the quality of goods, and over the environmental impact of the production process and the finished goods. The current attack on the welfare state is seen as an attempt to restore the conditions of capitalist profitability by returning the reproduction costs of labor to the private sector. With fewer and more stringent benefits, many unemployed people would no longer be free not to choose the most undesirable jobs. They would enter the labor market, thus exerting a downward pressure on wages which "ripples up" to the unionized employment sector. This effect would remove one fetter on capitalist profitability.

SOCIAL WELFARE POLICIES EXPLAINED: PARTY, IDEOLOGY, AND STATE DEVELOPMENT

The final major grouping of works shares the assumption that while socio-economic variables may be a necessary condition, there is ample room for the influence of political actors and ideals when social welfare policies are explained. Variables which are suggested as important include: patterns of state development, political parties, ideology, and actual or perceived power balances or imbalances. Charles W. Anderson provides a methodological underpinning for this perspective when he argues that to understand policy, one needs to investigate the actors' beliefs, values and understandings of political institutions and political processes.[60]

Writers who support this type of explanation tend to use a broad definition of welfare. They do not focus primarily on aggregate expenditures but concentrate, for example, on consideration of efforts to encourage full employment, regulation of private industry, quality of services, or reduction of oppression. What is important is less the level of spending than the question of who pays and who benefits from the expenditures. In contrast to an emphasis on convergence, this type of explanation tends to focus on divergences with an explicit purpose being to explain the differences that occur. Because of this focus on differences, researchers within this tradition generally need or choose to restrict their studies to a small number of countries. The focus is less on intervention *per se*, but on the reason for particular interventions at particular points in time, and on the qualitative characteristics of the interventions which occur.

Within works of this tradition there is often an emphasis on human decision and political choice. Rarely do writers argue that one variable can explain social welfare services, but different authors have focused on one variable more than another.[61]

Several writers have emphasized the importance of political variables such as the strength of Left parties. Gerhard Lenski in Power and Privilege: A Theory of Social Stratification investigates the pivotal importance of the strength of working class political organizations.[62] Similarly, Seymour Martin Lipset and Christopher Hewitt focus on the positive effect that socialist parties have had on the reduction of income inequalities.[63] In his work, The Social Democratic Image of Society: A Study of the Achievements and Origins of Scandinavian Social Democracy in Comparative Perspective, Frances G. Castles focuses on factors which account for the strength and success of Left parties. Castles asserts that there are two determinants of a democratic socialists party's potential for achieving reform: the size of its electoral support and its relative dominance within the party system of the country. These two determinants, in turn, are influenced by: the presence or absence of significant divisions within the working class; the ability of the social democratic party to make a cross-class appeal; and the strength and unity of the non-socialists. Finally, Castles argues that factors such as the strength of ties between organized labor and the social democratic party, the lateness and quickness of industrialization and the alliance of farmers with the social democratic party are important in explaining the success of Left parties.[64]

Somewhat similar to a focus on political parties is the emphasis on intentions or ideals. In The Case for the Welfare State: From Social Security to Social Equality, Norman Furniss and Timothy Tilton argue that different types of welfare states can be identified and that the types can be best differentiated on the basis of the aims of the governmental intervention in the economy.[65] The importance of ideological priorities as they relate to the objective strength of particular social democratic parties is emphasized by M. Donald Hancock who, in "Productivity, Welfare, and Participation in Sweden and West Germany," asserts that specific reform prospects differ in Sweden and West Germany due to contrasting ideological priorities and patterns of behavior on the part of Swedish and West German party leaders.[66] Similarly, Stephan Leibfried in "Public Assistance in the United States and the

Federal Republic of Germany" focuses on the correspondence between the theory and practice of social democracy.[67] Finally, the importance of ideas and ideals has been asserted by some writers.[68]

This third body of literature views the state as a key actor, not passively responding to demands, but actively intervening in civil society. For many of these authors such intervention can take place in accordance with certain ideological principles. These principles include equality, liberty, democracy, security, economic efficiency and solidarity. Social welfare policy is one specific policy commitment designed to realize these values. This view of welfare presumes that certain needs are so basic to all citizens that they should be provided as public services.[69] Much of the work within this view of the state is held together by a common critique of the distributional outcomes of the market and belief that the state must intervene on behalf of the citizenry to protect them from these market vagaries.[70] The welfare state is seen not as a mechanism which facilitates market forces but as a mechanism which interferes with market forces and effects some sort of redistribution of resources to those most adversely affected by unregulated markets (e.g., business cycles) and unregulated property (e.g., pollution).

Political ideology and internal policy-making structures are crucial in this view of the state because it is the ideological character of government which directs the goals of economic and social management. This state conception sees intervention not as a conservative force which institutionalizes class and interest group conflict nor as a mechanism which complements and directs the private market. The state can be a radicalizing force which mobilizes counter-elite support via policy, and subsequently subjects capitalist economies to a measure of democratic control. Andrew Martin in "Is the Democratic Control of Capitalist Economies Possible?" works with such arguments.[71] The continued successful mobilization of counter-elite support through the electoral process is crucial in fulfilling this ideological program. State outcomes basically reflect the distribution of power in civil society as refracted in state structures via the electoral process. Consequently, most analyses of the various dimensions of welfare state development emphasize the importance of the institutionalized agents of counter-elite strength, most notably, trade unions and labor or social democratic parties.

Recently, the viability of social policy based on social democratic values has come under attack by several authors. The sparks igniting the literature lie in the recent evidence of working class discontent with high taxes and public expenditures, unacceptably high and spiralling inflation rates, stagnating real wages, increased trade union militancy, increased support for anti-welfare state political movements, and signs of decreasing working class support for several social democratic and labor parties. According to this view of the state, these signs are not taken as evidence for political overload (as argued by pluralists) nor as evidence of the contradictory nature of the democratic state in capitalist society (as argued by Marxists). They are, rather, as Andrew Martin argues, evidence of the limits of the present stage of a social democratic policy logic.[72] In an environment of a strong trade union movement with ties to a social democratic or labor party, the present crisis of the welfare state is seen as the temporary inability of political leaders to effectively "deliver the goods."[73]

Andrew Martin, in "The Dynamics of Change in a Keynesian Political Economy: The Swedish Case and Its Implications," discusses the problems of Swedish social democracy. He argues that the so-called decline of Keynesianism (of which the crisis of the welfare state is a significant part) is not due to its inherent inability to offer any effective policy options. Instead, its decline is due to the absence of appropriate political conditions. In the Swedish case, this logic involved a transition from aggregate demand management to repressed inflation policy to income redistribution, each step involving a greater encroachment on the control functions of private capital.[74] The welfare crisis, according to this view, is a manifestation of the inability to successfully engineer the third stage of this policy logic -- public control over the amount, composition and pace of investment. The major factors which constrain the smooth flow of this logic are the degree of party-union strength and capital opposition.

That there are variable interpretations of what the welfare state crisis means, illustrates that a sensitivity to theories of the state is crucial in the identification of crisis symptoms, the causes of that crisis, and its individual- and structural-level consequences. We see this sensitivity as a necessary intellectual task. This task, however, takes on a practical importance when viewed in terms of future welfare policy prescriptions. For policy is not only described and explained in terms of different theoretical orientations, it is also changed according to those underlying theoretical conceptions.

CONCLUDING REMARKS

In this paper we have attempted to organize a significant amount of literature on welfare policy according to various descriptive and explanatory categories. Our review has been selective. It has been guided by our perceptions of major current themes in the welfare state literature. We have identified and illustrated how welfare policy has been described and explained, the theories of the state embedded in most explanations and, lastly, how the idea of welfare state crisis can be viewed from those welfare state theories.

As mentioned earlier, the term social welfare policy has escaped a generally acceptable definition. The variation derives, for the most part, from differences over why welfare policy is theoretically interesting. The three basic categories of explanation that we have presented need not be seen as antagonistic. Rather, we think that they are complementary. In the first category (the work epitomized by Wilensky), there is a major focus on structural factors that are not amenable to influence through policy (i.e., the aging of the population and the level of economic development). Within this category of works there is less interest in divergencies between patterns of social policy and less interest in the content of policy. This type of perspective answers questions about general patterns of development and raises questions about national variations on that development and the consequent policy-makers' options.

The second category narrows the focus to capitalist countries and explains social policy in terms of tensions endemic to capitalist society. It does little to explain, however, why different capitalist states produce different responses to working class pressures. The third category focuses on exploring these differences. It raises questions about the "autonomy of the state" and explores connections among party, ideology and policy. While the conceptions of the state underlying these categories appear antagonistic, they are, rather, a reflection of the varying influence of the state according to the level of precision used to define the dependent variable. As we move from the level of general patterns of development, through the level of capitalist society, to the level of the individual country, so the influence of the state increases.

With all of these different types of explanations and research interests it should not be surprising, then, that welfare policy "means" many things to many people. Nor should the apparent "disarray" be disheartening for welfare state researchers.

NOTES

1. Richard M. Titmuss, *Social Policy*, (London: George Allen and Unwin, 1977).

2. Harold L. Wilensky, *The Welfare State and Equality: Structural and Ideological Roots of Public Expenditures*, (Berkeley: University of California Press, 1975).

3. P. R. Kaim-Caudle, *Comparative Social Policy and Social Security*, (London: Martin Robertson and Company, 1973).

4. Martha Derthick, *Policy Making for Social Security*, (Washington, D.C.: The Brookings Institute, 1979).

5. Noteworthy examples of such a focus include: James B. Christoph, "The Advent of the National Health Service," in James B. Christoph and Bernard E. Brown, eds., *Cases in Comparative Politics*, (Boston: Little, Brown, and Company, 1976, pp. 35-74); Richard M. Titmuss, *Essays on the Welfare State*, (Boston: Beacon Press, 1958); and Brian Watson, *The National Health Service: The First Phase, 1948-1974, and After*, (London: George Allen & Unwin, 1978).

6. Arnold Heidenheimer, Hugh Heclo, and Jane Adams, *Comparative Public Policy: The Politics of Social Choice in Europe and America*, (New York: St. Martin's Press, 1975); see also the second edition, St. Martin's Press, New York, 1983.

7. Bruce Headey, *Housing Policy in the Developed Economy: The United Kingdom, Sweden and the United States*, (New York: St. Martin's Press, 1978).

8.Roger Duclaud-Williams, *The Politics of Housing in Britain and France*, (London: Heineman, 1978).

9. Bentley Gilbert, *The Evolution of National Insurance in Great Britain*, (London: Michael Joseph Ltd., 1966).

10. J. F. Sleeman, *The Welfare State: Its Aims, Benefits and Costs*, (London: George Allen & Unwin, 1973).

11. Peter A. Kohler and Hans F. Zacher, *The Evolution of Social Insurance 1881-1981*, (New York: St. Martin's Press, 1982). Within this tradition there are many fine works including: Jean Jacques Dupeyroux, *Securite Sociale*, (Paris: Dalloz, 1965); Maurice Rustant, *La Securite Sociale en Crise*, (Lyon: Chronique Sociale, 1980); Kurt Samuelson, *From Great Power to Welfare State: 300 Years of Swedish Social Development*, (London: Allen & Unwin, 1968); Herbert Tingsten, *The Swedish Social Democrats: Their Ideological Development*, tr., Greta Frankel and Patricia Howard-Rosen, (Totowa, N.J.: Bedminister Press, 1973); and Kathleen Woodroffe, "The Making of the Welfare State in England: A Summary of its

Origins and Development," Journal of Social History (Summer), pp. 303-323, (1968).

12. Neil J. Mitchell, "Ideology or the Iron Laws of Industrialization: The Case of Pension Policy in Britain and the Soviet Union," Comparative Politics, 15, No. 2, pp. 177-201, (1983).

13. Bernice Q. Madison, Social Welfare in the Soviet Union, (Stanford: Stanford University Press, 1968); and Robert Osborn, Soviet Social Policies: Welfare, Equality, and Community, (Homewood, Ill: Dorsey Press, 1970).

14. Larry Griffin, Joel Devine and Michael Wallace, "On the Economic and Political Determinants of Welfare Spending in the Post World War II Era," Politics and Society, 12, pp. 331-372, (1983); Francis Fox Piven and Richard A. Cloward, Regulating the Poor: The Functions of Public Welfare, (New York: Vintage, 1971).

15. There are many examples of such a perspective. Some of the finest include the articles in Peter Flora and Arnold J. Heidenheimer, eds. The Development of Welfare States in Europe and America, (New Brunswick N.J.: Transaction Books, 1981).

16. Wilensky, op. cit.

17. This objective derives from the theoretical and methodological concern with explaining persistent regularities in as many units as possible. In cross national comparative studies utilizing statistical methods, the causal concern is on concomitant variation between attributes within discrete systems in an effort to discover permanent causes that hold across all members of the population of units. Logically then, the bias in this method is toward many comparisons in order to control for any extraneous or accidental variation (e.g. cultural diffusion). For a discussion of the relative merits of statistical and historical comparison see Charles Ragin and David Zaret, "Theory and Method in Comparative Research: Two Strategies," Social Forces, 61, pp. 731-754, (1983).

18. Norman Furniss and Timothy Tilton, The Case for the Welfare State: From Social Security to Social Equality, (Bloomington: Indiana University Press, 1977). Bruce Headey's work has similar objectives though restricted to one policy area: Headey, op. cit.

19. P. R. Kaim-Caudle, op. cit.

20. Gaston Rimlinger, Welfare Policy and Industrialization in Europe, America, and Russia, (New York: John Wiley, 1971); see also Asa Briggs, "The Welfare State in Historical Perspective," Archives Européennes de Sociologie, 2, pp. 221-258, (1961).

21. Hugh Heclo, Modern Social Politics in Britain and Sweden, (New Haven: Yale University Press, 1974).

22. Nick Bosanquet and Peter Townsend eds., Labour and Equality: A Fabian Study of Labour in Power, 1974-1979, (London: Heineman, 1980).

23. Wilfred Beckerman and Stephen Clark, Poverty and Social Security in Britain Since 1961, (Oxford: Oxford University Press, 1982). Other studies in this area include those of B. Guy Peters, "Economic and Political Effects on the Development of Social Expenditures in France, Sweden and the United Kingdom," Midwest Journal of Political Science, 16, pp. 225-238, (1972); and Peter Townsend, Poverty in the United Kingdom, (Harmondsworth, Middlesex: Penguin Books Ltd., 1979).

24. Ivan Szelenyi, "Social Inequalities in State Socialist Redistributive Economies: Dilemmas for Social Policy in Contemporary Socialist Societies of Eastern Europe," International Journal of Comparative Sociology, 19, pp. 63-87, (1978); see also Alastair McAuley, Economic Welfare in the Soviet Union, (Madison: University of Wisconsin Press, 1979).

25. International Labour Organization, The Cost of Social Security, (Geneva: ILO, 1981).

26. Basic Statistics of the European Community, (European Community's Statistical Office, 1981); and Yearbook of Nordic Statistics, (Stockholm: Nordic Statistical Secretariat, Norstedts Tryckeri, 1985).

27. U. S. Department of Health, Education, and Welfare, Social Security Throughout the World, (Washington D.C.: U.S. Government Printing Office, 1980).

28. Brian Abel-Smith and Alan Maynard, The Organization, Financing, and Cost of Health Care in the European Community, (Brussels: Commission of the European Communities, 1979); and The President's Commission on Pension Policy: An International Comparison of Pension Systems, (Washington D.C.: U.S. Government Printing Office, 1980).

29. Some of these concerns are treated in Norman Furniss and Neil Mitchell, "Social Welfare Provisions in Western Europe: Current Status and Future Possibilities," in Harrell Rodgers (ed), Public Policy and Social Institutions, (Greenwich Conn: JAI Press, 1984, pp. 15-54).

30. Albert O. Hirschman, "The Welfare State in Trouble," Dissent, (Winter), pp. 87-90, (1981); Rustant, op. cit.; see also, as further examples, R. Emmett Tyrell, Jr., The Future That Does Not Work: Social Democracy's Failures in Britain, (Garden City, New Jersey: Doubleday, 1977); and Harold L. Wilensky, The 'New Corporatism', Centralization and

the Welfare State, (London: Sage Publications, 1976).

31. One example of this can be found in Norman Furniss, "Possible Futures and the New Order of Functioning," in Roger Benjamin, (ed.), The Democratic State, (Topeka: University of Kansas Press, 1984, pp. 213-236).

32. Wilensky (1975), op. cit.

33. Phillips Cutright, "Political Structure, Economic Development and National Social Security Programs," American Journal of Sociology, 70, pp. 537-550, (1964-65); Robert Jackman, Politics and Social Equality: A Comparative Analysis, (New York: John Wiley and Sons, 1975); and Frederic Pryor, Public Expenditures in Communist and Capitalist Countries, (Homewood, Illinois: Richard D. Irwin, Inc., 1971).

34. Wilensky (1975), op. cit.

35. Cutright, op. cit.; see also Peters, op. cit.

36. Larry Isaac and William R. Kelley, "Racial Insurgency, the State, and Welfare Expansion: Local and National Level Evidence from the Postwar United States," American Journal of Sociology, 86 (6), pp. 1348-1386, (1981).

37. Harold Wilensky (1975, op. cit.), however, does not posit this representational mechanism through which needs become translated into social welfare policy. He shows that not only is party ideology unassociated with social security spending levels, but also the political system (parliamentary, congressional, state socialist) has no effect on spending levels. The state, for Wilensky, needs no mandate but responds automatically to demographic shifts accompanying industrialization; whether that response is triggered from above or below is unimportant in affecting spending levels.

38. This view can be seen in the work of Alan T. Peacock and Jack Wiseman, The Growth of Public Expenditure in the United Kingdom, (Princeton: Princeton University Press, 1961).

39. Milton Friedman, Capitalism and Freedom, (Chicago: University of Chicago Press, 1962); For more recent elaborations on this line of thinking, see George F. Gilder, Wealth and Poverty, (New York: Basic Books, 1981); and Jude Wanniski, The Way The World Works, (New York: Simon and Schuster, 1978).

40. John K. Galbraith, American Capitalism: The Concept of Countervailing Power, (Boston: Houghton Mifflin, 1952); Charles Lindblom, Politics and Markets: The World's Political-Economic Systems, (New York: Basic Books, 1977).

41. Michel Crozier, Samuel P. Huntington and Joji Watanuki, The Crisis of Democracy: Report on the Governability of Democracies to the Trilateral Commission, (New York: New York University Press,

1975); Samuel Brittan, "The Economic Contradictions of Democracy," _British Journal of Political Science_, 5, pp. 129-159 (1975).

42. Colin Crouch, "The State, Capital and Liberal Democracy," in C. Crouch, ed., _State and Economy in Contemporary Capitalism_, (New York: St. Martin's Press, 1979, pp. 13-54).

43. Samuel Brittan, for example, argues that democracies have exposed crucial economic functions of the state to the "vagaries" of electoral politics. He uses the example of the money supply, and shows how exposing the money supply to pressure from organized labor has been the major cause of inflation in Great Britain: Brittan, op. cit.

44. Tyrell, op. cit.

45.Ralph Miliband, _The State in Capitalist Society: An Analysis of the Western System of Power_, (New York: Basic Books, Inc., 1969).

46. Nicos Poulantzas, _Political Power and Social Classes_, (London: Verso Editions, 1978).

47. Edward Greenberg, _Serving the Few: Corporate Capitalism and the Bias of Government Policy_, (New York: John Wiley and Sons, 1974).

48. James O'Connor, _The Fiscal Crisis of the State_, (New York: St. Martin's Press, 1973).

49. Alan Wolfe, _The Limits of Legitimacy_, (New York: MacMillan and Company, 1977); see also his article "Has Social Democracy a Future?", _Comparative Politics_, 11, pp. 100-125 (1978).

50. Piven and Cloward, (1971), op. cit.; and Piven and Cloward, _The New Class War: Reagan's Attack on the Welfare State and Its Consequences_, (New York: Pantheon, 1982).

51. Fred Block, "The Ruling Class Does Not Rule: Notes on the Marxist Theories of the State," _Socialist Revolution_, 33, pp. 6-28, (1977); Walter Korpi, _The Democratic Class Struggle_, (London: Routledge & Kegan Paul, 1983). In recent years, Theda Skocpol and her associates have distanced themselves from all neo-marxist approaches to the welfare state. They have developed a distinctive perspective with this work. With this perspective factors such as capitalist interests or policy-makers' concerns with business confidence do not explain different structures of welfare policy. Nor do they argue do different distributions of power resources in society. More generally, policy development is only marginally related to socio-economic interests; more importantly, it is due to the resources, capacities and structural arrangements of specific nation states. Theda Skocpol has discussed her ideas in several works including: "Political Response to Capitalist Crisis: Neo-Marxist Theories of the State and the Case of the New Deal," _Politics and Society_, 10, No. 2, pp. 155-201,

(1980); and Ann Orloff and Theda Skocpol "Why Not Equal Protection?: Explaining the Politics of Public Social Spending in Britain, 1900-1911 and the United States, 1880s-1920," American Sociological Review, 49, pp. 726-750, (1984).

52. John Westergaard, "Social Policy and Class Inequality: Some Notes on Welfare State Limits," The Socialist Register, 15, pp. 71-99, (1978).

53. Carmen Sirianni, for example, views the state as the major arena through which socialism will occur. The state embodies, at least in principle, values of democratic participation in decision-making and political equality. Richard Edwards, in contrast, focuses on the economy as the major arena of change. Control over the means of production, not control over political processes, is the goal of socialism for Edwards. See, Richard Edwards, Contested Terrain: The Transformation of the Work Place in the Twentieth Century, (New York: Basic Books, 1979); and Carmen Sirianni, "Production and Power in a Classless Society: A Critical Analysis of the Utopian Dimensions of Marxist Theory," Socialist Review, 11, pp. 33-82, (1981).

54. Samuel Bowles and Herbert Gintis, "The Crisis of Liberal Democratic Capitalism: The Case of the United States," Politics and Society, 11, pp. 51-91, (1982); and O'Connor, op. cit.

55. For discussion on this point, see Block, op. cit.

56. This point is made by Crouch, op. cit.

57. Thomas Weisskopf, "Marxian Crisis Theory and the Rate of Profit in the Postwar U.S. Economy," Cambridge Journal of Economics 3, pp. 341-378, (1978); and Bowles and Gintis, op. cit.

58. Weisskopf, op. cit.

59. William D. Nordhaus, "The Falling Share of Profits," Brookings Paper on Economic Activity, 1, pp. 169-217, (1974).

60. Charles W. Anderson, "System and Strategy in Comparative Policy Analysis: A Plea for Contextual and Experiential Knowledge," in W. B. Gwyn and George Edwards III eds., Perspectives on Public Policy Making, (New Orleans: Tulane University Press, 1975, pp. 219-241).

61. Anthony King is an exception to this general point. See, "Ideas, Institutions and the Policies of Government: A Comparative Analysis," (Part III), British Journal of Political Science, 3, pp. 409-423, (1973).

62. Gerhard Lenski, Power and Privilege: A Theory of Social Stratification, (New York: McGraw-Hill, 1966).

63. Christopher Hewitt, "The Effect of Political Democracy and Social Democracy on Equality in Industrial Societies: A Cross-national Comparison,"

American Sociological Review, 42, pp. 450-464, (1977); and Seymour M. Lipset, "The Changing Class Structure and Contemporary European Politics," in A New Europe? ed. Stephen R. Graubard, (Boston: Houghton-Mifflin, 1963, pp. 337-369).

64. Francis G. Castles, The Social Democratic Image of Society: A Study of the Achievements and Origins of Scandinavian Social Democracy in Comparative Perspective, (London: Routledge and Kegan Paul, 1978).

65. Furniss & Tilton, op. cit.

66. Donald Hancock, "Productivity, Welfare, and Participation in Sweden and West Germany: A Comparison of Social Democratic Reform Prospects," Comparative Politics, 11, pp. 4-23, (1978).

67. Stephan Leibfried, "Public Assistance in the United States and the Federal Republic of Germany," Comparative Politics, 11, pp. 59-76, (1978).

68. In this regard, see Anthony King op. cit. for a discussion of the importance of ideas to policies in the United States. In a somewhat similar vein, Timothy Tilton argues for the importance of ideology in the Swedish case in "A Swedish Road to Socialism: Ernst Wigforss and the Ideological Foundations of Swedish Social Democracy," American Political Science Review, 73, pp. 505-520, (1979). Other writers have asserted the importance of attitudes about citizenship or consensus and perceptions as to the reform possibilities at a given point in time. See, for example: Briggs, op. cit.; Albert O. Hirschman, Journeys Toward Progress: Studies of Economic Policy-Making in Latin America, (New York: Anchor Books, Doubleday and Co., Inc., 1965); and T.H. Marshall, "The Welfare State: A Sociological Interpretation," Archives Européennes de Sociologie, 2, pp. 284-300, (1961).

69. Such an argument is made by William Beveridge, Full Employment in a Free Society, (London: Allen and Unwin, 1944); Furniss & Tilton, op. cit.; and Alva Myrdal, Nation and Family, (Cambridge: MIT Press, 1968).

70. Such a critique is presented by Gunnar Adler-Karlsson in Functional Socialism: A Swedish Theory for Democratic Socialization, (Stockholm: Prisma, 1969); and more recently by Titmuss, Social Policy, op. cit.

71. Andrew Martin , "Is Democratic Control of Capitalist Economies Possible?" in Leon N. Lindberg, Robert Alford, Colin Crouch and Claus Offe, (eds.) Stress and Contradiction in Modern Capitalism: Public Policy and the Theory of the State, (Lexington, Massachusetts: D.C. Heath and Company, 1975, pp. 13-56).

72. Ibid.

73. This point is raised by Hugh Heclo in _Modern Social Politics in Britain and Sweden_, op. cit.

74. Andrew Martin, "The Dynamics of Change in a Keynesian Political Economy: The Swedish Case and Its Implications," in Crouch, op. cit., pp. 88-121.

Keith Fitzgerald

Economic, Social, and Political Indicators

The tables which follow present general comparative information about recent political and economic changes that are related to welfare state development. This information was compiled from the following sources:

International Labour Office (1985). The Cost of Social Security: Eleventh International Inquiry. I.L.O.: Geneva.

Mackie, Thomas and Richard Rose (1982). The International Almanac of Electoral History, second edition. New York: Facts on File.

Organization for Economic Cooperation and Development 1981). National Accounts of O.E.C.D. Countries, 1962-1979. O.E.C.D: Paris.

O.E.C.D. (1985). OECD Economic Outlook, 37 (1985). O.E.C.D.: Paris.

Taylor, Charles Louis, and David Jodice (1982). World Handbook of Political and Social Indicators, third edition. New Haven: Yale University Press.

Table 1: Political and economic variables and welfare expenditures in selected welfare states

	% Vote Major Party of Right 1945-72	% Vote Major Party of Left 1945-72	% Vote Major Party of Right 1973-81	% Vote Major Party of Left 1973-81	% Labor Force Union-ized 1975	Imports & Exports as % of GDP 1978	Energy Consump-tion per capita (Kilogrms) 1975	Public Educ. Expend-itures/ GNP 1978	Public Health Expend-itures/ GNP 1978	Total Social Security Exp./ GDP 1980
AUSTRALIA	46.2	46.5	38.1	44.2	44	33.4	6111	7.1	4.1	12.1
AUSTRIA	45.2	45.9	42.4	50.7	66	74.6	3724	5.8	5.3	22.4
BELGIUM	15.0	32.1	8.1	26.5	48	102.3	5712	7.7	1.1	25.9
CANADA	35.0	14.0	36.3	17.7	27	42.0	9835	8.0	4.4	15.1
DENMARK	17.6	38.8	10.4	32.7	65	57.3	5026	6.8	4.8	26.9
FRANCE	23.2	17.9	47.2	27.3	17	41.1	3939	5.8	5.5	26.8
GERMANY (FRG)	44.3	36.3	47.3	43.5	31	47.6	5358	5.2	5.7	23.8
ITALY	40.3	16.6	38.5	9.7	20	51.4	3106	5.4	6.5	18.2
JAPAN	43.4	24.6	44.6	19.9	35	25.7	3633	5.7	0.2	10.9
NETHERLANDS	10.0	28.8	17.6	31.5	33	95.3	6027	8.4	0.3	28.6
NORWAY	18.0	45.4	26.6	43.3	60	71.2	5106	7.7	0.6	20.3
SWEDEN	14.8	46.7	16.7	43.2	80	55.2	5569	8.6	6.2	32.0
SWITZERLAND	22.3	25.5	22.5	25.2	20	—	3419	5.2	2.1	13.8
UNITED KINGDOM	44.0	46.0	39.2	37.8	40	56.1	5268	6.0	4.8	17.7
UNITED STATES	50.0	0.0	49.4	0.0	23	19.2	10999	6.0	3.7	12.7

Table 2: Total expenditures of social security schemes as percentage of GDP

	1972	1973	1974	1975	1976	1977	1978	1979	1980
AUSTRALIA	9.8	10.5	11.0	10.7	12.4	14.3	13.0	12.6	12.1
AUSTRIA	18.2	18.0	18.2	20.2	21.0	21.1	22.5	22.5	22.4
BELGIUM	19.4	20.0	20.9	23.6	24.4	25.5	24.6	25.3	25.9
CANADA	12.4	13.9	13.9	14.7	15.2	14.5	13.9	14.2	15.1
DENMARK	20.5	21.0	21.0	22.4	24.0	24.0	24.7	25.5	26.9
FRANCE	20.4	20.9	21.6	24.1	24.7	25.6	26.2	25.8	26.8
GERMANY (FRG)	18.3	18.7	20.3	23.5	23.4	23.4	24.3	23.8	23.8
ITALY	20.3	19.6	21.4	23.1	22.8	22.8	14.7	14.9	18.2
JAPAN	5.9	6.3	6.5	7.6	8.9	9.7	10.0	10.6	10.9
NETHERLANDS	22.3	23.2	24.8	26.8	27.0	27.6	27.0	27.8	28.6
NORWAY	17.5	18.1	17.8	18.5	18.9	19.6	20.6	20.9	20.3
SWEDEN	20.7	21.5	24.4	26.2	27.4	30.5	30.4	30.5	32.0
SWITZERLAND	10.7	12.9	13.9	15.1	15.9	16.1	14.1	13.9	13.8
UNITED KINGDOM	14.3	14.7	14.6	16.2	17.4	17.3	17.2	17.5	17.7
UNITED STATES	12.1	12.3	12.5	13.2	13.9	13.7	11.8	12.1	12.7

SOURCE: I.L.O.

Table 3: Government disbursements as a percentage of GDP

	1973	1974	1975	1976	1977	1978	1979	1980	1981	1982	1983
AUSTRALIA	23.1	25.5	27.5	28.7	30.2	29.7	29.4	30.1	30.7	32.8	--
AUSTRIA	33.3	34.6	38.6	40.1	40.4	43.3	42.9	42.8	44.0	45.1	45.5
BELGIUM	35.8	36.4	41.2	41.7	43.4	44.8	46.2	47.7	52.3	53.0	53.5
CANADA	32.4	33.6	36.8	35.9	36.9	37.5	36.3	37.8	38.8	42.4	43.0
DENMARK	37.8	41.2	43.5	43.2	44.7	46.4	48.9	52.2	55.6	57.1	58.2
FRANCE	34.8	35.9	39.2	39.7	40.8	42.0	42.3	43.0	45.8	47.3	48.2
GERMANY (FRG)	36.1	38.8	43.3	42.6	42.7	42.6	42.3	42.8	44.3	44.8	44.4
ITALY	34.4	34.4	38.3	38.0	38.5	41.7	41.0	41.5	46.4	49.3	51.5
JAPAN	15.7	18.1	20.9	21.6	22.5	23.2	24.2	25.4	26.5	27.2	28.1
NETHERLANDS	44.3	46.8	51.0	51.5	50.3	51.8	53.5	54.1	55.6	58.3	--
NORWAY	39.9	40.0	41.8	43.8	45.3	47.2	46.6	44.8	45.0	45.5	45.9
SWEDEN	40.2	43.8	45.1	48.0	53.1	54.5	55.4	57.3	60.1	61.7	--
SWITZERLAND	24.2	25.5	28.7	30.2	30.4	30.2	29.9	29.3	28.9	30.1	30.8
UNITED KINGDOM	34.2	38.8	40.6	40.5	39.4	39.5	39.7	41.8	44.0	44.4	44.3
UNITED STATES	29.7	31.2	33.6	33.1	32.1	31.3	31.5	33.5	34.1	36.5	36.9

Source: O.E.C.D. (1985).

Table 4: Standardized umemployment rates for selected countries

	1973	1974	1975	1976	1977	1978	1979	1980	1981	1982	1983
AUSTRALIA	2.3	2.6	4.8	4.7	5.6	6.2	6.2	6.0	5.7	7.1	9.9
AUSTRIA	1.1	1.4	1.7	1.8	1.6	2.1	2.1	1.9	2.5	3.5	4.1
BELGIUM	2.7	3.0	5.0	6.6	7.4	7.9	8.2	8.8	10.8	12.6	13.9
CANADA	5.5	5.3	6.9	7.1	8.0	8.3	7.4	7.4	7.5	10.9	11.8
FRANCE	2.6	2.8	4.1	4.4	4.9	5.3	6.0	6.4	7.3	8.1	8.3
GERMANY (FRG)	0.8	1.6	3.6	3.7	3.6	3.5	3.2	3.0	4.4	6.1	8.0
ITALY	6.2	5.3	5.8	6.4	7.0	7.1	7.5	7.5	8.3	9.0	9.8
JAPAN	1.3	1.4	1.9	2.0	2.0	2.2	2.1	2.0	2.2	2.4	2.6
NETHERLANDS	2.2	2.7	5.2	5.5	5.3	5.3	5.4	6.0	8.6	11.4	13.7
NORWAY	1.5	1.5	2.3	1.8	1.5	1.8	2.0	1.7	2.0	2.6	3.3
SWEDEN	2.5	2.0	1.6	1.6	1.8	2.2	2.1	2.0	2.5	3.1	3.5
SWITZERLAND	--	--	0.7	0.4	0.4	0.3	0.2	0.2	0.5	0.9	1.1
UNITED KINGDOM	3.3	3.1	4.6	6.0	6.4	6.3	5.6	6.9	10.6	12.3	13.1
UNITED STATES	4.8	5.5	8.3	7.6	6.9	6.0	5.8	7.0	7.5	9.5	9.5

Source: O.E.C.D. (1985).

Table 5: Consumer prices (percentage changes from previous year)

	1973	1974	1975	1976	1977	1978	1979	1980	1981	1982	1983
AUSTRALIA	9.5	15.1	15.1	13.5	12.3	7.9	9.1	10.2	9.6	11.1	10.1
AUSTRIA	7.6	9.5	8.4	7.3	5.5	3.6	3.7	6.4	6.8	5.4	3.3
BELGIUM	7.0	12.7	12.8	9.2	7.1	4.5	4.5	6.6	7.6	8.7	7.7
CANADA	7.6	10.9	10.8	7.5	8.0	8.9	9.2	10.2	12.5	10.8	5.9
DENMARK	9.3	15.3	9.6	9.0	11.1	10.0	9.6	12.3	11.7	10.1	6.9
FRANCE	7.3	13.7	11.8	9.6	9.4	9.1	10.8	13.6	13.4	11.8	9.6
GERMANY (FRG)	6.9	7.0	6.0	4.5	3.7	2.7	4.1	5.5	6.3	5.3	3.3
ITALY	10.8	19.1	17.0	16.8	17.0	12.1	14.8	21.2	17.8	16.6	14.6
JAPAN	11.7	24.5	11.8	9.3	8.1	3.8	3.6	8.0	4.9	2.7	1.9
NETHERLANDS	8.0	9.6	10.2	8.8	6.4	4.1	4.2	6.5	6.7	6.0	2.8
NORWAY	7.5	9.4	11.7	9.1	9.1	8.1	4.8	10.9	13.6	11.3	8.4
SWEDEN	6.7	9.9	9.8	10.3	11.4	10.0	7.2	13.7	12.1	8.6	8.9
SWITZERLAND	8.7	9.8	6.7	1.7	1.3	1.1	3.6	4.0	6.5	5.6	3.0
UNITED KINGDOM	9.2	16.0	24.2	16.5	15.8	8.3	13.4	18.0	11.9	8.6	4.6
UNITED STATES	6.2	11.0	9.1	5.8	6.5	7.7	11.3	13.5	10.4	6.1	3.2

Table 6: Growth of real GDP at market prices

	1973	1974	1975	1976	1977	1978	1979	1980	1981	1982	1983
AUSTRALIA	5.5	1.9	2.4	3.2	1.0	2.8	4.5	1.7	4.0	0.0	1.0
AUSTRIA	4.9	3.9	-0.4	4.6	4.4	0.5	4.7	3.0	-0.1	1.0	2.1
BELGIUM	5.9	4.1	-1.5	5.2	0.4	3.0	2.0	3.5	-1.3	1.1	0.4
CANADA	7.5	3.5	1.1	6.1	2.2	3.9	3.4	1.0	4.0	-4.3	2.8
DENMARK	3.6	-0.9	-0.7	6.5	1.6	1.5	3.5	-0.4	-0.9	3.0	2.0
FRANCE	5.4	3.2	0.2	5.2	3.1	3.8	3.3	1.1	0.2	2.0	1.0
GERMANY (FRG)	4.6	0.5	-1.7	5.5	3.1	3.1	4.2	1.8	0.0	-1.0	1.0
ITALY	7.0	4.1	-3.6	5.9	1.9	2.7	4.9	3.9	0.2	-0.4	-1.2
JAPAN	8.8	-1.0	2.3	5.3	5.3	5.0	5.1	4.9	4.2	3.1	3.3
NETHERLANDS	5.7	3.5	-1.0	5.3	2.4	2.5	2.4	0.9	-0.7	-1.7	0.6
NORWAY	4.1	5.2	4.2	6.8	3.6	4.5	5.1	4.2	0.9	1.0	3.2
SWEDEN	4.0	3.2	2.6	1.1	-1.6	1.8	3.8	1.7	-0.3	0.8	2.5
SWITZERLAND	3.0	1.5	-7.3	-1.4	2.4	0.4	2.5	4.6	1.5	-1.1	0.7
UNITED KINGDOM	7.9	-1.1	-0.7	3.8	1.0	3.6	2.1	-2.2	-1.1	1.9	3.3
UNITED STATES	5.7	-0.9	-0.8	4.7	5.5	4.7	2.6	-0.4	3.4	-3.0	2.9

Source: O.E.C.D. (1985).

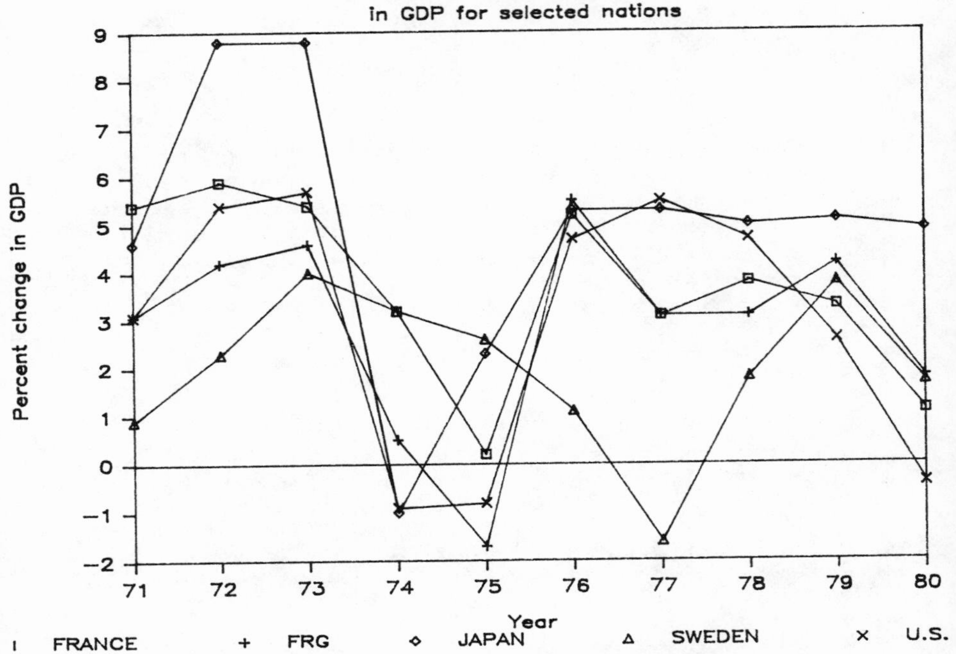

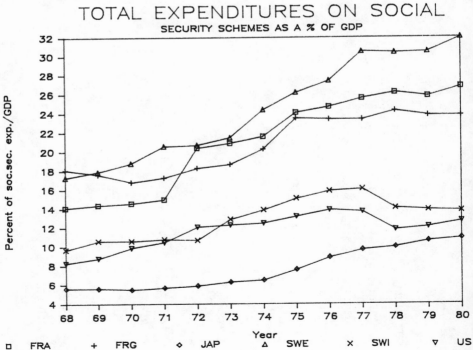

TOTAL EXPENDITURES ON SOCIAL SECURITY SCHEMES AS A % OF GDP

Percent of soc.sec. exp./GDP

32
30
28
26
24
22
20
18
16
14
12
10
8
6
4

68 69 70 71 72 73 74 75 76 77 78 79 80

Year

□ FRA + FRG ◇ JAP △ SWE × SWI ▽ US

CONTRIBUTORS

DOUGLAS E. ASHFORD is Andrew W. Mellon Professor of Comparative Politics at the University of Pittsburgh. His major interest in European politics has been in the areas of public policy and institutional change. His study of this relationship in center-local relations, _British Dogmatism and French Pragmatism_ (1982), will be followed by a study of social policy formation, _The Institutional Origins of the Welfare State_ (1986).

CAROL A. BOYER is a post-doctoral fellow in the Rutgers-Princeton Program in Mental Health Research, Rutgers University, New Brunswick. Her research focuses on the socio-historical determinants of government spending in the health sector, the organizational impact of the prospective payment system, and urban systems of care for the chronically mentally ill.

KEITH FITZGERALD is a graduate student in Political Science at Indiana University. He is currently writing his dissertation on the origins and genesis of recent immigration policy in the United States and Great Britain. His research interests focus on various aspects of state/civil society relations and their resolution in the policy process.

NORMAN FURNISS is Professor of Political Science and Director of the West European Studies Center at Indiana University. His current research focuses on the prospects for political change in advanced capitalist democracies.

LARRY J. GRIFFIN is Professor of Sociology at the University of Minnesota. His major research interests are in the areas of political economy, social stratification, and the analysis of social change. He is currently working on a comparative historical study of populist movements in the United States.

JERALD HAGE is Professor of Sociology and Director of the Center for Innovation at the University of Maryland. He is completing a study of _State Responsiveness vs. State Activism: The Rise of Social Expenditures in Britain, France, Germany, and Italy_. His next project involves labor unions and the determinants of their political effectiveness.

PERCY LEHNING is Associate Professor of Political Science at Erasmus University, Rotterdam. His main research interest is in the problems of normative political theory and their relation to public policy debate.

KEVIN T. LEICHT is a Ph.D. candidate in the Department of Sociology at Indiana University. He is currently finishing a project on "The Changing Class Character of Military Keyneseanism in the United States" (with Larry J. Griffin and Larry W. Isaac) and is in the process of writing his dissertation on the economic and non-economic consequences of union membership.

JOHN LOGUE is Associate Professor of Political Science at Kent State University and has taught at the Universities of Linkoping in Sweden and Roskilde in Denmark. He is the author of *Socialism and Abundance: Radical Socialism in the Danish Welfare State*.

LENNART LUNDQVIST is Senior Research Associate at the National Swedish Institute for Building Research and Docent in Political Science at the University of Uppsala. His major research is in the area of policy research with an emphasis on environmental and housing policy. His work in English includes *The Hare and the Tortoise: Clean Air Policies in the United States and Sweden*.

NEIL J. MITCHELL is an Assistant Professor in the Department of Political Science at Iowa State University. His current research is on the origins of public sector welfare provision in the United States and Western Europe, with a focus on the role of private sector welfare provision.

EDWARD MOOR is a graduate student in the Department of Sociology at Indiana University. His interests include political economy and the sociology of law.

PHILIP J. O'CONNELL is a doctoral student in the Department of Sociology at Indiana University. A native of Ireland, he worked at the Economic and Social Research Institute in Dublin from 1981-1983. His major research interest is in the comparative political economy of the welfare state, and he has written articles on income redistribution and on social structural change in Ireland.

BERNICE A. PESCOSOLIDO is an Assistant Professor in the Department of Sociology at Indiana University. Her work on the welfare state stems from a specific interest in government influence in the medical care sector. With Larry J. Griffin, she has recently completed an annotated bibliography and set of teaching materials on the welfare state, The Welfare State: Origins, Effects and Prospects (American Sociological Association, Washington, D.C. 1984).

HARRELL RODGERS is Professor and Chairman of the Department of Political Science at the University of Houston. His research specialities are in the areas of civil rights legislation and social welfare programs. His latest book is Poor Mothers: The Feminization of Poverty (Sharpe, 1986).

URIEL ROSENTHAL is Professor and Chairman of the Department of Political Science and Public Administration at Erasmus University, Rotterdam. He is the author of Political Order: Rewards, Punishments and Political Stability as well as numerous books and articles in Dutch on political administrative relations, the recruitment of government personnel, and the political role of the police. His current research interest is captured in the title of his inaugural lecture, The Political System and the State.

DON SCHWERIN is Docent in Political Science at Abo Akademi, Finland. He has also taught at Oakland University and the University of Oslo. He is currently working on the question of the economic viability of social democracy in Scandinavia.

TIMOTHY TILTON is Professor of Political Science at Indiana University. His main field of interest is the theory and politics of the welfare state. He is currently completing a project on the ideological development of Swedish Social Democracy.

ELIZABETH TROUSDELL is a doctoral candidate in the Department of Political Science at Indiana University. She is completing a comparative study on the social impact of steel mill shutdowns in the United States and Sweden.

WAI YING TSUI is a doctoral candidate in the Department of Sociology at Indiana University. Her research interests include include comparative health policies and the sociology of education. Her dissertation deals with the role of the state in developing vocational education policies in Japan and the United States.

PAMELA BARNHOUSE WALTERS is Assistant Professor of Sociology at Indiana University. Her primary research interests are in the sociology of education, the sociology of the family, and comparative historical sociology. She has written on school expansion in the United States and the cross-national study of development.